D0999242

SHOCK THERAPY

SHOCK
THERAPY

PSYCHOLOGY, PRECARITY, AND WELL-BEING IN POSTSOCIALIST RUSSIA

TOMAS MATZA

Duke University Press / Durham and London / 2018

© 2018 Duke University Press
All rights reserved

Printed in the United States of America on acid-free paper ∞
Designed by Heather Hensley
Typeset in Arno Pro and Helvetica Neue by
Westchester Publishing Services

Library of Congress Cataloging-in-Publication Data
Names: Matza, Tomas Antero, [date] author.
Title: Shock therapy : psychology, precarity, and well-being in
postsocialist Russia / Tomas Antero Matza.
Description: Durham : Duke University Press, 2018. |
Includes bibliographical references and index.
Identifiers: LCCN 2017049283 (print)
LCCN 2017056659 (ebook)
ISBN 9780822371953 (ebook)
ISBN 9780822370611 (hardcover : alk. paper)
ISBN 9780822370765 (pbk. : alk. paper)
Subjects: LCSH: Psychotherapy—Russia (Federation)—
Saint Petersburg. | Psychotherapists—Russia (Federation)—
Saint Petersburg. | Psychology—Russia (Federation)—
Saint Petersburg. | Psychologists—Russia (Federation)—
Saint Petersburg. | Post-communism—Social aspects—
Russia (Federation)
Classification: LCC BF108.R8 (ebook) | LCC BF108.R8 M38 2018
(print) | DDC 150.947/21—dc23
LC record available at https://lccn.loc.gov/2017049283

Cover art: Pavel Pepperstein, *Matryoshka* (detail), 2010,
© Pavel Pepperstein, Courtesy Regina Gallery

We believe that changes in a small group of people can contribute to major shifts in a society. At the same time we view changes in a small group as connected to the individual changes of its members. We trust that psychotherapy is capable of enhancing all these changes. From this perspective of personal and social interconnectedness, therapy is not only a tool for psychological help and change, but is also instrumental in bringing about social transformations. We are aware of our professional potential as well as our personal responsibility to promote humanistic values and make our world a better place to live.

—Psychotherapy Institute website, Saint Petersburg, Russia

The first motto of any self-emancipation movement is always the struggle against "selfishness."

—Jacques Rancière, "Politics, Identification, and Subjectivization"

CONTENTS

ACKNOWLEDGMENTS

Acknowledgments tell so many stories. They offer the genealogy of an idea. They indicate the intellectual community from which that idea emerged, and the institutional pathways it traveled on the way. They reflect a practice of gratitude. And they are passageways backward in time. These acknowledgments have been a pleasure to write, carrying me past the sequence of lovely and familiar faces that shaped my own development as the researcher and helped transform a nascent idea into the book you now hold in your hands.

I offer my deepest gratitude to the psychologists, psychotherapists, social workers, and coaches who invited me into their lives in Saint Petersburg. Without their willingness to take my calls, meet with me, help me make contacts, and open up their worlds to me, this book would not have been possible. I am humbled and touched by their generosity. I thank the psychologists of the organization I call ReGeneration for allowing me to take part in their work. I thank, especially, the people whom I call Tamara Grigorievna, Zhenya, and Aleksandr for inviting me to sit in on their trainings with children and for their friendship. I thank Vitya Markov for giving me so much of his time and helping me to understand what it might have been like to practice psychiatry in the late-Soviet period. I thank the psychologists of the Psycho-pedagogical Medico-social Center in X Region—especially the director, Tatiana Fedorovna, and the specialists Anna Andreevna and Vera. Each helped me better understand the nature of public psychological assistance and the challenges of that work. And I thank Zoya, who allowed me to quote from her reminiscences of work at the center. I am also grateful to the psychiatrists at the Psychoneurological Clinic in X Region for teaching me about how non-biomedical approaches have been incorporated into settings formerly dominated by psychiatry. Special thanks are due to Evgeny, who tragically passed away some years ago, for involving me in aspects of the daily life of the clinic, and to Olya, who allowed me to participate in her body-oriented therapy sessions and who sat down with me for many frank conversations. A special deep thanks to my friend Vera, who gave me insight into not just the Psychoneurological Clinic and the experience of being a patient there, but also her life in Russia as a musician, a daughter, and a sister. I am very grateful to Nikolai and Olessia at Verity for their hospitality and openness. They told me so many valuable things about their experiences in founding a psychological consulting company. To all of my Russian colleagues: I hope that I have captured faithfully the animating desire behind, and the struggles within, providing care to others.

Brilliant and wonderful mentors have nourished this project. I thank, foremost, James Ferguson, whose arrival at Stanford in 2004 could not have come at a better time for me. The lucidity of his thought, his monumental contributions to the discipline, and his kindness continue to represent for me what being a great scholar and mentor means. Jim also taught me to read theory closely and painstakingly, to attend to argument, and to approach what I write as if it will have effects in the world (even if it may not). I also owe much to Anne Allison, who became a spectacular mentor, co-instructor, inspiration, and friend during my three years at Duke. Many of the most mature arguments in this book benefited from exhilarating conversations with her while we were co-teaching the graduate seminar Precarity and Affect. But Anne's enviable attention to form and affect through writing were also guiding lights. Finally (and it may surprise her), I thank Caryl Emerson, my undergraduate thesis advisor at Princeton. She opened my eyes to the excitement of the interpretive act, the allure of theory, and the miracle of the written word.

Several others at Stanford University were crucial mentors at key junctures. I thank Matthew Korhman for orienting the project toward medical anthropology, for continually pressing me for argument, and for reminding me not to become overly enamored with theoretical paradigms. I thank Grisha Freidin for giving me the confidence to write about as complicated a place as Russia, and also for reminding me that the subjects of critical anthropology are, after all, people working on their own projects in the world. I thank Alexei Yurchak, whose postsocialism seminar at the University of California, Berkeley, was nothing short of an intellectual journey. The influence of Alexei's work in the field should be apparent in this book. I thank Sylvia Yanagisako for teaching me, just before fieldwork, that ethnography is the point of it all, and for encouraging me to push beyond theory. Finally, I thank Monika Greenleaf for her creative engagements with my project. Conversations with Monika reminded me to attend to the curious sides of social life, to moments of play, and to the things that don't fit.

Several other professors at Stanford were particularly supportive. Liisa Malkki has been a wonderful mentor and colleague over the years. I am so grateful for the many kinds of support she has given me, and for her reminder that fieldwork is life. I thank David Palumbo-Liu for his mentorship in Stanford's Program in Modern Thought and Literature (MTL), Akhil Gupta for his early mentoring and wonderful course on political economy, Sepp Gumbrecht for his receptivity to experiment, and Tanya Luhrmann for her constructively critical questions about my project. A big thanks also to two wonderful language teachers, Eugenia Khassina and Anna Muza, who together rejuvenated my love for Russian and helped me make some important breakthroughs. Finally, I thank Monica Moore—MTL's miracle worker, graduate-student ally, and holder of all keys to the castle.

It was a pleasure to have been trained in the Bay Area, a place so rich with anthropologists. I am particularly grateful to Li Zhang, Lisa Rofel, Lissa Caldwell, and Vincanne Adams for their collegiality and feedback, and for the invitations they extended me to share my work in their departments.

Graduate school was kept both sane and enjoyable by a collection of fantastic fellow students. I am so glad to have been a part of Stanford's MTL program with Nirvana Tanoukhi, Steven Lee, and Ulka Anjaria. Each of them taught me about committed, rigorous scholarship. Stanford's Department of Anthropology (once upon a time "CASA") was a warm and fuzzy second home. Numerous cohorts welcomed me as if I were one of their own. I am especially grateful to Tania Ahmad, Lalaie Ameeriar, Nikhil Anand, Hannah Appel, Elif Babul, Mun Young Cho, Jocelyn Chua, Maura Finkelstein, Ramah McKay, Zhanara Nauruzbayeva, Bruce O'Neill, Kevin Lewis O'Neill, Natalia Roudakova, Robert Samet, Rania Sweiss, and Thet Win for their ongoing friendship, humor, and creativity. I also thank Dace Dzenovska and Larisa Kurtovic at the University of California, Berkeley. Finally, I thank John Modern, Mark Elmore, Jon Platt, and Emily Newman, fantastic colleagues and dear friends: this book was made so much more possible with them in my life.

I am grateful to have spent time at the University of Cambridge's social anthropology department to further develop my research in the company of cultural anthropology's close British cousin. Special thanks are for Henrietta Moore, Nicholas Long, Caroline Humphrey, and Alexander Etkind for their engagement with my work and ideas.

For three exciting years I joined Duke's cultural anthropology department as an ACLS-Mellon New Faculty Fellow. The department and the university hosted a parade of amazing scholars and conferences, and I am fortunate to have spent time there. I am especially grateful to Orin Starn, who worked very hard to make me feel at home at Duke. Thanks also to Beth Holmgren, Ralph Litzinger, Anne-Maria Makhulu, Randy Matory, Laurie Macintosh, Louise Meintjes, Diane Nelson, Charlie Piot, and Naomi Quinn for an always exciting and generous exchange of ideas. In Durham I also benefited from reading the work of, and getting feedback from, Mara Buchbinder, Jocelyn Chua, Lauren Fordyce, Nadia El-Shaarawi, and Saiba Varma. Finally, extraspecial thanks go (again) to Anne Allison, as well as Harris Solomon, Rebecca Stein, and, at the University of North Carolina, Michele Rivkin-Fish. Each of them became especially close confidants, colleagues, and readers of my work.

Over the years I have had several amazing collaborators. I wish to thank Colin Koopman, whose Foucault across the Disciplines reading group at UCSC was a wonderful cross-pollination, and whose influence on my thinking with and through the work of Michel Foucault has been significant. Kevin Lewis O'Neill has been an incredible friend and collaborator and continues to amaze me with his willingness to pull me (and many others) into his magic. Kevin initiated a wonderful workshop on "the will" at the University of Toronto, and eventually a special issue that he and I coedited for *Social Text*. (I am also grateful to the Canadian Social Sciences and Humanities Research Council for funding the workshop, and to the participants in the workshop—

in particular, Tania Li, Mariana Valverde, Andrea Muehlebach, Naisargi Dave, Peter Benson, Daromir Rudnyckyj, Bethany Moreton, Katherine Lofton, John Modern, and Laurence Ralph. The feedback they offered at the workshop had an important impact on this book.) Finally, I thank Harris Solomon for his collaborative work on the *Somatosphere* project, "Commonplaces." I learned a tremendous amount from Harris's creative, groundbreaking approach to medical anthropology and his sharp eye for writing. On that score, thanks also to Eugene Raikhel for making space for that project in his journal, and for the many conversations about Russia that have surrounded it.

My years at the University of Pittsburgh have been incredibly fruitful. I owe a huge debt to Gabriella Lukacs for her insightful readings of late drafts of this book. I also wish to thank my colleagues Joseph Alter, Laura Brown, Heath Cabot, Nicole Constable, Bryan Hanks, Robert Hayden, Phillip Kao, Kathleen Musante, Andrew Strathern, Emily Wanderer, and Gabby Yearwood for making Pittsburgh a truly wonderful place to have completed this book.

Students at Stanford, Duke, and Pittsburgh have had a very significant impact on this book. Their questions about and interest in Russia and/or the politics of mental health have helped me to think more deeply about how to make arguments that both matter and remain accessible. Several seminar groups deserve special mention: postsocialism seminars at Stanford (2009) and Duke (2011, 2012) and the Culture and Politics of Mental Health seminar at Duke (2014) and the University of Pittsburgh (2015, 2016, 2017).

A number of organizations provided generous and crucial funding in support of this project: the Fulbright-Hays Doctoral Dissertation Research Award, the Social Science Research Council's International Dissertation Research Fellowship, and the Stanford Center for Russian, East European and Eurasian Studies. I also wish to acknowledge Stanford's Introduction to the Humanities program for postdoctoral support and, finally, the American Council of Learned Societies and the Mellon Foundation for the opportunity provided by the New Faculty Fellows Program. I would also like to thank the fabulous Center for Independent Social Research in Saint Petersburg, and especially Viktor Voronkov and Oksana Karpenko for their assistance.

Portions of this work were presented to some amazing audiences, including those at the University of Pittsburgh's Anthropology Department; the Institute of Sociology in Saint Petersburg; the University of Chicago's Center for East European, Russian and Eurasian Studies; Bard College's Program in Anthropology; Duke University's Global Health Institute; Harvard University's

Department of Anthropology; Duke University's Department of Cultural Anthropology; the University of California–Santa Cruz's Department of Anthropology; the University of California–Davis's Department of Sociocultural Anthropology; Stanford University's Center for Russian, East European and Eurasian Studies; and the University of Cambridge's Department of Social Anthropology. Thanks to the wonderfully engaged audiences at each of these places.

Several parts of this book appeared in journals and benefited from the close readings of reviewers. I wish to thank *Social Text* for allowing me to reprint portions of chapter 4, *American Ethnologist* for allowing me to reprint portions of chapters 2 and 3, and *Cultural Anthropology* for allowing me to reprint chapter 6.

Very special thanks are owed to Ken Wissoker, my editor at Duke University Press, for his steady hand in guiding this project toward completion, and for his faith that the end result would be a book worth publishing. I am also immensely grateful to the two anonymous reviewers whose comments provided such helpful guidance for refining the manuscript. I also thank Elizabeth Ault and the staff at Duke University Press for their invaluable assistance with all aspects of book production.

Finally, I wish to thank my family for their collective support of the dream to research and write. I thank, first, my amazing parents, Ike and Eila Matza, for teaching me about creativity and for never doubting my intuition that the life of the mind is worth trying to build a career around. Their love and confidence in me have been a steady and powerful force, and it has made all the difference. I thank my brother, Stefan Matza, for reminding me that there is a world beyond the book—a world of physical being. I thank my grandfather, Aarno Aaltonen, now long gone, whose memory is a powerful reminder that inquisitiveness, curiosity, and a sense of humor should be lifelong practices. I thank my father-in-law, Thomas Heller, who has shaped my thinking in so many profound ways, and my mother-in-law, Barbara Heller, whose practical knowledge of psychotherapy was as vital to this project as was her loving support. I thank Matt, Sharon, Amelia, and Zachary Heller for countless summers of inspiration away from research. I also thank my extended family, John and Libby Modern—two people who, I hope, will bring the joyful thought for the rest of my life.

I owe my deepest gratitude to my partner, Nicole Heller, and our two wonderful children, Aarno and Lilja. I have been so lucky to be able to turn from these pages into a world with them in it. They make life vibrate, they make me laugh, they never fail to lift my spirits, and they also keep me on solid ground. Nicole has not just read this project but lived it along with me, from prefield conceptualization, to fieldwork in a place cold and dark, to the many years of anxious writing that followed. Most important, she has shared the times that frame, and now exceed, the book. These pages are for you, my love.

FIGURE PRELUDE.1. "PEOPLE! Let's respect one another, please, and support [unreadable] . . ." Photo by the author.

PRELUDE

———

Bury That Part of Oneself

"It is windy. A blindfolded person is brought to a precipice accompanied by rhyth-mic blows on a tambourine. The rhythm quickens, and then stops. A command is given, and with a wild cry the person leaps down like a bird."

So began an article, entitled "From the Precipice into the Grave and Back," that ran in the newspaper Argumenty i Fakty (2001) (Arguments and Facts), which described a live-burial ritual known as "extreme training."

The article continued, quoting the coordinator, Aleksandr Savkin: "It's all very simple—in any situation a person is controlled by two forces. One [force] says, 'You are young, strong, beautiful—go ahead and jump, and everything will work out for you.' The other mutters, 'You are a bit old, you have no connections and very little money. What the hell do you need this for?' The question is, which force will win out? That's how it is. They bring you to the precipice and say, 'Change your breath-ing, change your consciousness, jump.' And in that moment there is an internal struggle: 'Oh God, I have a newborn daughter, a handicapped mother. What am I doing? Why do I need this nonsense?' On the one hand, it's intriguing; on the other, it's horrifying. But the person jumps, and at that moment something actually changes inside. What it is, exactly, is impossible to describe; nevertheless, some have *described it as a bit like sex. This feeling is recorded somewhere internally, on the physical level. And then every problem is resolved by remembering the jump. We have been leading people to the precipice for three years. They always jump."*

Savkin asserts, however, that true self-knowledge comes in the grave, in that "last refuge." As an air duct is installed, the person can "comfortably think," eventually falling asleep to the rhythmic drumming of the tambourine. On coming into contact with the "energetic body of the earth" through the grave, the person is given the strength to commune with himself or herself. The ultimate goal is to "bury that part of yourself that disturbs your ability to live, to love and be loved." Through the ritual, "the person is reborn to a new and better life."

/   /   /

The term *post-Soviet* invokes death and rebirth.[1] It marks a threshold and a kind of jump—from one system into another, from one life into another. Viewing 1991 as an opportunity to drive the final stake through the heart of communism, Western nations and international aid agencies made loans and grants of billions of dollars to help along economic restructuring in the 1990s. In accordance with the Washington Consensus, it was thought that marketization would naturally lead to democratic institutions and the growth of civil society (a view that proved to be wrong). Under Boris Yeltsin, reformers implemented "shock therapy," swiftly privatizing state assets at bargain-basement prices and enacting a variety of austerity measures, including reduction of budget deficits, the elimination of subsidies, price liberalization, and tightening of the credit supply, to free the economy from state control (Wedel 1998, 45–82). The reforms sent Russia lurching through a series of sharp turns. While some got rich quickly, many were left extremely vulnerable to massive inflation and diminishing savings, shrinking entitlements, currency devaluation, recession, and joblessness. As analysts put it sardonically after Russia's 1998 recession, the reforms turned out to be "too much shock, too little therapy" (Ledeneva 2006, 10).

During my fieldwork in 2005–13, the political order in Russia was still shaped by the legacy of the neoliberal reforms of the 1990s. In particular, the vast inequalities that emerged during privatization were still apparent. However, with the rise of Vladimir Putin in 1999–2000, a new political formation had also taken shape. Certain strategic industries, such as oil and gas, were pulled back into the state orbit. The oligarchy that had risen to power in the 1990s was entrenched and brought more closely into the fold of Russian state power.

The institutions with which people had contact, meanwhile (those dealing with housing, pensions, health care, and education), saw a new mixture of reforms that were not exactly neoliberal. Pensioner benefits were monetized in 2005; however, the cash payments were made by the state. Private insurance became more widespread; however, public health services, such as they were, remained available. Putin's merger of marketization with basic welfare support was accompanied by a more muscular discourse against the West; his popularity rose and has yet to wane. As I refine these pages, eighteen years after his rise to power, he remains in the Kremlin.

Russia's course from the Soviet collapse to the present is often discussed in these kinds of terms—that is, in terms of democratization, privatization, and liberalization—but it carved up lives, too. As Soviet life was "unmade" in the 1990s (Humphrey 2002), those reforms were projected into persons and communities, raising a series of fundamental questions about politics, the social order, and relationality in the context of a postsocialist market revolution. Those questions continued to be urgently present for those whom I met in the 2000s, who struggled both with what Russia no longer was and with what it could be under the Putin regime. *Shock Therapy* offers an account of some of the answers that people gave through an ethnographic inquiry into another fascinating post-Soviet phenomenon—the revitalization of psychologically oriented psychotherapies. In contrast to the biomedical materialist approach that had dominated Soviet psychiatry since the 1930s (Joravsky 1989), a psychology boom swept Russia in the 1990s, giving rise to new pop psychologies, markets for personal-growth seminars, and even publicly available mental health care.[2] A wide range of people found their way into psychological-service provision, and collectively their work spoke to new ways of understanding the self, the other, emotions, disorder, healing, and potential at a time when Russia was also transforming.

The title, *Shock Therapy*, is meant to be provocative. The therapeutic transformations I describe were not simply (or at least only) the neoliberal therapy that was said to be missing from the shock of rapid privatization. The variety of therapeutic practices that emerged in the 1990s and 2000s escape simple labeling; they were dynamic, eclectic practices that took shape in the context of the equally dynamic political conditions of the post-Soviet period, ranging from the wild capitalism of the 1990s and the unmaking of Soviet life, to the autocratic turn under Putin and the ongoing shocks of (un)employability, poverty, social risk, and rentier capitalism. I show how, in attending to the self in times of social change in Saint Petersburg in the 2000s, practitioners and clients asked a series of vital questions: How should I love and labor? What do I owe others, and what am I owed? What should I expect of my child? Who am I? What is our future? Who are "we"? What is a good life? Should the jump, as it were, be made confidently or hesitantly? The answers they gave, shaped by new psychotherapeutic modalities, reimagined the self, as well as the terms of political and social life, and of success and failure, in a changing Russia.

INTRODUCTION

And Yet . . .

It was 2005. The autumn morning was gray and damp. I met Lena near Udel'naia, a metro stop in the suburbs of Saint Petersburg.[1] The normally bustling labyrinth of kiosks and open-market stalls by the station was closed. A woman wearing the orange vest of the *uborshchitsa*, or street cleaner, brushed the wet pavement with a broom of bundled twigs. We wandered into a Blin-Donald's fast-food restaurant in search of a place to sit and talk. The *okhrannik*, a uniformed security guard, glowered at us even though we had bought something. Lena was about thirty-five by my estimation, with shoulder-length hair and a kind, tired expression. Her psychotherapy teacher and therapist, Vitya Markov, had put us in touch. He had told me that she was an exemplary student at his institute and could help me understand some of the ways in which people in Russia come to psychotherapy—a practice that, before 1991, was rare.[2]

Lena was startlingly open—a common quality among the many psychotherapists I would meet. As she told me her story, she glanced out the window, looking at nothing in particular.

"Many things have happened to me that were quite difficult [*tiazhelo*]. There were times when I thought of suicide."

The suddenness and weight of the last word stopped me in my tracks. As would often happen doing fieldwork in and around personal life, I put the pen down and began to listen, only picking it up again to jot key phrases. I reconstructed her account at home. She explained that what allowed her to "save herself" (*sebe spasti*) was a training course in psychotherapy that she "came across" (*stolknulas'*) and took for six months in 1997. It was an extremely significant experience. "It opened me up," she said. "It revealed me to myself. I began to experience changes that felt miraculous. My self-understanding changed so much I couldn't believe it. My family had difficulty accepting the changes." In 1998 she decided to study to become a psychotherapist. She thought, if she could change, then she might also be able to help others who are "suffering" (*v stradanii*). But later that year, her life changed once again. It was the time of the recession. She could no longer pay for school, and had to go to work. Soon afterward, she decided to travel with her son to the United States to get married. She had met a man. Lena left out the specifics of this decision, but at the time it was not uncommon for women to turn to international matchmaking services in search of romance, connections, and, often, a way out of Russia. I wondered whether this was the case for Lena.

Then came a tragic turn: the man she had met was killed in a car accident while she was in the United States. Devastated, Lena returned to Russia with her eight-year-old son. Her life's course seemed to have bounced, like a billiard ball, from one collision to another. Turning once again to psychotherapy, she resumed her studies at Vitya Markov's institute. This time she was especially struck by the human-potential writings of Carl Rogers and Rollo May, and the existential psychotherapy of Irvin Yalom.

"What was it that moved you?" I asked. I was interested in understanding how psychotherapeutic knowledge traveled in Russia.

She explained that what she liked most was the relationship between the client and the psychotherapist. She appreciated the fact that the interaction is situated "here and now" (*zdes' i seichas*), involving minimum questions, and that the therapist is only there "as support" (*kak podderzhka*), and to be completely open. I often heard the phrase *here and now* among psychotherapists and psychologists in Saint Petersburg. Associated with Carl Rogers, it signified a methodological rejection of Freudian approaches, which had sought the underlying causes of mental suffering not in the present but in the past and in the unconscious.

Lena gave me an example of one important insight. She said that at the start of her studies, she wanted to help people resolve their problems as quickly as possible, to tell them that they were not suffering alone. (It was an approach she attributed to her experience as an ER physician.) But when she tried to bring this approach to her psychotherapeutic work, she realized that it was not possible to solve a person's problems that way. "You have to simply be next to them," she said. "It's difficult. You can't just make a quick change. Instead, therapy should involve shared responsibility [*razdelennaia otvetstvennost'*]."

Her phrase, *shared responsibility*, was interesting. The word *shared* comes from the verb *razdelit'*, which can mean "to divide or share." It suggested two people carrying a burden together. It also suggested that some things might lie beyond the therapist's reach and, perhaps, beyond language. How is the balance between sharing and dividing struck? What is shared, and what does shared responsibility look like? To whom is one responsible? How had this realization shaped her path beyond suffering? And how does what is off-limits become part of the therapeutic encounter? I had so many questions . . .

Lena and I would not meet a second time. As I attempted to track the expansion of psychologically oriented, as opposed to biomedically oriented, therapies in Saint Petersburg, my fieldwork pulled me into other orbits—psychological-education camps and municipal counseling services for children, adult trainings (*treningi*)[3] and personal growth (*lichnyi rost*) seminars, advertising promoting particular kinds of psychologically-inflected child-rearing, talk radio, and a psychoneurological outpatient clinic (*psikhonevrologicheskii dispanser*, or PND). Yet Lena's story of suffering and psychotherapeutic healing echoed in my head. Her words would eventually push my analysis in new directions.

I had expected to understand the psychotherapeutic turn in Russia as a symptom of neoliberal capitalism's arrival. This expectation was supported by an extensive literature that describes how the neoliberal reforms of privatization and marketization are not just accompanied by but in fact depend on the cultivation of particular kinds of citizens—namely, self-sufficient, individuated subjects of freedom able to survive austerity measures such as the withdrawal of state social programs (Rose 1996a, 1996b; Brown 2003; Cruikshank 1996). The neoliberal polity, as Margaret Thatcher (1987) famously argued, is not a "society" (for that "does not exist") but rather a collection of responsible individuals. This assemblage of government, subjectivity, and political economy has been called *neoliberal governmentality*, and Western psychotherapies have played an important role in assembling that political rationality. The intuitions, habits, and modes of self-relation of the neoliberal subject, it is argued, are promoted nowhere as deeply as inside the consulting room.[4] Actually, this analysis *does* have explanatory force in Russia. As

I elaborate in *Shock Therapy*, discourses of individualism, responsibility, and self-sufficiency were abundant in Russia as state socialism ended and state capitalism began. What's more, many of the economic reforms of the 1990s *were in fact neoliberal* (see Wedel 1998; S. Collier 2011). There is also a strong institutional link between the arrival of capitalism and Russia's psychotherapy boom: markets created the infrastructure for new forms of psychotherapeutic work through the creation of human-resource departments, trainings for success, and psychological-education courses for children. By teaching things like emotion management, psychotherapists promoted the soft skills valorized in late-capitalist labor environments. Indeed, the conclusion that the psychotherapy boom helped disseminate neoliberal capitalism in Russia, one self at a time, is well founded.

And yet, when I confronted Lena's story, this account appeared partial. Confident assertions about the functional links among political economy, government, and subjectivity obscured the meanings that therapy had for Lena, not to mention the experience of living through the Soviet collapse and the rise of Vladimir Putin. What other ways were there to hear Lena's story, and to narrate an ethnography set in the midst of the Putin period in Russia? In trying to answer this question both adequately and critically, life histories like Lena's became a guide. As I learned more about how and why people turned to psychotherapy, what it had done for them and their social relations, I saw that they experienced social transformation in Russia not as a global phenomenon but as the ending of a way of life, and the start of something new and unknown, and that psychotherapy was a medium through which they came to terms with this experience. It seems obvious in retrospect, but at the time I struggled under the weight of assumptions. The diffusionist account of neoliberalism (see Kipnis 2008) obscured what was distinctly postsocialist in their stories. "We fell out of socialism and couldn't get used to capitalism," as one radio-show caller put the dilemma in 2005. While the analytic of neoliberal governmentality captured the effects implied in this statement, the nitty-gritty of "getting used to" something was more elusive. Ambivalence and contradiction rather than celebration or lament framed people's attempts to figure out how to live decently in precarious times.

Svetlana Alexievich's literary-ethnographic account of post-Soviet afterlives nicely captures the kinds of precarity that are specific to Russia: "My comrades met various fates [after the collapse]," says Elena Yurievna S., the former third secretary of the communist district party committee, who is quoted by Alexievich.

One of our Party instructors killed himself.... The director of the Party bureau had a nervous breakdown and spent a long time in the hospital recovering. Some went into business.... The second secretary runs a movie theater. One district committee instructor became a priest. I met with him recently and we talked for a long time. He's living a second life. It made me jealous. I remembered ... I was at an art gallery. One of the paintings had all this light in it and a woman standing on a bridge. Gazing off into the distance.... There was so much light.... I couldn't look away. I'd leave and come back, I was so drawn to it. *Maybe I too could have had another life. I just don't know what it would have been like.* (Alexievich 2016, 72; emphasis mine)

Collapse and the accumulation of conditionality—*maybe, could, would*. How should one respond to a world's unraveling? What could be, after all? At what point is it too late to change? These are practical questions, and as many people I met suggested, political collapse and the open horizon brought tantalizing but also terrifying possibility. Some found solace in religion or the bottle, some in entrepreneurship. Lena and others found psychotherapy. For them it offered mooring and, eventually, a professional identity.

This book, then, asks, how have those who turned to psychotherapy responded to the events in the decades following 1991? What does the psychotherapeutic turn—in the marketplace, the mass media, and state institutions—suggest about the renegotiation of key political coordinates, such as the individual, society, and well-being, as well as emergent political subjectivities? Finally, what does it reveal about political and existential conditions tied to the confounding promise of democracy?[5] To answer these questions, this book cuts a path through Saint Petersburg's "psy" landscape. I follow the movement of psychological knowledge from the Soviet period into institutions and bricks and mortar, over radio waves, and through minds and bodies. And I trace the new mental health assemblages and ways of thinking about selfhood, social relationships, and cultural understandings of success that emerged. Those ways of thinking, in turn, shaped the languages with which people worked to get along, and sometimes ahead. They also informed emergent configurations of the political.

The chapters that follow draw on extensive ethnographic research conducted in 2005–6, with follow-up fieldwork in 2007, 2010, 2012, and 2013. I did my research in Russia's second-largest city, Saint Petersburg, which has about six million residents. Termed Russia's "window to the West" by its founder,

MAP 1. Saint Petersburg, Russia's "window to the West."

Peter the Great, Saint Petersburg sits astride the Neva River at the mouth of the Baltic Sea and is about 120 miles from the Finnish border (see map 1). The city features an intriguing mix of neoclassical architecture, complete with canals and palaces, and Soviet-era constructivism, as well as shiny post-Soviet apartment complexes (see figures Intro.1 and Intro.2). In my fieldwork I traversed the city nearly daily, spending most of my time in two organizations that offered psychological services to children in different parts of the city. One of these, which I call ReGeneration, is commercial and offered me insights into the marketization of upbringing. The other, which I simply call the Psycho-pedagogical Medico-social (PPMS) Center, is municipal and offered me insights into how psychotherapy entered state institutions in the post-Soviet period. (I term the municipal network of which the PPMS was a part the "PPMS system.") The book also draws on ethnography in personal growth seminars for adults and a PND, as well as sixty life-history interviews with psychotherapists, like Lena. To provide context for this ethnographic work, my research included methods that are less conventional in anthropology: a survey of the Cold War–era historiography of Soviet psychology, and discourse analyses of the advertising culture of domestic services (of which

FIGURES INTRO.1 AND INTRO.2. The streetscape of the urban core and the periphery. Photos by the author.

psychotherapists are a part) and of a call-in psychological-advice radio program called *For Adults about Adults*.[6]

I show how what was at stake for both men and women caught up in the psychotherapeutic turn was not so much the construction of the deep psychological self that scholars term *neoliberal subjectivity*, but a search for modes of truth telling about experience, emotional harm, or violence, and a pursuit of sociality in the privatized spaces of postsocialism.[7] If state socialism posited a set of ideals for Soviet citizens about who they were collectively and what they should strive for, psychotherapy provided tools for reinvention, for better and for worse. Some turned to its humanistic orientation to process traumatic social memory and reimagine a postsocialist society in which inner freedom would be differently validated. Others drew on psychotherapeutic forms of sociality to create new quasi-publics. The effects of this work were not always salutary. As commercial and municipal organizations took up psychological diagnostics and idioms, they also helped reinstantiate social inequalities by grounding various kinds of difference in psychological terms. I argue that these efforts amounted to a tentative politics in Russia in which psychotherapists have reached for self-emancipation and equality but have sometimes stumbled over profit-motives and biopolitical norms. To put this in Jacques Rancière's terms, the psychotherapeutic vibrated between "the political" (*le politique*), or a pursuit of equality, and "the police" (*la police*), the order of domination (Rancière 1992; see also Chambers 2011). That vibration ultimately indexes the interplay of political rationalities—neoliberal, liberal-democratic, conservative, socialist—at a time of increasing centralization under Putin. And that vibration also indexes the fact that, as Rancière puts it, "the first motto of any self-emancipation movement is always the struggle against 'selfishness'" (1992, 59). I show how psychotherapists grappled with the implications of a new, much more self-centered discourse and its effects on personhood and social relationships.

The psychotherapeutic turn in the post-Soviet period has compelled me to rethink the relationships among care, ethics, and biopolitics. In Russia, humanistically oriented talk therapies have certainly been novel biopolitical forms of care that have yoked affects to the blinking consumer and state messages of the post-Soviet period. These findings echo many excellent studies of the antipolitical effects of care more broadly, especially under late capitalism (e.g., Cruikshank 1999; Rose 1998; Ticktin 2011; Zigon 2011). And yet these same forms of care helped many I met address existential questions and rebuild worlds. If we conceive of care, as Lisa Stevenson recently has, as "the way someone comes to matter and the corresponding ethics of attending to the other who matters" (2014, 3), then even within the confines of what she calls "bureaucratic care," care has ethical entailments. The practical ethics of care are thus not excluded from the biopolitical, nor are they simply derived from it. Care is a both-and proposition: it is internal to the government of populations, *and* it is a political and ethical practice. Care can either align with or diverge from biopolitical norms. In one instant, help can become harm. Care is precarious. In a similar key, Kathleen Stewart notes that precarity, written "as an emergent form, can raise the question of how to approach ordinary tactile composition, everyday worldings that matter in many ways beyond their status as representations or objects of moralizing" (2012, 519). This "mattering in many ways" is analytically vitalizing.

In the pages below, rather than seeking to elide the tensions among care, ethics, and biopolitics, I use the concepts of commensurability and incommensurability to describe the dynamics of those tensions. *Incommensurability* refers, in a Kuhnian sense, to the incompatibility of theories (Kuhn 1996; see also Halley 2006). But, in another sense, it identifies a moment before a radical world becomes domesticated, that is, made commensurate with hegemonic norms (Povinelli 2001; Dave 2011). This is the aspect of incommensurability that interests me. I suggest that the precariousness of care—the ways in which care oscillates between being commensurable and incommensurable with norms—is precisely the thing to analyze because it captures the ways in which those who give care struggle to do so under shifting and often difficult conditions. Michael Lambek's (2008) argument about the incommensurability of virtue and (economic) value is particularly useful here. He suggests that, in neoliberal times, a cornerstone of many of the governing projects social scientists have critiqued is making ethical and economic value—not to mention aesthetic or pedagogical value—commensurable. Concrete examples include the use of cost-benefit analyses and the creation of markets for the provision of public goods like education, health care, and welfare. It is the rendering of moral or ethical virtue in terms of economic value that leads to the demoralization of public life and, we might add, its depoliticization (Ferguson 2007). Tracing a lineage of resistance to such forms of rationalization through Georg Simmel, Karl Marx, and Max Weber, Lambek highlights a scholarly tradition of arguing *against* the commensurability of value and virtue, a kind of last stand against the grinding gears of capitalism. As Lambek puts it, "we must preserve another set of values or ideas about value with which to critically appraise the production and expansion of capitalist value" (2008, 135). Drawing on the Aristotelian-Foucauldian tradition of practical ethics, Lambek suggests that one way to augment incommensurability is to place the accent on considering human actions in terms of not ends but means. This perspective distinguishes virtue from economic value as well as absolute measures of virtue and the good. It is also anthropologically worthwhile to investigate how ends and means are articulated in practice. What kinds of choices do people make, and on the basis of what kinds of considerations? When scholars do not keep these distinct, Lambek says, referring critically to Pierre Bourdieu, "ethical practice appears to get subsumed within an agonistics of honor or taste, and an ethical disposition—to do the right thing, to be a good person or to lead a good life—is replaced by narrower instrumental and competitive calculations—to get what one wants and to do so ahead of, or at the expense of others" (2008, 137).

My focus on the incommensurability of care and biopolitics is more than an analytic framework. As I hope to show in this book, this approach was born from my encounters with Saint Petersburg's psychologists and psychotherapists. Many psychologists worked to articulate a vision of care in the face of market logics and/or biopolitical norms, and the work that I observed was, if not virtuous, then at least anchored in a complex universe of social meaning and relationships. They did so while often having to express those projects in terms of other types of (market) value. *Shock Therapy* tries to not only analyze but also reflect psychotherapists' struggles between virtue and value. Just as they grappled with the encroachment of a commercial biopolitics into their ethical projects, so I, analytically, resist subsuming those projects into another story of capitalist individualism spread through a psychotherapeutic medium. What follows, then, is an ethnographic account of the experts at the heart of a biopolitical endeavor that is unfinalized. By *unfinalized* I mean a mode of analysis that defers analytic closure.[8] Approaching experts in this way can be tricky in anthropology, especially when it comes to those in compromised positions. Therapists are not involved in direct action. They are not marginal, nor are many of them vulnerable. Many desire what Mark Liechty (2003) calls middle-class respectability, while contributing to projects of government. They are thus not the usual ethnographic subjects in whose name anthropologists write against neoliberalism, exploitation, dispossession, or antipolitics. Yet what I have also noticed is that experts often appear in such accounts as a faceless monolith ("the state," "bureaucracy," or simply "expertise"). Here I try to disaggregate the category of the expert to shed light on the commitments, desires, aims, and relations to power that animate caregiving.[9] I term this the *politico-ethical face of care*—a face that in Russia, looking Janus-like to the past and to the future, seeks the ground of healing and improvement. Seeing *that* face is crucial for attending to Lena's humanity, her struggle to locate the semblance of a life for herself and others, and also for understanding how people have responded to Russia's often-difficult post-Soviet decades.

In pursuing a different account of experts, I hope to contribute to a dynamic and important area of research engaged with care in its many institutional forms—humanitarian, medical/psychiatric, welfarist, developmental (see Ticktin 2011; Stevenson 2014; Davis 2012).

But do the "and yets" end? A critical anthropology premised on unfinalizability may seem lazy and dangerous. Many scholars have written with conviction against the obvious (and hidden) forms of oppression in the world. There should be nothing unfinalized about critiques of colonial domination, capitalist exploitation, slow death, racial and gender discrimination, or other systematic abuses. *Shock Therapy* draws intently from these critical traditions to discuss the regressive effects of the psychotherapeutic turn in Russia; however, it does so in a way that is also, I hope, productively "blasphemous."[10] For me, blasphemy is a rhetorical strategy that creates space in analytic fields. Care can be antipolitical. At its worst, care becomes dangerous and can harm. These are urgent, relevant insights; is this all there is to say?

Shock Therapy's organization relies on juxtaposition rather than neat resolution. Some parts explicate the link between talk therapy and the commercialization of upbringing. Other parts offer examples of how therapists linked their work to progressive political projects. Some parts analyze psychotherapy's antipolitical or regressive effects, demonstrating what Miriam Ticktin (2011, 223) terms care but not cure and a "medicalization of politics." Others focus on therapists' claims that their work on feelings and psychosociality was an important counter to forms of everyday brutality. My aim is for this account to be, much like the fieldwork that motivated it, alive to the social and political contours of psychotherapeutic care in Russia's second-largest city.

Precarious Care

Care, for Lena, began with herself but spiraled outward. In fact, many involved in talk therapy in Saint Petersburg associated their first encounters with social intimacy. They told me of thrilling stranger relations, and the new ideas about society that resulted. Six months after meeting Lena, I met Ira. At the time,

Ira was in her forties and was doing contract work as an "image maker" with a commercial psychological counseling organization I call Verity. We sat in the sun on a bench near St. Isaac's Cathedral in central Saint Petersburg, watching tourists pose for pictures, and Ira told me her story. When she graduated from Herzen Pedagogical University, her mother wanted her to become a teacher, but she had had such a bad experience in Soviet schools that the profession repulsed her. She complained that she was always made to feel like a black sheep. Instead, she got a job at an after-school program, and there her interest in psychology was sparked. She established close relations with the children and the parents, and she found that parents came to talk to her about their personal problems, something she said was rare at the time.

For a while, her therapeutic calling lay dormant. She was uninterested in Soviet psychology—it was "too theoretical" and not particularly focused on everyday problems. She put her interests aside and took time off work to help her husband with his burgeoning business in industrial supplies and to raise their child. By 1998, though, Ira felt she needed to do something for herself. She had stumbled on a psychology course in etiquette that also involved group therapy. *Etiquette* here meant not only a concern with propriety but an entirely new habitus. The idea was that low self-esteem could be boosted by bringing attention to one's self-image. Image making, Ira later reasoned, could be a useful thing to teach in Russia's emerging market society.

In the intervening years her husband's business took off, and he divorced her, leaving her with nothing. Letting out a sigh, she confessed that her work as a psychologist (*psikholog*) had since been sporadic. Few people were interested in what a middle-aged woman had to say about self-image. We turned and stared at the gold-domed church across the square.

"What was it like," I asked Ira, "in those first therapy sessions in the 1990s?"

She lit up. "It was a new way of thinking, a new point of view. We called each other by first name. It was a new social form. We used the informal 'you' [*my govorili na ty*]. I was crazy about it! I took all the psychology I could find. Sometimes without purpose. It was shocking how new it was. But I was ready. I felt very happy. I could be myself. It wasn't part of the Soviet system. It was for me."

Psychotherapy for Ira, then, began as a social practice. Her words expressed a desire for a new kind of sociality rooted in shared vulnerability. And so it was for many others who came to the new forms of talk therapy. Organized around psychotherapeutic idioms, the groups offered intimate, informal ways of being with strangers that they felt had not existed before. I term this *psychosociality*.[11] Care, then, was not only a professional pursuit or instrument but also an ethical practice aimed as much at the self as sociality. By *ethical* I have in mind Michel Foucault's late writings on the Hellenistic practices of the care of the self. Such practices, he notes, were ethical in the sense that they involved the everyday task of seeking well-being that aims at the good or the less harmful in ways that are not pure, nor perfect, nor overdetermined.[12] I draw on this conception of ethical practices to reframe caregiving.[13] Rather than operating within a total system in which actors play little to no role other than executing biopolitical plans, care unfolds in a social, biopolitical, economic, and cultural field.[14] Caring actions, while structured, are not necessarily scripted. Care does not spring forth, fully formed, from the head of Zeus, nor does it straightforwardly subjugate. Instead, care is an ethical practice with a politics through which people wrestle with social concerns, seek lines of flight, and, of course, sometimes marginalize others. Care is politico-ethical.

When it comes to approaching care in this way, context is crucial. In Russia, people's experiences with Soviet institutions—in particular psychiatric ones—deeply informed the ways in which they approached their work. For example, Lena's teacher, Vitya Markov, who cofounded one of the first psychotherapy institutes in Saint Petersburg, spoke to me at length about his experiences as a Soviet psychiatrist. To him, the abuses of Soviet medicine were a crucial part of his professional narrative. I finally heard that narrative one day in the spring of 2006, in his office. I had known Vitya for nearly eight months—I had been to his house for dinner, met his family, and had many discussions with him about the psychotherapy boom—but I had yet to hear his full story. I sat in the cushioned client's chair, and we laughed at the role reversal: this time he would do the talking. He told me that he had trained as a psychotherapist (*psikhoterapevt*) in the 1970s but was denied prestigious work because he was "Jewish by passport"; instead, he was placed in narcology, the Soviet psychiatric science dealing with alcoholism, which he described as a professional backwater. Scratching his salt-and-pepper beard, he told me about how Soviet medicine "broke the relations between patients and doctor":

My director [at the narcology clinic] would tell me how terrible [the patients] were. She hated them. Soon I saw that the patients [also] hated the doctors. Each one lied to the other all the time, and projected onto one other. The doctors would say, "Alcoholics are liars," but the doctors also didn't tell them the truth. So it was mutual lying. There was a Soviet joke [*anekdot*] about labor that went something like, "We pretend we are working, and the government pretends to pay us." In the clinic it was like that: one side pretends that they treat; the other side pretends that they get treatment. They were all playing a game. It was obvious. It was natural to want to stop it somehow, because it wasn't interesting to live that way. So I considered psychotherapy as a possible way of coming to something true.

Vitya and one of his colleagues would eventually reconceive therapy, at some risk to themselves. In their view, it should not be a "fight with alcoholism" (*borba s alkogolizmom*), as framed by the medical system, but a practice rooted in a "therapeutic community" (*terapefticheskoe obshchestvo*). By including patients, their doctors, and even the staff, this community ruptured the doctor-patient boundary. Speaking with enthusiasm about those early days, Vitya explained that they watched movies together and held gatherings in the evenings to discuss artists. "We basically looked at our patients as people who were going through difficulties, and whom we should help." Nevertheless, Vitya said, "I was called by my director once because the KGB said I mentioned Freud in one of these sessions." This was very concerning to him—not so much for his own safety but with regard to the integrity of the therapeutic space: "Should I really be exposing people to a situation in which one person could take what a person says and maybe tell someone about it?"

Whereas for Vitya the challenges of working within Soviet medicine were a crucial ethical pivot to his current work, others, like Nikolai Bazov, situated their therapeutic work in relation to the troubled present. I also got to know Nikolai well, eventually visiting his dacha, interviewing his wife (who was also a psychotherapist), and even helping him translate some of his writings into English. He was keen to know what people in the United States might think of his psychotherapeutic programs. A young psychotherapist focused on "harmonious relations" both inwardly and outwardly, Nikolai had co-founded Verity (the organization that at the time was sporadically employing the "image-maker" Ira) with his wife, Olessia. (I discuss their work in chapter 5.) In addition to leading personal-growth seminars, which I attended throughout 2005–6, Nikolai was also offering free trainings to public schoolteachers in an effort to address what he described as the legacy of an oppressive Soviet classroom environment.

We reconnected in 2007 in his office in the center of the city, and, over tea and crackers, our conversation veered to the fragmenting effects of Putin's authoritarianism. Citing the breakdown of the social fabric and the uptick in violence in Russia, Nikolai described his initial hope and eventual disappointment that psychotherapy could counter this brutality:

Many of the people around me have experienced terrible violence and beatings without cause. A neighbor from the middle of Russia suffered a fractured skull and eye problems after a terrible beating that landed him in the hospital for three weeks. This was unmotivated. It's just a release of aggressive tendencies in society. In the countryside people don't necessarily understand the source of this violence consciously, but they see it in the actions of our politicians, who operate on the basis of widespread fear and violence. Twenty years ago [when I started my work], I thought I would do something in Russia for the future of my children, to do what I could to build a better society. Now I understand that there is nothing here. Russia's future is in smog. I am afraid when my sons go out. I would like to raise them elsewhere, but there are not really any good possibilities. . . . I don't see a real way out. Meanwhile, I think that things will just get worse.

As Ira's, Vitya's, and Nikolai's stories indicate, talk therapy is *postsocialist*. For Ira, the groups that formed around the practice met a need that was unmet in late socialism. For Vitya, the Soviet collapse had made possible more responsive therapeutic forms that had previously been risky. And, for Nikolai, psychological training signified—at least for a time—the possibility to help rebuild society in the postsocialist period. These late- and postsocialist reference points are fundamental to the politico-ethical face of care.

What kind of care is involved here? Lena, Ira, Vitya, and Nikolai each used slightly different terms for what they do—Lena and Vitya called it *psychotherapy*; Ira, *image making*; Nikolai, *psychological training*. And sometimes they used the same professional designation, but in different ways: Lena and Vitya both called themselves psychotherapists (psikhoterapevty), but she had completed only postgraduate training, whereas he had a degree in psychiatry. Ira and Nikolai were both conducting psychological trainings, but Ira had had some certification training in psychology, while Nikolai combined such training with a medical degree (thus, he added the prefix *vrach*-, or "doctor," calling himself a *vrach-psikhoterapevt*). What was at stake in these distinctions, and how did they relate to care as a practice? The mix of terms stemmed from a fundamental contestation between Soviet and post-Soviet professional discourses. In the Soviet Union, and still officially today, a *psikholog* (psychologist) is a person who lacks medical expertise and works in either research or applied fields (testing, career counseling, some consulting). A *psikhiatr* (psychiatrist) is a specialist with medical training; this field was shaped by Soviet science and its materialist orientation to mental illness. Finally, a *psikhoterapevt* (psychotherapist) is a psikhiatr with additional training and is licensed to provide *psikhoterapiia* (psychotherapy).

Post-Soviet usage wreaks havoc on these distinctions. For ideological reasons that I detail in chapter 1, the sorts of talk therapy and self-help now popular in Russia were rare to nonexistent in the Union of Soviet Socialist Republics (USSR). As such, the psychotherapeutic turn has had an imported flavor, incorporating such concepts as *koyching* (coaching) and *Ia-kontseptsiia* (I-concept) (see Lerner 2015).[15] As Lena's, Ira's, and Nikolai's stories suggest, the rise of certificate training has democratized mental health expertise. Many people call themselves psikhologi, whether they have a degree or not. Some claim the title of psikhoterapevt even if they have not attended medical school. Another way to understand these differences is to map them onto a shift from more biologizing approaches to mental well-being under Soviet medicine to more psychologizing approaches. In that sense, when psychologically or psychodynamically oriented practitioners call themselves psikhoterapevty, they are appropriating a title that had been reserved for medical psychiatrists. Conversely, when psikhoterapevty deny another practitioner that designation, calling them, instead, a psikholog, they are seeking to reproduce a form of professional hierarchy established in the Soviet period.

The care I focus on, then, spans formal designations and spaces or practices (e.g., the clinic versus the consulting room versus someone's living room), but it shares one important thing: a talk-based, non-biomedicalized approach. In the pages that follow, I retain the transliterated emic distinctions for a person's professional positionality (i.e., the term each person uses to describe him/herself); otherwise, I use the *psychotherapeutic turn* to refer to the post-Soviet proliferation of talk-based forms, and *psychotherapy* and *talk therapy* as well as simply *care* to refer to the general talk-based approach.

Psychological Difference and Therapeutic Enunciation

In the ethnographic examples above, care was multiply precarious. It was provided to others living in precarious situations, and those who offered it did so under precarious material or political conditions. Seeing care as precarious illuminates its politico-ethical face as care takes shape in biopolitical schemes. *And yet:* care is also precarious in another sense. As many scholars have noted, its effects can flip between helpful and harmful; there is sometimes a great divide between intentions and results. As an organizing concept, *precarious care* also indexes psychotherapy's commensurability with social inequality, a particular risk that emerges when psychotherapy becomes a commodity or a technology of government. At the time of my fieldwork, Russia had seen new wealth and opportunity accompanied by tremendous new inequality (FRED 2018). Its Gini coefficient, a measure of income inequality, was significantly greater than those of other countries in the Organisation for Economic Co-operation and Development (with the exception of the United States) (OECD 2018). Those in a position to do well after 1991 did so with abandon, taking on the pejorative name "New Russians" (see figures Intro.3 and Intro.4). Elena Yurievna S., the same party committee member quoted earlier, describes her views of the Soviet period to author Svetlana Alexievich:

> No one wore Versace suits or bought houses in Miami. My God! The leaders of the USSR lived like mid-level businessmen, they were nothing like today's oligarchs. Not one bit! They weren't building themselves yachts with champagne showers. Can you imagine! Right now, there's a commercial on TV for copper bathtubs that cost as much as a two-bedroom apartment. Could you explain to me exactly who they're for? . . . They're renaming the streets: Merchant, Middle Class, Nobleman Street—I've seen "Prince's salami" and "General's wine." A cult of money and success. The strong, with their iron biceps, are the ones who survive. But not everyone is capable of stopping at nothing to tear a piece of the pie out of somebody else's mouth. (2016, 51)

Not everyone has iron biceps. A vast number of poor live at the dim margins of the glittering renaissance, and the social effects of Russia's capitalist revolution have been severe—high rates of suicide, alcoholism, early death, and divorce, as well as precarious living conditions.[16] In my fieldwork in a municipal psychological-assistance organization for children, I was able to see how children's mental distress could be a by-product of some of these demographic trends.

What is the politico-ethical face of care in these settings? A key finding is that, by pathologizing social suffering, the institutions providing psychotherapeutic care to the vulnerable tended to reinforce rather than mitigate social inequality. This was particularly surprising in light of the broader shift *away* from pathologization that the psychotherapy boom had brought about in Russia. As I discovered, the depathologizing forms of care focused on well-being were generally much more available to the better-off. Rather than pathology, these forms promoted highly market-oriented and gendered concepts of personal success and advancement.[17] The structuring of care also affected psychotherapists. Those working in municipal institutions, while

drawing much personal satisfaction from working with people that one social worker described as the ones "nobody needs" (*nikomu ne nuzhny*), struggled to do their work under more severe bureaucratic constraints and generally worked for much lower salaries. Those working in commercial contexts, by contrast, while able to develop a personal approach, were yoked to the logic of the therapeutic commodity. The mass of advertising materials in this context made clear that care became legible to others mainly as a lucrative endeavor. Care work also had an important gender component. There were disproportionately more women working in poorly paid municipal settings than in well-paid commercial settings.[18]

This distinction between kinds of care was not only a matter of professional structures. In fieldwork at two sites—a commercial organization (ReGeneration) and a municipal PPMS Center—I saw firsthand the ways in which social inequalities were recoded in expert languages to produce what I call *psycho-*

FIGURES INTRO.3 (opposite) AND INTRO.4. The fruits of (elite) labor and the ubiquitous cult of success. Photos by the author.

logical difference. For example, in January 2006 I spent a week participating in one of ReGeneration's psychological-education camps on the theme "controlling emotions and behavior" (*upravlenie emotsiiami i povedeniem*). ReGeneration served a largely elite clientele. This camp involved crossing the border to neighboring Finland for a mixture of a ski vacation and psychological lessons. I spent most of my days with eight adolescents in a small classroom at the camp compound for a several-hour-long *zaniatie* (lesson) led by Aleksandr and Zhenya, two young psychologists I got to know well. Each day, we moved through a workbook and different activities—emotional charades, sharing of our fears—meant to enhance self-regulation. In the activity I remember most vividly, we were asked to draw a map of our "internal emotional world." We worked on these for about thirty minutes, using large poster boards and colored pencils, and finally Aleksandr invited us to share. Gosha, age twelve, stopped playing with his cell phone and held up his internal world. He was the middle.

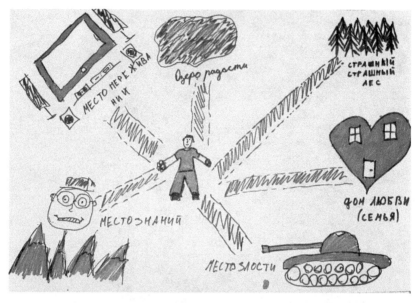

FIGURES INTRO.5 AND INTRO.6. The internal worlds of Gosha (top) and Tolya (bottom). Photos by the author.

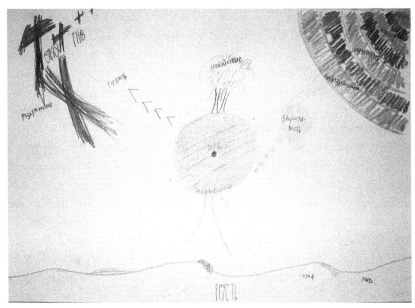

FIGURE INTRO.7. The internal world of the author. Photo by the author.

Lines led outward like spokes to different affectively charged locales, including "the lake of joy," "the scary, scary forest," "the place of emotional experience" (a home-entertainment system with a flat-screen TV), and "the place of knowledge" (with Tolya's bespectacled head skewered atop a mountain). I noticed that Tolya was sinking lower in his seat. He had folded his map into a square and had begun to tear it in half. Zhenya, the other psychologist, intervened, touching his arm. He refused to share, and only later did Zhenya show it to me. It was frantically drawn and divided into two halves. The top represented "reverie," but its pinks, greens, and blues drawn with erratic pen strokes suggested unease, or perhaps irony. Gray rivers turned blood-red in the lower, "dark" half and flowed into a red lake with black shores surrounded by jagged, cloud-enshrouded mountains. Two black towers loomed, one crowned with a brain sitting inside a movie camera, the other with a giant yellow eye surveying the landscape.

What I found interesting was that Aleksandr and Zhenya were not particularly interested in exploring the differences *between* our drawings. They did not focus, for example, on the fact that my internal world featured a sunlike object, whereas Gosha's did not. Nor were they particularly concerned with Tolya's complex representations (see figures Intro.5, Intro.6, and Intro.7). Instead, they were interested in self-knowledge and self-management as a means to success—psychology here was a tool for cultivating a particular habitus (Bourdieu 1984). Their promotional materials stated, "Knowledge is power. To be successful in life, a person has to understand himself, to know his plusses and minuses."[19] This is "the first step on the path to self-perfection [*samosoversh-enstvovanie*]. [Yet] knowledge alone cannot guarantee progress if it's not embodied in real results. And it's precisely through self-management that everything that a person knows about himself appears and is used."

Psychological difference played differently at the municipal PPMS Center. The center served "problem children," some of whom were living in precarious circumstances involving absent and sometimes disappeared parents, substance abuse, and so on. The center was staffed mostly by women between forty and sixty who were psychologists, educators, and speech therapists. Unlike at ReGeneration's camp, the child-client was off-limits to me. Not long after my trip to Finland with ReGeneration, I began attending PPMS Center's weekly meeting, or *konsilium*. One day, as snow covered the mud outside, Evgeniia Antatolievna, the psychotherapist overseeing the meeting, invited someone to share a case for review and discussion. As usual, there was a long, uncomfortable silence, a fear, perhaps, of the heated exchanges that could take place if a breach of protocol were accidentally revealed. Finally, Natalia Konstantinovna began to talk. A child's drawings circled the room. She offered a punctuated case history: "A boy, twelve years in age. First came into the center on a crisis call from his grandmother. He is unwilling to go to school and has nightmares. His father has left the family, and God knows what mother is doing. Binet test and Hand Test were administered, showing no psychiatric problems; however, on the drawing test he showed some abnormality, representing the leaves of trees with magical letters."[20] As for many of the cases I would hear, the specialists raised the specter of abnormality, with the drawings prompting further inquiry, further analysis, and a single clinical question: should the child be seen by a psychiatrist?

These two examples illustrate some of the ways in which psychological difference was produced in care contexts. As a start, ReGeneration worked primarily with the children of the elite, the PPMS Center with children living in difficult circumstances. Their therapeutic practices need not have been distinct, yet they were: while both were concerned with children's interiorities (in this case revealed through drawing tests), ReGeneration addressed the results in terms of potential, taking less interest in the particulars, and the PPMS Center brought the concerned language of (ab)normality to bear on the drawing. ReGeneration provided tools to a client; the PPMS Center used tools on a client. In fieldwork in these two organizations, which I discuss in chapters 3 and 4, I witnessed the powerful ways that practitioners could constitute psychological difference among children through therapeutic enunciation—that is, through attaching ideas about achievement or failure to psychological concepts. This, in turn, shaped institutional assumptions about ability and disability, capacity and incapacity, potency and impotency.[21] This articulation of psychological difference brought class and gender formations into being in the most intimate sites of interiority—the modes of knowing oneself—with the effect of turning some into potential immaterial laborers (Lazzarato 1996; Hardt 1999; Negri 1999), and others into risk factors.[22] How and why had the conditions of psychotherapeutic care come to intersect so neatly with social inequality?

Tactics and (In)Commensurability

Several structural factors oriented care toward managing population risk (delinquency, addiction, "asocial behavior") and harnessing human capital. As I detail in chapter 2, Putin's modernization policies, pronatalism, and the market logics of competitive advantage played a key role in making some kinds of care more practicable than others.[23] For instance, over the course of six months at the PPMS Center, I saw how dramatically modernization policies could affect the scope of care as the staff prepared to undergo *attestatsiia*, a periodic inspection of their services. Modernization, there, produced a wicked combination of decreased funding and audits. This combination hamstrung the psychologists and psychotherapists. As the attestatsiia dragged on, bureaucratic matters loomed ever larger, and the time available to provide care was diminished; the impulse to go above and beyond the call of duty was disincentivized. Care was pitched toward either highly abbreviated "correction" (*korrektsiia*) or a clearance approach—pathologizing difficult cases and referring them on to psychiatric services.

What theoretical concepts are appropriate for describing the structuring of care? Is this the symptom of an ideological formation whereby therapy extends the capitalist logics of austerity into the population? Are practitioners who try to work within these structures exhibiting false consciousness? Is this an instance of discipline whereby psychological expertise forms subjects of power through discursive incitement? Or perhaps, following Louis Althusser (1971), the relation between what psychologists do and the circumstances in which they work is one of overdetermination—a term that Kaushik Sunder

Rajan (2006, 6) usefully specifies as "contextual," not "causal." In fact, all of these are apt, but also partial. The concept I use to describe the relationship between biopolitics and care is commensurability. *Commensurability* refers to a process—commensuration—whereby particular sets of concerns or ethical practices are made commensurable with the world of norms. In contrast to overdetermination, commensuration is a subjective rather than a structural or determining concept. There is a dynamic at work, and it is a dynamic with potential effects. As Elizabeth Povinelli (2001) notes, commensuration, whether through "the efficiency of bureaucracies" or "economic transactions," domesticates and flattens difference. In the case of psychotherapeutic services for children, practitioners make care commensurate with the biopolitical economy by, for instance, framing their work as "improving human capital" (linking psychological *trening* to success) or, as at the PPMS Center, "managing social precarity and risk." Quantification and audits are thus instances of commensuration inasmuch as they render qualitative things (e.g., care, education, or student circumstances) on a spectrum of degree. Commensuration, as any ethnographer knows, frequently obfuscates the social and/or structural sources of suffering.

Concepts notwithstanding, how politically or socially salient is the politico-ethical face of care under such conditions? If my argument about incommensurability is to hold, the implicit and explicit claims about psychotherapy's moral legitimacy made by Vitya, Lena, and others ultimately have to be squared with the actual material effects of the work. That came with time in the field. In both contexts, therapists also deployed a range of counterhegemonic tactics (see Certeau 1988) against the biopolitical and/or economic norms governing their work.[24] At a basic level, psychotherapists across sites were acutely aware of the possible negative outcomes of their work. In the PPMS Center's konsilium, therapists frequently agonized over how an early-morning decision about a struggling child could move her to a special-needs school or place her *na uchet*—on the registry of psychiatric patients. They also frequently discussed the lasting consequences of being *na uchete* for the family and the child's development and peer socialization. In other words, the commensuration between children and the world of norms was made with eyes wide open.

There were also times when practitioners departed from the state mandate in order to provide what they viewed as better care, often at risk to their own livelihoods. In the PPMS Center, these tactics ranged from bureaucratic improvisation and working beneath the radar to ignoring specific aspects of the

PPMS network mandate overseen by state and municipal organizations. To give one brief example: Anna Andreyevna, a pedagogical psychologist (*pedagog psikholog*) at the PPMS Center, had invited me along on her school visits. These were meant to be rapid assessments of the children in each school, to identify children early on who might be showing signs of emotional distress or developmental delays. In the classroom I watched as she moved efficiently from desk to desk, administering various tests of memory, cognition, and emotion in search of potential problems. It was an exercise in bureaucratic quantification in which various diagnostics, including the Lüscher color test,[25] were used to collect data. There was something almost comical about how quickly she moved around the room with those color cards, dealing them out on each child's desk in three-minute bursts. But there was more to her work. Afterward, she invited me to lunch in the modest two-bedroom apartment where she lived with her husband and daughter. I spotted a copy of the Russian Federation's *Family Codex* (Russian Federation 2010) on the table. I remembered that in an earlier staff meeting she was exploring whether the PPMS Center could do anything more for a child than they were already doing, so I asked her about it. She told me that she was trying to reverse-engineer a legal justification for the extra work she was doing—work that she knew was outside the PPMS Center's mandate to "protect the rights of the child" because she was venturing into socially more capacious questions about the family. Later on, the director of the center would learn about Anna Andreyevna's tactic and berate her for it.

Tactics were evident in ReGeneration's daily work, too. There, practitioners spoke to me, not about promoting the success touted in their advertising materials, but about contributing to Russian democracy with a small *d*.[26] Their idea was that it might be possible to "civilize" the elite through reeducating their children outside the problematic forms of social reproduction inherited from the Soviet past.

Care practices, then, are contingent and may become *in*commensurable with biopolitical norms. *Incommensurability* here means providing forms of care that are, from the point of view of biopolitical and economic imperatives, off-kilter, even illegible. The PPMS Center's tactics opened up a gap between state policies (transmitted through the director's agenda) and children's needs as perceived by the practitioners. ReGeneration's tactics put psychologists at a distance from parents and the prevailing discourse of market success. At issue in each case was a struggle around how to understand social problems and provide care in the face of constraints.

Incommensurability also has an *affective* dimension. A mystery lurks at the heart of the biopolitical: any psychotherapeutic session hovers above the deep fissure between self and other. How certain can anyone be of the effects of any practice of care when knowing one another, and indeed ourselves, can be so elusive? This elusiveness resembles Elizabeth Anne Davis's (2012) insight about deception in clinical encounters, where misreadings can be abundant. The affective incommensurability I highlight here is also a kind of misunderstanding, but it stems not from deceit but from an intersubjective epistemic murk (Taussig 1987). Something dwells in the gap between what is shared and what is not shareable. It relates to the line that Lena described to me on that day in the BlinDonald's. I came to terms with affective incommensurability routinely as I subjected myself to the therapies about which I was writing. A particularly clear example came in a group therapy series I attended at the PND where I did some fieldwork. I had been invited there by Olya, a social worker, who had arranged a trening in what she called "body-oriented therapy" (*telesno-orientirovannaia terapiia*). By working in this way, Olya was injecting something new into the biomedically dominated practices of the PND, and her work was thus of interest to my project. Halfway through the trening, I found myself seated in a chair opposite my friend Vera, holding hands gently, if a bit awkwardly. Vera was a thirty-something patient at the clinic and was being treated for anxiety, depression, and other symptoms after being attacked by two men in a dark *podezd*, or underpass. Yet I knew Vera as a young composer who on occasion helped me with my Russian. Olya explained that our task was to make "hand sculptures": with our eyes closed, we would use our hands to make the shape of whatever emotion Olya requested. The therapeutic task was to find consensus and work together to make a good shape.

We sculpted words like *gratitude, comradeship, friendship, equality, jealousy, anger, woe, happiness, disbelief,* and *insult.* Some came extremely easily, such as *friendship*; others with much more difficulty, like *woe.* With each sculpture, Olya commented on our social-behavioral tendencies, putting me (at least) in a self-reflexive labyrinth from which there seemed to be no escape. Every successive move was pinned down by Olya's ongoing commentary. "Look at how Vera tends to withdraw from conflict. Look at how passive she is," Olya observed. In the next exercise, for *jealousy*, Vera responded by moving her other hand toward mine more deliberately. "Oh," Olya observed, "but she's very forceful when it comes to jealousy!"

Olya offered us our last word: *scandal.* Our hands began scanning one another's, mostly in confusion. Thoughts flickered past. "Does someone need to take the initiative? Should it be me or Vera? How should initiative be signaled? Is there such a thing as excessive assertiveness? What are the gendered dimensions of this exercise? What is Vera experiencing? Her hands feel tentative and stiff." Suddenly, out of the blue, there was direction. Vera slapped my hand as if to say, "Bad boy!," at which point I took the cue to play the role of the chastised offender, withdrawing in shame. After we opened our eyes, hands withdrawn, Olya asked me whether I often reacted to scandal this way—by retreating in shame. I answered no and suggested that I was responding in this way only in this instance, yet when I returned home to write my field notes, I wondered whether Olya was onto something. A certain affect from the session echoed beyond the moment of encounter.

This vignette gets at some of the murk involved in the clinical encounter. Olya could not be certain of the meaning of our actions; she could only gesture, as it were, with provocations. I did not really know what Vera was doing, and why; and vice versa. Nor was I even sure of the meanings of my own reactions. Therapeutic encounters, then, may well have effects, but those effects take shape within a wooly space in which people, feelings, multiple loops of self-reflection, and relations of force are brought into contact. Just as with its politico-ethical face, the murkiness of care has implications for the daily life of biopolitics. If one is not even sure of what happens in care encounters, then the biopolitical enterprise is destabilized, uncertain, perhaps also precarious.[27]

A Social in Search of a Politics

I have discussed how therapists used psychotherapeutic idioms to critique dominant orders in the socialist and postsocialist periods (albeit always within these orders' terms). In that sense, their practices were political, even if in a limited sense. But how is the political manifested *beyond* the confines of the consulting room or the training? What does that beyond suggest about emergent political subjectivities in contemporary Russia?

Recall Ira's and Vitya's rationales for pursuing therapy: they were both running from something—a felt lack of relations between doctors and patients, or between teachers and students, in Soviet times. But what they were running toward was less clearly formulated. Theirs was a politics in search of the social, and also the social in search of a politics. I found a similar impulse, or intuition, among other therapists and clients, who came together in search of an alternative kind of social experience. These *psychosocialities*, as I call them, were rooted in a heightened and excited form of togetherness. Sessions, I was told, sometimes delivered that experience and sometimes did not, but for the therapeutic community (or, rather, the community in therapy), a key appeal of any therapeutic encounter was that it always had the potential for such a heightened experience.

Psychosociality is a form of "social proxying," where imagined intimate stranger relations in public are mimicked in therapeutically attuned settings. What is essential to psychosociality is that participants feel the freedom to say things about themselves *as if* they were with intimate friends, but who are, in fact, in a room of people they may have just met. Another essential ingredient is that the others present pursue the same kinds of openness. Psychosociality, then, is a kind of togetherness through which people can enact forms of public intimacy that are otherwise rare. In Saint Petersburg, people involved in talk therapy were particularly keen for these kinds of social experiences. For example, psychosocialities were at play in psychological trainings for adults, such as the sessions offered by Nikolai (who previously spoke of his pessimism about Russia) and his wife, Olessia. Together they had founded an organization, Verity, which offered a variety of trainings in personal growth for adults—a project that stemmed, for them, from their own earlier experiences in group therapies. Olessia's work was particularly striking. At the time I met her, she was offering seminars in "systemic constellation" (*sistemnaia rastanovka*), in which she brought clients together to draw on an unseen *energiia*, or energy, as a guide to their problems. Their work summoned particular kinds of sociality (kin relationships, stranger intimacy) to help people navigate personal problems and even past political traumas.

I also found evidence of psychosociality in a virtual space: the liberal radio station Echo of Moscow (Ekho Moskvy). The station aired a weekly show called *For Adults about Adults* where the psychologist-host, Mikhail Labkovsky, offered on-the-air, live consultation. People from all across Russia could call in, share their problems, and enter the media stream. I tuned in whenever I could. Fascinatingly, Labkovsky was offering not just advice on personal problems but also a normative vision of how personal concerns should foster a new kind of public civility in Russia. Drawing on idioms like *self-esteem* (*samootsenka*), Labkovsky criticized the culture of corruption, selfishness, and indifference under Putin and advocated new political subjectivities and socialities rooted in psychological knowledge.

In the case of both Verity and *For Adults about Adults*, psychosociality was, indeed, only loosely political. Yet that is not the same as saying it was apolitical. I saw how different therapists used psychological idioms to articulate a postsocialist social body. It was a Frankenstein-like social body comprised of sewn-together parts—neoliberal emphases on self-esteem and responsibility (see Cruikshank 1999), consumerist emphases on lifestyle and affect (Patico 2008; see also Lukacs 2010), socialist ideals of intimate togetherness (see Yurchak 2006), liberal political ideals linking participatory democracy to public intimacy, and spiritual-cum-nationalist discourses that connected the soul to the motherland (*rodina*). But it was a social body nonetheless.

In the end, the political traction of these forms of coping and aspiration remains to be determined. But they were, for me, ethnographically important because they pointed to very real personal-qua-political dilemmas—between doing good and selling out, between being competitive and being socially caring, between being focused on oneself and being politically active—that are still being actively navigated in care work in Russia. Such tensions also point to the complexity of care as practice, including its historicity, its (in)commensurability with biopolitics and inequality, its affective and ethical excess.

As psychologists and psychotherapists have sought to care for (and in) Russia, then, they highlight some of the potentials, limits, and contradictions of a politics shaped by psychotherapeutics. They have helped clients locate self-esteem, empathy, and internal reserves in the face of a wide range of personal challenges and tragedies, including depression, low self-confidence, and social dissolution. By fostering psychosociality, they created connection in times of political isolation and anomie. Yet the promotion of self-esteem, empathy, and freedom had also been worked into the post-Soviet proliferation of market-based and instrumental understandings of self and other, producing forms of psychological difference among clients. Through the patrolling and management of affect, these very projects of freedom were simultaneously projects of constraint.

Thinking beyond the specifics of the psychotherapy boom in Russia, this study points to an emergent politics of the social—that is, a set of practical, everyday inquiries into postsocialist collectivity that, in this case, were articulated in psychological terms. What forms of togetherness were appropriate to the times, and how does one effect them in the presence of the money form and the biopolitical norm? These were by no means straightforward issues, and in my fieldwork in Russia I saw how they were contested, debated, and struggled over. What could supplement that lost ideal and counter the widespread perception of Russia as a carcass on which highly vulgar individuals preyed, while the rest, those who had a moral compass, were pushed aside to watch? How should individuality be respected in ways that retain a social valence? Care was not just a work of individual selves but also of a social body in which relationships were renegotiated under the shifting terms of post-socialism and state capitalism. As of 2013, when my formal research for this book ended, this was a complex field of practice, desire, and discussion with implications for what both care and the political could look like.

/   /   /

By inviting me into their worlds, the psychotherapists I got to know in Saint Petersburg certainly gave me a great gift. Yet, as Mary Douglas reminds us, "there are no free gifts" (Douglas 1990). Is the spirit of the gift operating in this book? Perhaps. But my task is to demonstrate how ethnography, like the many years of teaching that have grown from out of this research, is a practice that forces our paradigms into contact with the basic concerns of living and being with others. The message of *Shock Therapy* is one I learned from Lena: care—whether a therapeutic intervention or a writing of books—is precarious. It is perched between that which is divided and that which is shared, between closing down and opening up, between the normative and the potential, and between the reproduction of social hierarchies and their disruption. Starting with that acknowledgment opens a space for understanding, social connection, and yet also critique in precarious times.

BIOPOLITICUS INTERRUPTUS

What would an "and yet" history look like? In part I, I read with and against the grain of Soviet historiography to address a deceptively simple question: was there psychotherapy in the Soviet Union? As I show, both the topic and my ethnographic encounters circling around it were on vexed terrain and were muddled by the legacies of the Cold War. Chapter 1 attempts to address that vexation, while also providing essential historical context for the rest of the book.

FIGURE INTERLUDE 1.1. *Lenin's Haunts in the Petrograd Region*, depicting the addresses Lenin visited at different times. This panel, still intact, is half a block from Bol'shoi Prospekt, a shopping street featuring many luxury stores. Photo by the author.

INTERLUDE

Russian Shoes

I had arrived a few minutes early for my first meeting with Lena's teacher, Vitya Markov, with a copy of the Russian newspaper Izvestiia *[The News] tucked under my arm to pass the time. As I stood there reading, I glanced at two others standing around as if waiting for someone. The first was a woman, and so I turned my attention to the short man standing nearby. He had a salt-and-pepper beard and glasses and was wearing jeans, a knit ski hat, and a backpack. I studied him briefly and then dismissed him as an American tourist. Our meeting time came and went, and no one arrived. The familiar worry that I had gotten the meeting place wrong crept over me. From the corner of my eye, I saw the American tourist raise his phone to his ear. My phone began ringing. We turned to each other and laughed. "I was sure," Vitya said, "that you, with your* Izvestiia *paper and those shoes, were Russian."*

/   /   /

We often take one another for someone else. In Russia this commonplace misrecognition is often warped by the legacies of the Cold War. East-West discourses shape ethnographic encounters, the conclusions one draws from them, and, as I discuss in the first chapter of this book, the historiographical basis on which I sought to ground my research prior to entering the field. History, then, is not a background against which the present unfolds, but a conversational object with which ethnographers and their interlocutors do things.

The impetus for starting *Shock Therapy* with this awkward "and yet" history grew from the many instances in which psychotherapists rendered the Soviet past in contradictory ways. For example, questions about the nature of Soviet psychotherapy loomed large for me: What were its ideological and practical features? How was it different from current forms? To what degree was it an expression of the Soviet interest in constituting the so-called New Soviet Man (*Novyi Sovetskii Chelovek*; see introduction, note 19)? Perhaps my questions were just too stupid, but the way people responded could be frustratingly elusive: interlocutors might initially foreground the freedom to practice in the late-Soviet period, yet later on they would highlight party constraints.

I eventually recognized the opportunity in failure. By stepping back from my conversations with Vitya and others, I saw something else: a dialogical dance around contrasting historical imaginaries. My questions wavered between constructs of historical continuity and of rupture—in a few words, the *before* and *after* of 1991. And my interlocutors' contradictory responses were not a function of unreliable memory, increased rapport, or obfuscation but were patterned. They either rejected or embraced the Soviet past as a project and a moral community. The stance we each adopted depended, usually, on what the other had said, and on how our discourses fell on some tacit terrain of first vs. second world aggression, as well, perhaps, as a long-standing Orientalizing discourse of "Russia under Western eyes" (Malia 1999).

The contemporary and the historical were also frequently brought together in ethnographically meaningful ways. For one thing, traces of the Soviet past were ubiquitous, whether in the cityscape (as in the photo at the beginning of this interlude), in the mass media, or in everyday conversation. More specific to my ethnographic research, psychotherapists' oscillations about "what was" suggested an ambivalence about the status of the Soviet period that was also playing out in contemporary wars over memory and the meaning of the capitalist transformation, nationalist discourse, and political indifference (Oushakine 2000, 2009). Meanwhile, my own oscillation highlighted the political underpinnings of conceptual interrogation: my interest in postsocialism had been strongly shaped by prior historical, anthropological, and sociological inquiries. I saw what Talal Asad's interpreters have described as "the ideological character of objectification," that is, "the historical and political conditions of formation of the apparatuses of scholarly investigation" (Scott and Hirschkind 2006, 4; see also Buchowski 2004).

Chapter 1, then, is written with these lessons at the front of my mind. The aim is to characterize but also destabilize the historical frame in order to call attention to some of the problems in studies, such as this one, that seek to assess subjectivity as a biopolitical surface in motion. I also see this analytic practice as one that mirrors the ways that practitioners, through their own memory practices, sought to render care as being (in)commensurable with biopolitical norms.

Nonetheless, I do feel some obligation to give readers an idea about what the Soviet psy-ences were—at least approximately so (that is, how they have been described by various figures, living and dead). On that score, the following chapter also shows two things. First, psychotherapies resembling those found in the West were in fact ideologically anathema in the USSR. Second, such psychotherapies were nonetheless also present in the USSR. That these two points are partially contradictory is intentional—they are also the ways in which Western (largely American) and Soviet authors put matters. *The Soviet Union was unabashedly collectivist*, asserts one camp. *The Soviet Union was interested in individuals, just not individualism*, says the other.

The legacies of the Soviet period remain far from settled and are open to contestation. Any attempts at historical contextualization must begin with both an acknowledgment of this fact and an exploration of how, for whom, and in what ways the past continues to matter. I consider history as a performance, something akin to Johannes Fabian's (1996, 249) notion of historiology. As we tried to anchor ourselves someplace, my interlocutors and I entered into an eventful negotiation, fraught with conditioned assumptions deployed in both directions. Yet try as we might, slipping into the other's shoes always proved impossible.

Chapter 1

"TEARS OF BITTERNESS AND JOY"

The Haunting Subject in Soviet Biopolitics

If there were a single problem around which the history of Soviet psychology
could be written it would be the role of subjective factors in behavior.

—Raymond Bauer, *The New Man in Soviet Psychology*

In 1986 Carl Rogers came to Moscow. It was a few months after the Chernobyl
disaster and a few months before Mikhail Gorbachev's perestroika. The famous
American psychologist organized two four-day workshops on the suggested
themes of humanistic education, individualized instruction, and the fostering
of creativity (Rogers 1987). In a retrospective on these workshops, one participant, Ukrainian psychologist Alexander F. Bondarenko (1999), described his
experience there. His account begins with skepticism and disappointment. He
had hoped to learn "something 'scientific' . . . some new theories, experiments,
hypotheses and their proofs and disproofs [*sic*]," but, instead, Rogers had
mused about his youth and spoke in generalities about empathetic listening,
caring, and congruence (10). Then, on the second day, Bondarenko had a revelation: "I myself was the truth in the world, that was the essence, however
bad this truth might be" (12). He continues,

> It is difficult to render this in words, but this revelation came as a shock.
> From the time that I was a child, I had heard that I had to live for people. I
> was brought up with the idea that my life was necessary—to my parents,
> to the family, to the state, to the motherland. But it was needed as a part of
> a universal sacrifice or as a duty. And no one, myself included, needed my
> life as my own particular life, as the truth of my being in the world.
>
> I looked at Carl Rogers and I felt and I understood that this wise old
> man was neither adapting himself to the world nor adapting the world

to himself. He was being in the world. I knew I was lonely. I realized how lonely I had been. But I was feeling the truth of my being in the world and that feeling purified me and gave me strength to exist, and I sensed tears of joy as well as bitterness in my eyes. (13)

I would hear echoes of these words nearly two decades later, during fieldwork among psychotherapists working in Saint Petersburg. As I mentioned in the introduction, Ira the image maker contrasted the dry and theoretical Soviet approach to psychology with the revelatory sessions she attended in the 1990s. Vitya Markov had criticized the way the doctor-patient relationship was structured in Soviet psychiatry, and he took steps to humanize that relationship. In each case, a critique of the past was also important for situating current work. In this chapter I dive more deeply into this past referent. I discuss how psychiatrists trained in the Soviet period mounted bitter critiques against their former profession while praising the arrival of Western psychotherapies. Such descriptions raise questions both about the status of psychotherapy under Soviet power and its post-Soviet significance.

I understand practitioners' disdain for Soviet medical power, and Bondarenko's mixture of joy and bitterness, in terms of a story of haunting. Throughout the Soviet period, the subjective—that highly psychologized interior in Western psychodynamic theories that Bondarenko references—existed in a tricky relationship to Soviet power. Termed by turns "bourgeois," "idealist," and "pessimistic," the subjective was an ideological problem. And it was criticized most fiercely when psychology located the sources of affective disorder in the utopian social. Why? According to the American social historian Raymond Bauer, whose work dominates the United States historiography of Soviet psychology, the subjective factors of behavior—particularly in the forms of neurosis, depression, or anxiety—were always vulnerable to being read as symptoms of social dysfunction.[1] Far more ideologically preferable were clinical approaches that saw the psyche in materialist (psychoneurological) terms, and affective disorders as individual pathologies rather than signs of neurosis in an oppressive social world. As a consequence, the role that nonmedical talking cures played in the formation of Soviet psychology was minimal.

However, other materials suggest that the subjective never really disappeared from the Soviet psy-ences.[2] Instead, it haunted Soviet scientific psychiatry and research psychiatry, sometimes spilling over into clinical practice, appearing during the post-Stalin thaw of the 1960s and again under

Gorbachev. This story of burial and reemergence points to an important fact: the subjective has long been entwined with political liberalization in Russia—most obviously in the post-Soviet neoliberal reforms but also during "socialism with a human face" in the 1960s and perestroika in the 1980s. The core tension explored in this book—between recognizing individual emotional needs, on the one hand, and critiquing bourgeois social difference, on the other—is what emerged in each of these various moments when, after being buried, the subjective reemerged.

To explore these inflection points in more detail, I assemble a genealogy of applied psychology (*prikladnaia psikhologiia*). I draw from a historiography that is contested between and among Soviet and non-Soviet historians.[3] Why applied psychology, a branch of psychological work that refers to labor psychotechnics, psychotherapy, clinical psychology, applied developmental psychology, and mental hygiene, to name a few? In an early alternative to biomedical psychiatry, applied psychologists pursued work closer in approach and sensibility to the psychodynamic therapies that developed in Western psychotherapy. Moreover, applied psychology's many years of marginalization during the Stalinist period offer a fascinating account, in negative form, of the priorities and philosophical underpinnings of Soviet mental health care and the contours of the New Soviet Man within socialist biopolitics.[4] Through the institutional marginalization of applied psychology, it becomes evident what the New Soviet Man was *not*.

The genealogical account I offer here is also one among several. As a way to signal that, I crosscut the account that follows with interview fragments drawn from my fieldwork with practitioners trained during the Soviet period. These fragments indicate practitioners' ongoing dissatisfaction with Soviet psychology and psychotherapy in the late-Soviet period, even as the historical narrative I present appears to be one of decreasing state interference. At the same time as they provide a necessary grain of salt, these oral-history fragments themselves require seasoning. They, too, are performances that draw on remembrances of late socialism to do work in the present. Rather than seeking a single account of Soviet biopolitics, then, I am interested in the shifting relations between the ethics of care and biopolitics. Even under supposedly totalitarian conditions, there was room for maneuver, whether by departing from Soviet psychiatry's biological-materialist model of the person or by creating alternative kinds of therapy. To a degree, this room for maneuver troubles another claim practitioners made about the past—that the current "humanization" of psychology is an improvement over the harsh practices of the Soviet past. Nonetheless,

I am less concerned here with which claim is true than with the ways in which, no matter the biopolitical context, experts pursue discursive and also practical strategies for distancing themselves from hegemonic structures.

The twentieth century proved tumultuous for Soviet psychologists interested in the talking cure and topics thought too subjectivist for materialist research. Yet the intensification of interest around psychotherapy in the 1990s marks not so much a subjective revolution as a another remapping, under postsocialist capitalism, of the relationships among pathology, health, scientific authority, mental health, and interiority. This genealogy I trace here is crucial for understanding the personal and political stakes for those—like the joyful and embittered Bondarenko—who have been involved in the contemporary psychotherapeutic turn.

Soviet Psychology between Scientism and Marxism: 1917–1930

SOCIAL DETERMINATION: THE MECHANISTS

The types of applied psychology—mental hygiene, psychoanalysis—that in the West led to the development of client-based psychotherapy were present in the early Soviet period but disappeared by the late 1920s.[5] What put them on the wrong side of the Soviet project? One factor is practical: Soviet Russia had not undergone the bourgeois revolution that had gripped Euro-America; the February and October Revolutions of 1917, World War I, and the Russian Civil War (1917–22) had severely impacted Russia's industrialization, triggering famine, homelessness, and unemployment. Soviet authorities feared moral contamination from this violence, as well as hooliganism (Beer 2008). Production had fallen below 20 percent of the level it had reached in 1913 (Hosking 1993, 120). In 1924, seven years after the Bolshevik Revolution, only 23.3 percent of the population of the USSR was part of the urban-industrial matrix (10.4 percent workers, 4.4 percent white collar, and 8.5 percent bourgeois); more than three-quarters of the population were peasants. These figures were mostly unchanged by the end of the 1920s (518). Thus, the party's task of shaping new Soviet persons was as much socioeconomic as psychological, if not more. It involved turning peasants and the petit bourgeois into proletarians, and overcoming the Soviet Union's economic backwardness relative to its industrialized rivals (150).[6] Stalin's first five-year plan (1928–33; announced as having been achieved by 1932) directed tremendous resources into heavy industry as a means of economic development. The effects were significant. The size of the working class doubled during the first five-year plan and tripled by 1940 (154).[7]

According to Raymond Bauer, the Soviet psy-ences as a whole were given their fundamental shape during these same two decades. The future place of Marxism was central, as was the type of Marxism. Between 1917 and the early 1930s, experimentation was widespread in psychology, as it was in other fields (see Clark 1995).[8] There were efforts to join Freudianism and Marxism (until 1927 there was a Moscow chapter of the International Psychoanalytical Association; Wortis 1950, 72; see also Attwood 1990, 53–54), to develop behaviorism, to extend physiology to brain science, to create a system of mental hygiene, and to integrate the study of culture and history into human psychology. None of these was exclusively concerned with Marxist theory, though most were sympathetic to it as a sociological and/or philosophical position.

There was great interest in psychology's potential contribution to the uplift of the proletariat and the building of a socialist society (see M. Cole 2006, 12; Miller 1985). According to the orthodox Marxist principle of economic determinism, social conditions had held back the working classes and the Soviet Union's national minorities. The famous psychologists Lev Vygotsky and Alexander Luria went to Uzbekistan to study cognitive function among children. They found evidence of socioeconomic determinism: a "backward" upbringing or lack of schooling had indeed produced "lower" forms of reasoning that could be amended, they argued, through structural transformations and psychologically grounded pedagogy. (Motivated by a progressive interest in the way structural factors can lead to worse learning outcomes, the researchers nonetheless assumed a problematic ethnocentrism.)

By the mid-1920s, however, as calls for a properly Marxist psychology gathered force, the period of experimentation became hamstrung by philosophical debates. This especially affected categories like consciousness (*soznanie*) and psyche (*psikhika*) in both psychological research and Marxist theory.[9] Bauer writes that psychologists rejected introspectionism "because it reflected a contemplative approach to life, setting off thought from action, and because it was tainted with concepts like freedom of will and therefore was anti-deterministic.... Soviet psychologists, of the twenties, then, almost without exception, either rejected or did not deal with subjective and conscious factors in human behavior in a systematic way" (1959, 74).

This produced several ideas about human beings and behavior. Instead of attributing human actions to motivation or will, individuals were viewed, in

Pavlovian fashion, more deterministically: the person "was viewed as an adaptive mechanism that responded to external forces in such a way as to maintain equilibrium between himself and his environment" (75; see also Matza 2014). Little attention was given to "needs and interests," because these could all be described in the more precise language of reflexes. It was assumed that "the reshaping of human nature would take place automatically as the institutions of society were changed." For these reasons, psychology, which had already had a whiff of subjectivism, was vulnerable to being displaced by neurophysiology, the much harder and more materialist discipline of Ivan Pavlov. Researchers, who treated the mind as an empirically accessible part of the body rather than a metaphysical substance, stood more firmly on the soil of materialism. Indeed, psychologists like Konstantin N. Kornilov (the first to call, in 1923, for a psychology derived from Marxist tenets) asserted that consciousness was incompatible with materialist philosophy (Bauer 1959, 67–68).

THE DIALECTICS OF CONSCIOUSNESS: HUMAN AND ENVIRONMENT

Bauer suggests that this mechanistic trend lost its hold after Lenin's death in 1924. Still at issue was the relationship between materialism and the subjective. Bauer speculates that by the late 1920s, during the first five-year plan and the collectivization of agriculture, the mechanists' view became incompatible with a call for socialist initiative and creative thinking. Timed with the release of Lenin's posthumous writings, a more agentive view of the subject emerged. This view took up the Leninist line in philosophy, the "theory of reflection," which posited consciousness as a "reflection" of, but also action on, the objective world. This dialectical position drew subjectivist theories into Marxist terms.[10]

By the 1930s, after heated debates at various conferences and through polemical writings, the dialectical position had become dominant. This had several important theoretical consequences. First, researchers could now account for the psyche, albeit as a "qualitatively new synthesis of matter, the laws of which were not reducible to those of physiology" (Bauer 1959, 29). Second, consciousness, while carefully couched in materialist language as a form of "highly organized matter," had been assigned a relative autonomy from its material substratum and was "therefore restored to an important role in the direction of human affairs" (29).[11] In other words, in dialectical materialism psychologists had found a way to move beyond the subject-object dichotomy without dispensing with the subjective entirely. It offered them a material basis for the psyche, created an argument for the relevance of consciousness as an object of inquiry, and integrated the social into the individual in a way that did not, at the same time, reduce the individual to a mere function of environment. This enabled Soviet psychologists to move beyond the binary then defined by phenomenology, on the one hand, and objectivist materialism, on the other. In fact, the Russian scholar M. G. Yaroshevky (1996, 165) asserts that, far from hindering psychology, Marxism offered scholars a way of resolving the crisis between objective and subjective approaches in world psychology.

Consistent with the psychological model of active, conscious socialist workers, many speeches in the early 1930s were preoccupied with individual responsibility and initiative, marking an upsurge in the importance of "training" (i.e., various forms of self-discipline) in Soviet society (Bauer 1959, 46; Kharkhordin 1999). This was also the period of Stakhanovism, when party officials induced socialist competition by rewarding and celebrating workers who surpassed production goals.

Following the shift to dialectics, applied psychology enjoyed a temporary resurgence, peaking in 1932 and 1933 (Bauer 1959, 120; Graham 1987, 167). Nonetheless, as David Joravsky (1989, 335–54) notes, in becoming more vital to social policy, applied psychology also became more politicized. Along with the theory of reflection came an accompanying notion that theory should follow practice. According to Bauer, "In the early thirties, 'facts' themselves came to be scrutinized on a political basis, and 'objectivism' came to be a term of abuse" (1959, 105–6). "The more psychologists attempted to apply their techniques to concrete social problems, the clearer the political and social implications of their work became. In many instances these implications conflicted with the interests of the regime" (109).

CASE: SUSPICIOUS CONFIRMATIONS

"Was there psychotherapy at all in the USSR?" I asked Vitya Markov the day we met on the street corner.

"In the Soviet Union, there was no need for therapy," he replied as we were jostled back and forth in a silver subway car deep underground. "When you have perfected society and the person is a product of his environment, then the person needing counseling is mentally ill. He needs a psychiatrist, not a psychotherapist."

There was something terribly satisfying about his cut-and-dried answer. Yet I would realize only later that Vitya had offered me a simplified vision of Soviet psychotherapy. As I read the historical literature after my fieldwork, I saw that the greatest degree of party control over the psy-ences occurred during Stalinism, but also that the years after Stalin had been different. Why had this distinct, ideologically intense period stood in for the entire Soviet period? And was Stalinism, after all, as monolithic as Vitya's statements implied?

The Stalinization of Psychology: 1930–1953

According to Western and Soviet historians, the applied fields came under pressure in the 1930s. The results of empirical studies could pose ideological problems. Psychologists ran afoul of the increased attention to "party-mindedness" (*partiinost'*) in science.[12] Pedologists were scrutinized for accepting Jean Piaget's "bourgeois" concept of the "antisocial period of the development of the child" (Joravsky 1989, 108). Hit particularly hard were "attitude studies." Previously, at the start of the first five-year plan in 1928, such studies were thought important during periods of ideological transformation as a "guide to political reeducation of dissident groups" (Bauer 1959, 110). Psychologists queried people on the existence of God, and "which people are best" (110). But under Stalinist praxis, controversial findings were brushed aside or attributed to the researcher's reactionary tendencies.

In the area of psychohygiene, the early 1930s also brought to a close practitioners' concern to initiate mental health prophylaxis. Reports of neurasthenia after the civil war of 1917–22 and the stresses of collectivization had prompted this movement, and its leaders had looked to the United States' mental health services as a model, but this ended by 1931. N. I. Grashchenkov, a new leader in psychoneurology, phrased the new approach this way: "In our country, [the mental health movement] must be an instrument for mobilizing the masses for the execution of the tasks of construction, an instrument for creating a personality that fully meets the requirements of socialist society" (quoted in Joravsky 1989, 340). M. B. Krol', another psychoneurologist, was more direct: "The mental health of workers and collectivized peasants was assured by their dedication to labor as a matter of honor, glory, and heroism; by their participation in the sociopolitical life of the native land" (quoted in Joravsky 1989, 340). Socialist labor itself, not psychohygiene, should be the chief means for improving health (*ozdorovlenie*).

One of the most cited documents in the historical literature is Stalin's decree of July 4, 1936, criticizing pedology, the holistic field of child studies of which Vygotsky and Luria had been a part. Stalin accused pedologists of being better at finding defects than merits, noting that special remedial schools were growing alarmingly fast and that it was mostly the children of workers and peasants who ended up there (Joravsky 1989, 347–48). The decree also banned psychological testing, including intelligence tests, as based on bourgeois psychology that perpetuated class distinctions.[13] The decree also radically depsychologized the Soviet education system, replacing psychology with pedagogical expertise premised not on individuated approaches but on duty, discipline, and tough love.

Bauer links these transformations in applied psychology to Stalin's announcement in the same year that socialism had been achieved. Purges accompanied that declaration; once the utopia had been constructed, Bauer suggests, little room was left for divergence, lags, or difference. In criminology, for instance, he argues, "Stalin's declaration . . . meant that the social basis for crime had been eliminated, and that any subsequent deviations from the moral norm are an evidence of 'capitalist remnants in the consciousness of man' and must be eliminated" (1959, 42; see also Attwood 1990, 37–39). A psychology of difference had no place in such a society.

THE PROBLEM OF THE UNCONSCIOUS

The fate of Freudian psychoanalysis—both as theory and as clinical practice—in that period gives another clue to how the consolidation of Soviet-Marxist psychological theory impacted applied fields like clinical psychology and psychotherapy. In the United States' current age of managed care, it is easy to forget that psychoanalysis dominated US psychiatry from the 1950s until the 1970s, developing in the 1930s as it waned in the Soviet Union. By World War II it was viewed as cutting-edge science in the United States, offering a detailed and broad theory of mind (Luhrmann 2000). Many other theories and therapies developed from Sigmund Freud's ideas—those of Melanie Klein, Anna Freud, Alfred Adler, Erik Erikson, and Karen Horney—proliferated across consulting rooms. Grouped under the term *psychodynamic*, psychoanalysis shaped both the first and second editions of the *Diagnostic and Statistical Manual of Mental Disorders*, as well as the wide range of non-biomedical psychotherapies in the West (Hunt 1993; Young 1997).[14]

In the Soviet Union, by contrast, psychoanalysis followed a different trajectory. In the 1920s, the Soviet intellectual and political elite expressed a great deal of interest in Freudianism (Etkind 1997, 179–224; Miller 1985, 1990). Leon Trotsky and Nikolai Bukharin were both interested in wedding psychoanalysis and Marxism.[15] Although clinical practitioners were slower to take up psychoanalysis, in the early 1920s Luria used psychoanalysis in a psychiatric hospital in Kazan and later developed a clinical approach that combined psychoanalysis with physiological psychology (Miller 1985, 635–36).

Despite these synthetic efforts, the attack on Freudianism was well under way by the mid-1920s. Historian Martin Miller (1985, 631–32) cites one particular attack in 1924, by V. Iurinets, a party philosopher. Iurinets wrote sardonically that in reading Freud, "we are carried off into the semi-oblivion of a modern *Walpurgisnacht* [a pagan rite of spring], with its wild cries and frenzied dances, . . . on the waves of the unconscious contours of Prussian logic" (quoted in Miller 1985, 632). Iurinets also labeled Freud an "idealist," decoupling his work from materialism by claiming that Freud merely used biological analogies. Finally, he critiqued the social implications of Freud's work, especially his tendency to "generalize about unresolved sexual conflicts from questionable individual case studies." In the *Medical Encyclopedia* entry for psychoanalysis in 1933, another Soviet author, V. Vnukov, criticized the application of psychoanalysis to too broad a range of domains. Psychoanalysis "wipes away all the barriers between a neurotic personality and a healthy one" because "so-called" laws established from the study of neurotics "are then applied to healthy personalities." Psychoanalysis was a "fragment of bourgeois democracy," misreading "complex class relationships in primitive societies which emerged on the basis of definite socio-economic structures . . . as phenomena of neurotic mechanisms, as something biological in their very essence." Finally, psychoanalysis's effectiveness in treatment was "too complex." "Patients who are being analyzed for two years and more become too submerged in themselves, they are constantly stewing in their own juice and are torn away from reality" (quoted in Wortis 1950, 76).[16]

But it was psychoanalysis's central construct—the unconscious—that was most problematic for Soviet psychology. Unconscious desires were anathema to Stalinism's ideal-typic active, conscious person (Attwood 1990, 66). As an editorial in 1946 put it:

Soviet psychology and bourgeois psychology oppose one another in this respect: bourgeois psychology takes the "unconscious" as a point of departure, as though it were the basic determinant of human psychology, and as though it were the central core of man's personality. Soviet psychology has explicitly fostered the theory that consciousness is the highest, most specialized human level of development of the psyche and has indicated the dominant role which conscious influences play as compared with unconscious influences. In this regard *Soviet psychology is in accord with Soviet pedagogy.* Soviet pedagogy maintains as the basic principle of didactics the doctrine of *conscious instruction. And, in questions of training, it holds to the principle that it is the conscious personality of man, his conscious behavior, and his conscious discipline that are to be molded.* (Fomichev 1946, quoted in Wortis 1950, 119–20; emphases added)

Such critiques make it clear that by the time consciousness (soznanie) was reestablished in the official conception of the Soviet subject in the late 1920s, psychoanalysis had mostly been excluded from clinical practice (Etkind 1997, 225–85). In addition to the objection that psychoanalysis was idealist, Wortis argues, the materialist approach to psychology also "cannot conceive and does not accept a concept of mind which blocks off any large segment from interaction with reality" (1950, 71).

In contrast to Western private psychoanalysis, Soviet psychotherapy developed in psychiatric contexts as a junior partner to medical interventions. Its special feature lay "in [the] conception of how ideas can best be changed," and Soviet psychotherapy was seen as having much more limited use (Wortis 1950, 81). It was based on Pavlov's theory of higher nervous activity and the secondary signaling system. Within this framework, Soviet psychotherapy held its own conception of neuroses: consistent with dialectical materialism, neuroses were viewed through the prism of physiology—theories of and treatments for various neuroses were sought through Pavlov's model of cortical activity, stimulation, and the healthy versus unhealthy balance of excitement and inhibition.[17]

By the mid-1940s, one of Soviet psychotherapy's most fundamental methods was called *rational psychotherapy* (Lauterbach 1984, 69). As Wolf Lauterbach's immensely useful study, *Soviet Psychotherapy*, discusses, rational psychotherapy was developed in France, in Paul Dubois's *The Psychic Treatment of Nervous Disorders: The Psychoneuroses and the Moral Treatment* (1905), and appeared in Russia in 1912–13. The approach draws on Pavlov's theory of higher nervous activity and is based on the idea that "neurosis is the result of false reasoning, and the doctor can cure the patient by explaining his false notions to him" (Lauterbach 1984, 61–62) by means of "a direct appeal to rational consciousness [using] logic, persuasion, scientific enlightenment, group pressures and the creation of positive incentives" (Wortis 1950, 82).[18] The result should be a transformation in the patient's personality, his or her sensitivity to certain problems, and the resolution of "pathological ideas," all of which should be organized according to an "ethic of socialist society" (Lauterbach 1984, 63).[19] Soviet psychotherapists also frequently employed hypnosis and suggestive therapy. Derived from Pavlov's theories, these targeted "physiological factors which may support tendencies to persistent obsessive ideas" (Wortis 1950, 82). Once the patient was hypnotized, the therapist might use either direct or indirect suggestion or suggested dreams (Lauterbach 1984, 70–91). Finally, practitioners also employed "work therapy" and direct interventions in the patient's life with the goal of altering the patient's social environment (Wortis 1950, 82). Isidore Ziferstein's (1966, 1968) and Lauterbach's studies (1974, 1984), both conducted in the Bekhterev Institute in Leningrad in the 1960s and 1970s (see also Ziferstein 1966 and 1968), suggest that these techniques remained central to late-Soviet psychotherapy, confirming the ongoing centrality of the conscious, rational actor in Soviet psychological conceptions of the person, as well as the tendency to pathologize neurosis.

CASE: NOT THERAPY BUT "TEACHING"

I had heard Egor Eisenberg's name many times during my fieldwork in the PPMS Center. I gathered that he was a major figure in family therapy. I was finally able to interview him in the spring of 2006. A Soviet-trained psychiatrist, Eisenberg generally viewed his discipline's past in positive terms, emphasizing the professionalism of his colleagues, their commitment to curing patients, and the difficult material conditions with which they had to contend. He struck me as a man who, in contrast to Vitya Markov, had not been met with discrimination and had been able to work his way up to the top of Soviet psychiatry. Yet even he suggested that Soviet medicine had a problematic way of looking at the patient. Comparing today's practices to the Soviet period, he said, "[Today's patients] don't fear that they'll be presented as a laughingstock. You won't be given a moral lecture [*tebia ne budut vospityvat'*] or be insulted. There was an unwritten rule in Soviet medicine: [The task was] not only to care for, save, or cure but also to teach." He then gave the following harsh example of "teaching":

> A woman, our teacher, is administering abortions. We students are standing there, and the women were lying right there, being prepared for the abortion. The teacher says, "I will give her anesthesia; she has children, she's a good woman. But this woman"—she [our teacher] didn't explicitly say the word prostitute—"I am not going to use anesthesia, so she'll learn. She's always getting pregnant." And, you know, even though I was a completely green student at the time, I still felt that this was wrong. You can't shame a person publicly [*nel'zia pozorit' cheloveka publichno*]. The doctor could have discussed this with the patient later, saying, "Listen, why don't you use [caution] . . ." But why crucify her in front of everyone?

Eisenberg's story highlighted several things. First, he was referencing an approach to psychotherapy and behavior change that became common in the Soviet period—a practice oriented around moralizing and shaming. This was evident in his description of how the mentor here, the doctor, used a moralizing logic: "so she'll learn." Second, Eisenberg's story showed that despite the broad post-Stalin ideological thaw that took place after 1953, these kinds of problematic doctor-patient relations still existed. Finally, and crucially, Eisenberg (and perhaps others who pursued psychotherapy in Soviet times) nonetheless questioned those problematic attitudes and ways of promoting behavior change.[20]

De-Stalinization and the Thawing Psy-ences: 1953–1970

To summarize so far: the postwar legacy of the ideological debates of the 1930s was disciplinary narrowing, increased specialization, and the elimination of the conditions of acceptability for the emergence of what in the West is known as therapy. There are many accounts of how Stalin's purges prompted confusion, a closing of the ranks around Marxism-Leninism, accusation, denunciation, self-criticism, and purge. Concretely, there was also a shake-up of the heads of psychological academies and, ultimately, party officials closed the USSR's faculties of psychology, redesignating them as a subfield of philosophy, thus isolating psychologists from applied work (Bauer 1959, 128).

Things changed significantly in the year's following Nikita Khrushchev's secret speech in 1956 denouncing Stalin's cult of personality. In my interviews, without romanticizing the Soviet past, psychologists and psychotherapists described an emergent diversity of practices. Egor Eisenberg had been trained in psychiatry in the early 1960s at Leningrad State University. He told me how reading Harry K. Wells's *Pavlov and Freud* (1956) in the scientific library was a crucial moment in his development.[21] Emphasizing the official status of this text, he explained,

> This was not *samizdat*; this was an official publication.[22] I read it, and, of course, I understood what psychology is and psychiatry is. (At that time I didn't know the term *psychotherapy* at all.) And, naturally, this [difference] was really important. For me the main thing was that it was interesting. I had already been to the psychology department (then it was called the philosophical faculty) in order to learn who the psychologists were, how they are trained.[23] And, of course, I liked the fact that there wasn't some indiscriminate attack on Freud in this book, but a good biography of Pavlov and Freud. It showed that each was a genius in his own right: Pavlov as a

physiologist and Freud as a psychologist. . . . That's the impression I got from this book. And my impression was it was like that for many other psychologists my age and younger. They'd say, "You know, that book made a huge impression on me." Some started studying the physiology of higher neural activity, while others did psychology.

Eisenberg's story of reading Freud indicated, if not quite an ecumenicalism in the Soviet psy-ences, then at least a loosening of ideological strictures.[24] He also suggested that already in the 1960s the field had split between those who went on to study the problem of "higher neurological activity"—the Pavlovian approach to the problem of consciousness—and those who went in a "psychological" direction, including himself. What Eisenberg referred to here is a key moment when Pavlovian materialism began to lose its hold on the psyche in clinical practice.

In the second crucial moment in his professional development, Eisenberg cited his growing dissatisfaction with Pavlovian models in clinical work: "I was considered a good student, and a good young doctor, but I started to feel that something was missing in my work. . . . Just engaging with the symptoms, the prescribed biological methods of therapy, was really unsatisfying. Only then did I guess that, probably, it was unsatisfying for the patients, too. I then read somewhere that, it turned out, many psychiatrists, those who proceeded to become psychotherapists, both American and Russian, had had the same experience and had a similar fate."

Based on my survey of the journal *Voprosy Psikhologii* (Topics in Psychology), it is clear that there was often room for debate in Soviet psy-ence. As the Soviet psychologist Artur V. Petrovsky puts it,

> The fact that [since the 1940s] psychology was based on Marxism did not do away with the diversity of theoretical concepts, which evolved and interacted in Soviet psychology at one and the same time. Neither could it preclude the coexistence of various scientific schools and trends. This state of affairs was consonant with the creative nature of Marxism-Leninism—a circumstance which is sometimes ignored by Western historiographers of Soviet psychological science (Raymond Bauer, Josef Brozek, Gregory Razran and others), who attempt to present the matter as if Soviet psychology's shift to Marxist philosophy amounted to rejection of the struggle of views, termination of all theoretical debates, leveling of principled controversies among psychologists, and erosion of distinctions between different psychological schools. History has proved that such views are both erroneous and biased. (1990, 362)

Petrovsky's point is supported by other studies of Soviet practice, which suggest that the conditions for the acceptance of a psychodynamically oriented psychotherapy had already begun to emerge post-Stalin. This perhaps seemingly technical point forestalls the argument that the psychotherapeutic turn is exclusively post-Soviet. As I discuss below, before the Soviet collapse, the discourses of the psyche and personality had been in a state of flux for nearly three decades, reaching as far as the once-forbidden unconscious.

POST-STALINIST DEVELOPMENTS IN APPLIED PSYCHOLOGY

Lauterbach's previously mentioned *Soviet Psychotherapy* (1984), which Eisenberg had recommended to me, offers some concrete examples of the practices of therapy in the postwar period. Lauterbach, a German psychotherapist, had spent seven months at Leningrad's Bekhterev Institute in the late 1970s studying its methods. Lauterbach's account of clinical practice provides evidence that the critique of Pavlov, the partial rapprochement with psychoanalysis, and the emergence of new forms of psychotherapy had already begun in the 1960s. Even psychodynamically inscribed concepts like personality and the unconscious began to appear at that time.

A brief mention of the postwar social context helps to clarify the more general atmosphere of the thaw. Despite the ravages of World War II (in Russia, the Great Fatherland War), which included huge losses of life (particularly men) and neglected infrastructure and production systems (Hosking 1993, 296), the Soviet Union had been industrialized and urbanized. The rough ratio of proletarian to peasant in the 1920s had reversed: in 1959 nearly 70 percent of the USSR was made up of workers and bureaucrats, with only slightly more than 30 percent defined as peasants (518). In cultural terms, starting from this period, new personal practices emerged, including the pursuit of creature comforts that previously would have been deemed bourgeois. Vera S. Dunham (1990) notes a curious array of possessions, including perfume, colored postcards, embroidered pillows, and pink, scalloped paper in middle-brow socialist realist fiction. This marked a departure from Bolshevik asceticism, and an embourgeoisement of one segment of urban Soviet society. Dunham views this as a compromise the party leadership made with the ruling elite to allow the elite to develop their "middleclass values" (see also Boym 1994; Volkov 2000). According to Russian sociologist Vladimir Shlapentokh (1989), the rise of personal entertainment through the television, personal automobiles, and broader availability of consumer goods in the 1960s marked a kind of privatization. Alexei Yurchak (2006) notes that those who came of age in the 1960s cultivated a variety of personal styles, listened to American jazz music, and distributed pirated music and fiction.

Along with this proliferation of urban culture, personal style, and consumption, the psychological fields also underwent a degree of liberalization. After de-Stalinization was initiated in 1953, Soviet practitioners began to explore new approaches that resembled the West's psychodynamic forms. This was fed in part by academic exchanges with scholars from the socialist states of Eastern Europe (Vasilyeva 2005). In addition, researchers worked to further elaborate a Soviet-Marxist psychology, but without the pressure of purges (Graham 1987, 191). For instance, in the 1950s and 1960s, Aleksei Leontiev, a former collaborator with Lev Vygotsky on the studies in Central Asia, developed a theory of activity (*deiatel'nost'*) that became central to the post-Stalin Soviet psychological theory of the personality. For Leontiev, "social activity was the mediating influence forming the human personality" (Graham 1987, 212). Labor was the most important type of activity, but not the only one.[25]

Even the unconscious became a viable research topic through the work of the Georgian psychologist Dmitri Uznadze (Kozulin 1984, 95). Through experiments he had shown that an illusory effect in perception could be caused by prior conditioning, pointing to a *nonconscious* physiological basis for mental processes (98–99).[26] While not particularly Freudian, unconscious sensory-motor regulation flew in the face of the Stalin-era insistence that human behavior should be viewed as conscious activity.[27] In an indication of the much less charged atmosphere in the late 1970s, in an edited volume entitled *The Unconscious [Bessoznatel'noe]* (Prangishvili et al., 1978) put out by the Academy of Sciences of the Georgian Soviet Socialist Republic, both Uznadzeans and Leontievites confessed:

> It cannot be concealed that in those years [the 1930s–1950s] Soviet psychology made a mistake and threw the baby out with the bath water. The negative reaction of Soviet specialists to the defects of psychoanalytic methodology . . . was so strong that criticism of the weaknesses of psychoanalysis developed into a disregard for the very object of psychoanalytic studies. . . . Little by little, it becomes clear that insufficient elaboration of the problem of the unconscious and absence of appropriate methods of study retarded the growth of the most important fields of contemporary scientific thought within psychology as well as beyond it. (quoted in Kozulin 1984, 99–100)

On the practical front, the psychology faculties at both Leningrad State University and Moscow State University reopened in 1965 (Saint Petersburg State University n.d.), just a few years after Eisenberg had been making trips there to find out "who the psychologists were, [and] how to study them." This reversed the folding of psychology into philosophy that had happened after the debates of the 1920s and 1930s, reestablishing it as a distinct *social science*. The creation of a new university specialization in clinical psychology was especially significant. As mentioned, under Stalin, psychology had been pressed into being a research domain. Lauterbach noted, "The [Soviet] psychologist is not at all concerned with treatment. To him, treatment is a medical matter by definition. This attitude is logical in view of the Soviet notion that 'in a psychiatric illness it is not the psyche but the brain that is affected' and that the reason for the disturbance of normal psychological function must therefore be physiological" (1974, 483). The emergence of *clinical psychology* in the Soviet Union was thus symptomatic of a discursive shift in Soviet biopolitics, specifically a loosening of the grip that biomedical approaches had on mental health care. Its appearance implicitly deemed the psyche a possible seat of mental health problems, and it opened a new space for clinical practice. This would become one basis for the intensification of talk therapies in Soviet psychiatry—a trend that would last beyond the collapse of 1991.

CASE: THE THERAPEUTICS OF LYING

Vladimir Mikhailovich, who had cofounded with Vitya Markov the psychotherapy institute where Lena studied, was in his fifties when we first met. A former naval officer and engineer, Vladimir Mikhailovich had decided to study psychiatry at Leningrad State University in the late 1970s. Among the leading graduates of his cohort, he was nevertheless unable to get a job because of his papers' "fifth point" (*piatyi punkt*), which said he was Jewish.[28] In the end, he was able to find a job only in narcology (*narkologiia*), which he described as a low-status branch of psychiatry that worked with alcoholics; according to my research, many qualified practitioners designated as Jewish ended up in this field.[29] This encounter with professional discrimination would be the first of several for Vladimir Mikhailovich, and such experiences shaped his negative view of not only Soviet power but also its medical system as a whole.

Vladimir Mikhailovich's fundamental complaint with the Soviet medical system was that it positioned the patient and the doctor in a highly subordinate relation to the state, and in an adversarial relation with one another. As an example, he described the widespread use of placebo therapy in treating alcoholism, which made use of an implant, or *podshivka*, by which a substance called disulfiram was supposedly released subcutaneously. The patient was then told that if this substance came into contact with alcohol in the bloodstream, it could cause a severe physiological reaction and potentially lead to death.[30]

"Such methods," he said, "are very manipulative and are founded on the fact that the person is afraid. They created an awesome myth of death through drinking. Pills, injections—these were the symbols generally reflecting that myth. But the basis [was] deception."

Vitya Markov was also "Jewish by passport" and ended up at the same narcology clinic. He agreed with Vladimir Mikhailovich's harsh assessment of Soviet medical culture. Placing a lie at the center of the therapeutic relationship, he added, triggered further lying:

> This [lie] spins off all kinds of rumors because the sixth person to be administered the podshivka drinks and nothing happens. When you go in for your treatment, you tell this to the doctor, and he responds to your rumor with a lie: "Well," he says, "that may be true, but this other person did die." The key thing is that the entire relationship is based on a lie. There is no trust, and you play this strange game. The funny thing is that the essence of alcoholism is that it is based on lying to yourself, and here the method of treatment is to deceive. So you have mixed up the method with the thing that fuels the problem in the first place. . . . Of course this doesn't solve the problem. In a lot of cases, the lives of alcoholics were much happier when they were drinking.

Vladimir Mikhailovich told me that a related problem with Soviet narcology was that it did not see the patient; it saw only a "struggle with alcoholism" (*bor'ba s alkogolizmom*). Sensing this, patients "took the natural position of opposition [to the doctor]. The state, the medical system (narcology), combats alcoholics, and alcoholics combat them." Meanwhile, he asserted, "alcoholism has no relation to medicine; it is a social and psychological phenomenon."

Another clinical psychologist, Andrei Abramovich, who had worked at the famous Bekhterev Institute in the 1980s, described the elaborate performances that arose around the podshivka and its logic of deception, fear, and combat. He noted that doctors would sometimes create collective rituals before administering the podshivka, while the alcoholics would come up with ways to neutralize the podshivka, such as eating ten lemons. Placing a lie at the center of the therapeutic relationship, he said, "was the essence of the Soviet system."

Like Eisenberg's story of the public abuse of the "prostitute," Vladimir Mikhailovich, Vitya, and Andrei Abramovich offered uncomplimentary peeks inside the Soviet psychiatric system in the late-Soviet period. Here the discourse was not about abuse but about a lack of trust between doctor and patient, and a culture of lies and threat as the means of care.

In addition to changes in Soviet psychology and psychiatry, the scholarly literature points to a revolution of sorts within Soviet psychotherapy. A particular irony of Pavlovian psychiatry was that for all of the early Soviet critiques of psychoanalysis's asocial nature, Pavlov's approach, because of its objectivist-materialist parsimony, also downplayed the role of the social in neuroses. Starting in the 1960s, this model of the person and neurosis came under criticism. Vladimir Nikolaevich Miasishchev, a psychotherapist and educator, who directed the Bekhterev Institute, where Andrei Abramovich had worked in the 1980s, was among the most vocal and well-positioned critics. Miasishchev's work is significant because it was one of the first Soviet dynamically oriented approaches to psychotherapy (Lauterbach 1984, 108). (This transformation is interesting to consider in light of contemporaneous revolutions in Western psychotherapy, in which Freud was supplanted by Carl Rogers and the human-potential movement.)

What had happened in the USSR to bring about this shift? A student and colleague of Miasishchev, Ekaterina Yakovleva, put it this way: although Pavlov's theories of the "pathophysiological mechanism" of disorders were useful (i.e., a model of mental illness that takes the physiological characteristics of the brain as its object of diagnosis and intervention), "the clinical investigation . . . of . . . neuropsychiatric illnesses requires a knowledge not only of their pathophysiological basis, but also of the specific characteristics of the personality, its conscious relations, and other aspects of the psyche" (quoted in Ziferstein 1969, 352).[31] If biology was not enough to understand mental disorder, then what else was required?

Several aspects of Miasishchev's work are worth highlighting in answer to this question. First, his focus on *neurosis* was unique. He focused almost exclusively on what had until then been seen as a marginal disorder more or less solvable through rational and suggestive techniques. In the earlier Soviet psychiatric model, a patient suffering from a fear of public speaking would be "reconditioned" through some combination of rational psychotherapy and hypnosis. The assumption was that something neurophysiological—something in the brain—was interfering with his or her life and could be transformed rationally. Miasishchev was the first to "deviate from the conventional medical attitude of viewing the neurotic person as a patient who either lacks something which must be replaced through medication, information, supplemental training in rational thinking, or who must be operated on, repaired or modified through suggestion techniques" (Lauterbach 1984, 93). Second, Miasishchev introduced into Soviet psychotherapy a concept of personality (*lichnost'*), which had been out of place in the Pavlovian model.[32] He viewed the personality through the lens of one's relations, or *otnosheniia*, with friends, family, coworkers, society, and, ultimately, oneself. Relations defined one's personality and experiences in the world, and through otnosheniia, he also developed a language for discussing the concept of needs (Lauterbach 1984, 94).

This revised personality concept enabled a reworking of the theory of neurosis: neuroses arise when a conflict emerges in one's life that shifts, displaces, or disrupts one's otnosheniia, making a rational recovery impossible. For instance, a conflict between desires (what one wants versus what is possible) can lead to hysteria, and a conflict between internal needs (loyalty to the state versus loyalty to friends) can lead to obsessive-compulsive disorder (Lauterbach 1984, 105).

Miasishchev's suggestion that neuroses were disorders arising from social and other relationships (external pathogenic events) was a major departure: from the 1930s on, both the social and the subjective had been minor players in Soviet science's dialectical-materialist view; the idea that the psyche, not the brain, was the seat of disorder ran against the Pavlovian grain; and the notion of socially prefigured neurosis sat uncomfortably within Soviet utopianism (Lauterbach 1984, 106). Miasishchev therefore replaced the Pavlovian somatic conception of neurosis with one premised on the personality in interaction with the social world. Miller has argued that Miasishchev had in fact managed "to incorporate into his work on the neurotic personality many of Freud's concerns without making explicit use of psychoanalytic content" (1998, 121). Whether psychoanalytic or not, this also posited an actor somewhat less in control of his or her faculties, while implicating the social environment in disorder. At the height of Stalinism, when socialism had supposedly been achieved, the arrows of blame had pointed the other way.

CASE: THE CLIENT WASN'T IMPORTANT

As I mentioned in the introduction, Vitya Markov was questioned by the KGB for mentioning Freud in a group session in the narcology clinic in the 1970s (an agent had posed as an alcoholic). His colleague Vladimir Mikhailovich, calling the clinic a "theater of the absurd" (*teatr absurda*), offered another example of the politics and hierarchy at the clinic. While he was in the midst of a hypnosis session, with a "do not disturb" sign on the door, a head doctor on a tour of the clinic burst in. Rather than rising to show her the requisite respect, he asked her, politely, to leave so as not to disrupt the session. He was later reprimanded for his own (and his hypnotized patients') failure to show respect.

Soviet medical power could also be erratic and contradictory. Vladimir told me an amazing story about how he came to be hired, and fired, as the director of the city's first psychological-advice hotline. One day, out of the blue, he was called by a head doctor and asked to report to her office immediately. On his way, he noticed a line of people outside her door. The head doctor, Katerina Ivanovna, handed him the daily *Evening Leningrad* [*Vechernyi Leningrad*], which reported that the first walk-in psychosocial service and hotline in the country was opening. Vladimir narrated:

> "What do you think of this idea?" she asked.
> "I think it's a fantastic idea," I replied.
> "Good," she said, "start immediately."
> At first I protested. "But Katerina Ivanovna, I have a [therapy] group scheduled at three o'clock; they'll be waiting for me."
> "Don't worry about the group," she told me. "We'll cancel it. Begin."
> To this very day I remember what happened. I was sitting in the office, behind this huge Stalinist desk. People started coming in, and I remember one person who needed help, and I wasn't really prepared; I was thinking about my scheduled [therapy] group. Meanwhile, while consulting with this person, someone called on the hotline, and I was supposed to answer. It was horrible.

Vladimir Mikhailovich decided to "put things in order," dividing the walk-in service from the telephone service. But within a few months he ran into a problem. While recruiting staff, he chose a woman from his university days who turned out to be "Jewish by passport." He was pulled aside and told that while the director liked this person, "we already have a lot of Jewish people working in the hospitals." According to his recollection, she was eventually hired, but the event was very disturbing for Vladimir Mikhailovich. He felt he needed to share the story, so he called an old teacher.

> I had a good relationship with her; she was a normal person [*normal'nyi chelovek*]. And I told her what had happened. That's it. I didn't have some kind of active revolution in mind. The next day, our deputy director came up to me—someone with whom I had a good relationship—and said, "Vladimir Mikhailovich, I don't know how to say this, but you're no longer working on the telephone service. The head doctor has made the decision. I can't say what he said, but it was connected with your telephone call. It was bugged." Imagine! A therapist is supposed to guarantee the confidentiality of his clients but cannot because he's being bugged. This was a crisis counseling line [*telefon doveriia*] that was bugged.[33] It wasn't only me who was being bugged but also my clients.

He remained confused as to the meaning of this event. Was the party simply using the telephone line as a way to gather information on people? Was it a means to control psychiatry? Was it about Jewishness? "It's hard to say," he confessed, "but what is totally accurate is that there were no resources, and no accounting for the interests of the client. It was precisely the opposite. The client wasn't important."

Vladimir Mikhailovich's story cast the narrative of Miasishchev's innovations in a different light. Concretely, it raised questions about the practical scope of scientific revolution. Genealogy, in documenting inflection points in discursive practice, may, in fact, not offer much insight into practices. Miasishchev's increasing focus on the personality, relations, and neurosis did not, then, necessarily signal a broad institutional shift in doctor-patient relations. At the same time, Vladimir was no mere extension of Soviet biopolitics either. There remained numerous incommensurabilities between biopolitics and care.

Late-Soviet Liberalization and Perestroika: 1970–1991

New therapeutic modes continued to appear in the 1970s and blossomed into an ever more diverse range of practices in the 1980s. In fact, a homegrown New Age movement took root in the Soviet Union. Psychics and healers (*ekstrasenzy*), likely tied to the centuries-long tradition of Russian mysticism, appeared on TV (Stites 1992; Matza 2012). But the movement also included research scientists who began probing the field of parapsychology. In 1979 the International Symposium on the Unconscious was held in Tbilisi, Georgia, where a wide range of parapsychological talks were given (Kripal 2007, 326).

Late-Soviet education reform, discussed in the next chapter, was also crucial for the development of non-biomedical talk therapies. For much of the Soviet period, the Soviet Academy of Pedagogical Sciences (Akademiia pedagogicheskikh nauk [APN], established in 1943), charged with overseeing the upbringing of the next generation, was dominated by Anton S. Makarenko. Makarenko was a Ukrainian-born educator and vocal critic of psychology's "individualized 'child-centered'" approach to education (Rosen 1971, 35).[34] Drawing on Makarenko's pedagogical orientation, the APN oversaw the centralized, universal, and egalitarian Soviet education for most of the second half of the twentieth century (Dunstan and Suddaby 1992, 5; Gilgen and Gilgen 1996, 14; Kelly 2007, 95–96).

Yet in the 1980s, alongside other forms of liberalization in the psy-ences, there was a miniature revolution in the politics of Soviet education. The economic crises of the 1970s raised the issues of what constituted a proper education and whether the undifferentiated, centralized approach to education based on Makarenko's disciplinary techniques was addressing what Gorbachev suggested was the fundamental, and often-overlooked, aspect of the production process—the human factor. As Gorbachev remarked in 1985 to a meeting of the Central Committee of the Communist Party of the Soviet Union (CPSU), "Party work has to do with the human factor. . . . Hence the main task of this work today is to inspire, by all possible means, a change in the minds and moods of personnel from top to bottom. . . . Little can be changed in the economy, management and education without changing mentality and developing a desire and ability to think and work in new ways" (quoted in Rawles 1996, 103).

In a useful study entitled *Democracy in the Russian School: The Reform Movement in Education since 1984*, authors Ben Eklof and Edward Dneprov suggest that this late-socialist call to change minds and moods created the political conditions for the reform-minded factions in the APN to interject their own ideas for reform, which included psychological ideas about emotional needs. A famous meeting was held at the writer's colony at Peredelkino in 1986, and attendees developed a new rubric for education, called the Pedagogy of Cooperation. This approach advanced a liberal-humanist philosophy of "more humane relations between teacher and pupil," a "dialogue of cultures," "open schools," a more "democratic classroom," and a "greater respect for the autonomy of childhood and for the role of play in learning, and for freedom of choice as well as self-government" (Eklof and Dneprov 1993, 8–9). The Pedagogy of Cooperation was a departure from the earlier APN teaching priorities, which were based on the imposition of knowledge, skills, and abilities through rote learning. In the context of the conservative APN and its resistance to psychological expertise, this amounted to a psycho-ethical revolution.

As the chorus calling for the shift to differentiated, democratized education grew, those in power, keen to find ways out of economic stagnation, began to take note. Eventually, Yegor Yakovlev, an influential member of the Politburo under Gorbachev and the person in charge of education, assembled the Temporary Research Committee on the Schools (Vremennyi nauchno-issledovatel'skii kollektiv "Shkola" [VNIK-Shkola]), which eventually adopted the Pedagogy of Cooperation as its platform. Proposals were submitted in late 1987 and 1988 and led to the empowerment of "teacher-innovators," greater self-management of schools, the establishment of school boards, and the encouragement of diversity as opposed to leveling (Dunstan and Suddaby 1992; Eklof and Dneprov 1993, 12). This press toward differentiated education, decentralization, experimentation, diversity, and "humanization" (*gumanizatsiia*) (Eklof and Dneprov 1993, 5) redefined the schools. And the platform also introduced a new concern with the importance of individual needs into the heart of late-socialist biopolitics: now schools were supposed to "further the intellectual, moral, emotional and physical development of the personality, liberate its creative potential and shape a communist world-view based on general human values" (Muckle 1990, 79).

Psychologists played an important role in these reforms and helped pave the way for the psychotherapeutic turn. In giving their answers to pedagogical questions, the VNIK-Shkola group relied on clinical and other applied forms of psychology, in particular the developmental psychology of Vygotsky, which had been marginalized in 1936. Many of the reformers were themselves psychologists. In an interview in *Psikhologicheskaia Gazeta* (Psychological News), Aleksander Asmolov, the eventual head psychologist of state education in the USSR, recalled those years as introducing the liberal doctrines of education, or what he casts as the shift from "averaged" to "personality-oriented education" (2005, 10). Such programs laid the groundwork for the creation of "psychological services of education, aimed at prophylactic, diagnostic, correctional and rehabilitational work with the personality [*lichnost'*]."

To be sure, socialism remained a central premise in Soviet psy-ence and education, but as Jeffrey Kripal (2007, 331) reports, Soviet researchers had by then coined a materialist language that mirrored what was being called human potential in the United States. Two US psychologists from the Esalen Institute in Big Sur, California, who visited the USSR put it this way: "There is a remarkable symmetry between Soviet and American interests in this field. The Soviet term 'hidden human reserves,' for example, is almost identical to the American 'human potential' as a guiding idea. Soviet concern with 'maximum performance' resembles American investigations of 'peak experience.' Soviet studies of 'bioplasma,' 'biophysical effects,' and 'distant bioinformation interactions' resemble American studies of 'energy fields,' 'dowsing,' and 'remote viewing.' Training in 'psychical self-regulation' techniques is the Soviet equivalent of 'biofeedback' and 'stress management' programs in the US. In both countries these ideas have stimulated new approaches to education, health-care, and sports" (Kripal 2007, 331). (The parallel focus on human capital may also reflect the ways in which the new, neoliberal post–Cold War order, was dawning under Reagan and Thatcher.)

More frequent exchanges between American humanistic psychologists and Soviet researchers also spread new therapeutic orientations in the USSR (and influenced the VNIK-Shkola movement). Particularly influential was the aforementioned Esalen Institute, a retreat center and hub of the human-potential movement, which promoted "track-two diplomacy" under the Reagan administration. Esalen's director, Mike Murphy, initiated these visits in 1970. What began as a series of research trips to learn about Soviet work on the parapsychological was eventually formalized into the Esalen Soviet-American Exchange Program in 1980, which attained a high level of power and influence under Reagan. Alongside Esalen, the closely linked Association for Humanistic Psychology initiated its own diplomacy, sponsoring the trips of various famous psychologists to give seminars.[35] These visits, which would increase sharply after 1991, also fostered the development of nonmedical therapies.[36]

/   /   /

This brings me, finally, back to where this chapter began—the exuberance, the joy and bitterness, described by Bondarenko, the Ukrainian psychologist who had squeezed his way into Carl Rogers's Moscow workshop in 1986: "I realized how lonely I had been. But I was feeling the truth of my being in the world and that feeling purified me and gave me strength to exist, and I sensed tears of joy as well as bitterness in my eyes" (1999, 13).

Historians and scholars queried the why behind the spread of something resembling American human-potential psychology in the USSR. Such questions were premised on the idea that the movement's interests are ideological deviations from an assumed Marxist orthodoxy and therefore in need of explanation. For example, traveling to the USSR in the mid-1980s, American journalist Sheila Cole (1986) had set out to discover, "Why were the people in charge of the Soviet Union interested in Americans who are known in the United States for the extremes to which they have taken self-involvement?"[37] Cole's supposition, in the words of the historian Loren Graham, was that "the human potential movement fosters many attitudes valued by the authorities, such as expanded labor productivity, positive feelings about work and play, large families (at a time of declining birth rates), and close family ties (at a time of rising birth rates)" (1987, 219). Richard Rawles, a British sociologist, develops another related explanation: such trends were symptomatic of a larger reckoning under perestroika, whose political-economic counterpart appeared in Gorbachev's attempt to address the USSR's economic recession and perceived social stagnation through a renewed attention to the personality at the center of the production process.

In light of this chapter, the questions of Cole, Graham, and Rawles seem wrongly put. A great deal of attention and research had already been devoted to the subjective factors of behavior and the needs of the personality in the post-Stalin period within the Marxist tradition. Experiences such as Bondarenko's, then, may be better thought of as the *reactivation* (rather than introduction) of interest in the subjective. As the rest of this book will show, it is a reactivation that has been intensified, for better and for worse, under postsocialist capitalism.

CASE: "THE PEOPLE" IS NO ONE

In the introduction I briefly alluded to Vitya Markov's attempt to create a "therapeutic community" in the narcology clinic—a kind of quiet revolution that eventually got him reprimanded. His colleague Vladimir Mikhailovich elaborated on the story. He said that when he started working in narcology doing group therapy in the 1970s, he was instructed to follow the protocols, essentially a ten-lesson set of lectures.

"This [method] didn't propose [that alcoholics] rebuild relations," he complained, "or make a psychotherapeutic contract in which they would come to understand that they are responsible for themselves [*na nikh lezhit otvetsvtennost'*]. We were in white coats. To them we were people closely tied to the system [*priblizhat' k etoi sisteme*] in the struggle against alcoholism. In the best case, we were the people who knew something that they didn't know, and who would tell them what to do."

Vladimir Mikhailovich, Vitya, and others eventually formed a reading group in which they assembled the bits of Western psychotherapy they had gathered through samizdat. This included works by Gestalt founder Friedrich Perls, the humanistic psychologist Carl Rogers, and Freud. Through these readings they began to discuss what troubled them about the clinical protocols. Soviet medicine viewed the patient as someone to be "psycho-corrected," Vladimir explained. "This meant influencing minds" in keeping with "Soviet morals, ethics, and principles and a general devotion to the Communist Party." "The totalitarian system," he said, "presupposed that the most important category was the people [*narod*]. But 'the people' is no one [*narod eto nikto*]. And nobody was interested in the separate person, his aspirations [*chaianie*], his suffering, joy, inspiration, and soul suffering [*bol' dushevnyi*]. But that's what therapy is oriented toward. In providing therapy, what is most important for me is that very person [*dlia menia vot samym glavnym iavliaetsia vot etot chelovek*]."

Eventually Vladimir Mikhailovich and Vitya reoriented their care to the patient and the illness: "We took up the idea that you help people by reflecting what is happening to them, by helping them to understand that the problem is with how they live, how they build relations with themselves, with the world and other people; that, in fact, to a large extent the problem is a reflection of those difficulties that they encounter in life and that they can't overcome them using their own resources."

They formed one of the first outpatient clinics in the city, where patients could come and go as they pleased.

Looking Back

How should one understand Vitya Markov's, Egor Eisenberg's, and Vladimir Mikhailovich's stories, now in relation to a more substantial account of Soviet psychiatry, psychology, and psychotherapy? This chapter has illustrated a professionally bounded discursive formation in motion. In it, I have described what the conditions of acceptability within the Soviet psy-ences were and how, over time, "the subjective factors of behavior" (Bauer 1959, 68) haunted the formation of those fields.[38] These conditions have also had a bearing on the contemporary. They have shaped the interplay between materialist or scientistic discourses and clinical practice, as well as the consequences of debates around health and pathology, self and other, in shaping Soviet biopolitics, institutional configurations, clinical practices, and conceptions of the person. Whether faced with a demand for social uplift for so many living in illiteracy and poverty in the 1920s, or for ideological support for a particular vision of the human in the 1930s, or for post-Stalin liberalization in the 1960s, or for attention to the human factor of production in the 1980s, the psy-ences and their therapies have been, and continue to be, in a dynamic state of commensuration and incommensuration with biopolitical norms. This chapter also highlights the complex relationship among politics, therapeutics, and, as it were, the joy and bitterness of those confronting its new, "liberated" forms in the 1960s–1980s. If in the historiography the conditions of acceptability for the subjective, and thus also a more liberalized environment for doing mental health work, appear to have started expanding in the 1960s, the retrospective experiences of those I interviewed, including Vitya and Vladimir Mikhailovich, offer a different picture. Criticisms of the pathologization of difference; of the abuse, through "teaching," of patients by medical authorities; of the placing of deception at the center of the therapeutic relationship; of the neglect of the patient's concerns in the face of "the people"—these comments interrupt the historical narrative. They are, in an important sense, a part of this book's history of the "and yet."

If we set aside these ethnographic interruptions for a moment, it does seem that a broad narrative of the psy-ences can be sustained, even on the basis of a critical reading of the historiography. In particular, the more dispassionate works of Lauterbach (1984) and Petrovsky (1990) make it clear that there was a shift, over the course of the Soviet period, in the acceptability of concepts of subjectivity, health, and pathology. There was a move from a strictly deterministic view of subjectivity as almost exclusively shaped by the material environment, to a dialectical one situated between environment and consciousness, to, finally, increasingly subjectivist modes of understanding individual emotional needs. This gradual expansion of subjectivist and introspectionist orientations after the 1950s also brought new therapies, shaped at first by an evolving Marxist humanism and postwar contacts with European psychodynamic therapy, and later by American humanistic psychology. In other words, the story of the Soviet psy-ences over the twentieth century is a story of the increasing elaboration of interiority, emotionality, relations, and personality, even against the background of medically oriented practices' ongoing dominance.[39] As I will show in the next chapter, it is also a story of how postsocialist capitalism subsequently articulated with that process, driving forward ever more intense classifications of psychological difference. One could think of this broad shift in terms of the embourgeoisement of psychotherapy and Soviet society as a whole, heralding the celebration of emotions and the unique, while at the same time articulating the social as a potential source of disorder. This view is apt but also too narrow to capture the full scope of Soviet applied psychology. In the first place, it presumes, falsely, a lack of interest in individuality in the Soviet period. Unlike the many accounts of the Soviet period that frame intellectual debates as a binary agon between liberal individualism and Marxism, by the postwar period the Soviet sciences contained varying kinds of subjective emphasis and articulations of interiority as a category of analysis and target of therapy. To render this as a binary struggle, too, would mean to naturalize Western therapies and insinuate that the Soviet Union was gradually on a path to "normalcy" (see Krylova 2000; Yurchak 2006). As a consequence of a more refined view of postwar and late-socialist humanism, I suggest that the surge in humanistic, existential, and other subjective therapies under socialism had begun to take root in the 1960s, and again in the 1980s, during perestroika.

But there remains the curious puzzle of my informants' condemnations of late-Soviet psychology. Recall, for example, Vitya's broad-brushing of the entirety of Soviet psychotherapy as Stalinist. Many who had worked during the late-Soviet period were ambivalent about their past work, and their reflections could be compared to the Cold War–era critiques of Soviet psychiatry (see Bloch and Reddaway 1984). At their most extreme, these stories included accounts of KGB spying, bugged telephone advice lines, deception, anti-Semitism, lying, disdain for patients, and daily abuse and discrimination. Such stories prompt at least two readings—first, they are opportunities to interrupt historicization in the name of a history of the present, and, second, they are performances in the present. Following Lisa Rofel's work on cohort analysis, these stories are not simply "transparent descriptions" but also a "means through which postsocialist subjects are constituted" (1999, 14). They enable practitioners to constitute themselves as post-Soviet actors, and to render contemporary psychotherapy and psychology as part of the remoralization of not just Russian medicine but society as a whole. Looking to replace a culture of lies with truth, collectivity with the individual, and correction with care and self-responsibility, practitioners used the Soviet period as a pivot on which to simultaneously, if indirectly, say something about the present. What kinds of work do these stories about the Soviet past do for them? How do such stories stage the contemporary? If one reads psychotherapists' statements as a kind of negative image of the present, the therapists frame their vital point of intervention in the doctor-patient relationship. This entails the *humanization* (gumanizatsiia) of their discipline, a term that came up often in fieldwork, which was related to hostile Soviet-era therapeutic practices and the medical system, as well as the recalibration of subjectivity. Through implicit comparison with the past, these practitioners constructed themselves as agents in the face of Soviet constraint.

What they often left out of their comments to me, however, were critical views of capitalism, and the ways in which care and the subjective concerns of therapy continue to be warped, now by privatization. It was as if the critique of psychotherapy's past left little room for a more critical view of its present. Incommensurate forms of care, then, were subtly rather than overtly tactical. The weight of the past appeared to still be heavy.

As I discuss in the next three chapters, under postsocialist capitalism Bauer's so-called problem of the subjective factors of behavior was transmuted into a solution. In the wake of the New Soviet Man, there is now a psychological subject whose personality, relationships, emotional needs, unconscious desires, and self-fulfillment have become vital new areas of research, government, and investment. There is a great historical irony here. The "subjective factors of behavior" that Russia's first twentieth-century revolution critiqued have, since its second, capitalist revolution, returned with a vengeance, flowering into a care for the self that would make Lenin, bathed in red light and formaldehyde and on display in Red Square, spin in his mausoleum. And yet, as with their Soviet forebears, practitioners are constructively engaging with the problems of self and society, health and illness, and well-being in complex, unpredictable ways. The psychotherapeutic remains precariously political.

PART II

(IN)COMMENSURABILITY

What happened to the interest in psychological humanization—as both a disciplinary struggle and a social agenda—once the Soviet Union collapsed in 1991? And what does its afterlife reveal about care and mental well-being under the conditions of capitalism, consumerism, and democracy? Part II addresses these questions through an ethnographic examination of psychological services for children.

FIGURE INTERLUDE 2.1. First comes love, then comes Madonna: "8 July, Day of Family, Love, and Fidelity" (right), and "9 August, Gallery of Stars: Madonna" (left). Photo by the author.

INTERLUDE

Family Problems

It was day 2 of the Art of Parenting seminar offered by a rival organization of Re-Generation, PsyInc. I was there to get a sense of the variety of approaches to family-related psychological training.

There were eleven of us: me and another young man, plus nine women. In the first session we were asked to formulate our zapros—the problem on which we came to work. Many of the women had come because they were having difficulties with their children. One had an older son who didn't get along with her younger child and displayed aggression. Another admitted to having been excessively controlling and was worried because her children were doing poorly in school; she wondered whether she was the problem. Another had a toddler, like me, and was interested in learning how to be a good parent. She wanted to nip problems in the bud. The young man was an uncle. He was there to work on patience with his nephews. In short, we all hoped to be better adults with children.

Natalia, the psychotherapist, told us to divide into two groups. One group was told to pretend they were parents, the other children. Pretend it is bedtime, she said, and the children must be put to bed. Some in the kid group were pulled aside and told to be "bad"; the others would be "good." We began.

As in many treningi, there was a mixture of embarrassment, laughter, and discomfort. I was in the "bad-child" group at first, and it was awkward to see that my actions caused my partner all kinds of trouble. Fair was fair, though, and soon the tables were turned. My partner, now the bad child, crossed her arms and refused my pleading.

When we came back together again, Natalia asked each of us to talk about how it felt in that relation. In the cases of bad behavior, the "kids" spoke of being unneeded and not heard, the "parents" of being at their wits' end. One woman, Galya, said that she had failed as a parent. Natalia used this as an opportunity to comment that there are different ways to negotiate children's demands—totalitarian, anarchic, and something more democratic. She said that finding the democratic approach was the goal.

Some of the parents challenged Natalia, although in a democratic way, by claiming that they had already put all the lessons that she had given them into practice, but nothing was working.

"I've tried," said Masha, another mother, "but still my daughter is rude [ei khamit]."

"Remember," said Natalia, repeating her lessons about listening, "the problem child is just a child who needs something."

"What could she possibly need?" asked Masha.

Natalia fell silent for a moment. "Perhaps you yourself need to take care of yourself. If you aren't taking care of yourself, then that could influence the behavior of your children."

/ / /

Where is the problem in any family situation? Is it with the child or the parent? Or does the genesis of any problem lie in structural factors beyond the confines of the family? What does it mean to be *problematic*? In part II I discuss how commercial psychotherapy organizations and municipal psychological services addressed these questions. Their practices indicated a particular struggle to think about, and indeed redefine, personal problems—a struggle that became acute as children's well-being was redefined in a capitalist context and linked to the nation's future. Children's emotional worlds and the parenting practices assembled around them became new governmental concerns, vehicles for making money, and sites for managing risk.

Chapter 2

"WAIT, AND THE TRAIN WILL HAVE LEFT"

The Success Complex and Psychological Difference

By the time I started my fieldwork in 2005, the sprouts of interest in psychotherapy that appeared in the 1980s had grown, vinelike, into many cracks and corners. The new approach to psychology spanned commercial, state, and nonprofit contexts, reaching into human resources and personnel management, self-help, consulting services, outpatient clinics, schools, and nongovernmental organizations. The psychotherapeutic orientations varied (transpersonal psychology, existential psychology, humanistic psychology, and Jungian or Freudian psychoanalysis, as well as Russian social and developmental psychology), but despite this diversity much psychotherapy was being offered in one format: the *trening* (training). Less stigmatizing than therapy (*terapiia*) or counseling (*konsul'tirovaniie*), trening invoked a routine practice aimed at honing a skill or capacity—just the sort of thing needed in the new market economy.

Children's (and child-related) psychological services had also expanded considerably since the Pedagogy of Cooperation of the 1980s (see previous chapter). Several dozen commercial organizations worked in the city. They, too, offered treningi and appealed to parents' desire to manage their children's behavior. Some promised to help with life skills aimed at self-realization, others focused on school-preparedness, phrased in psychological terms. Some honed in on self-definition in professional contexts, while others simply promoted confidence building.

One of these organizations, ReGeneration, would become a key field site. I found ReGeneration through their website; they were one of the few with an Internet presence at the time. Nestled in a few rooms inside a public school in central Saint Petersburg, ReGeneration was run by Tamara Grigorievna, a woman in her fifties who had been educated in social psychology in the late-Soviet period and had gotten her start offering treningi to adults. A slight woman with a large presence who smelled faintly of cigarettes, Tamara Grigorievna welcomed me into their world. As she would later tell me, she saw opportunity in having me, a native English speaker, around. ReGeneration had between eight and ten psychologists on staff, depending on consulting needs, and held seminars and provided counseling throughout the year on topics such as self-confidence (*uverennost' v sebe*), developing behavioral and communicative flexibility (*razvitie povedencheskoi i kommunikativnoi gibkosti*), openness and making use of new opportunities (*otkrytie i ispol'zovanie novykh vozmozhnostei*), time management (*planirovanie vremeni*), and successful communication/socialization (*uspeshnoe obshchenie*). But their bread and butter was a sleepaway camp specializing in intensive psychological education (*psikhologicheskoe obrazovanie*). Modeled on the Soviet pioneer *lagery* of old, ReGeneration's camps took children either to the "near abroad" (Finland or Bulgaria) or to a campground in the Russian countryside and offered them a combination of leisure activities and behavioral lessons.[1]

What should one make of such programs? Why now in Russia? And why the prominence given to *psikhologiia* (psychology)? My many conversations with Tamara Grigorievna and two of her staff, Aleksandr and Zhenya, helped me to answer these questions. In broad terms, of course, ReGeneration was one legacy of the turn to emotional needs initiated by the APN reforms of the 1980s. But that prehistory did not really account for the contemporary popularity of the new psychology undergirding the psychotherapeutic turn—especially its commercial variants. As I would learn, this popularity stemmed from a widespread belief held by parents, and promoted by psychotherapists and psychologists, that in a market society the rules of the game are different. Paramount here was that the very notion of success had been culturally redefined, and achieving it required new ways of thinking and being, including psychologically inflected ones.

This brand of psychological work, meshed with commerce, could be an anxious place, especially for parents. I was particularly receptive to it because in 2005 my partner, Nicole, and I were new parents: our son, Aarno, was five months old when we arrived in Russia. I was often unsure of what I was doing, and this seemed apparent to passersby, especially *babushki*, or elderly Russian women. Having outfitted Aarno one day in what we thought was a snowsuit, we were scolded by a babushka wearing thick felt *valenki* (boots), who informed us that he was, in fact, wearing a "spring suit." Another day, a babushka stopped us on the windy Kamenoostrovskii Bridge. "Isn't he freezing?" she asked. "You should cover his ears. If they get too cold at this age, they will be cold for the rest of his life." Cold, clearly, was a thing of concern, and many older women took it as their duty to tell us—and most often me—that we were being lax.

The sense of being under the watchful eye of someone who knows better extended into fieldwork proper. One day, after having been advised by two babushki on the metro that Aarno's boots were on the wrong feet (this time, at least, they were not), Nicole and I joined our new friends, Irina and Vera, two children's psychologists, with our cranky one-year-old. Aarno was hungry and squirming irritably in his stroller. We struggled in front of them to calm him down. I felt the flush of embarrassment creeping up my neck.

"All children should be walking by his age," Irina remarked. "The reason he isn't might be your fears, which you project onto him." She added, "Children learn most of their emotions from their mother."

"Not from the father?" I objected, already sensitive to the gendered expectations around child-rearing in Russia.

"Yes, the father, too," she said obligingly. She fell silent.

My emotions got the better of me, and I couldn't help a curt reply: "I have noticed that many in Saint Petersburg fuss over children, even the children of strangers, and often micromanage [*melochnaia opeka*]. This is good for nothing other than irritation. It's my own business [*Eto moe lichnoe delo*]."

Vera, catching my frustration, tried to smooth things over. She agreed that it could be an invasion of personal space.

With the benefit of hindsight (and the waning of annoyance), the ethnographic relevance of these experiences came into view. In the first place, they exemplified the ways in which biopolitics—that is, a set of norms and techniques concerned with the government of life—filters into everyday life. Governmental concerns about population health are domesticated and circulate through the capillaries of stranger encounters through the mere expression of worry (or even exasperation)—in my case, at least, most often with babushki. Even more relevant to my project, the fact that psychotherapeutic advice differed from those old wives' tales indicated a contrasting biopolitics.

The first, condensed in the figure of the nosy babushka, expresses a kind of basic prophylaxis concerned with physical well-being. The second is relatively newer and is premised on an expert grid, developmental benchmarks, and a penetrative gaze, and it reaches beyond the physical to the psychological.

In comparison to grandmotherly advice, I found psychotherapeutic surveillance even more anxiety inducing. In the face of expertise, it could sometimes seem that children's development was a terrifyingly delicate enterprise. One false move—losing one's temper, being inattentive, being overly attentive, making approval conditional, or being too critical—and your child could be psychologically damaged! I imagined that other parents, confronted with the new psychological messaging that I found in Russia's public culture, might have felt such anxiety as well.

Indeed, as I surveyed the advertisements for children's psychological services, I found that the incitement of anxiety was common. One of my favorites was a brochure from an organization called FasTracKids, a trademarked franchise started in the United States that some psychologists were setting up in Russia (see figure 2.1). FasTracKids exhorted parents to "develop talents and abilities in your child" through programs in "Enriched Learning for Tomorrow's Leaders." "New research shows," they claimed, "that the first 5–6 years of a child's life are decisive. In the course of that time the neurons of the child's brain build connections. This moment should not be neglected; otherwise, the child will not be able to embody his or her [svoi] potential in full measure." This sobering advice was then supported by a quote from Newsweek: "Different areas of the child's brain achieve maturity at different times. As a result, every part of the brain is most susceptible to impressions at a given age. Give your children the necessary stimulation when they need it, and nothing will be impossible for them. Wait, and the train will have left."

The sense of "act now!"—thoroughly commercial in spirit—suggested that the trening's merger of child psychology with consumer culture had lent a distinct, capitalist edge to the usual parenting anxieties. As I hope to show in this chapter, the popularization and commercialization of the new psychology had reconstituted both the figure of the child and the act of parenting. Class and gender formations were particularly salient, contributing to the ways in which both childhood and parenting were conceived symbolically and performed (Salmenniemi 2013). No longer a Soviet institution for ensuring a moral upbringing, parenting had become resignified in commercial psychological contexts as an activity involving financial investment, expert knowledge, and careful planning.

Обогащающее Образование
FasTracKids®

FasTracKids® является революционной системой обогащающего образования. Данная двухлетняя программа разработана для того, чтобы обогатить уровень знании дошкольников.

Программа FasTracKids® подталкивает детей к тому, чтобы продуктивно думать, и одновременно с этим способствует развитию навыков речи, общения и лидерства.

Схема Типичного Двухчасового
Занятия FasTracKids®

20% ОБОГАЩЕНИЕ ПОЗНАНИЙ
Стимулирование способностей
и талантов

30% ПРИМЕНЕНИЕ ЗНАНИЙ
Решение задач
Обучение работе в Интернете
Творческие занятия
Проведение исследований

15% РАЗВИТИЕ ЛИЧНОСТНЫХ
И ЛИДЕРСКИХ КАЧЕСТВ
Самоуважение
Постановка целей
Построение отношений
Общение

20% 30% 15% 15% 20%

15% РАЗВИТИЕ ТВОРЧЕСКИХ
СПОСОБНОСТЕЙ
Мышление
Решение проблем
Принятие решений
Умственное развитие

20% НАВЫКИ РЕЧИ
И ОБЩЕНИЕ
Возможность выступать вживую
и с использованием видеозаписи
(по желанию)

FasTracKids® International, Ltd. ▪ ЗАО «Нежный возраст»®
Россия ▪ Санкт-Петербург ▪ Большой пр. П.С., д. 106
тел. +7(812) 973-99-99, 974-99-99
тел./факс +7(812) 346-16-97
www.fastrackids.ru
nv.spb@inbox.ru

РАЗВИВАЙТЕ
В СВОЕМ РЕБЕНКЕ
таланты и способности

FasTracKids®

«Обогащающее образование
для завтрашних лидеров»

FIGURE 2.1. The pie chart shows: "A Typical 2-Hour Lesson": "20% enriching knowledge (stimulating talents and abilities); 30% applying knowledge (task management, working online, creative activities, doing research); 20% communication and socializing skills (public speaking and use of video (optional)); 15% developing creative abilities (thinking, problem-solving, decision-making, mental development); 15% developing personal and leadership qualities (self-esteem, setting goals, building relationships, socializing)."

How about state institutions? Was the interest in psychotherapy and psychological *treningi* sustained in state institutions after the USSR's collapse in 1991? It took me longer to sort this out. State services had a minimal web presence, and most middle-class folk I queried had not heard of any. Eventually, through several unannounced forays into government offices, I learned that the psychotherapeutic turn had indeed made inroads into Russian institutions, particularly those that worked with children. A few months after meeting Tamara Grigorievna and her staff at ReGeneration, I discovered a network of PPMS Centers—what I term the PPMS system. There were nineteen of these throughout Saint Petersburg—one per municipality—and they offered psychotherapeutic consulting (as well as speech therapy, massage, and training in learning techniques) for children who had been identified by a school psychologist and/or teacher as having difficulties. The PPMS system was a public equivalent of ReGeneration.

I did my fieldwork in a PPMS Center in a working-class district of Saint Petersburg—outside the fancy and tourist-friendly center. I sat in on weekly meetings, accompanied staff on school visits, and participated in teacher trainings and interdepartmental conferences. I soon saw that humanization had taken a different form in the PPMS Center in which I did fieldwork. In comparison to ReGeneration's "enhancing" programs, their services were, at best, prophylactic, anticipating various possible problems—computer addiction, substance abuse, delinquency, various troubles at home. And, in the many instances where these possible problems had become actual, their services became largely reactive. As such, the staff at the PPMS Center made different assumptions about children. Because many of their clients were from poorer families in crisis, these differences in approach could magnify rather than mitigate already-existing social stratifications, producing what I call *psychological difference*.

Something biopolitical and postsocialist was afoot. The psychological shift to humanization in the 1980s had become something else post-1991. But what, how, and, more important, to what effect? The task of this chapter is to address these questions. First I situate my field sites in Russia's biopolitical economy. Through an analysis that mixes ethnography with secondary historical literature and advertising culture, I highlight several key discourses that structured psychotherapeutic work with children: market-mediated messaging about a competitive upbringing, glossy figurations of the child that conjure consumer desire and middle-class aspiration, pronatalism, and Vladimir Putin's economic modernization policies.[2] Next, I describe how psychotherapists, in seeking legibility within these discursive fields, have made psychological care commensurate with two partially overlapping sets of discourses—a neoliberal discourse of self-enterprise and the modernization discourses of the Putin administration. Through that process of commensuration, the psychotherapeutic sensitivity to emotional difference in the 1980s has become a mechanism of class and gender differentiation.[3]

For a parent navigating the new logics of parenting, the effects of commensurability could be compelling, anxiety inducing, or disorienting. For a psychotherapist seeking a way to offer care, the choice was often between making a living or not.

The Afterlife of Difference
FROM HUMANIZATION TO SELF-MANAGERIALISM

In January 2006 I joined ReGeneration at their camp in Finland, dragging along Nicole and Aarno. Tamara Grigorievna had agreed to let me sit in on one group's psychological-education lessons. In exchange, she would promote me to their parent-clients as the resident "native English speaker"—available to children to work on their language skills.

The campers came to see me as a kind of friendly curiosity. Some of them chatted with me about life in the United States. Others shared bits of their own lives. On the day the kids went skiing at a nearby hill, I became a kind of ski instructor, helping two ten-year-old girls learn how to snowplow. At times I was turned into an unwitting accomplice for dorm-room pranks that involved two tween boys insulting one of the male psychologists, who didn't speak English very well. I also spent a lot of time with ReGeneration's team of psychologists. Apart from participating fully in one of their group lessons, I also sat with the team late at night over brandy and cigarettes while they discussed the next day's plans.

The group of campers I got to know best consisted of eight tweens—six boys and two girls. I participated in their *zaniatii* (lessons), led by Aleksandr and Zhenya, the two young staffers I had met several weeks earlier. Zhenya was a recent university graduate and was interested in gerontological psychotherapy. Aleksandr was working on a higher degree, studying stress among soldiers. But at the camp and to the children, they were just "the psychologists" (psikhologi), as they called themselves. It was fascinating to watch them work. As I discuss at length in the next chapter, they created an intricate and well-planned set of lessons and activities about self-management. It was coherent, fun, and compelling, even for the kids. Through these exercises we were collectively led into our internal worlds and emotions, both graphically and through language. We developed ways to identify our fears and learned to discuss painful or limiting past experiences. We got to know ourselves, together.

But it was with a particular aim in mind: to become a more successful person. These psychological techniques for success were both extensions of and departures from the late-Soviet turn toward children's emotions. As the previous chapter discussed, economic stagnation had prompted Mikhail Gorbachev and others to call for institutions to attend to the "human factor of production" (Rawles 1996, 103). In response, reformers argued for a shift from "averaged" to "personality-oriented education" and a "more democratic and child-centered approach" (Asmolov 2005, 10). They hoped to shift attention to the child's needs and interests and to promote recognition of the "autonomy of childhood, freedom in choice, and self-government" (Eklof and Dneprov 1993, 8). As Aleksander Asmolov (2005, 10), who would later become the main psychologist in the Ministry of State Education in the USSR, argued, psychological services were vital in "differentiated education" (*variativnoe obrazovanie*). Psychology, he stated, would "open the line of possibility [*veer vozmozhnostei*] for the individual development of the personality in the world of culture." Emotions became a relevant area of educational concern, initiating the psychologization of upbringing (*vospitanie*)—an area that had previously been conceived of in moral terms (see Attwood 1990; Makarenko 1967; Bronfenbrenner 1970).[4] To be sure, the late-socialist reformers had in mind a form of success as well, but there was one key difference: success, then, was ultimately to be measured in collective terms.

The APN reformers had their critics, and in fact the critiques predicted some of the regressive directions that a focus on emotional needs would take under capitalism. The critics argued that because such reforms differentiated children, they were potentially exclusionary and violated a basic commitment of socialism, namely, eliminating class as a meaningful social category.[5] Differentiated education would amount to an ideological embrace of difference. Consider the language in this quote from Asmolov: "Gifted children [*odarennye deti*], children with disabilities [*deti s anomaliiami razvitiia*], and children with asocial behavior [*deti s asotsial'nym povedeniem*] are located on the extreme corners of a triangle, reflecting particular zones of risk [*zony riska*]. These raise the attention of the system of education" (2005, 10).

The institutionalization of differentiated education in the 1980s was accompanied by differentiation based on gender (Attwood 1990).[6] From its inception, the Soviet project was committed to the idea that gender roles were socially constructed (Attwood 1990, 66). Capacity was plastic, no matter who the person was. Early Soviet feminism (Kollontai 1990) made related arguments, particularly around women's labor, and propaganda posters of the 1920s exclaimed, "Down with kitchen slavery!" (*Doloi kukhonnoe rabstvo!*).

Correspondingly, psychological research on children tended either to assume a non-gender-specific child or else to deploy constructivist arguments drawn from Lev Vygotsky's theories of proximal development (Attwood 1990, 67–85). Starting during the demographic crisis of the 1970s, however, progressive ideas about gender and sex were sidelined by calls for biological reproduction. As Michele Rivkin-Fish (2010) notes, new campaigns emerged to both surveil reproduction and promote childbearing and child-rearing in the media as "women's mission." In 1986 one scholar at Moscow State University "portrayed small families (defined as those with one or two children) as a deviant and dangerous phenomenon that had arisen from the combination of two main factors: the loss of children's economic value to family survival and the rise of a destructive, self-indulgent consumer mentality" (Rivkin-Fish 2010, 708). Throughout the 1970s and 1980s, late-Soviet psychological studies of sex and personality development increasingly presumed an innate psychological difference between men and women (often relying on commonplace gender distinctions: active/passive, emotional/rational, competitive/cooperative).

These two developments in late socialism laid the groundwork for psychological difference. Fast-forward two decades, to the work of organizations like ReGeneration. The insistence on skills and capacity personalized what were previously sociological forms of differentiation. During the Soviet period, while the populace was differentiated on the basis of things like party affiliation, occupation, access to social networks, and the kinds of opportunities different people had, education was in principle undifferentiated. Under postsocialism, the differentiation of one child from another has been, via psychologists, more closely articulated with individual psychological traits, known now as *skills*.

In my fieldwork I was able to see the concrete forms that the turn to difference and emotions had since taken. ReGeneration and others had taken up the mantle of educationally attuned pedagogy and extended it. An ostensible sensitivity to different children remained. But something was new. Under the guise of an androcentric idea of success (*uspekh*) in the market economy, difference had become not so much appreciated as produced. Controlling one's behavior, knowing oneself, exhibiting confidence—such emotionally attuned techniques could make the difference between success and failure. As ReGeneration's program materials and lesson content suggested, for those in advantaged positions, difference was something toward which to strive. As the PPMS Center's work suggested, however, difference could also be a liability.

If psychotherapeutic work among elite children expresses a form of andro-centric, commoditized self-realization, public services had an entirely different cast. In the PPMS Center, I saw how psychotherapeutic expertise had taken shape in public mental health care. I sat in on the center's staff meetings for about six months in 2006 and almost always left feeling depressed. There were so many stories of family struggles: alcoholism, divorce, and death, and the children who suffer in ways large and small as a result; children suspected to be developing a mental disorder, and parents who were in denial or who legitimately disagreed with the diagnosis. I also noted that neotraditionalist conceptions of gender difference—that is, the kind that had emerged with the demographic concerns of the 1970s (Attwood 1990; Rivkin-Fish 2010)—were more prominent in the PPMS Center than in Re-Generation when it came to making sense of children's problems. As a result, I began to see the system of care in a new way—not as a responsive diagnostic body taking in children with clear troubles, but as a system that was also involved in the reproduction of troubles through the sometimes-hasty use of diagnostics.

The system of PPMS Centers has an interesting history. It was legally established in 1998. Whereas organizations like ReGeneration are only, loosely speaking, legacies of the late-socialist reforms of the APN, the PPMS system is a direct descendant: the Ministry of Education under which it sits is the successor organization to the APN. In the 1990s, the PPMS system was tasked with the psychological guidance (*psikhologicheskoe soprovozhdenie;* also *psychological support* or *accompaniment*) of children through the educational process (Molostov 2015).[7] As such, the system of PPMS Centers was one of the places where the humanization of mental health care took shape in state and municipal institutions by countering the tendency to pathologize psychosocial struggles (Pakhomova 2007). According to Elena Kazakova (personal communication, October 12, 2007), a professor at Saint Petersburg State University and a principal architect of the concept, soprovozhdenie would eventually also become a part of Putin's "modernization" reforms.

In contrast to that mandate, however, by the time I arrived in the PPMS Center where I did fieldwork, it seemed that pathologization had reemerged through referrals. Facing an onslaught of social and family problems, the PPMS Center's little army of psychologists sometimes resorted to referring tough cases to PNDs (outpatient clinics)—usually along with a suspected psychiatric diagnosis of some sort, in many cases suspected schizophrenia. This was not guidance so much as crisis management.

As I would hear from those who worked there, several factors beyond family precarity had pushed services in these directions. The combination of scant resources, federal policy requirements, and inspections hamstrung psychotherapeutic work. The form of care that resulted was starkly different from that at ReGeneration, although the PPMS Center's work, like ReGeneration's, had traveled some distance from the initial impulse of humanization.

Postsocialist Biopolitics

The difference between ReGeneration and the PPMS Center I visited was not just one of flush versus impoverished services, or different therapeutic philosophies, but was also profoundly shaped by a postsocialist biopolitical concern with children. I want to suggest that the difference in psychotherapeutic work reflects a bifurcation of the humanization of the 1980s in which the focus on emotions took divergent paths through the biopolitical economy. Two perceived crises—economic stagnation and demographic decline—were central to the biopolitical economy starting in the 1990s. The Soviet collapse in 1991 had effected a loss of geopolitical relevance and economic competitiveness.[8] Throughout the 1990s Russia's gross domestic product (GDP) fell well below Soviet levels, returning to the level of the 1990s only in 2007, late into Putin's second term (see United Nations 2014). Although Russia enjoyed high rates of GDP growth in the early 2000s—4.4 percent between 2003 and 2013 (World Bank 2016)—this was largely due to high oil and gas prices (McFaul and Stoner-Weiss 2008), a fact that even Russia's political elite saw as a vulnerability. The global recession of 2008 bore out many of these concerns as Russia fared far worse than the other BRICS countries (Brazil, India, China, and South Africa).[9] In response, policymakers discussed diversification, a goal linked to the cultivation of entrepreneurial labor. Not surprisingly, policymakers also turned their attention to children and education: their quality and capacity. The specter of the "human factor of production" had been raised yet again.

As for population decline, state officials, journalists, social scientists, and the public have been concerned about Russia's demographic crisis (*demograficheskii krizis*) since at least the 1970s (see Attwood 1990). An anxious discourse of "dying out" (*vymiranie ubyl'*) and "depopulation" (*depopuliatsiia*) continued into the post-Soviet period (Rivkin-Fish 2005, 1). Writing of the

1990s, Rivkin-Fish quotes two dramatic newspaper headlines: "Russia Has 100 Years to Live," and "Pediatricians Confirm That Russian Children Everywhere Are Physically and Mentally Deficient" (1). More recently, both Olga Shevchenko (2009) and Eugene Raikhel (2016) have discussed the tenacity of this *krizis* discourse in the 2000s. As Raikhel notes in his study of treatment for alcoholism in Russia, physicians drew on krizis discourses to index "socially destroyed patients," who "suggested an erosion that was simultaneously moral and bodily, in a way that was applied equally to particular persons and to the entirety of post-Soviet Russia" (31). Other grim social indicators, including low life expectancy (particularly for men), high infant mortality, abortion rates, and the incidence of alcoholism and heart disease, have added fuel to these anxieties.[10] The fact that the non-ethnic-Russian population in the southern republics continues to grow at a higher rate, in combination with increased in-migration from Central Asia and the Caucasus, has tinged discussions of the demographic krizis with a toxic ethnonationalism. Likewise, the demographic krizis is sometimes hyperbolically described by nationalists and the Communist Party as "the ongoing genocide of the Russian population" (Rotkirch, Temkina, and Zdravomyslova 2007, 351). The topic of demography is thus quite politicized. Rivkin-Fish notes that "demographers who prioritized reducing male mortality instead of promoting childbearing, on the basis that low fertility represented a trend common throughout the developed world and could not be effectively reversed, faced charges by nationalists that they were traitors with 'anti-patriotic' aims" (2010, 710).

When policymakers discuss these two concerns, they also reveal an underlying class and gender politics. For example, debates about pronatalist policies make assumptions about what kinds of families should be having children (and which ones should not), and also about whether one or both parents should be policy targets. Putin revealed his approach to these issues in a much-discussed annual address to the federal administration on May 10, 2006. "What is most important for our country?" he asked, and then gave his answer:[11]

> The Defense Ministry knows what is most important. Indeed, what I want to talk about is love, women, children. I want to talk about the family, about the most acute problem facing our country today—the demographic problem.
>
> The economic and social development issues our country faces today are closely interlinked with one simple question: who are we doing this

all for? You know that our country's population is declining by an average of almost 700,000 people a year. We have raised this issue on many occasions but have for the most part done very little to address it. Resolving this problem requires us to take the following steps.

First, we need to lower the death rate. Second, we need an effective migration policy. And, third, we need to increase the birth rate. (Putin 2006)

"Love, women, children": Putin's vision of the Russian family, presuming both sexual reproduction and an absent father, asserted that today's children are tomorrow's soldiers (the number of conscripts continues to fall) and workers.[12] This was evident in the way that the first-comes-love series follows on the heels of what the Defense Ministry "knows . . . is most important" (see also chap. 2, n. 12). Putin also linked children to Russia's "economic and social development issues"—both in the sense of "who are we doing all this for?" but also in the implied sense of *who will do all of this?* In the address, demographics were couched between calls for infrastructural investment, "technological modernization," energy efficiency, protection of private property, and the creation of an "innovating environment that will get knowledge flowing." He then announced his "mother's capital" incentive as a way to boost birth rates.[13]

Commenting on this speech, the sociologists Anna Rotkirch, Anna Temkina, and Elena Zdravomysleva (2007) have pointed out that Putin's maternity-capital program puts an interesting twist on the Soviet politics of gender and the family. First, it departs from a perestroika-era promotion of traditional gender roles by acknowledging that women's citizenship is premised on a dual identity as wage earner and mother, thus returning to the Soviet pattern of women's "double burden." Maternity capital is thus not intended to move women back to the home but to provide bridge funds while women are out of work. (Whether they can actually return to work is questionable.) The authors also argue that Putin's speech did not presume a heteronormative nuclear family, only a mother. Nevertheless, the program was not, therefore, "gender equal." Fathers were scarcely mentioned, possibly a sign of official acceptance of another krizis: the krizis of masculinity (Raikhel 2016, 43–48). In Russian politics, "parenting" is often a code for a politics of women. (And, if anything, the politics of the family in Russia has only gotten more conservative since 2006.)[14]

Class is most visible in policies around social reproduction. The relevant term here is *upbringing* (*vospitanie*), and Putin/Medvedev/Putin have addressed it through reforms to education and family law.[15] Like pronatalism, social reproduction was also framed as a matter of economic concern, and in discussions of the ideal citizen, there was little attention to inequality or mobility. Instead, the subject of modernization was an already well-positioned person. Consider the Ministry of Education's modernization drive (initiated on August 29, 2001), which was framed as a way to develop human capital in order to "overcome the danger of lagging [*preodolenie opasnosti otstavaniia*] behind global trends in economic and social development" (Russian Federation 2002).[16] The Ministry of Education's modernization criteria drew on the globally circulating language of the androcentric neoliberal subject and merged it with nationalism. In a report to UNESCO in 2004 on the progress of these reforms, the Russian authors argued that in the global economy there is a need for "moral, enterprising people educated in line with present-day standards who can make decisions independently in a situation of choice, can cooperate, who distinguish mobility, dynamism, constructive thinking, who are open for cross-cultural interaction, feel responsible for the destiny of the country. . . . [The] *Russian education system is called upon to prepare people who are not only able to live in civil society and a lawful state, but also to build them*" (Russian Federation 2004, 6). The report added that the project to "prepare people" is not a matter of "the assimilation of a certain amount of knowledge" (read: the Soviet Union's dominant model of undifferentiated education) but is oriented to "the development of their personalities, of cognitive and creative abilities" (8).

Psychologists were to be an important part of this work. As the report to UNESCO noted, reformers should build the modernized classroom on a "psychological-pedagogical conceptual base" meant to facilitate "the formation of common academic skills and . . . cognitive activity" (Russian Federation 2004, 13). This will "predetermine success" at subsequent stages in schooling. Psychologists working in schools and the PPMS system thus gave a social-scientific underpinning to the pedagogical objective of "the free development of personality" and the "personal orientation and individualization" of education (Russian Federation 2004, 11). Concretely, this has meant doing what one school psychologist I interviewed called "psychological enlightenment" (*psikhologicheskoe prosveshchenie*)—exposing parents and teachers to the basics of developmental psychology, as well as providing psychological soprovozhdenie to students.

In summary, then, the discourse of pronatalism and modernization indicate how Putin's early policies rearticulated the relationship between psychology and difference. Whereas during perestroika the psychotherapist was supposed to be responsive to different kinds of children, by the 2000s she or he was supposed to shape difference itself in accordance with the new biopolitical aims of national economic competitiveness and population growth.

CASE: "ECONOMIC PSYCHOLOGY"

According to Volodya Kozlov, an orthodox Freudian psychoanalyst, the rising biopolitical importance of psychological knowledge shaped the course of psychotherapy in Russia. I met with Volodya in 2006. He was extremely outspoken about how Putin's policies had altered the profession, in particular leading to Americanization, mixed with more highly instrumental kinds of work. He suggested that this was happening largely because of Putin's tightening control over education, which he likened to "vertical power" (*vertikal'naia vlast'*). He said that this vertical power was being exercised in psychotherapy through new certification procedures, accreditation, and the requirement for student projects to have a significant amount of empirical material and use statistics.

"Not even Freud could meet these requirements!" he said.

He claimed that by this point the reforms were coming from within the organization, "in a Foucauldian manner"—people were making changes in advance of being asked.

Volodya also told me that the standardization and institutionalization of psychotherapy had closed down the earlier proliferation of approaches in the early 1990s and the excitement about psychoanalytic work. What was happening by 2006 was a reining in of that diversity, an attempt to control it, coming from what he derisively called "state psychology." Within this new disciplinary space created by the state through the Ministry of Education, his colleagues tended to "first move from psychoanalytic work into Adlerian and Jungian approaches, then to Kohut and self-approaches, finally to some form of ego-psychology." He commented:

> They view Freud as being out-of-date. But their "post-Freudianism," which is influenced by American psychology brands (which have a Coca-Cola effect), is regressive and pre-Freudian. I don't interact with my colleagues in psychoanalysis anymore. They are uninterested in anything but earning more money through therapy. Thus, they see going to the cinema, for instance, as unproductive, even though it might help them to understand some problem better. Recently we had a visit from a famous psychoanalyst [who gave a lecture] but only two members of the institute attended. When I challenged the director about this, the director said, "You know how much money I lost to attend this thing? I had to cancel four appointments!"

In 2006, the institute had moved from offering only postgraduate (i.e., master's level) education to becoming an accredited university. Thus, the students there were obtaining their bachelor's degree as well, except that their studies were entirely in the area of psychology.

It is likely that this shift brought about tighter supervision of their activities. The institute, he said, was selling itself on the idea that "in three years we will transform your identity."

Lena, a student, entered the room and showed us her class schedule. It listed a class called Economic Psychology.

Volodya raised his eyebrows. "Economic Psychology—what the heck is that?"

The Success Complex

How do the biopolitical aims of pronatalism and modernization become part of psychotherapeutic work? I argue that psychotherapists themselves did the work of commensuration, and that this was not purely imposed on them from outside. That negotiation, whether one agrees with its ends, is also politico-ethical, as I show in subsequent chapters. Psychotherapeutic practices were *made commensurable* with the aims of Putin's political-economic agenda—in this case what I am calling "the success complex."

I borrow the concept of commensuration from Elizabeth Povinelli (2001, 325), who, in turn, draws on the work of Wendy Nelson Espeland and Mitchell L. Stevens (1998) to point out that one of the ways in which worlds are made unremarkable is through their commensuration with other epistemic and deontic horizons. By bringing difference into alignment with both dominant structures of knowledge (epistemologies) and assumptions about obligation (deontologies), commensuration domesticates difference through both "the efficiency of bureaucracies" and "economic transactions" (Povinelli 2001, 325). Commensuration operates through "a standardization between disparate things that reduces the relevance of context," "transform[ing] qualities into quantities, difference into magnitude" (325). Consider, as an example, the use of quantitative metrics in education in the United States, something I have been looking at recently. The "Great Schools" metric uses student performance on standardized tests to rate schools on a scale of 1 to 10. Parents, therefore, can compare very different kinds of schools at a glance, whether rural or urban, socioeconomically diverse or exclusively rich or poor, developmentally diverse or uniform. Both the creation of the metric and the act of comparison are practices of commensuration that align education with biopolitical aims. In this example one might argue that education as a practice is made commensurable with the aims of "school accountability," "raising the level of education through standardization," and "no child left behind." As the example also shows, practices of commensuration have significant downsides: legitimate differences in teaching and learning style, not to mention the merits of a diverse student body or school environment, are either neglected or intentionally marginalized for the sake of comparability. Commensuration, then, flattens a diversity of forms into a single plane. The consequences can range from compromised education policy, as in this example, to the forms of cultural imperialism that are found throughout the world.[17]

The practice of making psychotherapy commensurate with the success complex was visible when I visited a large expo for family products and services in March 2006. Called Childhood Planet (Planeta Detstva) and sponsored by the mayor's office of Saint Petersburg, the expo was an annual event held for several days at a famous venue on Vasilievsky Island. Inside were dozens of kiosks promoting everything from diaper cream to private schools, from governmental developmentalism to psychological training. I found abundant links to Putin's pronatalism and modernization policies at Childhood Planet.[18] For example, in one informational brochure, organizers suggested that the expo was oriented toward "the popularization of the old truth: 'it's wonderful to have children [*imet' detei—eto zdorovo*],'" and they explicitly stated that it was aligned with Putin's national projects (*natsproekty*), announced just six months earlier and set in motion that January. Another informational brochure suggested that in addition to featuring "every possible children's product and service," the expo would also include "educational and health programs— those that the President of Russia named as priorities." It was to be "not simply a commercial project but an important, socially meaningful event both for our city and for Russia as a whole," and even "a single professional space for bringing together the strengths of producers and commercial structures, specialists on children and the social sphere, educational associations, centers and clubs, representatives of educational programs."

In this "single professional space," parental (or, rather, because of traditional gender norms, maternal) responsibility was constituted as both a wisely exercised choice *and* a national responsibility. As the organizers acknowledged in the informational materials about the event, "with every year more and more products and services for children appear," facing parents with the question, "Which of these to choose, which of these are useful to me?"[19] Childhood Planet, they assured, "is designed to give you an answer." As a map through the labyrinth of choices, the expo not only enabled comparison shopping but also offered a chance to learn about "how the government of our city helps vulnerable families, how at the city level questions about the organization of medical services and the leisure time of our children are decided." Even would-be parents could learn about "social programs aimed at increasing the birth rates and what measures the governments of Russia and Petersburg are undertaking in this area."

I was intrigued when I learned that ReGeneration planned to go to the expo to promote their services. A few months earlier I had heard Tamara Grigorievna describing the market for psychological services to a group of university psychology students at a seminar. "We are for the most part inventing this market ourselves," she said. She described several obstacles, including the lack of a well-developed psychotherapeutic culture in Russia and a general tendency to associate anything with the prefix *psy-* with Soviet psychiatric abuse or pathology. The invention of a new market was, in a real sense, also a task of articulating an acceptable relationship between psychotherapeutic work and the economy of parenting. What would this market invention look like, exactly?

On the day of the expo, I found the staff wearing not the usual sweater and jeans but polished business attire. Marina and Katya, whom I had also gotten to know at the camp in Finland, were leaning over a small folding table, discussing the likely flow of visitors and the best orientation for their tables. As the expo opened and people started passing by, Tamara Grigorievna suggested that several staffers stand in the aisles to pass out promotional materials. Two psychologists stepped to the front of the stall and began handing out four-color brochures printed on expensive card stock to passersby. As part of their bid to circulate their name around the city, ReGeneration had also just completed work on their *Parent's Handbook*, based on all the questions about raising children they had received over their ten years in business. Their stall was a small island in a sea of other similar services, all in search of capitalized care.

I spent a long day moving slowly through the surrounding booths, collecting brochures and press materials to get a sense of the domestic-services market. I saw that the dream of a modernized Russia was alive and well in this glossy world. Magazine ads, how-to books, events, music, and other products deployed the imagery of success, along with a curious mixture of highly gendered and gender-neutral representations. Putin's modernization, in other words, was being imagined, authorized, and pursued in an environment of egregious splendor that spoke little to the everyday concerns of most Russians. These images also tied a middle-class, mother-centered approach to child-rearing to the logic of competition, advancement, and investment—a success complex.

The focus on elite culture at the expo was one of the clearest expressions of the federal imaginary. Consider this advertisement from a company called

МИР ЛИМУЗИНОВ
VIP ЛИМУЗИН СЕРВИС

Первый кортеж
в жизни Вашего малыша
всего за $99!

Встреча из роддома на лимузине!
Красиво!
Торжественно!
Комфортабельно!

Звоните: (812) 972-5000
www.limo-world.ru

АРЕНДА
VIP-ЛИМУЗИНОВ И
ЭКСКЛЮЗИВНЫХ
АВТОМОБИЛЕЙ

FIGURE 2.2.
Advertisement for
Limousine World:
"The first motorcade
in your child's life for
$99. Greeted at the
maternity hospital
by a limousine!
Beautiful! Festive!
Comfortable!"

Limousine World promoting "the first motorcade in your child's life for $99. Greeted at the maternity hospital in a chic limousine" (see figure 2.2). Such appeals created an atmosphere of consumer desire and pleasure, presenting visitors with a set of material goods, suited to their child, with which to dream. As a consequence, the child was also figured in particular ways: not just as a young person but as an object of adornment, education, preservation, concern, and presentation. One business, Carousel, specialized in children's haircuts and fashion, offering "outline sketches" for boys, and for girls over ten manicure, "face-art," and something called *vizazh* (defined as "a harmonic composition of makeup, hair, and overall look"). Studio K promoted its professional children's portraiture with an image of a girl wearing a white gown in an aristocratic pose (see figure 2.3). On the mezzanine, I found a pavilion for children's entertainment, a huge children's art exhibition, and later a beauty

STUDIOK

*Профессиональная
Детская
Фото-видео
Студия*

Москва 8 901 516 3036
Санкт-Петербург 8 901 370 1857
www.STUDIOK.ru

FIGURE 2.3. Advertisement for Studio K, a Professional Children's Photo-video Studio: "The traditional family portrait in Great Britain comes from the Royal Family."

contest to crown "Miss Childhood Planet, Miss Image, Miss Style, Miss Charm, Miss Extravagance, and, naturally, Miss Crowd Favorite."[20]

The gendered celebration of the child was complemented by an outsourcing of child-rearing, transposing what were once kin-based relations of care into the formal economy and, at least ostensibly, liberating elite women from the home.[21] Viewing the family as a corporate enterprise, firms called *agenstvo domashnego personala*, or domestic personnel agencies, offered nannies for mothers pursuing their own careers (see figure 2.4). One such company, Domovenok (House Elf), appealed to the working mother with the following words: "Career, ambition—the contemporary woman has something to lose. That's when the question arises: 'Where can I find a good nanny?'" Along with nannies, Domovenok offered other services, including the "Husband by the Hour," "Autonanny," "Sunday Father," and drivers and bodyguards. A firm called Dobraia Niania (Dear Nanny) assured its would-be clients, "We care

FIGURE 2.4. Page from a brochure advertising different "domestic personnel agencies," including "Your Auntie" (top left) and "Dear Nanny" (bottom right).

about your future!" Only Vasha Tiotia (Your Auntie) invoked a different, kinship-oriented language in its company name (and, to some extent its services): its "emergency nanny" would be prepared to "care for your child in times of illness."

The gender implications enacted the same schizophrenic dance that Putin had in his speech in 2006: advertisers presumed traditional gender roles in the family—it is the mother who is thinking about the children—while also giving lip service to women's careers. The advertising landscape also made it clear that class played an important role: in a patriarchal society, women's work becomes more feasible for those who can afford to outsource childcare. (Nonetheless, as I discuss below, the attempt to marry neotraditional gender roles with some measure of liberation through the market was rarely accomplished smoothly, a fact that had implications for the gendering of psychological care as well. As Rivkin-Fish elegantly puts it, in reference to Putin's maternity-capital program, "this gender-neutral language, while appearing universal and inclusive, obscures its own involvement in the power politics of neotraditionalist and pronatalist ideologies" (2010, 716).)

With sufficient funds, parents could also choose to privatize education. Appealing to parents' desire to get the best education for their children, these emphasized the virtues of choice and individual attention. Epigraf, a private kindergarten, asked clients, "Are you choosing a school? Do you want to know about private education? Does your child need an individual approach?" Petershule (Peter School), taking its prerevolutionary Russian name before it was closed in 1928, promised education in the German tradition in an "elite private *Gymnasium* (high school)." The private school Diplomat (see figure 2.5) boasted that its graduates had a 100 percent admission rate at the top Russian and European universities. The well-known business school Vzmakh (the name refers to a wavelike movement) targeted those eighth to tenth graders who are the "future bankers, top managers, and bigwigs of show business [*vorotily shou-biznesa*]": "Do you see yourself as a successful and confident person? Do you want to get more? That means that Vzmakh is the school that needs YOU. Take the decisive step—try to get into Vzmakh! Vzmakh is a school that really prepares students for work in the sphere of economics and entrepreneurship [*predprinimatel'stvo*]."

How did commercial psychotherapy organizations respond to the success complex? At least as a matter of advertising, they jumped right in, seeking to make psychological education an important product. In doing so, psychotherapists also lent potency, sustenance, and reach to modernization. That is, they effected at the level of interiority something akin to what geographer María Gutiérrez (2011) has described as "capital involution," whereby capital brings about increasing levels of internal complexity, intensification, and elaboration while forestalling a breakdown. What would a breakdown entail here? A public realization of the negative effects of the hypercommercialization of child development.

Uspekh, or success, was the alpha and omega of psychotherapeutic care in this context, linking confidence and achievement to products of a cognitive-emotional sort. An organization called 12 Colleagues, affiliated with Saint Petersburg State University, advertised that it could promote the "balanced development" of intellect, emotions, self-regulation, and conversation skills; the "growth of intellectual success"; obshchenie (communication; socializing) as a "laboratory of success"; acceptance of one's own uniqueness; and "preparedness for life's call [*gotovnost' k zhiznennomu vyzovu*]." Like ReGeneration, they

FIGURE 2.5. Advertisement for "Diplomat Private School": "The Best for Children."

also held camps on the "development of life skills for successful self-realization in a changing world." Other organizations offered courses on psychological preparedness for school, professional self-definition, and development of one's personality, where teens learn to "develop the skills of self-analysis, understand themselves and others, define their strengths and weaknesses, change themselves and their behavior, and develop conversation skills."

In this dense discursive network, the child was neither a Rousseauian innocent, a wicked Hobbesian, nor a builder of socialism but a bearer of talents to be harnessed, a bundle of brain connections needing stimulation, a creative resource for the nation, a person whose time is a career. "Time in bourgeois culture," writes Orvar Löfgren, "becomes geared toward the future, obsessed with development, and the goal is to gain control over it. The important new message is that people create their own future. Time is in short supply and must be properly managed" (Frykman and Löfgren 1987, 27). This temporal structure, yoked to success, also promoted a particular structure of feeling: anxiety. The more parenting necessitated management, foresight, expert knowledge, and even a bit of palm greasing, the more was it rendered as an uncertain and competitive enterprise.[22]

The Grammar of Difference

The success complex had also worked its way into therapeutics. A comparison of program documents from ReGeneration and the PPMS Center shows how success and its negative image—presumed failure—shaped things as basic as the grammatical constructions (passive or active voice), word choices, temporality of care, and intended audiences of statements about psychotherapy. As a form of commensuration, this grammar of difference indicates how class formations were brought to bear on children's interiors.

A few months after the Childhood Planet expo, I had time to read the *Parent's Handbook* that ReGeneration had been distributing. I was curious how the emphasis on uspekh might be merged with psychological advice. In a section entitled "Learning Self-Control" I found the following introduction:

> One of the most common parent misconceptions is that the primary concern with the child's development is intellectual or physical. We take pride in his successes [*my gordimsia ego uspekhami*] in school, his achievements in academic competitions or sporting events; we worry when he is sick or has lost. Before enrolling him in school, we teach him to read, write, and count. But we pay the least attention to what he feels when he experiences some event or other.... The realm of feelings [*sfera chuvstv*] is an important area of human development. The way a person is able to recognize and label his emotions is directly related to how he is able to cope with them, to control his state.... Emotional well-being primarily affects the person's self-esteem. By and large, self-esteem is primarily an emotional attitude about oneself: "Do I like myself or not?" and that means, do I believe in myself or not? To a large extent, adequate self-esteem affects self-confidence, the ability to set goals and reach them, and the ability to make friends and be a leader. At the same time, his own emotional well-being and ability to recognize and control his own feelings are the key to seeing and responding sensitively to the emotions of others. So, if we want to see our children be really successful [*uspeshnyi*], confident [*samouverennyi*], and happy, we have to be attentive and sensitive to his feelings and experi-

ences, accepting them, staying positive, and helping them cope with the negative.

This excerpt suggests a delicate dance around the question of uspekh. At first, there is a distancing from it—as if to suggest that success isn't everything and that parents should not focus too much on achievement and comparison. At the same time, the real problem is not that parents are oriented to Olympic heights but that they ignore the child's feelings (ReGeneration's area of expertise). The key to success turns out to be attending to this emotional realm. There is a tension here that recapitulates the late-socialist and postsocialist variants of psychological difference, which shifted from the recognition of difference to its production.

Given the consumer nature of Childhood Planet, it should come as no surprise that the representatives of the PPMS Center were not even, as it were, in its orbit. While there were a few governmental organizations scattered amid the commercial enterprises, these primarily represented the cream of the crop—institutions that had grown from the *Domy Kul'tury* (Houses of Culture) of the Soviet period—that is to say, extracurricular-activity centers that had received much money and prestige in the Soviet period and possibly still did. Nor was it clear why the PPMS system would have been represented. One afternoon I spoke with Vadim, who worked as a psychologist at the PPMS Center where I did fieldwork. He was in charge of its professional-development seminars (one of the few areas of "training" work). One day he told me that he was starting a little business on the side because he wasn't able to organize many "positive" seminars at the center. He complained about the red tape. Indeed, the day-to-day work of the center was too embroiled in crisis to devote staff resources to the sorts of forward-looking enhancement found at the Childhood Planet expo; crisis response was constantly being bumped ahead of other consulting work.

To illustrate the difference this makes in the constitution of the "unsuccessful" (*neuspeshnyi*) child, compare the entry from ReGeneration's handbook with this excerpt. The following, from an article "Lessons on the Development of Intellectual Abilities among Young Pupils" the PPMS Center referenced, addresses a similar set of concerns. It discusses success in school; however, it does so with very different assumptions about what is important and possible:

> Parents often turn to us when their child is having difficulty in elementary school. . . . The cause of these problems is usually that the level of development of abstract-logical thinking, memory, and attention is below normal

for that age. Our center offers classes using a specially organized program that is intended to promote the focused development of these functions in primary-school children. . . .

Before the start of the class, we conduct an in-depth psychological examination of each child, which reveals the level of development of intellectual functioning, and the particularities of the emotional-volitional sphere.

Then we design an individualized lesson plan. (For example, if a student struggles with math, then the emphasis is on developing the ability to establish cause-effect relations, reasoning skills, building inferences and drawing conclusions, knowing how to generalize, analyze, classify.) If it turns out that the underachievement is primarily due to distraction, forgetfulness, where the child is "listening but not hearing, or looking but not seeing," we offer more tasks and games to develop memory and attention. . . .

When carrying out remedial and developmental classes for children, we work constantly with parents. We give parents explanations and recommendations on how to explain tasks, how to teach poetry, what requirements are worthwhile, and which ones are unnecessary at a given moment.

After the end of the course (usually ten sessions), of course he does not become a straight-A student, but part of the problem with falling behind in school is resolved. Parents report that the child is now more able to cope with homework, and the teacher notices that the student is now able to give clearer answers and coherently express his thoughts. It's a great joy for children and their parents when the first "4" or "5" [B or A] appears on a test.

In the classes it is also possible to increase a child's confidence in his abilities and to create an active, positive relationship to learning.

This is very important. The unsuccessful [neuspeshnyi] young student often feels like a social outcast in school; he is continually told that he is worse than everyone else, is constantly getting scolded both at home and at school. Children react differently to this—some withdraw, become lethargic, passive, afraid to answer even if they know the answer. Others become irritable, aggressive, pugnacious. It's clear that nothing good will come of this in the future. After not finding a decent place in the class, and not having realized himself in school activities (which is really important in elementary school), the student will try to prove himself not in studies, but in something else. He can get involved with asocial teens, bad company, etc.

Our lessons help the child feel that he, too, can manage difficult exercises, that he, too, is no worse than others in taking on difficult tasks. It gets easier for the student to understand new material in classes; he starts to finish homework more quickly and easily. All of this helps reduce neuropsychiatric stress, improves his mood, and broadens the range of cognitive interests.

Thus, in developing the child's intellectual abilities, his psychological functions are also optimized, and his social-emotional problems are corrected.

In comparison to ReGeneration's text, the tone of this document is both more scientifically rigorous and more pessimistic. While both texts can be considered part of the discourse of uspekh, the discussion of abilities and skills is couched within a different problematic. If the first example takes as its object the child-agent on the path to success, the second speaks to the underachiever, and the term *uspekh* appears only in its negative adjectival form, *neuspeshnyi*. If the first orients the discussion of emotions to a relation to oneself through one's own efforts—supported, of course, by caring parents—the second orients it toward the efficacy of correctional-developmental lessons. Here, the emotional is not primary: if the child's schoolwork can be improved, his or her confidence is bolstered. Moreover, positive emotions are usually discussed in negative terms ("all of this helps reduce neuropsychiatric stress, improves his mood"). The locus of empowerment is different, too. It is not the client, assisted by his or her knowing parents, so much as the expert who is the doer here. Each also has a different relationship to science. ReGeneration eschews scientific discourses and, by extension, Soviet biopolitics, opting instead for the vagaries of emotional talk. The PPMS Center text draws on the power (but also the potentially negative associations) of a scientific discourse that is more systematic and functionalist. The place of the family is also different. ReGeneration's words are offered as advice to modify the parent's behavior. (As Tamara Grigorievna, ReGeneration's director, told me, the parent is often an obstacle to positive development—a source of bad social reproduction.) The PPMS Center text, contrastingly, aims to bolster the legitimacy of the service itself in the eyes of parents, to assuage doubts, while positing the parent as a necessary (and possibly the only) partner in the world around the child. The goals are also different. If the *Parent's Handbook* relies on a language of potential, the second deploys a language of potential insufficiency, along with a cluster of diagnostic terms: *level, in-depth psychological investigation, exercises, intellectual functioning, psychological functions*, and notions of planning and optimization.

The temporality of each example, finally, indicates how each child enters therapy under different expectations. Consider the way each child's outcome is temporalized differently. For the problem child, the therapeutic aim is that he or she be "no worse than others." The objective is not reaching goals but "manag[ing] difficult exercises" and lowering stress. The temporality here, we might say, is future imperfect in the sense that the effects of therapeutic work are framed as uncertain and of short horizon. By comparison, for the well-off child, there is a different sense of anticipation. Phrases like *the ability to set goals and reach them*, in conjunction with the ability to *recognize and control feelings*, index a change in state—a future perfect. As they write, "If we want to see our child as a really successful [*uspeshnyi*], confident [*samouverennyi*], and happy person, we have to be attentive and sensitive to his feelings and experiences."

It is not surprising to find these kinds of differences between paid and publicly available care. Chronic underfunding of social services around the world has unfortunately become commonplace.[23] Moreover, as many scholars have pointed out, the differentiated management of the population is a central part of modern governmentality under capitalism (Donzelot 1979; Procacci 1991). Effective social policy often depends on division and categorization. What interests me are the ways that expertise, class, and gender get linked together—how assumptions about individual capacity, worth, taste, and distinction are made commensurate with access to capital and social understandings of a person's economic and social value. Crucial here is the way that discourses of psychological difference have revamped assumptions about capacity, individuality, and futurity. These are patterned responses to the biopolitical economy, as opposed, for example, to projects motivated by equality, or safety, or fulfillment. And this emphasis on success in upbringing is not restricted to parenting in Russia—it is also part of a global "regime of anticipation" (Adams, Murphy, and Clarke 2009, 247) that stretches from health domains into financial services, disaster management, and preemptive national defense. As forecasting has made the future palpable, the human need to look ahead has become ever more elaborated and technologized. Such is the argument of Vincanne Adams, Michelle Murphy, and Adele E. Clarke (2009), who point out that prediction has become a widespread way of knowing "the truth about the future" (247). As a result, "speculative forecast . . . has been redirected as an injunction to characterize and inhabit degrees and kinds of uncertainty—adjusting ourselves to routinized likelihoods, hedged bets and probable outcomes. Preparedness is infinitesimally possible and infinitely malleable when one has a good working model of an anticipated 'future'" (247). They suggest that anticipation carries a particular affective state—a nervous anxiety percolating beneath the surface of our lives. The materials discussed in this chapter show how anxiety about the future was also central to messages about good parenting in Russia. Anxiety was an affect that psychologists seek to both produce and assuage.

Experts also summoned different kinds of anticipation, depending on the social group; the grammars of difference pointed to different discursive relationships between personal time and class. This observation resembles Anne Anagnost's (2006) claim that in China urban and rural subjects have been understood in relation to a discourse of human quality, or *suzhi*. Suzhi is a "value coding" of human capital produced through education and other investments. Through this suzhi discourse, some bodies are regarded as being of high value and worthy of investment, and others as being of low value.[24] In comparing commercial and municipal psychological enterprises, I saw a similar pattern, where one child was considered as worthy of cognitive and emotional investment, and another as requiring intervention and/or control. Crucially, this value coding was unfurled within different regimes of anticipation—one that hoped for the best, and one that feared the worst.

Conclusion: Class, Gender, and Commensuration

Many of the social and health values elaborated under socialism—including those concerned with differentiated education and psychological difference—were repackaged in Russia in the decades that followed. In psychological services, the market was a major force of change, foreclosing some psychotherapeutic idioms while enabling the rapid expansion of others. What was foreclosed were services linked to the initial impulse, developed in the 1980s, toward the whole child in the places where they were most needed—schools and public services. Whereas it would be too much to describe the late-Soviet Pedagogy of Cooperation as a "radical world," it was nonetheless not the mode of class and gender reproduction that its post-Soviet psychological forms became. With the benefit of hindsight, those late-socialist reformers, working to humanize socialist institutions and attend to the "emotional needs" of the child, look very much like a social movement full of a progressive, if also compromised, vision of what a child is or could be, psychologically speaking. In the years since their efforts, as the biopolitical economy enabled the psychotherapeutic idioms that were most commensurable with success, the problematic tendencies of attending to difference became more pronounced.

The commensuration of humanization with the biopolitical economy under Putin also gave psychological services a classed character, technologizing the government of (rather than the struggle against) inequality. As Jacques Donzelot (1979, xxi) suggests, the process of class production works through the ways in which psychological services help states manage the family as a "social surface."[25] He shows how social differentiation emerged in France along two lines—a bourgeois and a working-class pole. In the case of the first, "families willingly seize on medical institutions . . . constructing around the child an educative model" (xxi). Terming this "protected liberation" (47), he writes that the liberalization of relations was promoted, leading to greater individualization, a diminution of family roles, and fluidity in relational combinations. The working-class family, though, was "reorganized on the basis of a set of institutional constraints and stimulations that also make the child the center of the family, to be sure, but according to procedures much more deserving of the term 'supervised freedom'" (xxi). Under a relationship of tutelage, working-class families were placed in a relation of dependence vis-à-vis the state. This divergence had effects on children's worlds: "The home begins where the children are let out from school. There are those who go home all by themselves and those who are waited for at school. The first have the street, the vacant lot, the shop windows and cellars, while the others have yards, jungle gyms, afternoon snacks, and educative parents. Here the image is no longer of encirclement, but of preservation. Not suffocation, but liberation within a protected space" (4). Under Putin, psychological services also produced a bifurcated system of care.[26] In this instance, psychologists articulated idioms of success and achievement in ways that either drew those values into the substance of the self or posited them as being beyond reach.

Mark Liechty (2003) has argued that although class cultures have a structural character (and this is very much the style of Donzelot's analysis), they are also produced through local judgments about propriety and social location, and very often other symbolic encodings linked to ideologies of progress, development and modernity. In Nepal, for example, Liechty finds that the discourse of "suitability" and "modernity" is central to the production of middle-classness, and people actively engage in projects of respectability (25). Suvi Salmenniemi (2013), similarly, has argued that in Russia social class has reemerged as a salient category in a variety of symbolic encodings. Terms like *the unfortunate family* (*neblagopoluchnaia sem'ia*) and *the working-class lad* (*gopnik*) circulate widely and index social positions (Iarskaia-Smirnova and Romanov 2013). Direct transliterations of English terms such as *glamour* (*glamur*), *elegant* (*elegantnyi*), and *chic* (*shikairnaia*) indicate a substitution of social values (Salmenniemi 2013; see also Patico 2008). In the case at hand, psychotherapeutic expertise was one practice through which the symbolic codings of "the advanced" (or not) were also being produced, but not through the performance of seemly behaviors: as the psychotherapeutic messaging discussed above shows, propriety was also linked to an interior capacity, or habitus (Bourdieu 1984), that is, what Julia Lerner (2015) terms a "therapeutic habitus." As the Childhood Planet expo showed, children also became important vehicles *for parents* to perform class identities, even providing routes to possible social mobility. Indeed, one of the most successful marketing strategies Tamara Grigorievna and her colleagues found was to promote the fact that one's children might rub shoulders with the children of other important people at their camps. Psychotherapists also desired the kinds of global and flexible livelihoods that they promised parents they could cultivate in young clients. As such, selling psychological training was also a means to more travel and kitchen renovations—in short, a decent-paying job. As one PPMS Center psychologist (who eventually left for greener pastures) told me, she wanted a mode of living that that was *prilichnyi* (seemly, respectable).

All of these projects aspired to a globally circulating psychological culture associated with the governing modalities of liberal states, what Eva Illouz (2008, 60) terms "emotional capitalism." That culture prioritizes emotional intelligence, executive function, and sensitivity in ways that go beyond mere empathy; the slew of human-resource trainings, self-help tapes, and skills courses together constitute a kind of psychological lingua franca of doing business globally. The obverse side of this coin is that self-work is also a practice tied to the erosion of social programs and state supports. Success is a matter of the self. This is now present in Russia, too, where the forms of emotional intelligence, as imagined, were expressed by modernization projects to be crucial to the circulation of capital.

Among those who work with the working classes, however, an entirely different kind of class politics obtained. The psychologists themselves were not the young and upwardly mobile. They were middle-aged, and being a psychologist was often a second career; most were not in it for the money. Class-making projects were less central to their work and themselves. Yet class content was present in any case: rather than taking aim at emotional intelligence, they emphasized (lacking) learning and cognitive skills. The subject of care was spatially constrained: the child was limited to the realm of unruly affects located in the brain-body (as opposed to processed emotions), and the presumed spatiality of that child and family was regionally limited.[27] In a market economy, then, certain dispositions, in Bourdieu's (1984) sense, were predisposed to the benefits of flexible citizenship, while others, once caught in the nets of psychosocial services, were vulnerable to containment and decreased or downward mobility.

Gender also intersects with the success complex in important ways. As I suggested, the ostensible gender neutrality of commercial appeals was contravened by Russia's predominant patriarchal norms. Like the earlier tension in Soviet gender politics between feminist and pronatalist concerns, the underlying assumptions about sex-related personality differences that appeared in everyday conversations and therapies gendered the domestic versus market success in conventional ways. In other words, if commercial appeals to family life seemed to presume gender-blind children's abilities and gender-blind parenting, a variety of other discourses disciplined these messages. These included public discussions of the "feminization" of boys through psychological work, the "masculinization" of girls through their inclusion in the labor force and their separation from their "true" role of reproduction, and, finally, the "irresponsible mother" who spends too little time at home.

It would be too much to suggest a causal link between the temporality of descriptions of different children's lives via psychological difference and class and gender formations. As this chapter shows, there were far too many moving parts—ranging from federal policy, to underfunded services, to individual practitioners pursuing their own advertising strategies—to sustain a straightforward functionalist explanation. Rather, the production of psychological difference was an effect of various practices of commensuration. It is an example of what happens when demographic and economic concerns shape the techniques and practices of experts. As a consequence of this discursive and institutional conjuncture, the care that might help was organized in such a way as to delimit the therapist's horizon of possibility. Perhaps most troubling, the complex nature and structures of care could make it difficult to recognize how social inequalities were written into and produced through expertise. As subsequent chapters show, this success complex was also crystallized within institutional forms, legal codes, norms governing professionalism, and knowledge formations. It was underwritten by different availability of resources and constituted those structures within which psychotherapists' practices and tactics unfolded. Different from zones of social abandonment (Biehl 2005), the organizations that provided care were, rather, *zones of social investment and divestment* in which the psychological expert mediated social expectation. In each case the expectations woven around child capacity served a particular role of containment—either scripting (male) child development according to the anxiety-ridden competitive life of the bourgeois subject, or else dangling before the child and her or his family the forbidding and sticky webs of social services, pathology, and problems.

In closing, this inscription of difference into the substance of the self calls into question how effective the satisfaction of social needs can be through coordination between the state and the market in Russia. In the case of psychology, as attention to the whole child was made commensurate with the market, both the far-reaching logics of profit, investment, and success and the obverse logics of divestment and neglect, strongly shaped the work being done. In the next two chapters, I ask whether and how practitioners contested these effects in their work.

Chapter 3

"NOW, FINALLY, WE ARE STARTING TO RELAX"

On Civilizing Missions and Democratic Desire

> We thought we were on the frontier of a democratic revolution.
> We weren't. We were witnessing a market revolution.
>
> —Democracy promoter Sarah Mendelson,
> "Dreaming of a Democratic Russia"

It was January 2006, and Aleksandr, one of ReGeneration's young psychologists, was driving us toward the Russian-Finnish border in a *Zhiguli* sedan. After many meetings and discussions with ReGeneration's staff, I was finally on my way to one of their one-week camps, where a group of almost forty children between eight and sixteen years old would learn how to control their emotions and behavior. The drive through the undulating forests of Karelia was fairly long, and it gave me the chance to hear more about ReGeneration's programs from the point of view of one of its senior staffers. There was also something appropriate about the ride. Abandoned concrete lookout towers and rusting barbed wire at the border—monuments to the Cold War—marked the erstwhile ideological boundary between market democracy and communism. The border no longer took very long to cross. Since the collapse of the Soviet Union, the main impediment had become traffic jams caused by a bustling shuttle trade in luxury cars, Finnish agricultural products, and tourists. The porous border was also symbolic of the arrival of the very psychological ideas on which ReGeneration drew.

Aarno fell asleep in back, and as we rolled along, Aleksandr started venting about democracy with a capital *D*. Referencing the self-serving reform agendas of the US economic advisers who swarmed into Russia after the USSR's collapse, as well as the United States' democracy-building escapade in Iraq, he said, "Russian democracy has to follow its own course, like in the Islamic countries."

"What should democracy in Russia look like?" I asked him.

"A democratic Russia would mean being able to cross the border and not be asked lots of questions by the police; to be able to go to the housing authority, make a complaint, and know that something will be done about it." He was optimistic that this future would eventually come to pass.

His complaints about big-*D* democracy were familiar. After the wild capitalism of the 1990s, many Russians viewed democracy with understandable skepticism—much like victims of a bait and switch. Promises of freedom, equality, fair elections, and prosperity had been pushed aggressively by US economic advisers and their Russian contacts (see Wedel 1998). Yet what followed was bargain-basement sales of state assets, opaque transfers of wealth, massive currency devaluations, nonpayment of wages, empty store shelves, and a general feeling of *bespredel*—a lack of limits, rules, or obstacles (Oushakine 2009, 1). All sorts of wordplay poking holes in the neoliberal sheen followed. The word *privatization* (*privatizatsiia*) was resignified with the nearly homonymous *prikhvatizatsiia*, or "grabitization"; *democracy* and related terms like *liberal* (*liberal'nyi*) became dirty words; the abbreviated Russian equivalent for "liberal values" (*La-Ve*) became slang for "cash" (Oushakine 2009, 35). Vladimir Putin has achieved a long, powerful, and lucrative career by deftly exploiting this disgust to marginalize his political opposition by mobilizing a nationalist fervor against the "puppets of the West"—in reality, a small, disparate political coalition of liberal democrats and nationalists (see figure 3.1). In this way, Aleksandr's criticism of big-*D* democracy contained not only a critique of the Bush administration's maligned "democracy building" in Iraq but also something specifically post-Soviet.

As we crossed over into Finland, our conversation finally came around to the work of ReGeneration. He explained that the organization's young clients would spend a week learning self-management (*samoupravlenie*; also autonomy) by becoming more aware of their selves. He and his colleagues viewed this psychological education as a strategic tactic based on the eventual arrival of this future, small-*d* democratic Russia. "Psychological education," he said, "will be a necessary technology to succeed in the Russia to come." What, I wondered, was necessary about it? Was he referring to a tolerant attitude that, once spread across society, would render the rule of law operable; to liberal individualism in a market democracy; to mobility and opportunity; to fair

FIGURE 3.1. "Yankee-killers!" Pensioners demonstrate outside of Saint Petersburg's shopping arcade, Gostinniy Dvor. Photograph reproduced with the kind permission of Mark Elmore.

elections? The answer depended on what kind of Russian future, and indeed what kind of democracy, Aleksandr had in mind.

The answer was not obvious. My fieldwork in several of ReGeneration's camps suggested that their strategic efforts were not explicitly concerned with democracy, let alone the political. Tamara Grigorievna's staff never discussed institutional reforms, elections, or political parties. Nor did they discuss their views of Putin very often. (As I learned, this was not due to indifference or support. They were critics, but not particularly vocal ones.) The lack of explicit politics notwithstanding, they did use a constellation of terms—*freedom* (*svoboda*), *self-management* (*samoupravlenie*; also autonomy), and *responsibility* (*otvetstvennost'*)—that broached the political. These terms anchored the skills they worked to instill in their child-clients—knowing and arresting one's impulses, listening to others, being personable, being a leader, speaking in public, managing one's time, and quelling aggression. As such, they implicitly tied psychological education to a range of concepts specific to liberal political subjectivities.[1] Rather than politics writ large, therefore, ReGeneration was concerned with micropolitics. They were intervening at the level of intra- and interpersonal relations. The scalability of those efforts remained, for me, an ethnographic question. But what was also important was that their psychological education drew on discourses more similar to those of the 1990s than to Putinism.

Their work also had particular social and material features. The children at ReGeneration's camps were largely ethnic Russian and from the families of the new elite. During the camp I conducted a small survey of the attendees. I learned that of the thirty-eight campers in Finland, twenty-nine had one or more parents working in finance or law or running their own businesses. Twenty-eight were from either Saint Petersburg or Moscow, Russia's two biggest and wealthiest cities. Their socioeconomic status was also evident in how, back in Saint Petersburg, some were dropped off by their parents' drivers. ReGeneration's programs were expensive and often involved foreign travel, as in this case: at that time, a weeklong camp in Finland cost approximately two months' salary for a white-collar worker. Aleksandr echoed the social positions of their clients when he told me that while some kids have behavioral problems, many are sent because the parents want their children to learn particular skills for taking over the family company. This located the clientele squarely among those known as "New Russians"—a post-Soviet nouveau riche known for their political connections and consumption habits.[2]

What kind of democracy was this, then? In this chapter, I use this question as a leaping-off point to explore ReGeneration's work and some of the social and political implications of the psychotherapeutic turn among the upwardly mobile in Russia. At issue here is the conjuncture of the practitioners' particular democratic desire, the relationship between what they tried to teach their clients and the micropolitics of neoliberalism, and the elite status of their clients. In one sense, the social profile of the clientele and, indeed, the words ReGeneration used to describe their aims suggest that this psychological education is a form of elite polish in neoliberal times. This interpretation is consistent with my argument in the previous chapter about how psychological difference intersects with class and gender formations. Thus, psychological education delivers the skills necessary not so much for democracy as for what Julia Paley (2001, 6) calls "marketing democracy," a democracy infused and shaped by neoliberalism and promoted as such.

And yet ReGeneration's director, Tamara, put it differently. Responding to my direct question about the class status of their elite clientele, she replied frankly, "We hope to work with the 20 percent of Russia that will make decisions for the other 80 percent." It was their intent, she suggested, to transform the elite—and thus the country's future—through their children. Acknowledging the status and political power of ReGeneration's clientele, she imbued their work with a particular moral significance that pivoted on the social difference between her staff and their clients. The question is, to what ends? They—and I (analytically)—were apparently *caught*. On the one hand, psychotherapists made their work commensurable with biopolitical norms, delivering technologies of the self that taught the already well-positioned to manage themselves in and for the global economy. This was a project of governing capitalized selves through freedoms that only some can afford, in a society in which full democratic citizenship is selective. On the other hand, in casting their work as a moral intervention, the psychologists also articulated an incommensurability between their work and those biopolitical norms. That incommensurability started from a stated difference in status between themselves and their clients and included a critique of the cultural norms of the nouveau riche. Also, as I show in later chapters, psychotherapists mobilized the language of the self as a critique of Putinism.

The play between commensurability and incommensurability mirrors the tension between the biopolitical and the ethical in precarious care. Often conflated in accounts of governmentality under neoliberal conditions, the biopolitical and the ethical are in a tensioned relation.[3] People can manage themselves and others in ways that may simultaneously align with power and capital and also run against its grain. Focusing on how ReGeneration's staff worked between the biopolitical and the ethical is crucial to making sense of psychotherapeutics as a contemporary, political site of subject formation in contemporary Russia. I acknowledge, though, that there is some reason to be suspicious of a distinction between biopolitics and ethics. Biopolitics, after all, often relies on moralizing and draws subjects into state aims by constituting them as caring subjects (see also Ticktin 2006; Bornstein and Redfield 2011). Andrea Muehlebach (2012) has argued this, pointing out that ethical projects are not antithetical to neoliberalism; on the contrary, they are central to it. She notes that in Italy the mobilization of moral sentiment in and through unremunerated social work and other sorts of affective labor dovetails with the gutting of state welfare. Thus, charity—or, in my case, socially intentioned care—is not a departure from the rapacious market; rather, it serves it. Muehlebach's concern is tracking the enfoldment of charity into the neoliberal political economy. At the same time, she adds that charitable practices and their moralities are politically multivalent: "Morality allows members of the Left to participate in the moral neoliberal in both wholehearted and yet also critical-complicit ways, and to forge out of this historical moment practices that are both oppositional and complicit at the same time" (9). She concludes, "There are thus moments where ideologies of charity coexist with the gift as truly reciprocal act, disembedded action together with a tight circuit of obligatory giving and receiving. The ability to discern the one from the other, and to have charity morph into solidarity, is a struggle and a question. And it is perhaps the beginning of another story" (228).

That other story is the one that interests me. As I showed in the previous chapter, there is ample evidence that psychotherapists are complicit with the production of class and gender formations in neo-authoritarian, semi-neoliberal times. Here I am interested in the phrase "critical-complicit" and the tension between biopolitics and ethics that is congealed in its hyphen. To be sure, psychological education may not contain the kinds of radical political solidarity that Muehlebach has in mind and that animates so much critical anthropology; nor is it unremunerated. Nonetheless, I follow here Tamara's and Aleksandr's sense that psychological education is a micropolitical response to the problems in Russia that had stemmed, in part, from the neoliberal shock therapy of the 1990s and the other shocks that have followed. They did not see themselves as engaging in bourgeois culture building but as repairing broken social relations, whether by countering harsh parenting with new models of care or by promoting tolerance. They spoke of transforming the elite, not simply cultivating that elite. In exploring this work as critical-complicit, I show how the tension between biopolitics and ethics is made manifest in spaces of social difference: the psychologists' perception that they are working across and also with a social divide between themselves and elite others produces this tension. And on that basis they, as caregivers, also negotiate their complicity in the reproduction of psychological difference. Ultimately, I find the nuances of their responses worth dwelling on because they illuminate the ambiguous nature of democracy in Russia—the ways in which democracy both is implicated in the expansion of social inequality and also underlies some leftists' radical critique of the neo-authoritarian turn under Putin. Critical complicity is thus a feature of precarious care, as well as a condition of post-Soviet politics.

The Freedom Lab

ReGeneration's camps were places to learn how to be a kind of political subject. To train children in these new subjectivities, practitioners deployed a range of techniques, including the careful creation of atmosphere, a hermeneutics of the self, and what I call "regimes of rule breaking." Tamara specialized in the creation of social atmospheres and viewed their camps as a place to allow children to experience freedom and autonomy in the midst of different norms, expectations, and disciplinary forms—specifically, ones she argued are still uncommon in Russian households. By invoking keywords like *autonomy, freedom, self-sufficiency,* and *individualism* ("in the good sense"), she also implied a link between their efforts and what Barbara Cruikshank has called "technologies of democratic citizenship—discourses, programs, and other tactics aimed at making individuals politically active and capable of self-government" (1999, 1). Couched in psychological languages, however, these technologies were not so much about political action as about a relation to oneself involving forms of self-management, candor, confession, and, as Tamara indicated, even relaxation.

With reference to a variety of studies linking the psy-ences to neoliberal governmentality, the camps can easily be read as places where the spread of Western self-help and therapy (not to mention diagnostics and psychopharmacology) constitutes a subject of, and for, governance (Burchell 1996; Cruikshank 1999; Dean 1996; Foucault 1991; Rose 1996a). That Russia's youth is the target is also part of a trend in which educational-developmental psychology is offering tools for defensive parenting under austere economic conditions. In the search for a competitive edge in the face of economic volatility and exhausted social supports, the child's interior is the next frontier.[4] My observations of the day-to-day events and activities at the camp suggest that Aleksandr's psychological education was, indeed, very much like an elite finishing school for a neoliberal age. The desired subject was self-managing and autonomous—qualities that were amplified by ReGeneration's implicit critique of the family, which was understood as a source of bad social reproduction and a brake on self-sufficiency. The psychologists drew on their rising stock as experts to reconstitute their clients as the self-knowing, androcentric "feeling subjects" I encountered at the Childhood Planet expo. The underpinning of success, in turn, projected those subjectivities into the global marketplace, instantiating a future-oriented anxiety concerned with competition and planning ahead. Viewed in these terms, ReGeneration's work sought to shape both interiority, through the technical rendering of the self, and the kinds of interactions and opportunities made possible by having the right kind of polish. In the pages that follow, I detail how the psychologists used two key technologies to effect (and affect) this particular feeling subject: lessons (zaniatii), in which focused psychological education took place, and a general assembly, in which the children gathered for socialization. These technologies constituted a kind of freedom lab.

On Monday morning I joined Aleksandr and Zhenya's zaniatii and, along with eight eleven- to thirteen-year-old children, became a feeling subject. During the week that followed, we were led from constituting and exploring interiority to intervening in it with our faculties of reason. Our journey inward began with an affirmation of our emotional ignorance: "How are you?" Aleksandr asked, turning to Gosha, a boy with stylish hair highlights. "Normal'no," Gosha said, momentarily lifting his eyes from his cell phone. He had used the Russian equivalent of "fine." In response, Aleksandr drew a bell curve on the board. "This is the full range of human emotions, and this," he said, pointing to the middle 60 percent, "is what most people call 'normal'no.' It's quite a wide range. So how are we really feeling?"

We were then paired and told to respond to our partner's question, "How are you?" for a full minute without saying "normal'no." The results were remarkable. In describing how I was to Tolya, a small boy with glasses, I quickly ran out of things to say. Others, too, soon fell silent, illustrating the paucity of our emotional vocabulary as well as, perhaps, a discomfort with solipsism. Aleksandr and Zhenya then began to demonstrate that our current states, for which we lacked words, could be broken down into layers and levels.

Beginning with this sense of limitation, they would try to provide us with resources for self-investigation using a series of interpretive and representational exercises that helped us first constitute, then turn out, our insides for examination and, finally, develop skills of self-management. We drew pictures. We modeled behavior. We played emotional charades. We completed and then shared such sentences as "The scariest time in my life was . . ." We were encouraged to discuss instances in our lives when we lost control of our emotions. We used our bodies to represent various emotions.

These exercises often produced fascinating results. In one, we were handed a lump of clay and told to mold our "deepest fear" with the idea that materialization would neutralize it. As an expression of my own anxieties about social judgment, I made a little green man with a mean expression and an oversized index finger pointing mockingly (figure 3.2). Gosha, who was obsessed with electronics, surprised me with his poetic (albeit claustrophobic) sensibility, making a "house without any doors or windows" (figure 3.3). (In another exercise where we were supposed to describe our ideal inner state in terms of weather conditions, he described his as "a single tree on a snowy hill under a clear, starlit sky.") Sasha, a brash thirteen-year-old jokester, made an "animal

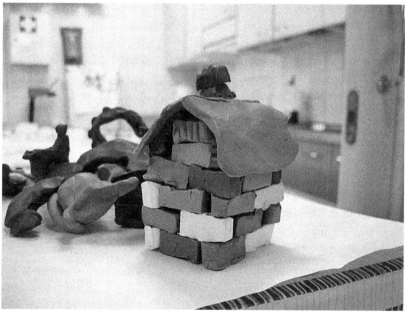

FIGURES 3.2 AND 3.3. Clay representations of the author's (top) and Gosha's (bottom) deepest fears. Photos by the author.

claw that can expand and oppress but also contract and disappear." Igor had made a simple, mysterious black box representing darkness, and melancholic Tolya made a green "alien" holding guns. (When he saw my little green man pointing and laughing derisively at me, he remarked wryly, "Tomas, we are brothers.")

In another exercise, we drew maps of our "internal worlds." Serafima's was a harmonious composition (figure 3.4). "The sun," she explained, "is a manifestation of joy that gives off ecstasy and enjoyment, but also nervousness and anger." Ilya, by contrast, drew a chaotic map in motion: a tangle of roads, passes, and dead ends, complete with a "mood teleport," that showed his changing moods as a journey (figure 3.5). Gosha put himself at the middle of his picture, with lines leading outward to different emotionally infused locales, including "the place of emotional experience," designated by a home-entertainment system with a flat-screen TV.

As diverse as these results were, we spent little time delving into the details. The point was to constitute a relation to oneself, rather than to submit anyone to particular scrutiny. (I learned that some of this individual attention was handled outside the zaniatii, beyond the view of other campers [and anthropologists]). Having created an internal world, we were then taught to intervene in it, to control its atmospheres and movements, to mobilize reason over knee-jerk behavior. As ReGeneration had promised in their promotional materials, we were being moved beyond the Socratic imperative of self-knowledge (*samopoznanie*) into the terrain of *doing*, toward the management of self (samoupravlenie).

"What things do you do to help you through tough situations?" Zhenya asked us one morning. "What do you do when you feel uncomfortable?" When Gosha, Ilya, and Grisha cited playing with, throwing, or just pushing the buttons of their mobile phones, Zhenya observed that these actions could be thought of as forms of self-regulation. We were then asked to draw a picture of a person who is self-regulating—what is she doing, how does she handle herself? I worked with Serafima and Lara, and we drew a person who was calm, wearing comfortable clothes and slippers and reading her favorite book. Realizing that disturbance is what necessitates self-regulation, we added some distractions—loud music, a cat scratching at her leg. When we were all finished, Aleksandr asked us to derive "a formula" for self-regulation, which my group did using the analogy of a scale with two arms—the tools used for self-regulation should always outweigh the impact of the distractions. Another group had counterposed brains (*mozgi*) and will (*volia*), both of which were

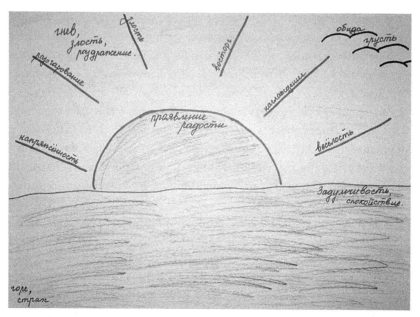

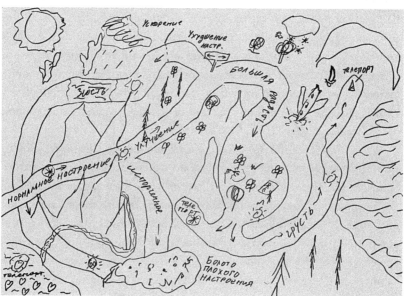

FIGURES 3.4 AND 3.5. Serafima's (top) and Ilya's (bottom) emotional worlds. Photos by the author.

to be mediated by self-regulation. A third group put forward the less intuitive formula "emotions + thoughts = self-control." It was unclear what general formula could be drawn from this hodgepodge of drawings.

Aleksandr and Zhenya then offered "the answer": a circle composed of the words emotions, thoughts, and behavior, linked with bidirectional arrows. "This is the 'eternal engine,'" said Aleksandr, "and is what drives the human being."

We nodded, jotting this in our workbooks. On the next page we learned more about the elements of this eternal engine. Emotions (*emotsii*) are "our appraisal [*otsenka*] of and personal attitude toward the signals of the external and internal world [*sreda*]." Compared to thought, emotion in these terms is something closer to an unmediated response. Thoughts (*mysli*), in contrast, is more mediated: it is "a mental representation, idea, judgment, opinion, reasoning, conclusion or supposition." Finally, behavior (*povedenie*) is "a person's conduct and actions" and the way in which "the person's personality, the particularities of his character, temperament, his needs and tastes, are manifested."

We were then asked to list all the emotions we could think of. We made all kinds of guesses, ranging from ecstasy to dreaminess and confusion. I paused and pondered, tripping over my analytics (see Massumi 2002; Briggs 2000; Lutz 1988): Is an emotion "feeling," unmediated by thinking? Or do cognitive processes have a role in emotion? What is the role of language? Is love, which is both feeling and thought, an emotion? Aleksandr explained that love is actually not an emotion and that there are ten basic emotions, according to the source they were using: happiness, surprise, interest, sadness, wrath, disgust, insult, fear, shame, and guilt.

The workbooks in our laps had linked emotion, thought, and behavior, roughly corresponding to feeling-thinking-acting, with bidirectional arrows, indicating circulation without a necessary point of origin; it became clear over the week, however, that the basic model of experience with which we were working was the following:

external stimulus → emotional response and/or thinking → behavior

"All we do depends on how we feel," said Aleksandr. Indeed, he seemed to mean this not only in the mundane sense that feeling depressed means acting depressed but also in the technical sense that emphasizes the instrumental nature of feeling: *how*—meaning, by what means—and *where* do we feel? By using reason to bring emotional responses under control, we could also control our behavior. The relationship that they offered between the terms rested on two assumptions about human experience. First, by isolating an intervening process between stimulus and response, it broke experience down according to the division between thinking and doing, where thinking precedes doing (leaving aside kinds of doing that may be constitutive of thinking, like ritual prayer or yoga). Second, by delineating that internal process, it posited the Enlightenment distinction between reason and passion. The result was to assert an autonomous subject on whom was bestowed the capacity for intervention at multiple levels of experience—not just feelings and actions but also thinking itself.[5]

We spent the remainder of the week discussing the techniques of self-regulation. One could do a variety of practical things to make oneself feel better, but all of them relied on a single proposition—one first had to train oneself in the art of "reading" oneself by honing skills of self-observation and interpretation. This took on interesting dimensions when projected into social situations. Zhenya started by writing five emotions on the board and giving a corresponding color: sadness (blue), irritation (red), wrath (black), happiness (yellow), and satisfaction (green). She told us to use this key to note our current mood. I made a yellow and a green box for "happy" and "satisfied" in my workbook, as did most others. Then, in answer to the complaints the kids had been making that the lessons did not include enough games, they told us that if we could reach consensus, we could plan the rest of the day. If not, they would decide for us. Several of the more boisterous kids immediately began talking about just playing games. One suggested one game; another, another one. Then they began to argue over which game was good and which stupid. Sasha began making lewd jokes with two others. Serafima and Lara, not participating, provided an amused audience. Tolya, the only serious one, protested, saying, "Our parents didn't send us here to play games but to learn." Sasha threw some crumpled paper at him.

The psychologists, who had been sitting back and watching in silence, instructed us to stop and note our emotional state. I scratched a red box for "irritation" and continued to watch in dismay as my classmates squandered their chance to address their own dissatisfaction with the trainings. As things continued off track, so did my emotional barometer—using the color code I noted irritation, wrath, and sadness. The lack of agreement went on for fifteen painful minutes, until finally some of the class clowns began to shift roles. Gosha was the first to say that perhaps Tolya was right, we shouldn't just play games. He reminded his cohort that they might lose the chance to decide the day's schedule. The joking slowly ebbed, and more became attentive. Zhenya asked us again to note our emotions, and I noted satisfaction mixed with a lingering irritation. Ten minutes later we had come to an agreement—we had proposed a mixture of games and lessons. We did our final emotional check, and I had again returned to a state of happiness and satisfaction.

This exercise demonstrated how much an emotional barometer could say about ourselves and the situation. It charted a trajectory of emotional experience for the group and also showed that everyone, regardless of their role in the mayhem, had experienced the exercise similarly. This seemed to offer a kind of disciplinary lesson: in showing us our emotional interdependence, we also came to appreciate, perhaps more profoundly, the importance of personal responsibility—crucially, even the clowns ruined the experience *for themselves.* Further, self-regulation appeared as a natural outcome of self-knowledge: the curvelike movement of the group dynamic—traveling from positive to negative to positive—suggested that the collective realization of dissatisfaction had helped bring about a change in behavior. It was a perfect expression of the camp objectives. Zhenya also pointed out that these kinds of skills of observation and self-control could be helpful in influencing other people's states. "What bothered you in the exercise?" she asked rhetorically. "Your mood may have been affected by your level of nervousness in making your ideas heard; by certain new, unfamiliar ideas; by your personal point of view; and by social conditions." She said that if we exercised self-regulation, and moderated the influence of our experiences on our emotions, our self-regulation would also feed back more calm into the collective discussion.

In later days this link between self-control and social control was posited in the context of other techniques. For instance, we were given some tricks for avoiding fear and anger. To be less afraid, one might "orient oneself to success" by thinking about one's achievements, "sing a happy song," "list one's strengths mentally," or "draw that which scares you, look at it from another angle, and then destroy it." And to be less angry, one might "break something unneeded or tear a few sheets of paper into tiny pieces," "punch a pillow," or "stamp one's feet." We were also advised how we could help others to calm down: "respect the person's point of view," "use humor," "discuss your own mood and the other person's mood," and "use I-statements." Like the techniques of self-regulation, these also rested on a kind of hermeneutics. We were told that it was possible to read how a person is feeling, or even what they are thinking, by paying attention to how she or he moves or looks, how she or he speaks, and what she or he says—what they called the nonverbal, paralinguistic, and verbal levels. What makes a calm person, noted Aleksandr, is called "congruence" (*kongruentnost'*). He singled out Ilya as someone with good congruence in that these different behavior cues aligned in a way that was consistent with how he was feeling.

Governing Subjects

The zaniatii, drawing on a range of cognitive-behavioral techniques (positive reinforcement, role playing, and the rehearsal of past negative experiences; see Sheldon 1995), had armed us with emotional intelligence, giving us a range of tools for affective management. To what ends? One way that I have answered this is to begin with the clientele's elite status. In light of the combined focus on competition and uspekh (success), it was not simply self-realization that was valorized but self-realization that would bring about a competitive advantage. Affects were not managed simply to cope with the world but to succeed in it. For example, as a capstone to Aleksandr and Zhenya's zaniatii, the discourse of uspekh emerged in the final pages of our workbook. Several figures were presented for us to emulate now that we had developed the skills of self-management. All were famous athletes and were associated with short quotes about working hard, trusting in oneself, and achieving. One quote was from David Beckham: "Manchester's trainer played a huge role in our success. He inclined us toward winning, forced us to believe that we are the best. And so we really were."

This embroidering of uspekh into the micropolitics of self-management was reinforced in the general assembly, where Tamara gathered the children three times daily. These meetings were organized by scorekeeping, friendly competition, and a range of individualizing practices that began the day the children arrived at the camp. This form of socialization, signaling an evaluative gaze, was tempered with a permissiveness intended to instill internal discipline and a structured freedom—a kind of *regime of rule breaking*. Children could leave their seats and walk around, have side conversations, and even taunt the psychologists. All that was expected of them was that they participate in the activities. When things went awry, the psychologists rarely yelled. Instead, they modeled patient but firm interpersonal relations.

The camp's orientation to uspekh, along with its emphasis on competition, individualization, and self-management, thus aligned this work with neoliberal political rationalities, which are premised on governing free individuals, who are "induced to self-manage according to market principles of discipline, efficiency, and competitiveness" (Ong 2006, 277).[6] ReGeneration pushed self-responsibility even further by seeking to circumvent the family, the last bastion of care in the face of privatized social support (Garcia 2010). As Anne Anagnost (2006) has observed of China's recent turn to youth development, under such conditions "profit and loss" become one's own problems, wholly dependent on individual "quality."

I also found that ReGeneration's work linked freedom to a particular economy of desire for the West.[7] This relationship was nicely summed up by a Megafon cell phone company billboard I saw in central Saint Petersburg in which a man held a cell phone aloft in front of the Las Vegas version of the Statue of Liberty, mirroring the statue's iconic pose. The text on the billboard read "Roaming for Travelers." Despite ongoing critiques of US and European Union policies, the symbols of bounty, fashion, and style from *zagranitsa*, or abroad, continue to entice many Russians through what Caroline Humphrey has called "content consumption," in which "the goods themselves confer their identity on people" (2002, 176). As an example, she cites the villas of the New Russians, which become "the ground for two specific self-images, that of an haute bourgeoisie within an imagined 'historical' empire and that of sleek, efficient Europeans within a globalized vista of modern business elites" (176). Similarly, the term *evro-remont*, literally "Euro-repaired," circulated throughout the 1990s and 2000s as an index of good-quality apartment renovations—with double-paned glass, private water heaters for showering, and personal water filters because the Saint Petersburg water cannot be consumed without being boiled first. Perhaps the clearest indicator of this link between the West and social mobility in Russia is seen in the new leisure class's ability to flock to Turkey, Europe, the United States, and points beyond (and this includes sending one's children abroad for psychological education). Many of the wealthiest continue to hold their substantial riches—in some cases wealth from the theft of state assets in the 1990s—in offshore bank accounts.

As a sales tactic, ReGeneration has drawn on this form of content consumption as well as other popular state discourses about modernizing subjects. This commensuration with the biopolitical economy helps to bring ReGeneration's aims under the sign of flexible citizenship (Ong 1999; Dunn 2004). Moreover, there is a particular masculinist, elite, and rational disposition that can be read through their efforts: their work entails "a bifurcating and Western cast of mind" (Rosaldo 1984, 137), in which reason is separate from and mobilized against emotion to intervene in experience and behavior. As Pierre Bourdieu (1984, 34–41) has observed in his analyses of social distinction, the privileging of reason over passion suggests a "bourgeois ethos of elective distance," whereby contemplation is superior to action. This privileging is also classically gendered: feminist anthropologists have demonstrated how this dichotomy underlies other gendered social distinctions such as private-public (Gal and Kligman 2000; J. Collier and Yanagisako 1987) and nature-culture (Ortner 1974). Indeed, even though ReGeneration's staff was predominantly female, the subject that the staff sought to constitute resonated strongly with the figure of the male entrepreneur in Russia (Yurchak 2003). Finally, consider the suspension of the rules in the name of liberation and positive reinforcement. Such practices could be read as sanctioning the well-to-do's sense of entitlement to misbehave without consequences. In light of all of this, ReGeneration can be glossed as a finishing school for an emergent elite in which psychological education offers the means of competitive advantage, leadership, and distinction.

Democratic Sentiments

In my conversations with Tamara, Aleksandr, Zhenya, and others both during and after camps, they offered me an alternate understanding of both the motives for and the effects of psychological education. They saw their work as promoting a socially attuned and gender-sensitive empathy (based on the idea that "if my feelings matter, so might those of others") rather than an instrumental technologizing of the self. They saw themselves as intervening in social relations, whether through injecting new models of care into families or promoting tolerance, rather than as engaging in the production of young entrepreneurs. Instead of simply cultivating an elite, they spoke of transforming that elite. Their claims rested on a single foundation: a pathologization of the Soviet past and a critique (if muted) of the post-Soviet elite. On the basis of that foundation, they endowed their work with moral and social legitimacy. For them, self-work was a response to deeply rooted social problems, whose contemporary manifestation lay in the callous attitudes and lack of concern for others among the elite.

Taking this perspective into account poses productive challenges to analyses of neoliberal governmentality and biopolitics. In one sense, it highlights a disconnect between the way governmentality studies—especially in their sociological vein—approach experts and the way anthropologists encounter experts in the field. As Dominic Boyer has put it, we ought to treat experts "not solely as rational(ist) creatures of expertise but rather as desiring, relating, doubting, anxious, contentious, affective—in other words as human subjects" (2008, 38). In another sense, it offers a corrective to the "diffusionist" models of neoliberalism critiqued by Andrew Kipnis (2008) and more recently, in the Russian context, Stephen J. Collier (2011). Finally, the historicity of the psychotherapeutic turn complicates the view that expertise is exclusively regressive and in the service of power.[8] Instead, it may be critical-complicit.

In wrestling with these issues, I have found the Foucauldian concepts of subjectivation and ethics helpful. Focusing on subjectivation (rather than *neoliberal* subjectivation) broadens the inquiry to other governing projects and historical formations. Becoming a subject of something, and to oneself, entails multiple forms of knowledge, power, and "games of truth." It unfolds in relation to various institutions and discourses and according to multiple modes, domains, and goals (Foucault 1990b, 25–32; 1997a, 290). Subjectivation is thus neither a matter of simple indoctrination nor an exercise in Promethean agency; it is a situated process through which the pushes and pulls of the everyday are negotiated. As Saba Mahmood succinctly puts it, "the capacity for action is enabled and created by specific relations of subordination" (2005, 29). Subjectivation is also ethical. Jarrett Zigon (2011) has pointed out that, while shaped by moral assemblages, self-constitution always entails questions of how best to live.[9] The concepts of subjectivation and ethics bring a dual focus to the fact that experts must navigate ways of knowing, being, and living that are overdetermined and may entail an unpalatable complicity but are, nonetheless, not dictated.[10]

A sense of historical location was particularly salient for ReGeneration's psychologists. If subjectivity, as Michel Foucault puts it, "is the way in which the subject experiences himself in a game of truth" (1994, 260), then the project of psychological education was a matter of inciting others (and themselves) as subjects not only of neoliberal capitalism but also of history. Relatedly, it was not only an expression of relations of power but also a form of care. This particular form of historical awareness mixed with care took shape predominantly through the invocation of a conception of post-Soviet democracy, as well as particular imaginings of what the postsocialist everyday should look and feel like, affectively speaking.[11] Many psychologists, like Aleksandr, saw their work as having some connection to democracy. Over time, it became clear that they meant not only a form of freedom expressed through consumer choices and success but also membership in a particular liberal imaginary in which basic rights to security, dignity, and responsive institutions were possible (see Ferguson 2007).[12] As psychologists, they hoped to lend content to this loosely specified desire for their clients and themselves.

Consider Igor, another ReGeneration psychologist. One day, he told me of his brother's recent death in a car accident. Igor thought that he could have been saved if not for the slow emergency response; it took over an hour for the ambulance to arrive. Organized around an experience of safety and calm, his alternative future was expressed affectively: "I want to live in a place where basic life services like that are faster, more responsive. I was recently in Helsinki. One night I went for a walk on the empty highway. I would never do this in Russia, but in Finland there was the silence, a passing car. Nobody was paying attention to me. It was a safety that was calming, unusual. It's a safety that you have in the United States, too, and I envy it."

The desire for security was complemented by a particular interest in reshaping the disciplinary expectations around children and adolescents. I observed this at another ReGeneration program, a three-week camp on friendship held at a former leisure compound for Leningrad State University workers. Unlike at the camp in Finland, where ReGeneration was the sole tenant for the week, here it shared the grounds with other groups, including a soccer team. At lunch one day, I joined Anna, a psychologist in her mid-twenties. As we took our places around the table, campers trickled in for the meal. The young soccer players, dressed in tracksuits, calmly sat down and waited for the bell to signal that they could eat. A few moments later, loud noises erupted from the doorway as a group of ReGeneration campers burst in, laughing boisterously. They played musical chairs and flirted. Some started eating before the bell. Others scooted their chairs back into passersby or flicked around bits of food.

"Just look at our kids," Anna said approvingly. "They are so filled with life. Not like those kids from the soccer camp."

Anna's view surprised me. The contrast seemed to highlight the disrespectful and spoiled nature of "our kids." Yet her statement was more than what a parent, blinded by love, says to justify bad behavior. The disregard for discipline was cast in positive terms. It was part of what ReGeneration was trying to accomplish. A follow-up conversation with Tamara made this desired transformation clearer. She said that she and her staff aim to reverse the totalitarian parenting styles of Soviet upbringing, or vospitanie. She is especially interested in allowing children to behave in ways that would be strongly disciplined at home or in school. She confided that the administrators of the campgrounds often say that kids in her programs "lack discipline" and are given "too much freedom [svoboda])." But she countered,

We are creating an atmosphere where the children have more freedom than they do at home so they can find their own way, become more self-sufficient. . . . The cultural norm in Russia until perestroika with regard to vospitanie was very strict and directed. There are still multigenerational families living under one roof, and nobody learns to practice autonomy [*samostoiatel'nost'*; also self-management]. Children get married and then move in with their parents. But things are starting to change for the better, like in Europe, where everyone . . . is so free, all so relaxed. Now, finally, we are starting to relax. It's a form of individualism in the good sense of the word.

Tamara and her colleagues thus viewed their camps as places to intervene in historically constituted social relations by allowing children to experience new expectations and forms of sociality. Couched in psychological expertise, freedom (svoboda), for Tamara, was a relation both to parental and teacher authority and to self that involved management, independence, and even relaxation.[13] It also involved the creation of particular kinds of affective atmospheres. In an exercise typical of their group meetings, for example, the psychologists invited the children to pay each other compliments. They had cut out little squares from construction paper, written a superlative judgment on each, and asked the children to pick one and present it to someone while the group looked on. This exercise involved them in the creation of particular kinds of socialities, inducing them to rescript their interactions with one another according to particular normative sorting and classifying operations (prettiest, handsomest, funniest, smartest).

While "the West," as mentioned earlier, continues to structure the discourse of freedom and relaxation, ReGeneration's interest in molding alternate subjectivities had important historical components that had less to do with the West as a desired other. As Vitya Markov, the man whom I had mistaken for an American tourist, had complained to me some weeks earlier, Soviet psychotherapy had been hemmed in by "ideological purity," was abused as "a tool for 'reforming' patients and correcting 'wrong' behavior," and lacked a "concept of internal human experience and humane therapeutic relationships." The attention to confidence and relaxation was thus also premised on rescripting the relationship of the therapist to the client and offering an alternative concept of interiority.

The political specificity of this interest in alternate psychological subjectivities is made clearer with reference to the time during perestroika when the Soviet approach to education was challenged by a group of philosophers and psychologists (discussed in the previous chapter). Before the 1980s, psychology in its client-based, nonmedicalized forms had played no role in communist pedagogy, let alone daily practice, in the Soviet Union. Rather than emotions, the disciplined will was at the center of communist sciences of behavior (Matza 2014). This emphasis on will had been institutionalized by the APN, which held sway over Soviet public schools and influenced styles of upbringing. The academy had long shunned child-centered approaches to education in favor of more disciplinary and undifferentiated approaches (Asmolov 2005). In the 1980s, however, as Mikhail Gorbachev shifted attention to the "human factor of production" (Rawles 1996, 103), a group of scholars staged a revolt within the academy. Drawing on Western psychotherapies—especially human-potential psychology—this group called for the humanization of Soviet public schools (Eklof and Dneprov 1993). We should therefore understand the practitioners' interest in freedom and self-cultivation in relation not only to market democracy but also to a particular, late-socialist perestroika progressivism.

Progressivism notwithstanding, it was clear that ReGeneration was primarily reaching only the children of the well-to-do. Recall Tamara's response to my comment that her clients' privilege would seem to narrow the staff's social-reform efforts or even undermine them entirely: "We hope to work with the 20 percent of Russians who will make decisions for the other 80 percent." The elite target population was integral to their vision of the utility of psychological education. Her statement also suggests an important distinction not just between segments of the Russian population but also between psychologist and client (who lacks something). I encountered it in another conversation, when, responding to my request for access to clients' parents, Aleksandr demurred: "They have no interest in seeing us; we are their employees."[14]

This difference between we and they indexes contested power relations between the post-Soviet elite and the mass intelligentsia (Shlapentokh 1989; see also Patico 2008), that is, teachers, doctors, engineers, and, indeed, psychologists. In the Soviet period, the intelligentsia had become accustomed to a certain material privilege while occupying the role of moral standard-bearers. Jennifer Patico (2008) and Michele Rivkin-Fish (2009) have argued that as their material means disappeared in the 1990s, all that remained for the intelligentsia was cultural capital.[15] Affronted by the materialistic values of the so-called New Russians, the intelligentsia has struggled to maintain a place in the national imaginary and, at the same time, has issued frequent critiques of the corruption linked to the new elite. In light of this, Tamara's targeting of that consequential "20 percent" is part of a civilizing project aimed at the elite, long considered by the intelligentsia to lack manners and ethics (Humphrey 2002).[16]

This general civilizing concern took various forms—most often outside the group lessons, in one-on-one interactions. Aleksandr told me that Sasha, who loved to disrupt his own (and others') psychological education, had calmed down a lot since first coming to the camp, when he was like "a scared animal." Invoking the critical discourse of the crass New Russians, Aleksandr painted a picture of home neglect, saying that Sasha, whose parents are divorced, almost never sees his mother, a high-powered executive, and spends most of his time with his grandmother. The psychologists have thus been helping Sasha to build sustained, trusting relationships with adults rather than to respond to them with a defensive sarcasm masking fear. Over time, Aleksandr noted, Sasha has come to identify closely with him. As Tamara told me, many children begin "living from camp to camp," identifying more strongly with the camps than home. In these examples, one can also see how psychological education is also form of self-work for the psychologists. Armed with the premise that they were intervening in both historical and contemporary problems by helping children develop their own self-management skills, they simultaneously constituted themselves as social reformers.

The psycho-ethical reeducation of the elites has a particular urgency given that elites continue to be viewed by many ordinary Russians as hopelessly corrupt. Each year Russia's president announces a war on corruption, but little seems to change: Russia continues to be hounded by poor corporate governance, selective law enforcement, and extortion, not to mention state graft. In the words of Boris Yeltsin's prime minister, Viktor Chernomyrdin, regarding the reforms of the 1990s, "We hoped for the best, but it turned out as it always does [*khoteli kak luchshe, a polichilos' kak vsegda*]" (quoted in Ledeneva 2006, 11). Alena Ledeneva suggests that Chernomyrdin's words summarize a sense of "Russia's entrapment in its own ways," "allud[ing] to routine practices of the elites—from local bosses to transnational networks—that continue to benefit from such an order of things" (2006, 11).

Many scholars have written about the vacuum in social trust after the collapse of the Soviet state (see Humphrey 2002; Oushakine 2009; Shevchenko 2009; Verdery 1996; Volkov 2002). The idea is that the perceived solidity of late-Soviet institutions had anchored a wide variety of social practices. Its absence in the 1990s and the lack even of any succeeding national idea had thus given rise to the variety of improvised structures that many anthropologists have noted. These include suzerainties, private security, and mafia bosses, as well as, at the symbolic level, conspiracy theories and a new habitus structured by a logic of permanent crisis. The experience of the 1990s thus continues to pose questions about how to structure new forms of social constraint, social order, and trust as a way to arrive at increased social equality—a goal that has remained, up until the present day, elusive. In effect, what reformers of all kinds in Russia seek are the kinds of institutions that have served as a sociopolitical guarantor in other states, what Aleksandr may have meant by small-*d* democracy.

In the face of problems of social trust and inequality, ReGeneration and its staff appeared to believe that psychological education had both a moralizing and a socially reordering potential, operating one self at a time. Their efforts to constitute particular kinds of subjectivity can thus be connected to a long tradition of civilizing projects in Russia.[17] Their efforts shared not only the tendency to compare Russia with the West, but also an economy of desire, where particular symbols, whether material or subjective, take on value in and through their association with a generalized West. Their work was also endowed with a particularly comparative, and forward-looking, temporality, in which it was not just a few kids but Russia's very future that was at stake. The practitioners even suggested that there were old habits that had to be overcome through their work, a suggestion that resonated with the centuries-long political anxiety about Russian "backwardness" (*otstalost'*). Many viewed the parents as the problem in that they were the vehicles for social reproduction that made the psychologists' work—the work of reforming social relations—difficult. For that reason, the separation of children from their parents in camps was fundamental to disrupting the reproduction of bad habits. Such were the ways in which ReGeneration's psychologists framed their work in class terms.

What, finally, of gender in their promotion of a "feeling subject"? Commercially available psychological services intersected in interesting ways with gender formations. On the one hand, there was the matter of public responses to the psychotherapeutic turn: as one psychologist who worked for a diagnostics company told me, people view the spread of psychologists as bringing about the feminization of boys. She suggested that there was something about "the psychological," in other words, that was viewed as being feminine. Whether this was because the majority of psychologists in Saint Petersburg were women, or because emotion talk was associated with femininity, remained unclear to me. On the other hand, there was the question of how psychologists themselves engaged with gender discourses in their work.

Recall the two discursive formations concerning gender in Soviet Russia—the gender-neutral ideal of Soviet labor, and the demographic discourses that actually reified gender distinctions via the imperatives of biological reproduction and male heroism (Kaganovsky 2008).[18] These two poles have historically come into conflict around projects to either transform or reassert a structural opposition between the domestic and the public/economic: Soviet women in the workforce were, at once, signs of socialist progressivism and a threat to traditional kinship orders. In the post-Soviet period, it could be argued that this dynamic has continued: the supposed gender-blindness of market messaging discussed in the previous chapter (both boys and girls can be entrepreneurs) runs up against a countervailing set of conservative expectations that young women will eventually fight the demographic crisis by having children. A telltale sign of this tension is that the imperative to commercial success, while ostensibly ungendered, is often gendered masculine (Yurchak 2003). The presence of women in business and politics is also viewed as curious. One psychologist commented, speaking of Valentina Matvienko, Saint Petersburg's mayor from 2003 to 2011, "She appears ill at ease with her femininity because she is playing a man's game." These normative attitudes are buttressed by dominant conservative messages in which women who are seen as working too hard, or else as seeking "domestic personnel" to relieve themselves of child care, are portrayed as either unfeminine or potentially selfish (it is assumed that the nannies are standing in to raise children while the mothers go shopping). As such, ReGeneration's effort to create "feeling subjects" potentially resignifies gender in Russia. Promoting emotion talk *and* also promoting entrepreneurship (at least ostensibly) among girls and boys cuts across at least two conventional gender formations—that linking femininity and emotion talk, and that linking masculinity and the market economy. We are dealing here with matter out of place (Douglas 2002), and both the market and the place of emotionality in commerce have posed new kinds of possibilities for feminist politics and labor, as well as new kinds of sources of tension for conservatives.

Critical-Complicit: Between Ethics and Biopolitics

If the gap between the two characterizations of psychological education reviewed above cannot be chalked up to false consciousness, then I ought to have observed some instances of recognition, discomfort, or ambivalence among practitioners about their work. In fact, many psychologists working commercially in Saint Petersburg described a struggle to find the right balance between work that was viable but also "for the soul" (*dlia dushi*). At issue were competing questions of value (Hemment 2004; Patico 2005; see also Anagnost 2008; Lambek 2008).

As an example of this ambivalence, I noted the various ways in which ReGeneration's employees mobilized different, and in some ways competing, discourses to describe their work. In some cases—especially when promoting their services—they described their work in the for-profit terms of success formulas, as they had at the Children's Planet expo. At other times—especially when interacting with children, among themselves, or with me—they drew on the nonprofit discourse of social work. This flexible repertoire offered them not only symbolic resources for advertising but also a set of frameworks within which the tension between biopolitics and practical ethics was negotiated in practice. This can be thought of in terms of an appropriation of commercial languages and modalities in order to effect change, and vice versa.

The organization's hybrid positioning in between the market and the nongovernmental sector seems central to this flexible language of legitimacy. As anthropologist Julie Hemment (2004) has noted, post-Soviet Russia has seen a growth (and subsequent shrinking) of the so-called third sector (*tretii sektor*), or "civil society," of which organizations like ReGeneration are a part. The third sector began to consolidate in the 1990s, largely as a legacy of both late-socialist progressivism and post-Soviet Western aid imperatives: comprising various social organizations (*obshchestvennaia organizatsiia*), the third sector was viewed by Russian reformers as a staging ground for social solidarity, and by Western reformers as a way to circumvent government-to-government aid disbursements (much as was the dominant neoliberal mode of development work in the 1990s) (Hemment 2004, 218–19). In theory, the third sector was to compose one of the three legs of a stool on which a new Russian liberal-democratic society would sit, the others being the state and the market.

Both the historical context and intervening events have moved Russian politics and economy in new directions. Early reforms sought to constitute and bolster the boundaries around the formal economy and the third sector; however, the diminution of Western aid dollars in the late 1990s, and Putin's reining in of nongovernmental organizations following the various "color revolutions" in the Commonwealth of Independent States (CIS), has strategically maintained the fuzzy boundaries between these supposedly distinct institutional domains, allowing the state a greater scope for controlling the third sector. ReGeneration reflects another piece of this story particularly well: the overlap between the third sector and the market. For example, when describing their financing, Tamara and her codirector, Ivan, both referred to ReGeneration as a "commercial organization" (*kommercheskaia organizatsiia*). By this they meant that they were not dependent on grants and operated on the basis of their own sales. Yet when describing their institutional location, they described themselves as "nongovernmental" (*negosudarstvennyi*). By this they meant that their organization was not subject to bureaucratic requirements and structures. In short, the organization shifted between designations, depending on context.

This institutional background brings to light one important context within which the blurring of the languages of capitalist subjectivation, on the one hand, and civility and tolerance, on the other, is taking place.[19] The lack of distinction between commercial and nongovernmental enterprises in the post-Soviet context has contributed to their melding into a conflated nonstate domain consisting of both commercial and third-sector activities. But there may be an even stronger reason for the psychologists' ambivalence about the work of subject making. One day, over coffee, Aleksandr painted for me a sobering picture of what young people in Russia face today. Without a hint of nostalgia, he said, "In the Soviet Union you didn't need to think about the future. You went from university to the institute, or from the army to work." With few choices, the route to self-fulfillment in Soviet times, he said, was "freedom inside." He then drew two pictures of the individual surrounded by what he called "society" (*obshchestvo*). He continued, "In the Soviet Union everything was absorbed, except the elite, by the state. The smallest unit, the individual, was part of a structure that included work and life, and there was little place [outside this]. These structures were fairly stable." Today, he said, the society surrounding the individual is "a zone of conflict and choice that also brings a higher degree of freedom." Stopping short of condemning the former to glorify the latter, he added, "Each brings its own challenges to the task of self-fulfillment. Today the problem is choice and unpredictability. The problem is that it is too easy to make no choice about your future. If you do this, you get left behind."

This sense of contemporary life as a perpetual race that one has no choice but to enter came up in a discussion with Tamara. I had asked her about ReGeneration's reliance on competition as a means of discipline and socialization. At the camp on friendship, I had observed a singing contest between two teams of children turn sour. The exercise was meant to teach the concept of chivalry (*rytsarstvo*) and involved a heteronormative courtship ritual in which boys sang a love song to a girl seated passively in a chair (an example, also, of the general traditional gendered norms at the camps). With the psychologists acting as judges, the score was kept neck and neck, and the kids became engrossed in the competition. But there could only be one winner. When the winning team was announced and the prize—a large bottle of Coca-Cola and plastic cups—distributed, Misha, a hyperactive twelve-year-old in loosely tied high-tops, began to throw a fit. "That's unfair!" he complained, circling the room. "Our songs were better. You're biased," he added, pointing at the psychologists. As the winning team enjoyed their soft drink, he stormed out of the room. Didn't the reliance on competition undermine the goals of the camp, namely, social connection, empathy, and friendship? If there are winners, there must also be losers, I asked. In response, Tamara explained, "In Europe and America, the main tendency, unfortunately, is a model based on good behavior—reward, bad behavior—punish. The kids already have this in place." She added thoughtfully, "A lot of good things can come from competition. For instance, the child has to study the situation where he loses, to learn from it. He has to learn to lose."

Unpredictability. The burden of choice. Not getting left behind. Learning to lose. These phrases illuminate the realities of the world in which psychological education was playing out during my fieldwork. They also illuminate the contexts within which ReGeneration's interest in a therapeutics of history and care is made commensurable with the neoliberal calculus of self-management. In search of a middle ground between market gain and social work, Tamara and her team faced the challenge of offering psychological education and teaching empathy in a context in which such things were legible only in terms of competitive planning for the future. In terms of practical ethics, they were seeking a "capacity for action" that was "enabled and created by specific relations of subordination" (Mahmood 2005, 29). This capacity for action was one they sought for themselves as possible reformers of Russian society. It was a capacity they sought as business professionals interested in making a living. And it was a capacity they sought for their young clients. At the same time, this capacity for action was also enabled by relations of subordination. Within ReGeneration's mise-en-scène, the client was subordinated to the psychologist, who was subordinated to the parent-client.

Conclusion

This was what small-*d* democracy looked like. It rested on technologies of citizenship that disclosed a particular liberal political imaginary. Further, ReGeneration's micropolitics revealed the various ways in which democracy was being envisioned by experts living and working during the early Putin period. On the one hand, there was an unmistakable "managerialization of personal identity and personal relations" and "capitalization of the meaning of life" under neoliberal conditions (Gordon 1991, 42, 44–45; quoted in Yurchak 2003, 75). Market mechanisms are central to the ways in which other liberal modalities—autonomy, governing through freedom, particular psychological techniques to constitute emotionality, self-esteem, and self-governance—are imagined. Their practices also disclosed particular classed and gendered features in which content consumption was operative. From this point of view, psychological education was a technology of democratic citizenship that resembled the patterns under neoliberalism.

But through its work ReGeneration also offered technologies of democratic citizenship in a country that was at that time, and still is today, living under neo-authoritarian rule and in search of its small-*d* democracy. ReGeneration aimed at constituting subjects that were different from the crude *sovok* (hyperbolically crude Soviet person; Pesmen 2000) and the New Russian. They pursued alternative socialities (more tolerance, less corporal punishment) and affects (more joyful, less austere) that were specific to postsocialism. And through the gender-neutral promotion of emotion talk they also ran against the grain of neotraditionalist gender formations. Democracy, then, was an imagined polity that these practitioners sought to bring into being that resonated with both neoliberal and postsocialist social formations at once. Economic and political liberalisms, and, indeed, questions of biopolitics, care, and ethics, were being negotiated on the terrain of the self. Moreover, these negotiations were also symptoms of a broad struggle over social norms and dispositions whose stakes were cultural, and even economic, ascendancy.

This chapter has thus shown how psychologists continued to have an alternative, if somewhat undefined, politics of the self that merged with but also departed from a neoliberal governmentality. Their interest in a repaired sociality, self-sufficiency, and self-worth rooted in self-knowledge shared features with, but was not the same as, such a governmentality. This was illuminated through an appreciation of the ways that these projects were socially and historically specific, reaching back to discussions during late socialism about the emotional needs of the child, empathy, freethinking, and supportive environments. This is what I took Tamara to mean by "individualism in the good sense." Situated at the intersection of these two modes of subjectivation (neoliberal and postsocialist), the self became an important object of experimentation. At stake were competing visions of Russia's political future.

And yet . . . and yet this particular vision of social reform also appeared vulnerable. Market demand and state priorities offered less traction for discourses of care and respect than for the (male) feeling subject primed for success.[20] Through commensuration, then, what was understood by practitioners as a politico-ethical project was translated into a variety of other forms—a defensive mode of parenting based on an anxiety-ridden future; forms of self-sufficiency that appeared to deny social relatedness; new biopolitical modes of constituting entrepreneurs while managing the rest. Class and gender formations take their clearest forms at the moment psychological education is instantiated as a technology of government. As I have suggested, however, these two rationales were neither mutually exclusive—as if tolerance, empathy, and freedom have nothing to do with capitalism—nor homologous. Psychological education, like other forms of self-work, continued to be a practice by which persons also sought to constitute themselves and others as ethical subjects.

It was far from clear whether psychological education could offer a robust alternative to the expansion of possessive individualism in Russia. At the time of my research, much about the expansion of self-work—ReGeneration's emphasis on self-sufficiency, empathy, self-management, freedom, relaxation, communication of feelings, and civility—was defined in a subtractive way, in opposition either to a particular version of the Soviet past or to the perceived manners of the Russian elite. It was clear, in other words, what they were against. But what were they for? These materials only hint at the beginnings of an answer. At best, one can say that such projects were critical-complicit. Yet if we are to examine these projects as governmental, this may be a good place to begin. It was certainly a question that Russian psychologists were exploring through their work.

In the next chapter I turn to the practitioners at the PPMS Center to examine the ways in which they navigated the biopolitical economy.

Chapter 4

"WHAT DO WE HAVE THE RIGHT TO DO?"

Tactical Guidance at a Social Margin

> Facing . . . disarray, there is only the little army of counselors and
> psychologists, and they are always insufficient in number to meet the
> demand of defenseless parents, of lost children and unhappy couples, of the
> misunderstood, of those who have not learned how to live.
>
> —Jacques Donzelot, *The Policing of Families*

Tatiana Fedorovna, the director of a PPMS Center, invited me for an interview on an odd day—New Year's Eve. I was interested in the center's work because centers like these were among the first in Russia to offer free psychological counseling to children. The PPMS system as a whole is part of a network of public institutions that was created in the mid-1990s and legally established in 1998. At the time of my research, there were approximately 750 such centers in Russia, employing sixty-four thousand specialists nationally (Zabrodin and Watts 2003; Fedotova 2006), and 19 of them in the city of Saint Petersburg. The center where I did research employed approximately twenty specialists in children's health.

This particular center was in an outlying district of the city, and as I trudged through the snow on New Year's Eve, I paused to look at a large, weathered building, hanging in the heavy winter mist (figure 4.1). It reminded me of the Russia I first encountered in 1994, before advertisements, full-glass storefronts, and consumer culture flooded the city. This building had about fifteen stories. Its sides were a patchwork of concrete siding. Balconies were adorned with dangling wire and satellite dishes, each with a face turned to the sky. Signs of life inside glowed dimly through the windows. Smokestacks in the distance coughed a thin gasp into the cold air. Unlike the adorned city center, the buildings and sidewalks were caked with dirty snow. In the fading light

FIGURE 4.1. Beyond the city center. Photo by the author.

of 4 p.m., the headlights of a trolley blazed over a billboard showing a sun-tanned couple riding a Vespa in white shorts.

I met Natalia Ivanovna, the center's part-time accountant, by a cell phone store at the corner of two massive roads. Tatiana Fedorovna had told me I would never find the center on my own, and she was right. Natalia Ivanovna led me through a maze of buildings to the center, inside a modest concrete structure in a quiet and brambly courtyard in the midst of a sprawling Soviet-era apartment block. An unlit vestibule with a wet rag, or *triapka*, partially stapled to the floor lay beyond the front door. We wiped our feet, and Natalia Ivanovna handed me a pair of worn blue covers, or *bakhily*, for my shoes. Standard in most clinical settings, bakhily always made it clear who was the clinician, and who was not. Inside, I noted that many were still wearing their winter coats as the heating wasn't working too well. Then I waited.

When Tatiana Fedorovna finally arrived, she seemed distracted. I asked her about the nature of the center's work and the length of time it had been open, and she answered brusquely. I wondered whether I had offended her. Meanwhile, people kept ducking their heads in and out of the room. I started to sense that something else was happening in the center. Eventually she told me that they were having their holiday party and that if I wished, I could join them and then we could speak afterward.

I found myself thrust unexpectedly into a parallel universe. There was a large room with six tables that had been set for a light meal, complete with Sovietskoe champagne, plastic cups, and snacks. About twenty people were scattered around the room. As I entered, a woman with long, dark hair and glitter eye shadow was assigning people to different tables after guessing who they were. Another woman, the emcee for the evening, took me by the arm and corralled me into the first. Not knowing what was happening, I stepped on the latter's feet. There was laughter and mayhem, and she proclaimed, "Table five!," at which point I was led to a table with two other women. We were quizzed on what 2006 signified, and the emcee tried to give us clues that it was the year of the dog, at which point Igor Filippovich, one of the male practitioners, emerged from inside a pile of stuffed pillows configured to look like a doghouse, wearing a hat with dog ears. Soon remarks were made about how 2005 was passing and how this time of year was a chance to put things behind you. We were given a piece of paper and a pen and told to write something that we wanted to leave behind. We then crumpled the paper into a ball and tossed it into a plastic bag.

The emcee asked, "What should we do with it?!"

One young woman said, "Burn it!"

We formed a circle; we would take care of matters with our feet. Soon the bag of bad memories was in the center of the room, being kicked around like a soccer ball. Some people, particularly the few men there, tried to juggle the bag or kick it forcefully. Sometimes the bag went airborne and landed on someone's head. People's faces became red with excitement, wet with sweat, and in some cases almost mad.

The mood in the room had been extremely energetic, but over the next hour it dropped like a stone, particularly after the first sips of champagne.

This group of psychologists, psychotherapists, speech therapists, and social workers suddenly appeared overworked, tired, and melancholy. Some, I noticed, hardly said a word at all and sat with their heads supported by an arm on the table. At several points the emcee motioned to have the music turned up to mask the silence. Perhaps it was not so easy to leave the troubles of 2005 behind. A heaviness settled over the room like a winter mist.

/ / /

Help can hurt those meant to receive it. This is one of the resounding messages of recent anthropologies of care—humanitarian, biomedical, psychiatric. This chapter takes up a related but less explored question: how does harmful help affect those who offer it, and what do they seek to do about it? These are important ethnographic questions motivated by an interest in rendering those working in public assistance in complex terms. My analysis aims to recognize the moments of positive encounter, assistance, and attunement while at the same time carefully tracking the dangers—in particular care's problematic enmeshment in relations of power. What might an anthropology of danger *and* possibility in the therapeutic encounter look like? Drawing on fieldwork in the PPMS Center in X District, this chapter follows the pathways of psychological expertise into public assistance. I examine the post-Soviet shifts in mental health care in relation to inequality while attending to the fact that therapists and their clients were caught up in a recognizably human endeavor—an effort to ease pain, to offer and seek out more healthful outlooks, to carve out a life that was neither radical nor complacent but somewhere in between. As I describe, many receiving psychological assistance at this center were living in difficult material and/or social circumstances. Meanwhile, a number of bureaucratic processes tied to Vladimir Putin's modernizing reforms—audits, standardization, and systematization—colluded with these conditions to shape the way affect was enunciated therapeutically. In contrast to their private-sector peers, the PPMS practitioners were turned away from emotions and toward cognitive function. The effect of this shift was to render the "problem child" of public services in discursive terms that were even less open to social context, emotional experience, and, indeed, the more humanized psychotherapies used by the psychologists' commercially based peers. As such, therapy appeared ever more constrained in the face of social vulnerability, and the practitioners who sought to work around these constraints put themselves at risk.

I bring these critical observations into contact with another kind of account: at the PPMS Center, the practitioners were, along with their clients, the victims (rather than the puppets) of a governmental strategy to reduce costs and the scope of care. The specialists also pursued care beyond cognition, developed their own institutional networks, and provided assistance in cases where, legally speaking, they were not allowed to do so. To conceive of the PPMS Center as a space of both biopolitical commensuration and ethical practice recasts the production of psychological difference. Rather than a subjectification enacted between psychologist and client, I propose an account of what I call precarious care in which the dangers of intervention are constantly funneled down to the therapeutic encounter. This view of shared precarity also captures the nature of public social work in the Putin era. This era has been a time in which the advancement of the petro-economy has not been matched by an improvement in the lives of many citizens, nor in the services that are meant to help them. Precarious care, then, refers to the risks and opportunities involved in assisting others in Russia today.

This analysis has implications for studies of care delivered under precarious conditions. In an immediate sense, it proposes an analytic approach for rendering those forms of care in more complex terms. And in another, more theoretical, sense, it raises questions about the degree to which neoliberal governmentalities (under which these forms of care are usually grouped) are necessarily a form of "govern[ing] at a distance" (Rose 1996a, 43), achieved through shaping the conduct of conduct (Foucault 1991). The cases under investigation here show, instead, the "government of indifference." Indifference was produced by the imposition of new norms of efficiency under conditions of severe constraint. Disaster, in this context, was just waiting to happen, and experts were left either going along with it or pushing against it. And when they did push back, they partook of the risk experienced by their clients. By viewing care as an unfolding ethical practice, it is possible both to capture the dilemmas involved for those involved in such endeavors, as well as to sharpen the analysis of how care circulates through different biopolitical economies.

Inside the PPMS Center

After the New Year's Eve party, Tatiana Fedorovna invited me to sit in on their weekly staff meeting, or *konsilium*. Along with attending these meetings, I would also interview the staff, sit in on several interdepartmental meetings, accompany one specialist on her rounds at the local schools, and participate in both a teacher training and several Balint groups.[1] Unlike at ReGeneration, I was not given access to the children and their families, nor to any *treningi* or counseling sessions with them. The materials in this chapter are limited to encounters with the staff in particular spaces and contexts, including outside the center. The Wednesday-morning staff meetings in question took place in a small conference room. On the first day, I entered to find a group of specialists gathered around a table. As I would learn, these psychologists—mostly women, mostly middle-aged—used the meetings to discuss their difficult cases, seek and give advice, and vent. The meetings featured many cases that reflected the risk factors families in the community were confronting: alcoholism, suicide, divorce, and abuse. And the PPMS Center's client waiting lists were only growing. According to center estimates in 2006, it took about a month to get an appointment, and the staff could see only about a thousand children over the course of the year (in a region with sixty thousand children). As I would later learn, the system as a whole had contracted by about 15 percent a few years earlier owing to budget reforms (Zabrodin and Watts 2003). Uncertain at first of what to do at these meetings, I began making a field-note catalog, jotting as much as I could about the cases as I heard them:

> CASE: Story of a feud around a daughter between a mother and aunt. The mother was described by the aunt as being irresponsible, inviting strange men to the apartment, and drinking. Initially the daughter was mostly cared for by her grandmother, but the grandmother died when the daughter was four. Then the aunt wanted to take over, and did for a while. There was a subsequent struggle around the administration of several different apartments. At a certain point the mother began to express more interest in caring for her daughter. Thus, the daughter appeared in the center as the one with the problem, but it turned out that she was caught in the midst of a feud over her custody between her mother and her aunt. (The father appeared to be absent.) The center suggested that the two parties talk with one another and offered itself as a mediator.
>
> CASE: A catastrophic event occurred in a family. A brother fell through the ice to his death. The other child felt tremendous guilt. He didn't see any reason to go on living.

CASE: Boy came in with difficulties with pronunciation, mild cerebral trauma and a fever.

CASE: A mother was arrested for striking with a Hugo Boss umbrella two religious missionaries who had been let into her home by her daughter.

CASE: A mother made a crisis call. She was unable to control her son. He was seventeen.

CASE: A boy was having nightmares. His mother called. It turned out Dad was playing video games that may be causing the nightmares. Dad turned off the sound, but the boy still liked to watch. He was drawn (*pritiagivaet*) to it. The nightmares hadn't stopped. There was a daughter. She was seven. She was still sleeping in the bed in between the parents. The boy's view of the parents was that Mama is "beautiful" and Dad is "evil." The practitioner said that she conducted the "[Paired] Hand[s] Test," a test meant to assess the projection of aggression. In the test, nine cards were shown to the child, and he must say what the hands are doing. The answers were recorded verbatim and scored. Despite the boy's apparent resistance to tests, it was generally fairly easy to track his aggression—"the hand is punching someone," he said. He did not do very well on it. The leader of the meeting said that it will be necessary to observe the interactions of the family. She agreed to take the case from the younger practitioner.

CASE: A girl was brought into the center two years ago with speech problems, but underlying emotional problems were soon diagnosed. She had no friends at school and difficulty relating to others. (Papa was where?) It turned out that the mother disappeared without a trace and was gone for about two years. Eventually she returned. Why did she leave? A story is told about the mother's fixation on "going to New Caledonia." After this, the mother wanted the daughter back. In principle, the daughter also wanted to go back, but the grandmother was fighting this.

CASE: The child cries when his father drinks. Where can the child be sent for help?

At each meeting I noted my gathering gloom as I confronted these snapshots of families getting pulled, with an almost gravitational certainty, into the webs of social services. Many involved situations in which one or both parents were on the razor's edge of something—whether alcoholism, a job loss, depression, domestic abuse, gambling, or suicide. These were not so much cases of catastrophe as the sorts of quasi-events (Povinelli 2011) that flit beneath the radar of national health reports, offering glimpses of how the USSR's matrifocal family, which had emerged after the loss of male soldiers in World War II, was in a state of uncertain transition. Other cases involved more typical kinds of family struggle—working parents, an anxious child, the cloud of abnormality. Regardless of severity, however, the practitioners confronted these broad social problems through a single symptom: a child experiencing anxiousness or fear, or exhibiting antisocial behavior, or appearing in school with mysterious bruises, or having a penchant for playground fights, or seeking pleasure through addiction, or some combination of these.

It became clear over those Wednesday mornings that the PPMS Center was a site of therapeutic enunciation, wherein phenomena were converted from one medium into others. Once crossing the threshold of the center, social suffering (Obeyesekere 1985) was individualized.[2] Then, in therapy, individual (affective) experience was translated into emotional problems, behavioral problems, cognitive malfunction, or even possible pathology.[3] These forms of enunciation seemed to lead away from the child-client's social world and into asocial domains of measurement, assessment, and referral. To be sure, the diagnostics were a last refuge for frustrated and over-tasked specialists, but they also created filters through which the more complex forms of social suffering I heard about were less likely to pass.

The Wednesday meetings also gave me a profound appreciation for the difficulty of the practitioners' work. As I watched the staff discuss cases as a group, I saw how care was itself an affectively saturated practice, rooted in a muddle of intensity, which often appeared as pity, courage, sadness, frustration, feelings of being overwhelmed, and anger. But that complexity, too, was transformed through the therapeutic protocol, which, over the course of my time in the center, was becoming ever more narrowed. That is, structured around the collaborative ideal of guidance, or *soprovozhdenie*, and framed by a federal discourse promoting creativity, self-realization, and innovation through psychological assistance, the center's actual work was quite different from that ideal. Almost exclusively focused on crisis cases, the center had instead become a site for testing and diagnostics, as well as a transfer point to more serious psychiatric institutions. If organizations working with elite children—across both commercial and state contexts—were in the business of personal enhancement, the PPMS Center was largely playing defense. It appeared to me, observing from the side, that the weight of these enunciations was also felt by the practitioners.

> **CASE**: A mother's child was placed in a sanatorium. She was instructed to stay away from the child. There were charges of neglect. To what extent should the municipality get involved? She was initially against placing the child in the sanatorium because she feared her son being placed *na uchet* [on the state registry of committed patients].

Social Precariousness

To what extent did "the case" as described in the konsilium, and in staff meetings and conversations with staff, mirror the social reality out there in the surrounding district? I could never be completely certain, as I did not have access to the clients and their lives. My portrayal of the center as a kind of affective atmosphere (Brennan 2004), and my description of the cases I heard, should be read with these limitations in mind. Nevertheless, as I began investigating demographic context, I became convinced that the center was one place where those getting left behind Russia's oil-fueled boom were surfacing. Digging into statistics on Russia gave context to what I learned in my fieldwork in the center. At that time, many Russians were living in significant poverty, there were high male mortality and suicide rates and low birth rates. In 2004 the top 10 percent of income earners had 29.8 percent of the total pie, whereas the bottom 10 percent had 2 percent. Although the number of people living below minimum subsistence levels had fallen by 8.5 percent between 2002 and 2006, the global financial crisis of 2008 would later reveal the fragility as well as the patchy nature of this recovery. Even at the height of oil prices in 2006, roughly 20 million people, or 15 percent of the population, were considered poor, living on less than 5,083 rubles ($169) a month.[4] Children—the main subjects of this chapter—have been especially vulnerable to poverty. In 2005, the overall poverty rate was 19.6 percent, but among children it was 26.7 percent (Organisation for Economic Co-operation and Development; Manning and Tikhonova 2009). By 2011 Russia's Gini coefficient, a measure of income inequality, was significantly higher than those of other countries in the Organisation for Economic Co-operation and Development (with the exception of the United States) (OECD 2018).

Social mobility was also highly uneven. The lion's share of those lifted out of poverty during 2002 and 2006 were the "transient poor"—people already

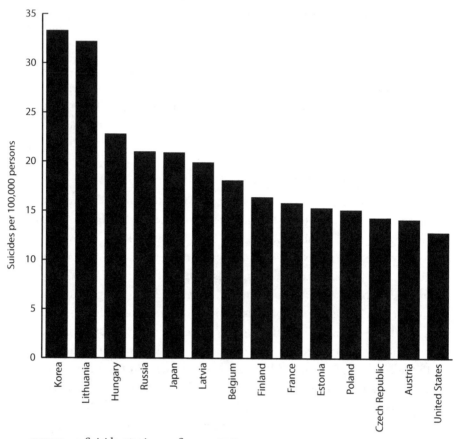

FIGURE 4.2. Suicide rates in 2011. Source: OECD 2017a.

clustered around the minimum subsistence line. Meanwhile, the "chronically poor" rose as a percentage of the total poor, from 40 percent to 60 percent, and they had no prospects for mobility, even during Russia's years of relative economic prosperity (World Bank 2009a, 18). Also worth considering is that another quarter of the population was considered vulnerable to poverty (defined as having an income less than 150 percent above the minimum subsistence level). Relative to rural areas, poverty reduction was three times better in cities; poverty rates could be an astonishing forty-five times higher in rural areas than in cities like Saint Petersburg and Moscow (World Bank 2009a, 17). The populations that were being treated in Saint Petersburg's marginal PPMS Centers, while not a majority of the urban population, were in fact quite representative of Russia's population as a whole, which is still, at the time of this

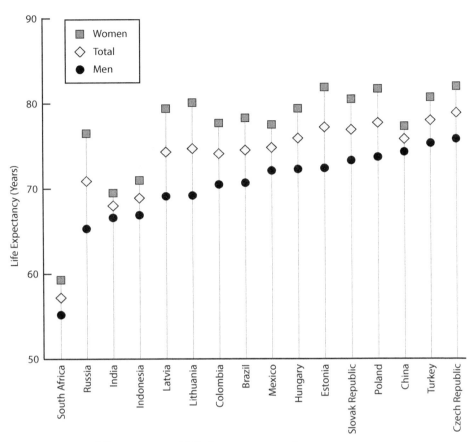

FIGURE 4.3. Life expectancy at birth. Source: OECD 2017b.

writing, beset by high poverty rates and vulnerability. Perhaps no indicators were as potent as Russia's health and well-being statistics (figures 4.2 and 4.3): suicide rates in Russia were among the highest in the countries in the Organisation for Economic Co-operation and Development. The same was true for mortality, especially male mortality. Birth rates, a topic of governmental concern since the 1960s, have since the 1990s been discussed in terms of a demographic crisis. While it is true that birth rates have climbed in recent years, fears continue to circulate in the popular press about the dying out of the Russian people.

By 2005–6, the federal wheels had already been set in motion against this demographic crisis—the center where I did research, it seemed, was one of its contact points. The PPMS Center was located in one of Saint Petersburg's remoter and poorer districts (*raoiny*) and, as such, catered to a vulnerable population. Districts like this one were filled with the mixed signs of the post-Soviet economy. During my initial fieldwork, Russia had been enjoying a five-year surge in economic growth due to high oil prices (McFaul and Stoner-Weiss 2008). New construction was everywhere, and cranes could be seen all over the city.[5] The spread of cozy cafés, restaurants, fancy cars, and a semblance of middle-class life in the city centers could make it difficult to see the flip side of the Putin era. Yet whenever I ventured beyond the sheen of the city center I saw the variety of decaying structures from the late-Soviet period, such as that massive apartment building that I passed on my way to the center on New Year's Eve. A range of other "invisible" phenomena were equally common, including problems of homelessness, dispossession, and unemployment (Höjdestrand 2009; Humphrey 2002).

> CASE: Eight-year-old boy. Fears. Bad self-image. Screams at school and can't be re-strained. Parent sought advice. Practitioner was unable to help. Dispatched to another school.

Becoming Psychological

As I learned more about the founding of the PPMS system and saw the kinds of psychosocial work being done outside state services, I began to wonder how this all-too-familiar patterning of public assistance and pathologization of social vulnerability had come to be. After all, the psychology boom that had swept into Russia ten years earlier had augured a broad turn toward holistic, humanistic services. If they were not exactly attuned to sociality, as their late-socialist predecessors had been, those early practices were at least premised on *the whole child*. Meanwhile, the marketplace for psychological trening, despite its problematic commodification and instrumentalization of self-work, at least remained a place in which the young client was enunciated as a subject with potential. How did public institutions' narrowed focus on cognitive function come to be? What had shaped that process, and to what possible effect for the child-client, the practitioner, and the state?

Part of the ethnographic task here is to identify the infrastructures, whether semiotic or material, that enable the translation (and also management) of affect.[6] Affect, as Lauren Berlant (2011, 16) has argued, points to an important juncture between history and experience: "[Affect's] strength as a site of potential elucidation comes from the ways it registers the conditions of life that move across persons and worlds, play out in lived time, and energize attachments." It "communicate[s] the conditions under which a historical moment appears as a visceral moment." I take Berlant's point to be that affective response contains a certain social reality—if not an essential one, then at least one that speaks before being translated into something else by experts (including, I should add, anthropologists). How, then, is affect met—by experts, in genres, by friends? Berlant argues that it is through intuition, that locus where affect and history meet. Viewed from this vantage, the weekly Wednesday meetings pointed in two directions at once: to some prior affective experience and, through intuition, to a means of engagement with the presenting child.

One way to trace the shift from emotion to cognition is to look to a series of ministerial reforms begun by the Putin administration in the early 2000s, termed *modernization* (*modernizatsiia*). Educational institutions (*obrazovatel'nye uchrezhdenii*), of which this center was one, had come under bureaucratic scrutiny at the same time that the social problems associated with inequality were growing. I came to see the shift to cognition in the PPMS system as a governmental answer to a biopolitical question: how should state institutions address, in practical and effective ways, the social vulnerability that had been prompted by the ungluing of the family? Modernization was one such answer. But in my work in the PPMS Center I also saw how modernization enabled forms of bureaucratic performance in which municipal officials and scholars working to maintain the PPMS system could invoke systematicity and accountability without necessarily having the corresponding resources to support the work of the centers. Such performances, while apparently administratively productive, had less positive effects in the center. In conjunction with difficult material conditions of care, governmental imperatives pushing toward efficiency and order constrained the therapeutic scope of the center's work and shaped the subject positions of care recipients as risky and functionally broken (see Castel 1991). Ultimately, this allowed children and their problems to fall through the cracks. To arrive in a PPMS Center was to be seen in a particular way. Again, the contrast with commercial services is instructive. There, the young client was figured as filled with potential and in need of a bit of emotional intelligence. This contrast amounted to a differentiated management of affect—in one case, affective experience was rendered as cognitive (dys)function; in the other, it was rendered sensible as emotion. This difference reflected in particularly intimate terms the class differences among Russia's youth.

A look at the origins of the PPMS Center system brings into relief the nature of their current work, as well as the degree to which the social landscape has changed since psychological work was first introduced. As discussed in previous chapters, the years between the perestroika of the 1980s and the mid-1990s promised a sweeping humanization of social institutions. This was certainly rooted in the economy; the USSR's economic stagnation had prompted Mikhail Gorbachev to announce that more attention had to be given to the human factor of production. But it was also rooted in an interest among Soviet educators and psychologists in what they called "more humane relations between teacher and pupil" (Eklof and Dneprov 1993, 8). Focused on a more "democratic classroom" (9), they agitated for "greater respect for the autonomy of childhood and for the role of play in learning, and for freedom of choice as well as self-government" (8).

Their efforts were also situated within a broader interest in non-biomedical talk therapies in mental health care that would eventually also feed the growth of the market for psychological services. The psychologist had a central role in all of this, and once Soviet education began to emphasize differences among individuals and in education, the psychologist's expertise became more indispensable. The PPMS system that would emerge in the 1990s was thus an outgrowth of those late-Soviet discussions around education, subjectivity, and, vitally, economy. Centered on the core concept of guidance, or soprovozhdenie, which was developed in the late-Soviet education reforms, the system was tasked with carrying further the emphasis on the humanistic, psychologically attuned, child-centered classroom.[7] By the time a federal resolution establishing the PPMS system was signed into law in 1998, a number of such organizations were already in operation.

In its early form, soprovozhdenie meant assisting children with problems in development, studies, and social adaptation by offering "individually oriented teaching, and psychological, social, medical and legal help" (Russian Federation 1998, 1). Indeed, the very name of the PPMS system—Psycho-pedagogical Medico-social—indicated a holistic (and novel) biopsychosocial approach to mental health care (see Kitanaka 2011). At the heart of the PPMS concept was the premise that a multidisciplinary team (psychologists, pedagogues, medical doctors, social workers, and speech therapists) would essentially reassemble the figure of the child and her or his individual needs through a holistic approach to care. Elena Kazakova, a scholar who had been involved in the formation of the PPMS Center system and an important theorist of soprovozhdenie, told me, "The 1990s was a really romantic period in Russia. The period of the rise of humanism [*uvelichenie gumanizmom*]—humanistic ideals. We turned toward the person in absolutely every way [*Eto povorot k cheloveku absoliutno vo vsekh*]. I am not speaking abstractly; it was real. And at that time, the discussion was about the fact that the child needed to be helped. They didn't place him under a standard [*oni ne podvadit ego pod standard*] but tried to search for the origin of his problems."

The humanistic origins of the PPMS system bring into relief the retreat from the child-client in the decade that followed the 1990s. Children remained at the center of federal biopolitics as economic objects—just as they had appeared as the human factor of socialist production. Their psychological well-being was still highlighted. What changed was the emphasis on humanization. Under Putin, the interest in humanization (and, with it, emotionality) diminished in state services. The priority became modernization—of not only education policy but also technological development, housing infrastructure, and, indeed, subjectivity. What was modernization in these contexts? Its early rhetoric disclosed a primarily self-reliant person. According to a document prepared for UNESCO, modernization ought to lead to the production of "moral enterprising people" who "make decisions independently in a situation of choice" in a system oriented toward "the development of their personalities, and cognitive and creative abilities" (Russian Federation 2004, 6). Boilerplate rhetoric notwithstanding, underlying this technical shift there was a pessimism with roots firmly ensconced in the soil of economy. In the words of one psychologist writing in 2002, while "the child's right to full-fledged and free development" remains central to modernizing education, "unfortunately, currently more and more children are found in a position of acute social trouble. Bad ecology, the growth of social aggression, economic problems, the spread of narcotics, the increase of migration, instabilities of the family, parent and teacher incompetence—these and many other factors are becoming external boundaries of the process of development of the child" (Sartan 2002). In essence, the humanistic, emotion-centered approach to children, not to mention their "full-fledged and free development," was rendered impractical in the face of an overwhelming "bad ecology."

This pessimism was also translated into revised therapeutics. A methodological document in 2005 about reforming the PPMS system dismissed the earlier emphasis on humanization and put forward a new, more practical vision: "However much psychologists talked about the importance of optimizing the education of pupils for emotional stability, positive self-value, self-confidence . . . , the fundamental burden in the learning process falls not on the emotional-communicative but on the intellectual sphere. . . . It would be better to emphasize not the formation of the personality of the child, the systems of his communication and emotional contacts, but in the first instance the development of his thinking [*myshlenie*]" (Iasiukova 2005, 3). The author's point is that poor performance in school at an early age can have a magnified effect over time; thus, the therapeutic emphasis should be on early detection and cognitive interventions—training memory, building logic skills, and keeping an eye out for brain dysfunction. Notice, however, the author's insistent negation of prior forms: learning depends *not* on emotion but on cognition, psychological work should target *not* the personality but thinking. Regardless of emotional well-being, it is thinking (myshlenie) that is of interest. This redirection of the reason-passion dichotomy shifts the psychological enunciation of affect-as-emotion to affect-into-cognition. In practice, struggling children were given diagnostic tests of their attention, cognitive reasoning, and spatial and mathematical logic, and the tabulated results then discussed with their teachers. Beyond school diagnostics, the PPMS Center where I did fieldwork was also offering a range of programs that responded to particular kinds of deficits—deficits of attention, memory, or clear speech; problems with writing; weak communication among asocial teens; or emotional instability. Thus, the PPMS system had been induced to approach the child not as an emotional being full of potential but as a kind of machine in crisis whose function must be improved.

The modernization of psychosocial services and the translation of affect into cognition in Russia is consistent with global trends. The appearance of managed or administered care in societies subjected to various kinds of economic austerity has placed a strong emphasis on evidence-based practices, pressing the therapeutic increasingly toward measurability (see Strathern 2000; Luhrmann 2000; Adams 2013).[8] In the Russian context, the policies governing the PPMS system's operation contain a similar prioritization of measurement. One study issued by the Committee for Education of Saint Petersburg noted that in the absence of practical standards, it had become "necessary to evaluate the results of the activities from the point of view of their social effectiveness" (Zimina 2003, 4–5). Such systematicity (*sistemnost'*), the author concluded, would be crucial to the legitimacy of mental health services and could be achieved through an audit process, or *attestatsiia*: "There is a real opportunity to assert the rights of the institutions of psycho-medico-social assistance in the education system through attestation and state accreditation" (Zimina 2003, 11).[9] Given this emphasis on measurement, it is not surprising that more cognitively oriented approaches, such as that of Liudmila A. Iasiukova, were taken up in the PPMS system: Scholars have generally noted that cognitive-behavioral approaches have grown in popularity around the world because of their short-term, structured nature and their accessibility to empirical studies (Gaudiano 2008, 5).[10]

Anthropologists writing on other dimensions of post-Soviet public policy have noted a more general shift to a neoliberal-like audit culture in Russia. Stephen J. Collier (2011) has shown how the neoliberalization of the post-Soviet social has included the monetization of social benefits and new budgetary practices.[11] Jane R. Zavisca (2012) highlights the turn away from municipally maintained housing stock to housing associations. Anna Rotkirch, Anna Temkina, and Elena Zdravomyslova (2007) describe how monetization has entered family policy via the maternity-capital program (see Rivkin-Fish 2010). Audit cultures were, of course, no stranger to the Soviet period. Eugene Raikhel (2016, 70–72) details the use of the registry (*uchet*) and the "dispensarization" of alcohol treatment (i.e., the use of psychiatric outpatient clinics for treatment) to measure effectiveness in the 1970s.[12] Yet the differences are in the ends, not the means. As Collier notes, the goal of socialist planning was the production of particular social goods; under Putin, one could argue that the goal is the cost-effective management of social risk. Modernization, then, might be better described as a form of calculative care, which seeks to replace the socialist citizen with the consumer-citizen. What is interesting about the modernization of mental health care, however, is the particular way that this consumer-citizen has been figured as an end of policy. As I elaborate below, in contrast to the neoliberal "entrepreneur of the self," in the PPMS Center the child was figured pessimistically, as an isolated individual with potentially faulty thinking. Only some could be entrepreneurial.

> **CASE:** A mother routinely came home late. She was unable to watch her children. She asked the neighbors to do so. She returned, and the child had been beaten. Ended up in the hospital. He was twelve. She was raising the child alone. Father left for work in the north. Remarried. It was the mom, son, and granny. The child was a smoker, as was the mother and grandmother.

The Vice of Modernization

In 2005–6 I saw how modernization was brought to bear on the daily practices of the PPMS Center. Squeezed by high-flying policy rhetoric and a call for audits, on the one side, and difficult conditions of care, on the other, the PPMS Center's work and its clients were placed into a precarious situation. When I began my fieldwork, I was not immediately aware of the difficult process that lay on the horizon for those who worked there. *Attestatsiia* (*attestation*) was the official word for it. Formally speaking, attestatsiia referred to a process, initiated several years earlier by the municipal authorities, in which the operations of public institutions offering psychosocial services would be scrutinized every five years. It involved a lengthy inspection lasting anywhere from several weeks to several months. This process, it was argued, was necessary to ensure the standardization of psychosocial services, and also to promote efficiency and accountability. But it was also attestation in the fuller sense of that term—an expectation that practitioners would affirm institutional truth through rituals of verification. Unfortunately for the staff, attesting to the truth of their work involved them in a game whose rules were not fully known, and therefore whose truth could not be fathomed.

Viewed from the ground, it seemed that attestatsiia did little that was good, neither for the center, nor for its practitioners' work, nor for those whom they served, the youth living in that district. Worse, during the most intense moments of attestatsiia it appeared that the main charge of the center—to provide guidance (soprovozhdenie) to their clients—became less and less practicable. Attestatsiia demanded a slew of bureaucratic testimonials—case documentation, description of programs and correlation to staff hours, staffing salaries and hours—that were extraordinarily difficult to provide. I observed how, as winter turned to spring in 2006, work hours and weekly staff meetings meant to advise one another on difficult cases were colonized by administration. The municipality's procedure for improving "guidance" had the ironic but not wholly unexpected effect of leading practitioners further afield from those they were charged with guiding, and further into the thickets of the bureaucratic testimonial. This emphasis on attestatsiia bore striking resemblances to other discourses of auditing circulating during Putin's second term; these indexed some of the places where neoliberal policies were in fact being enacted. From a certain point of view, then, this center appeared to be caught up in a bureaucratic trap—wanting, perhaps, to do a particular thing (more "positive" work, as psychologist Igor Filippovich had put it) but

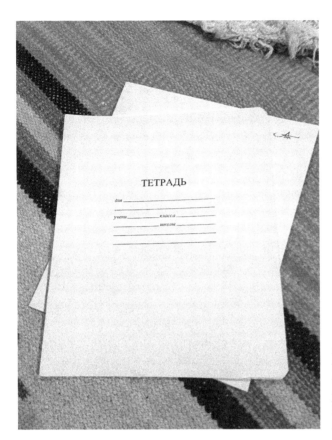

FIGURE 4.4. Attestatsiia's object: the tetradka. Photo reproduced with the kind permission of Emily Newman.

unable to do it because of structural constraints. One of this book's organizing concepts, precarious care, was in fact first inspired by my work in the center. It describes both the client (who is often working class, or at least a so-called problem child) and the practitioner (who is working without much financial support). Both are precarious under the conditions of care.

As the center geared up for attestatsiia, it became apparent that it was a source of great anxiety. Tatiana Fedorovna showed me the thick binders they had to put together in preparation. Meanwhile, the case documentation alone was cause for alarm: lacking computers, the case histories were recorded in blue exam booklets, or *tetradki* (figure 4.4). It was from a stack of tetradki that practitioners read when they came to the staff meetings; it was into a tetradka that they wrote during consultations; and it was with the tetradka that any client's case moved among specialists. Thus, the most important part of the center's work was stored in notebooks kept in piles in the staff coffee room. The vulnerability of such a system caused the specialists to worry.

As the months wore on, the Wednesday-morning meetings became increasingly charged with concern about administrative legibility. One day, for example, I observed a heated discussion about a case involving a seven-year-old boy of Iranian heritage. Based on the tetradka, the boy had been in the center before; he was struggling with feeling like an outcast. He wanted to dye his hair blond, make his name more Russian sounding, and become Orthodox Christian; to his parents' dismay, he had started crossing himself. The attending specialist added that there was also a situation around the fact that the father, "who isn't just Iranian, he's also a doctor," left on a trip without kissing the child. At this point, Evgeniia Antatolievna, an outside specialist who often oversaw the meetings, interrupted: "How does this have anything to do with the child's memory and logic problems?" She asserted that what was emerging from the case file was that the child had been transferred internally with everyone disagreeing about the problem and "nobody feeling any guilt about it." In the midst of all of this back-and-forth, it was striking that nobody had even discussed the boy's troubling desire to efface his Iranian identity. Rather, the problem was defined in cognitive terms, and then even this issue was eclipsed by accusations of bureaucratic "buck-passing" (Herzfeld 1992, 4). Such tensions between procedure and care were a leitmotif at the center. They also highlighted how the push toward audits reached into the therapeutic practices by shaping which ways of discussing cases were considered appropriate in the staff meetings.

Another way that a general atmosphere of audit shaped the center's practices was through the policy emphasis on systematicity and legal norming. Practitioners often found it necessary to offer holistic care but risked running afoul of the center's mandate to remain focused exclusively on the child and work on issues of cognitive function. As is evident from the examples given in this chapter, however, many of the cases crossing the PPMS Center's threshold were entangled in issues far bigger than thinking problems. In one case involving a mother-son relationship, the son was skipping school, had developed a computer addiction, and was spending the whole day in gaming halls. When the school called and someone was sent to the boy's house, he was found to be living in squalid conditions and sleeping on the floor. His mother also regularly locked him in his room. The specialist commented, "This is concerning—what if there is a fire? Is he is able to go to the bathroom when he needs to? The recommendation from the sitting specialist was to get to work on the question of computer addiction." After the case was reviewed, Anna Andreyevna brought the conversation back from the narrow question of computer addiction to the safety issue: "Some of the details of this case remind me of one of my own," she said. Noting her deep concern, she added with exasperation, "It's difficult to know what to do and where to turn for help." (Anna Andreyevna, I would later learn, had been trying to offer her clients legal advice while also offering therapeutic services that went beyond the strict constraints of the center.) Tatiana Fedorovna, the director, became very upset. "Too much time has been wasted on this! The work that Anna Andreyevna is doing is not our responsibility. We should have written a letter to the local inspector long ago to absolve us of further responsibility." She then turned the discussion to "results." She pressed Anna Andreyevna to describe what had actually come of all her extra efforts. Anna Andreyevna sank into her chair in silence.

A similar scene took place in discussions of the next case, which involved a five-year-old. The practitioner, a young psychologist named Diana Ivanovna, was unsure whether her group work had had any effect. The child, she reported, still had very "sharp reactions": "She does everything out of spite and sees it as being correct." One of the few male specialists, Vladislav Efimovich, suggested that perhaps some observation by the regional outpatient clinic (PND) would be appropriate. Again, Tatiana Fedorovna interrupted: "What do we have the right to do?" In continuing to try to resolve things falling outside their mandate, she said, "we have taken the child's time and wasted the state's money. We have committed a breach (*narushenie*) of protocol."

These examples illustrate how the ad hoc nature of the PPMS Center's legal structure, combined with attestation, contributed to intrastaff conflicts. Meanwhile, though charged with protecting the rights of the child, specialists quickly found that the problems they faced were much larger than what their legal mandate allowed them to address. When they tried to act in accordance with protecting the rights of the child, following leads beyond their mandate, they risked reprimand. However, from the director's point of view, their work was primarily a matter of results and protocols. In a rare lapse into candor with me, some weeks later Anna Andreyevna, who had borne the brunt of the director's criticisms on several occasions, vented about the push to just "count statistics" like some kind of *chinovnik* (the demeaning term for a lowly civil servant); she pointed to an important difference in the kind of work she does. On that particular day we were discussing the fact that Anna Andreyevna was expected to generate reports on the total number and types of problems they consult on. I asked her what the center does with them.

"I really don't know," she replied, somewhat exasperated. "We are asked to turn these in, and then I have no idea what happens with them."

Around this time, the results of the attestatsiia were just coming back, and they were not glowing. Anna Andreyevna confessed that they had found mistakes—though primarily matters of improper documentation. While hesitant to agree when I suggested that this bureaucratic procedure seems to miss the point of their work, she did admit that the laws and ways of structuring things inside the Ministry of Education change so quickly that it is difficult to stay on top of them. Tatiana Fedorovna, she said, had taken the results very personally and was embarrassed. Of course, since she was responsible for reporting to the city officials, and ultimately for the center's work, the issue of the center's institutional mandate, obligation, and boundaries was essential for her. Observing these boundaries allowed the center to exist. It also kept its employees out of trouble and employed.

The attestatsiia also had particular social effects inside the PPMS Center. These included wasting of time and resources, as well as conflicts between administrators and therapists. This sense of extra demands on one's time was something I witnessed in a konsilium after the poor results of the attestatsiia had come in. As the year wore on, practitioners spent less and less time discussing cases, and more and more time on procedural matters. The PPMS Centers were being pushed further in the direction of crisis management and were being told to prioritize crisis calls, exclusively if necessary—a statement of the dire family situation in Saint Petersburg. These shifts in priority, then, soaked up even more time in the konsilium; in one case the entire three hours were devoted to going over the new system they would be implementing for their crisis books, all of which was to be done by hand. The results of the attestatsiia had also prompted Tatiana Fedorovna to insist that the specialists keep journals, in which they were now expected to account for all of their time.[13]

Vera, a young psychologist, confided to me after leaving the center, "It was a hard place to work. You were constantly being pulled in two directions at once. On the one hand, you were expected to plan your work carefully. On the other, there were always new demands being made on your time by the events [e.g., on drug addiction or healthy living] that the center is expected to provide for the region."

Ultimately, the push for efficiency also created a bitter atmosphere. As Vera continued to tell me about leaving the center, she let loose her discontent. One person, she said, was "two-faced: she'll flash you a big smile while holding a knife behind her back." Another "for some reason was telling me all the time not to write the full details of the cases in my tetradki and seemed extremely nervous." And yet another was "emotionally closed and extremely difficult to work for. Most of the other specialists who could leave have."

What, then, were effects of modernization on the work at the center?[14] What I observed in the staff meetings and the life of the center was that modernization in general, and auditing in particular, combined with under-resourcing, pressing social need, and constrained legal mandates to make the practitioners' work extraordinarily difficult. Further, modernization structured the translation of a range of children's difficulties in particular ways, figuring them as treatable through shorter-term cognitively focused interventions and measurable care. Finally, what was left of the child and his or her social worlds was primarily a brain with memory problems, contained in a small blue note-book stored in a pile in the staff coffee room.

The narrowing nature of this work (affectively, subjectively, socially) is made particularly clear when it is contrasted with the psychological work for elite and middle-class children. At ReGeneration's psychology camp, in which Russian kids were taken over the border to Finland (discussed in the previous chapter), the young clients were often invited to constitute and en-counter their own "internal emotional worlds." This often took place through drawing, similar to the assessments used in the PPMS Center. Yet the locus of interpretation remained with the child rather than a group of gathered spe-cialists. The aim of ReGeneration's work was a cultivation of emotional intel-ligence rather than diagnosis and correction.

> **CASE:** Could not process lessons. Felt alarm all the time. Father and uncle recently died consecutively.

Ethics and Incommensurability

In the face of these structural constraints, did state psychologists blindly enact the modernization of care? What moments of slippage existed? In fact, practi-tioners took initiative beyond the view of the state inspectors and apparently also the center director. For example, it was possible for practitioners to con-tract with other centers, establishing, quite apart from the city government, an improvised system to coordinate work on shared cases, thus effectively supple-menting the lacking administrative structure. As Anna Andreyevna's response to the case of the boy locked in his room and sleeping on the floor shows, the legal mandate to protect the rights of the child could be creatively, if surreptitiously, reinterpreted, leaving room for how a practitioner could intervene. These were instances of legal indeterminacy in which a gap opened up because of poorly articulated legal regimes. Such gaps made it possible to authorize a wider array of practices and kinds of care.[15] There were also forms of therapeutic indeterminacy. As I got to know the practitioners, I began hearing of the improvised techniques they used in care that were, so to speak, off the books.

There are some important ways, discussed below, in which the practitioners' work in the PPMS Center became productively incommensurable in the sense that the practitioners' creativity circumvented the boundaries of modernization's "calculative care." Practices that are incommensurable with governing norms can operate as productive forms of improvisation and constrained agency (Heath Cabot, personal communication, October 25, 2013; see also Cabot 2014, 9–10). A precondition for these kinds of incommensurability was the indeterminacy that resulted from loose legal and therapeutic norms. At the same time, as I show below, once improvisation is captured administratively, it can just as easily turn problematic. Together, the following examples show the various ways that indeterminacy also makes incommensurability less possible, and makes care encounters precarious in the face of the law—turning care into something always poised between neglect and possibility.

INSTITUTIONAL INDETERMINACY AS A SPACE FOR IMPROVISATION

Consider, first, a small instance of bureaucratic improvisation. While Olga Zimina, the author arguing for attestatsiia, had hoped for a certain systematicity, the reality of the situation was quite far from this. Part of the problem lay in the fact that the mental health system as a whole was not particularly well integrated. I spent several weeks learning how a severe case would travel through the system, starting from a concern in school and scaling upward. In theory, this case could start with a referral from the school psychologist to the PPMS Center, and then move to the PND and perhaps even a psychiatric hospital. But when I asked whether this picture of the system was accurate, most said that while it was right "in principle" (*v printsipe*), the links between services were actually still premised on personal relationships. Thus, to a significant degree, because of the lack of definition offered by the state and municipal authorities, the system was being built from the ground up.[16] At the same time, these very same centers remained fundamentally responsible to those authorities and could be called on at any time to document their activities.

Near the end of my time in the PPMS Center, I was invited to a meeting between Tatiana Federovna and Lena Aleksandrovna, the director of a sister organization affiliated with the local police that worked with juveniles. Lena Aleksandrovna had contacted Tatiana Fedorovna to discuss the fact that they were working with some of the same children. They wanted to see about developing a collaboration, so that, as Lena Aleksandrovna put it, "the left hand would know what the right is doing." The reason for the overlap was that the center got word of all its young clients through schools or caretakers, while the sister organization was fed through the police. At least as of that time, no federal or municipal system had been designed to address this. In the meeting Lena Aleksandrovna asserted her main needs. She said that her organization was limited in the amount of time it could spend with any client—just six months—and that this made it difficult to do anything sustained at the level of emotional or intellectual support. In particular, she singled out support for kids with conflicts that rest inside the family. All they can do is inquire about upbringing but not really investigate (*rassledovat'*). This was the gap that the PPMS Center might fill, she explained. They agreed to meet once a month to begin to discuss the children they were sharing.[17]

Having in about thirty minutes settled on the ways in which they would collaborate, they spent the next hour figuring out how to make it look bureaucratically legible, anticipating official processes like attestation. As Lena explained to me, since they are both municipal organizations, it was important that they give the impression of "working and not just sitting around talking." They eventually identified the proper piece of paper for noting their activities: a yellow form with a serial number on top that both parties seemed to be quite familiar with. Of chief importance in their negotiation in this process was getting "the stamps"—of both organizations, plus various government authorities. For Lena Aleksandrovna, the stamp of the PPMS Center was as important as the actual work. There was quite a bit of discussion about whether or not the center should then write therapy recommendations on these slips. Tatiana Fedorovna quickly jumped in, saying that they don't have the right to do that. They talked for a while about what to write on the form. After saying that PPMS could write nothing, they decided to sign the specialists' names and write "oral recommendations given." When the meeting was over, Lena Aleksandrovna sat back in her chair and sighed. "I've just about had enough of our bureaucratic ways. Sometimes it makes us fail to see the forest for the trees."

The exasperated sigh notwithstanding, municipal employees were able to leverage an indeterminate legal structure (one might also call it simply an under-resourced structure) as a way to craft such services themselves, maintaining a sense of doing something that was responsive to needs on the ground, despite the municipal codes.

Especially interesting were the stories of therapeutic indeterminacy. As I got to know the psychologists, they began telling me about the improvised techniques they used in care that were, so to speak, off the books and that effectively thwarted the mandate to focus more singularly on cognitive function. These stories were often moving tales of interpersonal connection in which clients, too, "flipped the therapeutic script" (Carr 2011, 196). For example, in the summer of 2015 I reconnected with Zoya, a young psychologist who had just been training when I began my fieldwork in 2005 but who had gone on to become a staff psychologist at the center. When we spoke, she shared with me her therapeutic experience with a young girl, let's call her Ksenia, which she had penned in a thoughtful essay reflecting on the experience. (What follows is drawn from that essay.)

Ksenia had spent many years in social services, including the PPMS Center but also a special-education school and an orphanage. She had first come to the center as an unruly, misbehaving child and was assessed as having language deficiencies and developmental delays. Zoya related to me that she wore old, soiled clothes and had a homemade haircut. Her mother was in remedial school herself and worked sporadically as a street cleaner (*uborshchitsa*). She had certain unspecified neurological difficulties, and her family background, while somewhat unknown, was suspected to have included alcoholism and abuse. By the time of Ksenia's birth, her mother had endured some unclear hardship, and Ksenia spent some time in an orphanage. "Their relationship," Zoya writes, "wasn't easy. Ksenia's mother was warm, but her own neurological problems prevented her from being a stable, safe resource. They survived on insufficient welfare payments. . . . Her mother unknowingly [*sic*. Zoya here means that Ksenia's mother did so without knowing she was hurting her daughter] teased her about being overweight and repeated her demands, often shouting. Ksenia described her mother as if describing a spoiled little child—lazy, eating sweets, put out."

For a while Ksenia attended normal schools, but she was eventually put into special education. Zoya, the psychologist, found this peculiar. Aware that she might have been rationalizing on Ksenia's behalf, she wrote, "Her intellectual ability is still puzzling for me. Our record contains results from different testing methods, but I suspect that even if we exercised the fullest diagnostic battery available, it would say little about her ways of learning." As she got to know Ksenia, she found her to be extremely intelligent, struggling only with some attention deficit, poor eyesight, and hearing. Her cognitive function, in other words, was only part of the story.

To meet this child where she was, Zoya and her mentor, Vladislav Efimovich, developed certain tricks. Departing from standard protocols and exercises aimed at bolstering memory and numerical skills, they taught her to play cards, chess, and checkers; taught her English; and engaged with her not as a child with a cognitive impairment but, in Zoya's words, "as a person." As a young woman living in "heartbreakingly difficult conditions," Ksenia nonetheless became very capable over time. She often defeated the staff at the games, and her confidence grew.

Zoya would later wonder about the degree to which Ksenia's experience in the orphanage had affected her. In therapy sessions Ksenia would at first throw soft cubes at Zoya and other therapists. One day, though, Zoya writes that Ksenia "started to build secure fortresses, dividing the room, and inviting me in." Another time, at age fifteen, Ksenia "meticulously . . . re-created a version of a happy nursery—sun beaming in through the window, a wall of rainbow-colored cubes." Zoya entered to find Ksenia lying on the pillows with a teddy bear. "I almost felt tearful at the scene and told her about my impression. She nodded, smiling, and never returned to this game."

Ksenia referred to Zoya, somewhat obstinately, using the diminutive form of address. Meanwhile, she "opposed the idea that she needed psychological help," redefining the terms of her encounters with Zoya and her mentor on her own terms, as a kind of friendship. Zoya wrote, "We often tried to discuss what was going on in [her] life (and mine), and though she opposed my 'psychologist' role and expressed her annoyance frequently ('don't ask me your psychological questions'), later she asked my opinion on her relationships with friends, teachers, her mother."

Zoya's account also described a series of horrible events in and out of public services. For instance, on one occasion while living in a residential school (*internat*) Ksenia was accused of trying to drown another student. In fact, she was trying to wash the child in the showers, but the damage was done and she was moved to a remedial school. For her part, Zoya also overruled certain legal norms governing her work in an effort to overcome some of the bad tendencies of social services for children. "One time," she writes, "I broke conventions very consciously (we did things like that in our center, but extremely rarely). Ksenia asked me to go to professional school with her and her mother, who wasn't of real help, to apply. I did, and I don't regret it. That was an expression of trust, and they needed a calm companion, a presence. Of course, it gave me tremendous gratification [to know] that I could be of 'real' help."

/   /   /

Zoya's story was a bit of a revelation to me. The creative techniques she employed, the refusal of the category of the cognitive and the hierarchies therein, the committed care: while these may not have been the rule, they indicated moments in which the center's work became visible in ways that would not be legible—indeed, could even be problematic—in the attestatsiia. There was a domain of excess at work where human interactions and negotiations—in a word, sociality—resulted.

INDETERMINACY AND DANGER

Yet, if fuzzy or lacking legal norms could become sites of possibility for responsive care work, so could they also become a source of danger. As I observed in the konsilium during the height of the attestation, legal indeterminacy could also transform improvisation into mission drift. When practitioners encountered a child exhibiting difficulties in school and suspected that something at home was causing it (e.g., the father's drinking), two questions immediately came up. First, was the PPMS Center even the correct institution to deal with the issue? Second, did they have a legal right to follow their cases beyond the child-school context, as Zoya had done? Although the PPMS Center system was by then eight years old, these questions were still very difficult to answer. From a legal point of view, practitioners sometimes found themselves stumbling over conflicts between the child's legal rights and the parents' rights. The system's primary task was to ensure every child's right to a good education and well-being. Yet given the social nature of the problems they confronted, this mandate could sometimes run afoul of what parents thought was appropriate. In some cases, parents would even refuse to come in for a consultation, leaving the practitioners in serious doubt as to how to proceed.

If this legal indeterminacy enabled improvisation, it also created risk. Recall the case of the boy with a computer addiction, who was skipping school and spending all day in gaming halls, and whose mother had locked him in his room. In the course of the konsilium, Anna Andreyevna revealed that, in a similar case, she had followed her therapeutic mandate beyond the child, reading up on family law and trying to offer the family legal advice. Yet divulging this led to an argument between administrator and practitioner. Something similar could be said about therapeutic indeterminacy. Zoya's interventions with Ksenia created possibilities for herself, as a psychologist, to "speak back" to state protocols. This also enabled Ksenia to speak back to psychotherapeutic authority. Yet what was preserved between client and practitioner was an unequal power relationship. Clients could improvise, speak back, find breathing room, and rescript, but always with some possible danger—especially in the case of the problem child, over whom hangs a decision about being sent to an institution. Similarly, in instances of therapeutic improvisation, the specialist was always in danger of being found out, being accused of wasting resources or not producing measurable results.

As a governmental form, what does indeterminacy do? To be sure, indeterminacy enables alternative kinds of practices, improvisations, and the like—offering up a particular brand of circumscribed agency, a set of possibilities to make what one does incommensurable with the governing norms. At the same time, as a productive form of government (rather than an absence), indeterminacy also shifts the responsibility for any action from the institution to the individual. Thus, there can be some important dangers involved for a psychologist who takes the initiative. These dangers can range from internal reprimands and an unpleasant work environment, to failure to pass subsequent state inspections because one's creative response to state indeterminacy is itself legally illegible and thus potentially illegal. As a result, when placed within the juridical frame of illegality, incommensurability can pose problems for those who pursue it. Once captured by law, the incommensurable is made commensurable with governing projects—and, in this case, to the possible detriment of the client and/or the psychologist.

CASE: Mother-son. Mom complained that her life is terrible. She had no work, no husband (he was addicted to drugs), no mother to help with her son. Very demonstrative. All was very sad. She had a disabled son. Evgeniia Antatolievna remarked that it reminded her of the story of a director and an actress who met and fell in love and decided to move to the country to start a new life, have lots of children, etc. They do this, and then something goes wrong. They get expelled from the village and end up back in the city. Very sad history. The case was brought up by Anna Andreyevna just so that the people in the room know that "they exist."

Conclusion: Zones of Social Divestment

This chapter has painted a tensioned portrait of one psychological assistance center through which psychological care was being offered for free to Russian children. The PPMS Center was defined early on as a place that would provide humanistically oriented care, but that aim shifted in new directions under Putin's modernization programs. In particular, structural forms and administrative processes came together to narrow the subject position of both the care provider and the recipient. From the standpoint of administrative legibility, the child was not so much a social being as the seat of an underperforming brain in need of assessment and correction. And the psychologist was not a caretaker so much as a node of state efficacy.

Whereas psychology for the working class and the poor was figured by the state in increasingly bare terms, translating affect as cognitive failing, psychology for the elite continued to render affect sensible as emotional potential. In contrast to the forms of cognitive management at play in this center, the emphasis on emotional management and self-realization at ReGeneration certainly appeared preferable—as both a form of capacitation and a technology of self. To judge from the financial gains possible from being a competent affective laborer (i.e., providing service with a smile), the production of emotional intelligence in commercial psychological spaces would seem to better prepare young people for a successful life in Russia, as well as for the kinds of affective and spatial mobility recognized as recipes for and results of success. The contrast points to the ways that class difference was at play in and through the shifting logics of psychosocial care. Gender, too, was often approached in highly normative terms. In comparison to ReGeneration's play with gender normativities, the diagnostics at the PPMS Center tended to weld traditional ideas of masculinity and femininity onto the problem children.

At the same time, here and there around the staff meetings and through the therapeutic encounter itself, specialists were engaged in a range of ethical practices that were not only administratively incommensurable but also, potentially, analytically illegible. These were engagements premised on a commitment to care over and above the protocols; they were efforts to make do within less-than-optimal circumstances. Stories like that of Zoya's encounter with Ksenia, though, in which Zoya worked against the pressure to convert persons into particular kinds of human capital, made these aspects of care work analytically legible. It was not simply the case that the PPMS Center enacted the biopolitics of cognitive assessment. Rather, there was a tension between techniques of rule and practice. And that tension, productive as it was of institutional incommensurability, allowed for the exercise of a circumscribed agency.

It remains important to repeat, however, that instances of improvisation were hardly reversals of relations of power. Danger was involved for those concerned—and often in ways that seemed to spiral downward to those who were least empowered. In closing, it is worth asking how institutional and therapeutic incommensurabilities might also do a particular kind of governmental work on behalf of states (Cassandra Hartblay, personal communication, October 28, 2011). In fact, as much of the scholarship on neoliberal austerity has pointed out, calls to efficiency under austere conditions are themselves modes of rule that seek to remove social support on the grounds of apolitical, technical reasons (Ferguson 1994). A concept of precarious care, I suggest, can help capture the problematics and potentials of care work, while at the same time directing our critical gaze to the structural problems that psychologist and client alike face.

At the close of Zoya's essay, she notes that her mentor once asked her what she most respected about Ksenia. "My answer," wrote Zoya, "is that she wants to be as good as others. While demanding the rights that society continuously failed to protect, Ksenia never wanted to be pitiful. . . . She didn't want to make a plea for disability, or look weak. She strove for good grades, sometimes frustrating teachers with her stubbornness. She wanted to be honest, to get a job, to support herself and her mother, to be 'like everyone.'" Commenting on Ksenia's amazing resilience and ability to not become bitter, Zoya concluded, "When I think of her everyday struggle, and my very easy life compared to hers, I feel shame—different from the kind that I felt in the [center's] corridors. I don't have half of her self-sufficiency and desire to live 'correctly' in a world that isn't kind to her."

/   /   /

Noting that "virtue cannot be totally prescribed or predetermined," Michael Jackson suggests that "much ethical activity is best understood as a function of the *relationship* between unpredictable situations and extant moral norms" (2011, 8–9). The moral worth of any action, he adds, "lies in what we achieve within the limits of what is possible." In the space of the PPMS Center, conditioned by modernization and audits, the limits of what was possible appeared to be not only narrow but also shrinking. And yet it was from within the government of indifference that practitioners sought, for better and for worse, to make a difference.

PART III

IN SEARCH OF
A POLITICS

In part II, I described the relationship between psychotherapists' efforts to provide care and the bifurcating effects of Vladimir Putin's biopolitical economy. I showed how psychotherapeutic care had come to be both classed and gendered, but also the politico-ethical dimensions of caregiving as a practice. I understood this as an interplay between commensurability and incommensurability. In part III I turn to a different question: do psychotherapists envision their work as having a politics *beyond* the confines of the psychological-education camp and the psychosocial center? I suggest that they do and that new, fraught forms of psychosociality and public intimacy are fundamental to that vision.

FIGURE INTERLUDE 3.1. Moving through public transit. Photo by the author.

INTERLUDE

―――

Public Spaces

1

While awaiting the metro in Gostinnyi Dvor station: a woman is hurrying after a young man, waving a glove after him. The young man is trying to get away from her. Together they are causing a minor stir. He says, "For the last time, it's not my glove!" He waggles his own gloves in her face.

She shrugs her shoulders, drops the glove on the ground, and dashes through the metro doors, which will soon close.

Moments later, another man sees the glove, picks it up, and runs after the woman. "You dropped something! You dropped something!" he says urgently, holding the glove in the air. She shakes her head and shrugs through the window, as if to say, "No, it's not mine."

The original suspected owner, the young man, smiles and says to himself, "That glove will just not go away!"

The glove ends up back on the platform, and the announcement comes: "Caution, the doors are closing [Ostorozhno, dveri zakryvaetsia]*."*

2

An afternoon outside Lomonosovskaia metro station: pigeons scatter underfoot. An old woman is ambling across the square. She is carrying a plastic satchel from the perfumery and cosmetics store Riv Gosh, whose name is a direct transliteration of the French phrase for Left Bank (Rive Gauche). Judging from their ubiquity among babushki, these bags, often wrinkled from frequent use, appear to have great functionality. Perhaps they are also a kind of ironic status symbol.

She walks with her head tilted down and is visibly shocked when a car confronts her in this pedestrian space. Car ownership has ballooned in the last decade, and parking has gotten tight. The city is being converted into a giant parking lot.

"Soon they'll be driving through our apartments! [Skoro oni budyet ezdit' v nashikh kvartirakh!]," *she yells, shaking a fist in the air.*

3

Listening to the radio station Echo of Moscow: the host, psychologist Mikhail Labkovsky, is fielding phone calls on the question "What would you change in yourself if you could?" Tatiana phones in.

TATIANA: *Good evening. You know what I would like to change . . .*

LABKOVSKY: *In yourself.*

TATIANA: *Well, probably . . . In myself?*

LABKOVSKY: *Yes.*

TATIANA: *Well, in myself, probably, no.*

LABKOVSKY: *Well, we would all love to change something in the country, for example, or in the world. But how about in yourself?*

TATIANA: *Well, basically, not in the country, because change in the country . . . I don't know when it will happen.*

LABKOVSKY: *It's always happening.*

TATIANA: *The reforms . . . well, they've been going on for so long . . .*

LABKOVSKY: *So you don't want to change anything in yourself?*

TATIANA: *No, I would change the country. I'll explain why.*

LABKOVSKY: *Explain.*

TATIANA: *You know, I'll be sixty soon. When perestroika started twenty years ago, that was the age when I wanted to change something in my life, but these twenty years, they have simply weakened me.*

LABKOVSKY: *And into what country would you change this one?*

TATIANA: *A European one.*

LABKOVSKY: *Which one? They are all so different.*

TATIANA: *I know Denmark a little, because I have a daughter there. She married; she lives there. But which country is not essential. It's simply another way of life. It's not because they are richer, no, no. It's more about culture, the culture of human association. So to speak. They don't have the sort of problems that we have, say, that arise at every step. On the everyday level, I mean. This rudeness . . . it's not somehow global, just daily. And when would this [change] be—it's unknown.*

LABKOVSKY: *Thanks.*

/ / /

The everyday events I noticed while in transit to fieldwork, or when listening to the radio, were reminders that "human association," as the caller Tatiana put it, was constantly being negotiated, and not always through the self. A dropped glove, and an attempt to find its owner—this was a gesture that moved from an awareness of the dearness of warmth, to, perhaps, an attempt to build solidarity. On the other hand, nearly getting run down by a car in the square exemplified the ongoing privatization of public space. Soon, the old woman lamented, they'll be driving through our apartments. Psychotherapists, too, were engaged with sociality within the cracked spaces of capitalism. I draw on fieldwork in adult treningi and an analysis of a popular talk radio program to document some of the psychotherapeutic means for reimagining social and public life, and the implications these practices have for politics under Putin.

Chapter 5

"I CAN FEEL HIS TEARS"

Psychosociality under Putin

Diana, a young, fashionably dressed woman in her mid-thirties, took a seat next to Olessia, the psychotherapist.

"What do you want to diagnose, Diana?" Olessia asked.

Diana answered ritually, "A symptom [*simptom*]." She was then told to choose a "substitute" (*zamestitel'*) from among us. She stood, chose, and then pressed her substitute forward with two hands at her back. They paused together. Diana bowed her head in silence for a few moments and then, gently patting the shoulders of the substitute, said, "You are 'Diana.' " Going through the same movements, she selected someone to personify her symptom. She then returned to her seat.

The "symptom" and "Diana" (the substitute) were now standing in the middle of the room. Olessia, the therapist, instructed them to attune to an energy (*energiia*) that would move them in certain directions and change their personae into what or whom they represented. "Diana" began to make faces. Standing before the "symptom," she coyly averted her gaze. She clasped her hands behind her back and stared down at her feet, tracing a semicircle with her big toe. The unnamed "symptom" stared back at her determinedly. Olessia occasionally made some comments about this or that behavior. After a few moments, Olessia rose and chose another person, placing him at a distance from the "symptom." She did not say whom (or what) he represented.

"How do you feel?" she asked "Diana" and the new figure.

"Better, of course," both said, "or at least different." The "symptom" reported a desire to move in the direction of the new addition. For "Diana" this was "comfortable." As the figures shifted positions, Olessia leaned over to the real Diana, seated next to her: "This addition is your 'sexual desire.' You need to listen to it. You need to follow it, to allow it to move." Diana nodded, taking this in deeply. This concluded Diana's session.

Other sessions followed. Participants queried various personal questions—often related to some indecision about money and work. One woman asked whether she should become a hairstylist or stay in school. A man wondered whether he should continue living in Saint Petersburg, where the money was good and he had a love interest, or return to Ufa, the home of his kin. Another woman, also a psychotherapist, brought up a dilemma she was having in her consulting: "What does the client want?" Olessia herself asked about whether her oldest son should go to a *gymnasium* or a *lyceum*, two schooling options in the city.

/   /   /

These episodes took place at a psychodrama session called Systemic Constellation (Sistemnaia Rastanovka), which I attended on a follow-up visit to Saint Petersburg in 2007. Systemic constellation (also family constellation[s]) is a therapeutic method based on the theories of a German psychotherapist, Bert Hellinger (Cohen 2006), which has been imported into and adapted to Russia. Like other forms of psychodrama, it rests on the premise that personal problems can be modeled for the client in a performance, or "constellation," rendering them legible and thus therapeutically operable. To this idea Hellinger adds another element—an unseen force external to the scene that moves bodies and is linked to the client's genealogy. Olessia called this element energiia.[1] Energiia reveals whatever it is that troubles the present—and that troubling thing is often buried somewhere in the person's familial past.

Systemic constellation was very popular in Saint Petersburg in 2007. Many young urban professionals were turning to it for guidance. Why, I wondered, would clients and therapists seek capacitation through displacement—first onto the body of another, who stands in as a substitute, and then through an ineffable power tied to the past? Given its prominent, social nature (the practice is essentially staged for the others in attendance), what might this practice reveal about the sociality of psychotherapy, and the kinds of problems people deemed worth sharing?

I want to use Olessia's practices and reflections on energiia as a leaping-off point to discuss something that I noticed repeatedly in my experience in therapy sessions—a perceptible form of intimate sociability that formed among participants. In this chapter I focus on the social dimensions of therapeutic work. Those dimensions were, I argue, sociopolitical gestures. That is, by drawing on idioms of psychosocial resonance like *energiia* (energy) and *garmoniia* (harmony), psychotherapists invented and circulated languages for thinking about sociality—or what I term *psychosociality. Psychosociality* refers to a form of association and solidarity that took shape in, around, and through psychotherapeutic groups.[2] These idioms and forms of association, in turn, could become staging grounds for participants to formulate concepts that touched on broader political questions in Russia: What is value? How can human intimacy be maintained? What is mental well-being?

The search for answers to these questions was striking when contrasted with another set of discourses I often heard, those about *strakh* (fear), the lack of *stabil'nost'* (stability) in life, and the violence and isolation in Russia during Vladimir Putin's rise. Psychosociality was not a direct response to these discourses, but at a time of increasing anxiety, such groups were nonetheless socially and politically salient, and therapists like Olessia described their work to me in terms that reached out into the world. For that reason, in this chapter I pursue a symptomatic reading of psychosociality. I interpret the effort to affect psychosociality as an attempt to find links between therapeutic social forms and a politics at a time of widely perceived dissolution.

Past Effects and Affects

I first encountered systemic constellation while researching Verity, the organization founded by Olessia's husband, Nikolai, in 2006. When I met them, Verity was offering other therapeutic services besides Systemic Constellations—most especially Nikolai's long cycle of programs, Harmonious Relations. Verity pitched these at upwardly mobile urban Russians. Initially convinced that Systemic Constellations was a fringe movement, I was surprised when a therapist at a competitor organization had not only heard of it but also thought it quite therapeutically legitimate.[3]

Nikolai was the first to tell me about Systemic Constellations. We met in his office one day, and he explained to me that a client volunteers to have a personal concern modeled via a constellation of social relations. This constellation can include one's ancestors. According to the method, personal problems experienced in life are often genealogically motivated. One carries the wounds of the past within oneself. He told me that some of our problems could not be solved "here and now," referencing the famous phrase from Carl Rogers's client-centered therapies. This was because there are problems that are tied to one's roots (*rod*) and that, if left unrecognized and unresolved, could be reproduced across the generations.

I must have looked a bit skeptical, because Nikolai added that he was unconvinced at first. He said:

> I thought that most psychological problems could be solved by a good psychologist, and that when a problem can't be solved, it's because of the psychologist's skills: with a good frame, the problem can be solved. Now I know I was wrong. Because half of our problems are not our own. It's to do with our roots. For example, a girl might repeat a situation in her life, with men or money. This [pattern] started in the life of some person in her roots. It was an accident many years ago. So long as the situation is in the [older] generation, we can't solve it without contacting that generation.

He gave me an example of what is meant by generational "contact": people come in and take a short test. "If it is your problem, you can solve it in the usual way. If it's from your roots, you do a constellation." This information from one's roots can be transmitted because we all carry it inside of us. "As we know, the past and the future come together at this one point, in the now. Information about you and your relations are in you," he said, adding that many things can be addressed in a constellation, including physical symptoms or diseases.

There was undoubtedly an element of the miraculous at play in this otherwise-secular middle-class practice. He told me a fantastic story in which one of the substitutes—representing a client's father—kept calling himself "Ivan," although the woman's father's name was Piotr: "This happened enough times that the client became confused. She went home and asked her mother, 'Who is Ivan?' Her mother went pale, and only after an hour came back to her senses. 'Ivan is your real father. But nobody knows about Ivan.'" I also witnessed a moment of contact with the past in Olessia's session (albeit in less dramatic fashion). One female client's inability to relate to men, it was revealed, was connected to an abortion her mother had before she was born; someone else's decision was supposedly haunting her.

Hellinger's systemic constellation (also called "family constellation") is grounded in the epistemology of both existential phenomenology and a

"Zulu-influenced ontology of trans-generational connectedness" (Hellinger spent fifteen years in South Africa as a Catholic missionary) (Cohen 2006, 227). Drawing from this experience, constellation theory proceeds as a form of "somatic psychology" that assumes that "the knowledge of trans-generational loyalties are [sic] held not in the mind but from a deeper level of systemic, genetic, or cellular consciousness" (Cohen 2006, 226). The therapeutic task, as practiced in Saint Petersburg, was to unearth these deeper levels of consciousness, wherever they might lie, and come to terms with them.

One author writes, "In the silence and stillness of the constellated scene, the client and representatives are able to tune into the unconscious, collective will of the family system.... From within this knowing field (Laszlo, 2004; Sheldrake, 1995), the interplay among the *conservative forces of systemic integrity* (balance, bonding, and order) and the expansive forces of animated existence (physical survival and reproduction) come [sic] momentarily into conscious awareness. The client is able to perceive both a pre-reflective, systemic connection between the ancestral field and the presenting issue and a possible healing movement" (Cohen 2006, 226; emphasis mine).

Beneath the miraculous, though, various kinds of normativity were also at play. In the example mentioned above of the woman's mother's abortion, a moral discourse opposed to abortion was fused with a set of gendered assumptions about the task of "meeting the right man." These struck me later as the "conservative forces of systemic integrity" just referenced. There were also examples in which the very solidity of the normative was in question. Participants were deeply uncertain about value, and the role that money should or should not play in important life decisions. Finally, because of systemic constellation's focus on purging a haunting past, it was also clear that therapists were potentially sorting norms of value and morality against the backdrop of historical memory.[4] Inna Leykin (2015) has found something similar in her research on a self-help movement in Russia called Rodologia, in which genealogy is the crucial therapeutic modality. In these social groups, Leykin notes, genealogy provides the means for navigating post-Soviet memory. In many instances, a family trauma linked to collectivization, World War II, or imprisonment figured in people's efforts to renegotiate their own heritage and, thus, their relationship to post-Soviet Russia. While systemic constellation was less clearly historical and political than Rodologia, the appeal to energiia was undoubtedly a post-Soviet memory practice.[5] It operated as an imagined mode of transfer between present and past, naming a space in which clients might, as part of a group, reconcile their lives with their family histories—in particular those traumatic events that may have been, in some real sense, haunting the present.

Breakdown: Fear and Isolation

If the past haunted, the present seemed saturated with fear. Another prominent set of discourses I encountered in my fieldwork concerned anxiety and social breakdown. For example, I often heard a great deal of discussion among therapists about an unidentified fear (strakh).[6] At the PPMS Center, I heard about many cases in which children were gripped with fear: the boy with an unidentified panic or fear; the child with inexplicable fears of death and loss; the girl who easily manipulates her parents and has become fearful that she will somehow be responsible if they die; the preschooler who fears Baba Yaga (a Russian fairy-tale witch); the boy with "internal feelings of fear" that have "different sources"; the child who clings desperately to her mother and fears being abandoned; the boy whose father and uncle recently died who feels fear all the time and cannot do his schoolwork; the boy who missed school all of January, who draws himself as two people, light and dark (one is at home and scared; the other wants to ride his bicycle), and has a spontaneous fear of death and cemeteries; the tenth grader who fears water and open space; the boy who is afraid to be at home alone and draws UFOs.

Adults, too, were fearful. Psychotherapists told me that Russians "fear change" and "fear loss," that "their fears interfere with their own ability to live," that "they are afraid to smile," that "they fear opening up." One psychotherapist working with a university-linked clinic made a direct connection between the anxious experiences their patients reported and a "growth in society of fear, alarm, dismay, and aggressiveness." At times, fear crept into psychotherapeutic practice. In a Balint group, Vera Aleksandrovna, a psychologist working at the PPMS Center, remarked about a case she was working on, "Whenever I encounter this case, I am filled with strong emotions—fear, pity, wrath." Her colleague Svetlana suggested that she reflect on the experiences in her own life that were causing her fear. In another staff meeting, after a practitioner pointed out that a particular boy was "unable to explain the sources of his fear," Vladislav Efimovich turned to his neighbor and remarked, "Who can?"

Who can, indeed? But this was precisely what practitioners were tasked with doing—finding fear's source. Their pursuit of that source could lead to discussions of Russia's contemporary social problems (alcoholism, poverty) and, more often, of a general anxiety about the future and social order, two things that were upended with the collapse of the Soviet Union and that have remained in a state of anxious suspension under Putin.[7] For example, one afternoon after the PPMS Center's konsilium, Anastasia Fillipovna, the doctor-psychotherapist and children's specialist who often oversaw the meetings, sat down with me for an interview. I was curious to hear what she thought about all the instances of fear among the center's clients. She explained that two words in Russian are commonly confused: *strakh*, or fear, and *trevoga*, which might be translated as "anxiety" or "alarm":

> We need to speak more about anxiety [*trevoga*] than fear [*strakh*]. Anxiety is directed to the future, a concern that situations are undefined, so that something can happen, and can make one's own position unstable. I would say that that's more like anxiety than fear. [Our anxiety] can be explained by the fact that society is going through an ongoing state of change, and people still cannot assert or confirm that their situations are stable. They have no savings to help them in a moment of need, or property to sell to support them. They do not know what kind of political society exists, and they worry about their children. And so it is really anxiety, caused by uncertainty. But in the Russian language, fear and anxiety are often not differentiated. Fear is a response to something happening, for instance, a barking dog. With anxiety, nobody is barking.

Like the difference between mourning and melancholia (Butler 1997), Anastasia identified a crucial distinction between the presence and the absence of the object of fear. To conflate one with the other, as one might do by scapegoating, gives a more material (but ultimately falsely attributed) existence to future uncertainty, as if uncertainty could somehow be located in relation to an imagined object, as well as anchored in the body.

In another conversation, Olessia's husband, Nikolai, described some of the possible dangerous effects of this future-oriented anxiety. Speaking about the increase in random violence in Russia, he said:

> I am afraid when my sons go out. I would like to raise them elsewhere, but there are not really any good possibilities. . . . I don't see a real way out. Meanwhile, I think that things will just get worse. Olessia is willing to move, but her feelings are more mixed. She argues that our world is a mirror of our mind. But I think about the twelve people I know who were beaten on the street, in the middle of the day, good people. [The idea that] by changing our thinking nothing will go wrong—we can see that this isn't

totally true. I can't even think of a family around me that has not had some recent encounter with violence.

Nikolai's stories of violence resonated with the findings of anthropologist Serguei Oushakine, whose work in provincial Russia uncovered a tendency among his informants to respond to political collapse and trauma through conspiracy theory and ethnonationalism—what he calls a "patriotism of despair" (2009).

Since Nikolai related these stories to me in 2007, everyday violence has only gotten worse. Putin's popularity has hinged in part on a cynical deployment of Slavic nationalism and xenophobia. While this has helped bolster his ongoing support, it has also unleashed a string of violent assaults against non-ethnic-Russian citizens, members of the political opposition, and members of the LGBTQ community. Public spaces have become more and more patrolled: the law against "gay propaganda" has been interpreted as meaning that any public demonstration in support of LGBTQ rights is illegal on the grounds that it promotes a homosexual lifestyle to children (Chan 2017). Journalist Masha Gessen (2013) fears the law could also be interpreted broadly as a threat to gay couples with children. With regard to violence against those who are not ethnic Russians, between 2014 and 2016 friends living in Russia were condemning on Facebook a string of disturbing videos, entitled "White Subway Car" ("Belyi vagon"; see Bulakhtin 2017), in which groups of young men indiscriminately attacked people on the metro who appeared to be from Central Asia and the southern republics while onlookers yelled encouraging patriotic slogans and the police stood and watched.

In an interview in 2014 on *NewsNet*, Oksana Karpenko, a Russian sociologist and head of the Center for Independent Social Research, described a situation of apprehension under the law:

There is no total prohibition or open repression. Repressive laws have been passed, but in "good" tradition, they are applied selectively, and if you don't "stick your neck out," you can violate them all you want. It is this unpredictable application of the repressive measures that creates, on the one hand, a feeling of lawlessness in society, and on the other hand, a fear of standing up for something [*strakh vysunut'sia*]. It resembles a rolling back to the Soviet societal contract: the state does not touch those who support it or at least do not touch it. The state and citizens are separate. (2014, 6–7)

The Social Energy of Psychosociality

Psychosociality was, of course, not a direct answer to these social problems, but it did involve creating novel, intimate forms of human association in a context of widely perceived social breakdown. In that sense, then, idioms like energiia were also proxies for social life. Volodya, a transpersonal psychologist (and developer of the live-burial technique mentioned at the beginning of this book), instructed clients in a three-day training entitled "The Psychotherapist as Shaman" to "get in touch with our energiia and become more rooted." He added that this energiia also flows between people in consulting work, animating connection. Energiia prepared the ground for psychological intimacy by creating an immanent substance for interconnection, and also the invisible medium for unreserved and excited exchange. Groups could have it or lose it. Olessia told me at length about her growing frustration with her other courses on women's sexuality because, lacking any men in the room, things seemed somehow flat. "We would gradually go along, and there is no anger, no energiia. Instead, it's a certain state [*sostoianie*]; it's like ... [she inhaled and held her breath]." She explained that "when there are women and men together, they drive each other along [*oni sami drug druga goniat*]," and that the presence of both "helps the group energy [*grupovaia energiia*]," creating a "spark" (*iskra*) that "adds something unconscious ... an instinct; it's human nature." Further, without this spark, "it's harder to see [*uvidet*] the true natural essence [*istinaia sushnost' prirody*] of these women." Energiia was thus an imagined substance, often very gendered but not always, that drew people into contact with their familial pasts and with others, into a kind of heteronormative collective effervescence.[8]

Through the current of energiia, psychotherapeutic work became affective social work. Neither object nor subject, energiia was a change in state, a way of thinking about social transfer or exchange, rather than just a discipline of self-cultivation. Most obviously, it was external to the subject, initiating the capacity to act from without. And energiia's focus on the past, on one's roots (rod), created a link between the self and a (familial) other.

How might energiia be theorized? As akin to power? According to Michel Foucault (1990a, 92–93), power is also immanent to the micropolitics of daily life and fundamentally social. Yet power constitutes the social differently— as a series of relations of force rather than as a circuit or set of flows. Energiia seemed to be less about agon than attachment—both harmful and sustaining.

In relation to rod, energiia signified a historically mediated sociality, marking a charge between bodies and times (see Warner 2002). From that standpoint, affect may be a better correlate concept to energiia. Affect is understood, in contrast to emotion, as a feeling in the raw. Prediscursive but not presocial, affect is sensation as registered on/in the body before being semiotically fixed (Massumi 2002). Affect is also social, referring to the feel of a room when you walk into it—anxious, intense, celebratory (Brennan 2004). It is, in Gilles Deleuze's (2007) words, "the melodic line of continuous variation of the force of existing." Affect is both within the body and also between bodies, passing back and forth through words, actions, and postures. It is the circuitry of the social, and also the source of a power to act or to strive (for Spinoza [1993], *conatus*).

Read in these terms, energiia posits a conception of agency as affective and social in nature. It takes the affective energies of these social practices—rather than just individual desire or disciplined will—as the impetus and force of life. Similarly, theorists of affective labor look to affective and affecting networks as sources for commons (see Hardt and Negri 2005). In this conception, a sense of political possibility and connection is attributed to the circulation of unstructured feeling.

An ethnographic example might help: recall Ira's story about her first taste of group therapy in the early 1990s, a time when such social practices were rare. The euphoria she described was as much about personal revelation as about a new social encounter, and it pointed to an exuberance that I, too, sometimes experienced when participating in and observing group therapy sessions. In her memorable words, which I quote again: "It was a new way of thinking, a new point of view. We called each other by first name. It was a new social form. We used the informal 'you' [*my govorili na ty*]. I was mad about it. I took all the psychology I could find. Sometimes without purpose. It was shocking how new it was. But I was ready. I felt very happy. I could be myself. It wasn't part of the Soviet system. It was for me."

What possibility emerged from this experience for Ira? From the standpoint of psychosociality, not only the therapeutic experience but also the languages and social practices associated with it were new. For Ira, and, indeed for many others, psychotherapeutic intimacy created the possibility for other, more open and informal kinds of social relations.[9] More concretely, for Ira these groups also opened onto a career path at a time when such paths for recently divorced middle-aged women were rare.

Psychosociality as a Proxy for Social Absence

In conversations about energiia, practitioners often invoked a partner concept. *Dusha*—loosely "soul"—was the instrument that people needed to rely on, not only to sense this energiia, but also to find direction in their life. If energiia was intersubjective, moving across and through persons, dusha was more internalized. As Olessia explained to me, in her work she drew on the power of *zadushevnost'* (literally, "behind-the-soul-ness") to feel the soul suffering of another. Recounting a story of an experience doing individual consulting, she said, "[The client] is sitting there, and he has no emotion on his face. He sits, talks about these things that are unpleasant, even heavy. But he reflects no emotions. He speaks with a calm voice, no intonation. But inside of me everything is being squeezed, and I can feel his tears. I don't feel sorry for him. I have caught his condition [*Ia lovliu ego sostoianie*]. So I say to him, 'You want to cry right now.' And he says, 'Yes.' Because it's like I feel his tears. I have this ability."

What makes this work, she says, is that the situation "calls to the soul [*vyzyvaetsia k dushe*]," and that, with dusha, she can "feel his condition" and "catch its field [*lovliu polia*]." Olessia's imperative to "work with the soul" (*rabotat' s dushoi*) meant drawing on this compass as a counseling resource and as a way to discovering what is "true" (*pravda*) for that person, without any particular need to arrive at what is universally true (*istina*):[10] "Everyone has their [claim to deep] truth [*istina*], and that's fine. I steer away from that. I try to say, what are you feeling? What is happening now? How is it reflected in your body [*kak v svoim tele otrazhaetsia*]? Where is this hurt located in your body?" To illustrate the relevance of dusha's relative truth (pravda) and importance in therapy, she mentioned the approach to group therapy of the American human-potential psychologist Carl Rogers. "He didn't dictate a direction for psychological work [*vector dvizheniia*] to the group. The group would begin to interact, and certain problems would appear through interactions, certain emotions would appear [*rozhdaetsia*], and he would work with these emotions, with these soul conditions [*s sostoianiami dushevnimi*]—in other words, *that* power chooses [*etot vlast' vybiraet*]."

Nikolai was also explicit about the role of dusha in orienting oneself in the world. He told me he was experimenting with a new psychological theory called "transurfing reality," developed by a Soviet quantum physicist turned self-help author named Vadim Zelind. Drawing on the analogy of the pirated compilation DVD, a mainstay of Russian street kiosks at the time, the idea was that one's life is a DVD filled with different movies. One can choose any number of movies. The question, Nikolai said, is how to choose, and most people are not sufficiently attentive to dusha. "We can't understand our path because we look from the mind—only our dusha can point the way to happiness—we can't hear dusha. Dusha doesn't choose the goal. It can only give advice. We can choose whatever we want, but only dusha can see the disk. The problem is that we are all sleeping. We need to become more aware."

Olessia's and Nikolai's reliance on dusha for advice is interesting in light of the concept's cultural meanings in Russia—namely, its simultaneous individual and social dimensions.[11] Folding into itself notions of both an internal emotional world and intimate sociality, dusha is immanent; it is that thing on which one can rely for continuity and direction when facing uncertainty. According to the linguist Anna Wierzbicka (1992, 47–52), *dusha* cannot be explained by direct reference to English terms like *soul, mind,* and *body*.[12] Like the Cartesian binary mind-body, dusha is also counterposed to body (*telo*), and is thought to be a source of insight for the person; however, unlike mind, it "focuses mainly on values and emotions" (47). It is "an internal spiritual theater" (50), where feelings are prominent and events can take place. It is deep and cannot be easily observed in oneself; meanwhile, "these events are unknowable to outsiders ('*chuzhaia dusha potiomki,*' the proverb says, 'another person's *dusha* is unfathomable')" (50). Nonetheless, it can be a source of intuition, as in knowing something in one's soul—a knowledge that is not purely factual but "somehow linked to values and to a person's hidden inner world" (51). Dusha is also a locus of human will, as in "soul strength" (*dushevnaia sila*) (52). When one is depressed, it is the soul that is in trouble: a term for being mentally ill is *dushevnobol'nyi* (literally, "soul sick") (52). "Thus," Wierzbicka suggests, "the Russian *dusha* is used very widely and can refer to virtually all aspects of a person's personality: feelings, thoughts, will, knowledge, inner speech, ability to think" (52).

I mentioned earlier that the idioms of *energiia, garmoniia,* or *dusha* were not just concerned with psychosociality, and that there was also a normative dimension to this work: for example, therapists appealed to *energiia* and *dusha* to sort through questions about value. Of the twenty people participating in the Systemic Constellation session I attended, about half had questions about money, career, and other problems of personal choice. Which is the better thing to do? What is better for me? Not only for money but also for me as a person, for my soul? One client, for example, wanted to work through a career decision. She was a translator of legal documents into English, work that paid very well, but she felt that it was not her "soul's work." She told Olessia that she had other, more soulful interests, including being a graphic designer, but was uncertain about whether to act on her intuition to leave her current job.

After she finished describing the simptom, two people were picked from among us—one to represent lucrative work, the other to represent the soul's work. Olessia reasoned that, perhaps, the soul's work could also be more lucrative. Then, alarmingly, she selected me to play the role of money. We three stood together in the room; it was up to me to choose which profession. At first I stood, rooted. Then Oksana reversed the positions of the two careers. And she again asked me, "Money, where do you want to go?" Feeling pressure to do something, I chose the girl who was smiling most pleasantly at me. She represented graphic design. "Wow!" said the woman. I'm not sure why, but Oksana concluded that it might be that something would need to change in her life—perhaps she needed to find a husband and have a child—in order for her to make this career change.

By invoking dusha in relation to the market, therapists and clients used these psychotechnical idioms in ways that diverged from the dominant story of instrumentalizing the self for the labor market. The psychological invocation of dusha and energiia could just as often be used in opposition to market rationalities. I came to see these terms as speaking to the instability of questions of value—whether economic or ethical. The anthropologist Michael Lambek (2008, 136), paraphrasing Georg Simmel, notes that "money transforms quality into quantity," or, in Kantian terms, dignity into price. Energiia and dusha were discussed in this psychodrama setting as alternatives to the conversion, through the market, of value into a purely economic significance.

Dusha was also often described in ways that implied a social dimension, and it could be invoked in the same breath as other concepts denoting intimacy, including obshchenie (communication or socializing, often of a deep type), kukhonnyi razgovor (kitchen talk), and svoi (one's close friends or circle) (Yurchak 2006; Pesmen 2000; Ries 1997). Also, unlike in Protestant and Catholic contexts, where souls are possessed and individualized, dusha is immanent. It is a force that may or may not be connected to the person. For this reason, coming to know one's dusha can also be a kind of social communion. As Wierzbicka (1992, 57–58) notes, in Russian there are many phrases that suggest a desire to share one's inner states with another, to "exteriorize them": ilit' dushu (to pour out one's soul), otvesti dushu (to relieve one's soul), otkryt' dushu (to open one's soul), dusha narapashku (a wide-open soul), razgovarivat' *po dusham* (to talk from soul to soul). "What these expressions suggest is that although other people cannot know what goes on in a person's dusha without being told, *there is an expectation that normally people would want, and need, to tell someone what goes on there*" (Wierzbicka 1992, 57; emphasis mine). Hiding dusha from friends is seen as bad social form. Rather, one must strive for what Olessia described to me as zadushevnost' ("behind-the-soul-ness"), which is what one does when really letting friends in on something intimate.

In conjunction with *energiia*, then, *dusha* articulated a communal and affective basis for psychological knowledge. Rather than expressing life's direction as a matter of individual uniqueness, these concepts pointed to some external force or measure—often brought into focus through social interaction—that at the same time constituted a form of sociality, a psychosociality.

Perhaps the most explicit idiom of psychosociality I encountered, though, was *garmoniia*, or harmony. Many psychological trainings invoked this word in their titles. There were courses on "harmonious relations," an institute called Harmony, and even the Ministry of Education had termed the work of psychologists working with problem children in schools as *soprovozhdenie*, a term that means not only guidance and support but also a form of accompaniment that characterizes two instruments playing a duet harmoniously. Together with *energiia* and *dusha*, *garmoniia* articulated a social circuit through which one person's inner well-being could be linked to another's in a state of "harmonious relations" (*garmonichnye otnosheniia*).

Nikolai was the keenest theorizer of garmoniia I encountered. He had for the last decade been teaching his psychological theory of human personality types and harmonious relations. His work drew on theories first developed in 1988 by a Russian psychologist named Viktor Tolkachev, which extended Sigmund Freud's theories of the oral, anal, and genital stages of child development to a grand psychological theory (Tolkachev 2008). Tolkachev's idea was that our personalities are organized by eight "openings" in the body—the eyes, ears, mouth, skin, navel, anus, urethra, and nose—which are our points of contact with the world. Each person is genetically more oriented to some "vectors" than others (think of Freud's anal type).[13] Psychological problems in the form of dissonance occur when a person fails to recognize and accept his or her predispositions. His course, Harmonious Relations, sought to bring this to light and thus constitute inner harmony. (For a graphical representation of the results of my personality test, rendered in vectors, see figure 5.1.) When these two dimensions of the personality—genetic potential (*genetichekii potentsial*) and

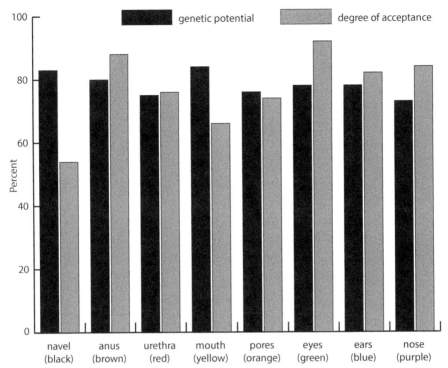

| | navel (black) | anus (brown) | urethra (red) | mouth (yellow) | pores (orange) | eyes (green) | ears (blue) | nose (purple) |

FIGURE 5.1. My vector analysis. Each bar refers to a vector linked to one opening in the body. The darker bars (left) indicate my "genetic potential" in these areas—essentially an indicator of which vector is most dominant in my personality. The lighter bars (right) indicate the degree to which I accept this aspect of myself. Harmoniousness pertains not to genetic potential but to the degree of self-acceptance.

acceptance (*priniatie*)—are in a state of harmoniousness (*garmonichnost'*), then one is more likely to be both happy and successful. As Nikolai repeatedly told me, the level of genetic potential was not what was important for a person's happiness, well-being, or success; rather, it was the degree to which that person was aware of his or her inclinations in and toward the world. "The ideal is when all eight vectors are in harmony. Realization, manifestation, harmony—this is my work," Nikolai said.

Like energiia and dusha, garmoniia is also a social concept. Through its focus on the body's openings to the world, the theory is focused on self and the world. Moreover, discussing the importance of acceptance (priniatie) for harmony, Nikolai said that if a person "can understand and accept the vectors in another person, then harmony in the family results. If you can do this at work, then there will be harmony in the collective. And then on the planetary level if you can understand and accept other countries, then harmony will be planetary. I consider this system to be very holistic [*ekologicheskaia*]."

These ideas of inter- and intrapersonal harmony were also redirected to address some of the challenges specific to the post-Soviet period. For example, if garmoniia entailed a particular alignment of energiia, then the existence of racism, ethnocentrism, or male chauvinism always had the potential to adversely influence one's garmoniia. Commenting on the oppressiveness of gender identities in Russia, Olessia remarked, "There are very few harmonious women in Russia who are just fine with who they are [*khorosho shto im kakie est'*]." She described the enormous expectations placed on women—in the workplace, for example, or in public—to look a certain way. Nikolai also discerned a problem of garmoniia specifically for women: "The big question for women in Russia is that they have no harmony in their private lives, in sex, in relationships with others. Many have sexual problems."

Even Tamara Grigorievna, ReGeneration's director, viewed garmoniia as fundamental to new ways of being. In describing their efforts to provide psychological education to children, she told me, "[In our work] we take less of an interventionist approach, and try to develop the values of development, garmoniia, success [*uspekh*], and self-confidence. We are teaching new values and a new language in Russia."

The Precarious Politics of Stability

The focus in this chapter has so far been on psychosociality as a heightened form of human association. Yet Verity's work (as well as ReGeneration's) often vibrated between different kinds of economies, ontologies, and effects (see Ahmed 2004). While at times it was premised on noncommodified social practices, at others it was captured by capital. If psychology presupposed social idioms, so, too, were they sometimes individualizing. And if one effect of psychology was pleasure, another was surely a reactionary fear that tended to extend, rather than disrupt, problematic social orders and political outlooks. This was apparent to me in the inherently conservative politics of social stability that therapists often mentioned.

For example, psychotherapists indicated that stabil'nost', or stability, was necessary for fostering good psychological work. Aleksandr from ReGeneration told me that social stability is necessary for their profession because the work of the self cannot take place in unstable societies. Citing Abraham Maslow's (1987) hierarchy of human needs, with self-realization as the highest level, he suggested that only after basic needs are met (food and shelter, security, love) can one attend to questions of self-realization. A stable society was a prerequisite for these basic needs to be met. Others read the increasing interest in psychology as an outcome of stability and prosperity. For example, Tamara Grigorievna told me that the fact that more and more people were valuing not just higher education but also psychology was "a good sign of stability." Conversely, Olya, the social worker running body-oriented therapies in one of Saint Petersburg's PNDs, told me that she preferred not to invest time in developing her professional qualifications. "In the face of an uncertain future, why invest in self-development?" And Aleksandr, speaking of the conditions for self-realization (*samorealizatsiia*), commented on several encouraging signs in Russia, including the fact that "the state can make a budget for more than one year" and that "politics are more stable—we know that there will be a presidential election." As Nikolai put it, "stability means you can run your business, and that your clients can afford to come to you."

At the microscale of self-work, therapists also invoked stability as a safeguard against the fearful emotions that the collapse of social order had triggered. Daria, a school psychologist working in the area near the PPMS Center, suggested as much when she told me that psychologists might play a stabilizing role in this context: "The great social change we have experienced is reflected in the growing demand for psychologists and religious figures." Addressing matters at a markedly more fine-grained level, Irina Pavlovna, a psychoanalyst who had invested a great deal of her own money in a small family practice, insisted that proper relations between parents and children must be based on a number of "stabilities": the parent must be dominant, and "dangers can result from an imbalance or instability in gender relations and identities."

Stability as an interior state was also a capacity that could be developed. The PPMS Center I visited offered several programs aimed at the "development of capable stability." I also observed a female client in a training who, when asked to describe her goal for the session, responded, "I want to become more sure of myself, more stable on the inside, more steadfast [*tverdyi*]." Vladimir Mikhailovich, Vitya Markov's partner, who had been trained in the Soviet period, told me that "psychology is a way toward self-fulfillment [*samosovershenstvo*] and self-development [*samorazvitie*] that allows a person to feel more confident, more even-tempered, more stable [*stabil'nyi*], more independent."

He added, "Everyone wants to be better [*vsem khochetsia byt' luchshe*], more stable, confident. . . . People really want to be stronger."

To be sure, the psychological discourse of stabil'nost had a politics, but it was an inherently conservative and foreshortened one. Igor, the young psychologist at ReGeneration who had lost a brother in a car accident because the ambulance took so long to arrive, told me that given the choice between a more democratic Russia and Putin's model of central control, he would still choose the latter "because people need stability in their lives in order to begin to live." He continued, "When I look around the city, I like what I see. There are renovations, the improvement of daily life, a rising quality of life, and cafés." He said that stability was the quickest way to arrive at a Russia where he would feel safe raising a child. He added, "After spending just one week in Finland, I no longer throw cigarettes on the ground. But I look around me, and that's all I see. In general, Russians show a lack of personal responsibility. This needs to change, and stability is a way that this might happen. When free of fear, Russians will be able to rely on the government."

Participants in Nikolai's harmonious-relations seminar described stabil'nost' in similar ways. Whereas Nikolai was interested in fostering more holistic, or ekologicheskie, global relations, his clients had a narrower view of what this knowledge could enable. I spoke with Lara, a participant who worked for a multinational company, after the session on the vector of the ears. She told me that she had signed up for the course because she had "seen the results with her own eyes": she and a male friend who had previously taken Nikolai's course were pulled over by a police officer, who tried to shake them down for a bribe. After ten minutes of talking with the officer outside the car, though, her friend returned without having to pay. She explained that in the course on harmonious relations, her friend had learned how to manage others through understanding their personalities. Thus, Lara had translated Nikolai's aspiration for holistic global relations into a strategy for dealing with corrupt police officers.

Teresa Caldeira (2000, 34–37) has written of the prevalence of fear talk in contexts of urban social transformation. When "violence disrupts meaning" (34) she argues, the narration and signification of discourses of fear can counter perceived disruption through the reestablishment of order. Referring to the work of René Girard and Mary Douglas, she notes that "danger is controlled and social order maintained by clear categorizing" (36). Fearful talk, then, is productive in the Foucauldian sense. It brings into being concrete effects, such as inciting further violence, criminalizing certain social groups, transforming policing tactics, and so forth. Beyond these kinds of effects, fear talk can also spur inherently reactionary norms that maintain, rather than disrupt, social orders—a prime example being traditional gender or race relations. In Russia, inasmuch as fear circulated through psychotherapeutic milieus, it was also a possible source of retrograde defensiveness, as was seen in the way that conservative norms around abortion and gender could also be inscribed into the emergent psychosociality of Olessia's Systemic Constellations session.

This vibration among fear and connection and possibility and danger is also an aspect of what I have been calling precarious care. In its most specific sense, of course, *precarity* refers to the unstable and temporary nature of employment and daily life that characterizes contemporary labor markets (see Standing 2011). Recently, Judith Butler (2010), Anne Allison (2013), and others have also extended the concept to an existential register—precariousness: as the means of survival are rendered increasingly precarious, so, too, is daily life colored by anxiousness, fear, and uncertainty. Despite the efforts to constitute social connection in Russia—through psychotherapy or otherwise—precarity and precariousness continue to shape conservative and market-friendly ideas about value, social life, and fellow feeling. Precarity and the concomitant desire for stabil'nost' has also been productive of a rising tolerance for increased security. Referring to political institutions, the economy, and the rules of daily life, the desire for stabil'nost', present in some form at least since perestroika, has intensified under Putin. It is now mobilized as part of a broader politics of quiescence that also justifies political domination by threat: "stability under me, or else." The implied threat is a return to the tumultuous 1990s, which most remember as being lawless, chaotic, and even shameful.[14]

In her research in Moscow, Russian sociologist Olga Shevchenko (2009) also found an abundance of discussions of stability in daily life. She characterizes the postsocialist condition as defined by the discourse and practices of "total crises" (2) Likened to "living on a volcano" life required "unceasing labor of remaining attuned to what could be the ominous rumblings of coming calamity" (8). "Change . . . was almost never a good thing" (8). Her informants' nervousness about change was so intense that faring well in the postsocialist period was not the mark of achievement. "Rather, they praised themselves for being successful in the preservation of their families' peace and well-being, a preservation which, could, of course, bring unforeseen and pleasant advances, but which was valuable primarily for its own sake. *Improvement was a by-product; stability was what counted most*" (8; emphasis mine). She identifies two proving grounds for finding stability: domesticity and the assertion of autonomy and competence.

The desire for stability in the face of precarity thus has a deeply conservative aspect. And in the scope of psychosociality, it can be rather limiting, leading those interested in social transformation to paradoxically accept the status quo in the name of overthrowing it, and producing what Shevchenko calls, in another context, "an incentive for creating defensive institutions" (2009, 14). To the point: in 2010 in a *New York Times* commentary on the occasion of the twenty-fifth anniversary of perestroika, Mikhail Gorbachev remarked, "What's holding Russia back is fear. Among both the people and the authorities, there is concern that a new round of modernization might lead to instability and even chaos. In politics, fear is a bad guide; we must overcome it" (2010).

Traversing Hierarchies of Value

I end this chapter with a portrait of Nikolai because the tension between the noncommodified and the commodified, between sociality and individualism, between pleasure and fear, was particularly evident in the ways he explained his work to me. At stake for him, it seemed, was a desire to constitute psychosociality in ways that would subvert its capture as capital and its rendering in particular gendered orders. Nonetheless, his efforts continually ran up against those very hegemonic processes. Ultimately, at issue for Nikolai was a fundamental question: what is value?[15]

Nikolai was extremely generous with his time with me. He was about my age, spoke some English, and was eager to meet with me and learn about what I was seeing in Saint Petersburg. In our conversations his dilemma around value was particularly apparent. For him, value was challenged by a tension around turning the politico-ethical project of garmoniia into a commodity, and by a particular gender-class configuration—in this case, one in which masculinity and entrepreneurial success were aligned. These two contexts, ironically, seemed to push a man interested in harmonious relations in the direction of instrumental forms of work, as well as social isolation.

Our first meeting took place in Nikolai's office, which sat in the back of a labyrinthine renovated building in the city center. Its interior was, I thought later, a kind of a material manifestation of the ongoing efforts to reconstitute life from within the ruins of state socialism. The building seemed to have joined together several structures built at different times. A complex system of arrows for navigating its halls and levels was tacked to the concrete walls.

Over our many conversations, Nikolai made it clear that the vector system was not only something he tried to teach others but also an analytic lens he used to understand his own life's potential. Especially in our early meetings, Nikolai described himself as possessing a "high genetic potential" in the urethral vector—a clear sign of leadership and hot-headedness. Keen to assure me (and perhaps also himself) of the explanatory power of his theory, he would at times make grand claims, asserting that his vector system was universally applicable and could help people understand themselves and others, bring them success in love and money, and even bring about world peace. His desire to succeed was apparent: he asked me what modifications would be necessary to sell this system in the United States. Would it be possible to join the faculty of a university? How much money did psychologists make in the United States? Would people pay to come to his workshops? This assertiveness carried over to his seminars, where he would try to attract clients by conjuring the image of a shaman with X-ray vision, who could see into the dark recesses of the psyche. Only through his expertise, he implied, could his clients come to terms with themselves and harmonize their social relations.

In one conversation I asked him whether a harmonious person could be recognized as such. "He is completely sure of himself [*on dovolen soboi*]," he replied. "He is happy with himself, comfortable, harmonious; he doesn't fall into depression from some kind of failure; he knows what he wants. Second, he has the ability to build harmonious relations with his surroundings—with the family, work, business, and so on."

In another conversation he told me that since "money [is a] a variant of energiia," there could also be something called "money garmoniia," whereby the same energy that flowed within and between people also flowed through relations structured by money and sexual desire. The harmonious disposition of these relations could lead to all kinds of success, he said. In short, Nikolai's interest in harmoniousness was at times overwhelmed by instrumental concerns, just as it was in Lara's story of the police incident.

Nonetheless, alongside his efforts to build a trening business, another story remained. Referring to his experience during perestroika, Nikolai told me how, after attempting several failed business ventures and falling into depression, he resolved to leave Russia and go to Europe. He recounted a dramatic scene in which he said goodbye to his family and drove to the border. Then, while stuck in line, he had a revelation. "I suddenly felt free," he told me. "I realized I did not need to leave Russia, and that what was important to me was not money but what's inside." He returned home. The path that followed was premised on resignifying his past. He described how, as a child, he had been routinely abused by his teachers. "Imagine the boy," he said, "to whom a teacher says,

'You are nobody.' This boy will develop many psychological problems. For the rest of his life, he will feel that professional success is the way to overcome this feeling of inadequacy. . . . This is not the path to harmony."

I sometimes worried that Nikolai was reading between the lines of my questions and telling me what I wanted to hear. But I later learned that he was offering free sessions for Saint Petersburg's teachers to help them better understand their students and, ultimately, respect them. Over our meetings, the two sides of Nikolai—the salesman and the social worker—could seem to be in tension. One day he announced he had decided to change his professional priorities; he had become more interested in giving harmony to others than in chasing corporate clients. Psychological training in Russia, he said, had become an instrument of manipulation, not connection. He gave Olessia's experiences as an example. "She wanted to teach women about their bodies, their senses, their sexuality, feeling more comfortable with themselves, but all they wanted to know was how to manipulate their husbands." Statements like these remained tempered, however, by a gendered understanding of accomplishment. He admitted that Olessia had been making more money for Verity than he, and that this made him feel ashamed. He then boasted that Verity had won an account in a competition with four other firms and was then given the opportunity to assess several midlevel managers. This probably led to their firing, however. He then quickly changed the subject back to his desire to shift his emphasis away from corporate work. On another occasion, he laid out a general critique of those who would define their garmoniia in relation to success: "Every achievement opens a vista onto a new level of achievement. What makes a person finally harmonious is the realization 'I'm human.' It's at this point that he may find some sense of garmoniia inside himself and with others."

These conversations took place over several years. They reflected Nikolai's sense of his work as much as the particular ways in which we came to know each other between 2005 and 2012. Nonetheless, they indicated to me a challenging, and familiar, struggle among various social identities in a market economy. This struggle seemed to produce in Nikolai an ambivalence toward his psychological work, his homeland, and its shared future. It was an ambivalence that remained unresolved. He spent most of our early time together trying to convince me that his system was capable of solving personal, social, and even geopolitical problems, but when I met with him again years later, I found a person questioning everything. "With the vector system," he confessed, "if you have a problem in your life, it's your fault. But with [the new system I'm studying], it's not your fault." At least partly for economic reasons, Nikolai had been reconsidering the nature of value and well-being—things that he, apparently, had difficulty harmonizing in Russia's market.

And Yet: Domesticating Psychosociality

Nikolai and Olessia, like their colleagues at ReGeneration, seemed trapped within the language of success and self-promotion. The social promise of therapy was haunted by its capture as capital. As is often the case with affective economies, the capaciousness of energiia, dusha, and garmoniia also made them consistent with the spectral nature of what Karl Marx famously called "the social hieroglyphic" (1990, 167)—the commodity. On receiving my payment for her psychological training course, held in her living room with just a handful of close friends, Valya, a former psychotherapist from the PPMS Center, beamed: "When you pay a lot of money for something, it means you really value it. Your money—it's like energiia; you're giving me your energiia." Indeed, even in Olessia's systemic constellation seminar, many of the symptoms that clients had seemed only tangentially related to family problems. Instead, participants sought help in figuring out which career to choose, whether to follow what was good for their soul or what was good for their wallet, whether to uproot themselves from their community in search of a job. The range of issues, focused as they were on questions about work and money, suggests that energiia, an affective resource for social effervescence, was also an idiom for navigating the market society. Psychotherapists, then, could just as easily channel this willful energiia, as a kind of capacitation, into the invisible hand of the market, a force known only through its emergence via the choices of self-interested subjects.

Others also invoked energiia as a force that could be harnessed for mastery over both self and other. One therapist explained that whereas fear inhibits people by making them less confident and unhappy, learning how to channel energiia was often discussed as a way forward. Nikolai spoke a lot about "the rule of moving energiia in human relations" and often suggested that if one learned to master this rule, various forms of good fortune—financial, social, sexual—would follow. He mentioned something called a "pendulum" of "special psychic energiia": "When many [people] want something [at the same time], they provide a special energiia to a pendulum" that can make things happen. He added, "Many people in our life want to take our energiia through making rules. One must destroy one's connection to those people." Energiia was thus also a sensitive and valuable commodity, subject to imbalance, disturbance, and corruption. The centers of conflict in the world are places where there is "a diversion of energiia from its realization."

This gets at a critique of psychotherapy more generally. That is, in helping clients to accept who they are without interrogating the cultural patterns, forms of knowledge, and relationships that may have led them there, psychotherapy may reproduce relations of inequality. Perhaps one of the greatest ironies was that, in envisioning his own successful future, Nikolai, who spoke so often about harmonious relations spreading across Russian society, sometimes dreamed of himself sitting alone somewhere, on a beach, communicating his ideas to the world through his laptop.

Conclusion: Psychosociality beyond Security

This chapter began with two questions: What do we make of the fact that the clients in the systemic constellation seminar were seeking capacitation through displacement—first onto the body of another, who stood in as a substitute, and then into an ineffable power? What role did relations of kin and history play in the sense making of, and for, the self? Energiia, dusha, and garmoniia, I argued, are idioms of psychosociality that Nikolai, Olessia, and others mobilized as a kind of social proxy. Crucial to their efficacy as social forms was the coproduction and circulation of affect. Psychological therapy in Russia has not, therefore, been a solipsistic process, but rather a mode of social engagement and a struggle with social difference and distinction. It is also a site for examining how personal growth and/or socially meaningful work ought to be related to exchange value. "Growth" here involved an "aspirational normativity" (Allison 2013, 47) in which a future fantasy was premised on an increasingly elusive middle-class life, reproducing a structure of feeling that Lauren Berlant (2011) calls "cruel optimism." Market conditions thus shaped, but did not always determine, the terms by which sociality was negotiated and produced through self-work.[16] Not quite radical, these practices were nevertheless politico-ethical. If the polluting influence of the commodity was part of the terrain in which "the self" became a socially relevant ethical substance, it was not encompassing. As Michael Jackson (2011, ix) puts it, human well-being is not a "settled state" but a "field of struggle."

To say that the therapeutic turn has resulted in psychosociality does not necessarily challenge the critique of psychotherapeutic practices and their role in reproducing class difference. That particular effect is clear enough and was discussed at length in part II. Yet through a greater understanding of the key concepts used by psychologists, psychotherapists, and social workers, the social significance of psychological work as something happening in Russia becomes clearer, I think. This chapter also echoes earlier arguments in this book about how expertise is not primarily a matter of *transmitting* some political rationality (neoliberal, socialist, etc.) but is negotiated in practice at the intersection of a series of situated choices, dreams, actions, and normative frameworks. Such choices, dreams, and actions have implications for the ways in which one life is made more valuable than another, and they are unquestionably ordered in particular ways, mediating selfhood and the production of gender inequalities. At the same time, the search for psychosociality also demonstrates a continuous interrogation of the terms of that mediation. Along the way, these psychotherapists and their clients asked themselves, what is most important in life? How shall I live? In that sense, energiia's decentralized form of self-orientation contained tools for questioning some of the models of successful life that were in circulation in urban Russia.

Expertise is thus both a means of domination and a situated ethical practice—a practice by which one establishes a relation to oneself in and through modalities of power. Foucault (1997b, 225) writes that practical ethics "permits individuals to effect by their own means or with the help of others, a certain number of operations on their own bodies and souls, thoughts, conduct, and way of being" in order to transform themselves into the willing subjects of a particular moral discourse. The analytic promise of situated subjects for anthropology is that an ethical practice can, at the same time, push toward desubjugation. Here the Foucauldian "limit-attitude" is operative, by which one constantly presses beyond that which one is told one is. Lambek (2008) has pointed out that a focus on ordinary ethics may also offer anthropologists a way to write against the hegemonic commensurability of virtue and value.

This notion of a practical ethics has descriptive force in considering Olessia's and Nikolai's efforts to constitute psychosociality. It highlights the interplay between biopolitical norms and ethical practices, and the ways in which ideas about human association were actively discussed in psychotherapeutic contexts. Investigating the relationship between biopolitics and ethics is a way to trace the relationships of subordination as well as the conditions of possibility in any politics of living. They are "experimental," in the way Lisa Rofel describes, in that they took place "in a multi-dimensional and shifting field of interpretive practices" (2007, 23).

Energiia, I suggested, offered a way to reckon with the past and family history. Garmoniia was something psychotherapists used to articulate a link between the social world and the inward turn through psychological reflection. Dusha provided people with a language for interrogating the supposed link between value and economy. All of these idioms circulated in settings premised on intensely intimate relations—places where complete strangers might, after just a few hours, feel an unparalleled form of closeness. And yet all of these idioms were bedeviled. Binary gender norms, the moral sanctions against abortion, the hegemonic association between growth and financial success—these surfaced periodically, disturbing the smooth surface of improved social relations.

I view the contestation between these forms of striving and bedevilment as nascent political forms that indicate some of the idioms, ideas, and aims—for better and for worse—that this particular community expressed in its search for a form of political subjectivity. They indicate a politics in search of the social, as well as a form of sociality that has, as yet, only a loosely defined politics. Their nascence notwithstanding, they are also undeniably possible critical sources for commonality and solidarity in the face of Putin's neo-authoritarian turn.

In the next chapter I turn from a consideration of human association to the question of what kind of political body is being imagined through psychotherapeutic means. I draw on an analysis of a radio show called *For Adults about Adults* and describe how the host used psychological thinking to outline a civic public premised on new forms of public intimacy—a public that was met, nonetheless, with suspicion.

Chapter 6

"HELLO, LENA, YOU ARE ON THE AIR"

Talk-Show Selves and the Dream of Public Intimacy

The woman cooking cabbage. The man who wishes he could be done with
drink. They are the game's remoter soul. Connected by the pulsing voice on
the radio, joined to the word-of-mouth that passes the score along the street
and to the fans who call the special phone number and the crowd at the
ballpark that becomes the picture on television, people the size of minute
rice, and the game as rumor and conjecture and inner history.

—Don DeLillo, *Underworld*

I don't want to call the broadcast, but I want to talk about my phobia. It's a fear
of death, fear of the unknown, what comes next. I think that many have this.

—Sergei, text message to the Echo of Moscow, July 2, 2005

The rise of the talk show, or *tok-shou*, in Russia has been impressive. Beginning with perestroika in the mid-1980s, and accelerating with the arrival of
the market economy, talk shows now occupy a central place on Russian TV
and radio.[1] Part of their attraction resides in what Michael Warner (2002,
168) terms the "appeal of mass subjectivity," where by entering the uncanny
feedback of a mass public—that place where radio callers hear themselves
hearing themselves as the host asks them to turn down the dial in the other
room—audience members can experience the fantastic contradiction of
being embodied and self-abstracted simultaneously.[2] But talk shows are also
popular in Russia because they offer audiences a chance to speak and be
heard at a time when there continues to be much to say about politics, the
economy, and everyday struggles. This chapter is about the emergence of a
new style of post-Soviet talk show—one that offered its callers and listeners
psychological advice—and the political work it does. It takes up a concept

that has been lurking in the background of the other chapters—neoliberal governmentality—and investigates the ways in which, by disseminating neoliberal-like techniques of the self and organizing listeners into live publics, the talk show articulated a political vision of the self and a normative public.[3]

The television programs airing at the start of my fieldwork in 2005 revealed that psychotherapeutic expertise had risen to a place of prominence in the studio.[4] Consider Channel One's daytime lineup: on the program *Lolita: Without Complexes* (*Lolita: Bez Kompleksov*), where the pop singer Lolita Miliavskaia aimed to "discard the masks that hidden feelings lurk behind" and help guests "change their lives," "professional psychologists and psychotherapists are always present to give . . . concrete advice and help them to find the path out of their most hopeless situations." In the slot just prior, on *Understand. Forgive.* (*Poniat'. Prostit'.*), the guest entered the spotlighted office of two psychotherapists and was given not only a consultation but an expanded investigation of her life, including televised visits to her home, her work, and "those places where conflict happens." "It's not just an office visit, but many meetings, many conversations, a concrete problem and its real resolution. The reconstructive story of the cure of a patient takes place on one program."[5] One of the most successful hosts of this genre was the psychotherapist Andrei Kurpatov, a household name among practitioners and laypeople, whose Channel One show, immodestly titled *We Will Solve Everything with Doctor Kurpatov* (*Vse Reshim s Doktorom Kurpatovym*), was the first to open the therapeutic session to viewers. Seated opposite his guest, the "pale youth with the burning gaze" (Stepanova 2006) provided couples therapy and treated irrational phobias.

Such programs, distinctly post-Soviet in their emphasis on mass-mediated personal disclosure, composed 13 percent of the weekday broadcast minutes between nine o'clock in the morning and nine o'clock at night on Russia's five main channels at the time (Channel One, 5, NTV, Domashnii, Rossiia). More strikingly, during those hours the chances were one in four that the state-run Channel One was airing an advice talk show.[6] As an *Izvestiia* writer put it in 2006, "Channel One has taken the healing of the population seriously" (Petrovskaia 2006).

The emphasis on psychotherapy on talk shows in those years is another important part of the complex story I have traced in this book about how the new forms of psychotherapeutic care have unfolded at the intersection of market forces, biopolitics, and the desires of the expert. This chapter approaches the talk show as a lens onto what a psychologically sensitive public might have looked like during the early Putin period, a period which is ongoing. I focus in particular on a radio talk show, *For Adults about Adults* (*Vzroslym o Vzroslykh*), hosted by psychologist Mikhail Labkovsky, and show how the program became a staging ground for various conceptions of political life. One such conception is that of a neoliberal governmentality.[7] In offering advice, Labkovsky deployed techniques of the self, like self-esteem, as well as a proposed reinscription of relations of intimacy that resonated with the autonomous forms of civil association promoted in neoliberal policies (Cruikshank 1999; Donzelot 1979; Rose 1996a, 1996b). His vision was also reinforced performatively and in virtual form by the synergistic combination of psychotherapy and the media. The voice speaking its woes on the air sutured together subject and public, constantly (re)fusing the boundaries between interior and exterior in a way that is consistent with neoliberalism's dispersed governmental energy.

And yet Labkovsky's advice was also multivalent. While much of what he prescribed resonated with a neoliberal governmentality, he was less interested in shaping his listeners into rational-choice actors than into particular kinds of postsocialist liberal citizens. Using the psychological as a staging ground, he advocated a vision of a new kind of public in Russia—one premised on respect, freedom, and civility. In many respects, Labkovsky's advice straddled a divide between political and economic liberalisms.[8] Finally, another political conception was apparent in the way that callers responded to Labkovsky's prescriptions. Many were outright resistant to, even offended by, his social commentaries. Their critical engagements proposed other postsocialist solutions to personal problems, along with other understandings of selfhood, intimacy, and politics—that is, ideas in which socialist values were perceptible but also transformed by the logics of market conditions. This political multivalence, I argue, is a good indicator of some of the discourses shaping political subjectivity in Russia. Caught between differing conceptions of liberalism and democracy, persisting socialist ideals, and the lessons of everyday experience, callers and host together brought into relief Russia's complex political landscape.

Labkovsky's show also offers clues about how projects that may appear in one sense to be neoliberalizing actually articulate with other political rationalities to produce novel formations. This multivalence is helpful for analyzing the nature of liberalism in Russia, which often appears contradictory; that is, *liberalism* in reference to a political stance remains a dirty word in Russia, while neoliberal rhetoric surfaces in federal pronouncements pertaining to economic policy and the development of enterprising persons. A close attention to the exchanges on *For Adults about Adults* suggests that we need to think about *liberal assemblages* that combine and recombine a range of technologies and rationalities (welfarist, advanced/neoliberal) with other political orientations.[9]

Ultimately, this chapter shows how psychotherapeutic ideas were used to imagine political life at the start of Putin's second term. Psychotherapeutic advice was a form of care that seemed to provide a thoroughgoing model, including ideas about the interior of the citizen, his or her intimate relations, and the kinds of publics appropriate to postsocialist times. Nevertheless, Labkovsky's psychotherapeutically inspired, egalitarian, liberal-progressive vision of a future Russia appeared to serve Putin's call to sacrifice all for the economy. In a context in which the neoliberal economy is divorced from liberal-democratic politics, one is left with neoliberalism without liberals, a situation that may characterize contemporary capitalism more generally and that testifies to the flexible promiscuity and discursive power of austerity.[10]

For Adults about Adults

For Adults about Adults aired on the politically liberal, private, nationally broadcast radio station the Echo of Moscow (Ekho Moskvy).[11] The show aired from 2004 until it was taken off the air on September 1, 2012, in response to a conservative law on the protection of children.[12] During its eight years, the program was a clearinghouse for personal problems, a place to hear the sad details of the alcoholic's life, to be amused by the pugnacious pensioner, to find something that might be usefully applied to one's own life, and perhaps even to call and enter the media stream. In the hands of Labkovsky, the sympathetic host with the soporific voice, the chaos of life could seem momentarily calmed, secured by advice that was as consistent as the program's regularly scheduled slot, Saturday night from ten o'clock to midnight.[13]

Labkovsky was educated at Moscow State University and also collaborated with the Canadian Family Mediation Practice. His political views on issues such as sexuality, gender norms, and child-rearing were liberal-progressive. Drawing on the psychotherapeutic sensibility of American humanistic psychology, he offered his callers a hopeful perspective on their problems: no matter what the problem—dependence, lack of confidence, dispossession, overwork, domestic abuse—change can begin within oneself.

Labkovsky's program was organized thematically, and its topics generally concerned either family life (children and divorce, marriage problems, property and gender relations, alcoholism, mental illness) or personal issues (self-transformation, mental health, feelings of unfulfillment, psychological dependence, fear). The four months of shows I analyzed aired in the first half of 2005 and included over five hundred calls and text messages from men and women of diverse ages (three women for every two men).[14] The average stated age was forty-eight for female callers and thirty-seven for male callers, but there were also many calls from pensioners and students. As for socioeconomic status, while it is generally assumed that psychotherapy is an elite activity, the data suggest that the program drew listeners of diverse backgrounds: of those who provided adequate information to permit a guess, a slim majority described themselves as somewhere between working and middle class, owning property and living well enough to have some disposable income, but not without financial woes (43 percent). Slightly fewer were poor, describing dire living conditions (40 percent). Finally, 17 percent were relatively wealthy, mentioning multiple properties, managerial positions, businesses, and travel.

A slate of recent reforms was at the front of callers' minds at the time. On January 1, 2005, pensioners, veterans, and others with a privileged social status in the USSR saw their social benefits (e.g., free rides on public transit) monetized. More details on the legal process of privatizing an apartment were issued, stirring anxieties about housing that stretched back through the housing shortages, shoddy construction, and expropriation and communalization of the Soviet period. In March a new law was ratified allowing people to create housing associations and select alternatives to state-provided maintenance services. A revised family codex amended the rules for the division of assets in case of divorce, as well as procedures related to child visitation and child custody. Together, these reforms reflected Putin's hallmark mix of neoliberal-type social policies and ongoing centralization of state power. They also introduced new uncertainties into the management of life, rolling back decades of state social support and services, introducing new opportunities for citizen initiative, and transforming kinship formations.

Labkovsky's dual expertise in psychology and the law facilitated a discussion of problems at the seam of the personal and the political. Following suit, many treated the program as a place to ask questions, to express worry, to vent, or just to be heard. "I want to say that no one belongs to the world now [*mir seichas nikomu ne prinadlezhit*]. Neither the young, nor the old," said Tatiana (May 7, 2005, caller 9). Another complained, "In the last fifteen years, millions have left Russia. No one is needed other than floozies, oil workers, and street sweepers" (April 16, 2005, caller 3). And Valentina said, "For me it started in 1992 when all stability crumbled, when organizations started to fall apart, when there was nothing to eat, my husband took to the bottle from grief [*muzh zapil s goria*], and there were two children who needed to be fed, and there really was no time to think about defining who should do what. . . . We fell out of socialism, and no one could get used to capitalism" (July 9, 2005, caller 30).

Labkovsky assisted his listeners in getting used to things—depression and divorce but also capitalism and new laws—by recommending psychological techniques. These techniques had an expansive quality, triggering the rearrangement of relations of intimacy and assembling those relations into particular social formations that were addressed to not only personal but also political problems. Finally, Labkovsky prescribed methods for conflict resolution and norms of politeness that produced a particular vision of Russian civil society. In the pages below I first elaborate on the nature of these techniques, focusing on self-esteem and self-possession, and the way private property relations appear to have been "folded in," in the Deleuzean sense, to create subjectivities with a particular sense of possessive interiority.[15] I track, in particular, the slippage between Labkovsky's political liberalism and the forms that neoliberalism has been described as taking on the surface of the self. Next, I examine how, by bringing intimate relations into psychological grids of perception, the techniques also ordered a particular kind of public and politics. This normative public resembled a civil society, of which the radio program, as a mass public, became a virtual version. Finally, I turn to the social problems frustrating the construction of the neoliberal subject and the liberal-democratic public. Despite Labkovsky's orientation to a psychotherapeutically mediated individualism, many callers contested his political vision, offering glimpses of competing ideas about the political in Russia, as well as the place of psychotherapeutic knowledge in those visions.

The Echo of the Self: Talk-Show Technologies

On March 5, 2005, Labkovsky greeted listeners this way:

My friends, if we are asked today what we are unsatisfied with in our lives, then there will be many calls, and much dissatisfaction. Many organizations studying public opinion talk about what percentage of the population is dissatisfied with pension reforms, with the housing law, with the president, with the government. I want to ask a different question. What would you change in yourself if you could? [*Shto by vy izmenili v sebe, esli by u vas byla takaia vozmozhnost'?*] . . . Usually we search in our own way [*svoistvenno*] in our surroundings. It's not constructive and generally ineffective in the sense that nothing changes in our lives; nothing is added to it besides gradual irritation [*postoianno rasstroistvo*] about the fact that we don't like our surroundings. And if we ask the question in this way, "What would we change in ourselves?" then it gets interesting.

In the face of political disenfranchisement, a felt inability to "get used to capitalism," and a host of other problems, Labkovsky was inviting his callers to consider another kind of solution: self-transformation.

The volume of responses was the highest of any program analyzed—some eighty calls and text messages in two hours:

I want to change my internal world and how I think.
I want to feel less worried when alone.
I want to be less affected by rudeness.
I want to be less lazy.
I want to be less defensive and stop covering up my inadequacies with snobbishness.
I want to learn to shut my big mouth.
I want to be less angry.
How can I be less hypochondriac?
How can I develop love of self?
How can I learn to say "no" without worrying about disappointing others?
I want to love others even more.
I want to escape this emptiness.
I want to reach my artistic potential.
I want to be able to self-regulate.
I want to know how to live.
I want to lose weight.
I want to be taller.
I'd like to become the governor.
I'd like to change my name to Aleksandr—Aleksandrs are more effective in life.

Like cosmic dust orbiting a black hole, call after call brought out the features of an invisible gravitational center, the self. In inviting his listeners to consider self-transformation, Labkovsky wasn't just making a common psychothera-peutic suggestion; he was also initiating them into thinking of everyday prob-lems in a particular, self-centered way. As the list above makes clear, the self could be many things: an internal world to be changed; a thing to be coaxed to perform in order to achieve something; a locus of worry, insult, defensiveness, or anger; a domain requiring control in the face of external challenges; a site of potential action where one can train oneself in something; a store of desires to be other than what one is; a container for normative values. What is impor-tant is that through the simple question "How would you change yourself?," the self became an it.

Labkovsky's concern was not with specifically defining the self but rather positing it as something to which one relates, whatever it is. His concern was a technology, which involved the proper attitude, or relation, to one's self, which he often defined as a relation of esteem, or *samootsenka*.[16] As a practice, samo-otsenka relied on a differentiation between interior and exterior domains, and careful mediation between them. Thus, samootsenka was, first, a matter of proper orientation: a self-esteeming person should look to himself or herself when faced with a problem. The lack of samootsenka, Labkovsky explained to a caller named Alexei (January 15, 2005, caller 15), is "when a person is not ori-ented to himself but to the opinion of others." Second, samootsenka emanates outward into the world; it can have effects, such as increasing (or decreasing) the respect one receives from others. As Labkovsky told Nikolai (January 1, 2005, caller 11), "When you love yourself, then you look at the surrounding world the way you look at yourself, and, correspondingly, if you don't love yourself, then that also flows from you. You produce the impression of a person with problems, who is unsuccessful, who has complexes [*cheloveka problem-nogo, neudachnogo, zakompleksovannogo*], and due to that, correspondingly, there will be many problems."

Putting these techniques into practice, Labkovsky's samootsenka could then overcome a range of problems, including a lack of confidence, domestic disputes, and addiction. For example, in a call from sixty-seven-year-old Larissa Konstantinovna, samootsenka was a way to be liberated from the op-pressive judgment of others. A man had recently asked her to marry him, La-rissa Konstantinovna explained, and she questioned Labkovsky's advice that people should live together before marriage. "Understand, I am a teacher at a college, and I am a social person, to a degree. Immediately it will become known. We'll start to live together, and then it won't work out, and everyone will know. . . . I am afraid of what Maria Nikolaevna will say" (January 15, 2005, caller 2).

Labkovsky retorted unsympathetically that if she was "more interested in Maria Nikolaevna," then she needed to forget about the boyfriend and "live in order to gather impressions about [herself] and [her] surroundings." He continued, "And don't allude to the difficult Soviet period, when this kind of thing was impossible. Now you can allow yourself [to do this] if you wish. So allow it. And try to live together." "One more curious detail," he added, "there is this understanding, samootsenka, are you familiar with it? . . . So, samoot-senka is how you value yourself. You are reasoning as a person who has no samootsenka. That is, your respect is based on the evaluation of others. Feel the difference [*pochuvstvuite raznitsu*]. It's better if you yourself investigate whether it's good or bad. In evaluating your life you are not resorting to your own values, but to what you think others think."

"But that's how we were raised. [*My tak vospitany.*]"

"Well, Larissa Konstantinovna, well, give it up, you're not at an interroga-tion. What does 'raised' mean? You are your own boss. [*Vy sami sebe khozi-aika*]. 'We were raised this way' or 'We are a product of a certain time . . .' You are completely, I would say, a little cunning. You can do it if you want to."

In a Foucauldian moment, it is the host who most fervently asserts Larissa Konstantinovna's autonomy, who appeals to her inner reserves, who rejects the idea that she is a product of a certain time, who encourages her to take time to learn about herself, and, finally, who tells her, in a complex phrase, "Vy sami sebe khoziaika," that she herself is the governor or master of herself. This demonstrates how samootsenka works as a political technology. As Barbara Cruikshank has noted in her study of the self-esteem movement in the United States, "by isolating a self to act upon, to appreciate and to esteem, we avail ourselves of a terrain of action, we exercise power upon ourselves" (1996, 234). The exercise of power upon oneself, even a liberatory power, is a form of sub-jectivation situated in relations of power.

It is worth lingering a little longer over the term *khoziaika* (proprietress, or owner)—and *khoziaistvo*, the implicit internal domain over which one ought to be a master—because it hints at the specificity of those relations of power and the terrain of action that samootsenka involves. Caroline Humphrey has linked the cultural concept khoziaika to a discourse of political power in Rus-sia according to which "socio-political order is brought about by the exercise of centralized and personified power, not by law, the observance of principles, or the existence of civil society" (2002, 28). In other words, people "seek order not *in* themselves but *for* themselves, that is, from powers [*vlasti*] conceived as above" (29). Humphrey's contention casts samootsenka, which in this context would mean, "You're not a slave to anyone," in an interesting light. Specifically, it suggests that it involves an *internalization of external authority*, which is then exercised over oneself.

This form of samootsenka also appears to invert its socialist counterpart.[17] Oleg Kharkhordin (1999) notes that in the Soviet self-training literature, *samootsenka* meant not "self-esteem" but "self-*evaluation*" and was the first step toward becoming a better communist. One was supposed to take stock of oneself as compared to the ideal of the New Soviet Man in order to recognize one's deficiencies and prepare the way for self-compulsion (*samoprinuzhdenie*), enacted through particular ways of training the will (*volia*). In this process, so-called pointless self-rummaging (*samokopanie*) was to be avoided. Rather, through training the will, one would come to a state of self-control and self-possession (*samoobladanie*). All of this, Kharkhordin argues, was aimed at "a transformation of the self that would make self-sacrifice possible" (241–55), or what Oushakine calls the "self under erasure—the void subject" (2004, 395). In contrast, Labkovsky's model of samootsenka urged listeners to *ignore* social judgment in forming a view of themselves and the world, thus changing the source of authority from the collective to the ideology of the autonomous subject. It also shifted the object of self-work from the will to feelings, and the technique from one of explicitly normative comparison to self-knowledge (which is, of course, normative in its own, implicit way). Finally, he offered listeners an alternate telos of self-realization, replacing self-control and self-sacrifice with a kind of eternal self-return.

In light of discussions of property, Labkovsky's assertions that his listeners should heed only their own inner voices took on a possessive relation to the self, suggesting a resonance between Labkovsky's samootsenka and postsocialist discourses of property.[18] Recall C. B. Macpherson's (1962) concept of possessive individualism, which argues that the property form instantiates the idea that what a person owns, in the first instance, is himself or herself. This ontological sense of self, according to Macpherson, derives from the a priori of private property as a natural right, which is "read back into the nature of the individual" (3). As this particular relation to self takes root in liberalism, he argues, ownership comes to ground freedom itself and the realization of one's potential. Citizens come to feel that not just possession but also self-possession is the precondition for both their freedom and even their humanity. Being a free individual, for MacPherson, means being the "proprietor of his own person and capacities, for which he owes nothing to society" (263). And what makes us essentially human is "freedom from dependence on the wills of others," a freedom that "is a function of possession" (3).

For Adults about Adults was filled with examples where property concerns were enfolded, constituting this particular notion of, and relation to, the self. Obsessively technical legal questions about property law (often exasperating the host) and the *lack* of property expressed the link between property and selfhood.[19] That is, the threat of *dispossession,* itself a harrowing and painful experience many in Russia had suffered throughout the last century, appeared to link sympathetically the status of one's material khoziaistvo to the status of one's self-as-khoziaistvo. As Humphrey (2002, 21) notes, dispossession strikes at personhood because it strips a person not just of their possessions but also of their social status, a dual fear that Labkovsky's callers frequently cited, especially in calls where kin had competing claims to property. In many cases, anxieties around gender appeared in instances where only one spouse owned the apartment. These calls prompted Labkovsky to formulate his samootsenka model in terms of a more explicit form of possessive individualism, but the calls also seemed to flow from that model of subjectivity.

In a call from Vladimir (May 28, 2005, caller 35), for example, we learn that the opportunity to privatize the family's municipal apartment has created a conflict. He and his mother are registered there. Presented with the option to legally reconstitute the apartment as property (and therefore to really own it), his mother has decided she'd like to privatize it in her own name (which depends on Vladimir waiving his right) in order to bequeath it to both him and his sister, who currently has no rights to it. "My mom," he said, "wants to convince me that she will distribute everything fairly."

"Well, Vladimir, here it's up to you," Labkovsky replied, taking an almost parental tone. "I can't give you advice about how to act; you need to decide yourself. Because we are not talking about the fact that after the death of your father an inheritance was created, but about the fact that two registered people remain in the apartment, one of whom wants to privatize it for themselves so that the other registered person will be refused their right to property in this apartment. How you should act is for you to decide. I can't give you advice. If you refuse [to privatize], you are automatically stripped of your right to this apartment. That is, you will be registered there, but nothing more. You will not be an owner."[20] (See figure 6.1.)

"And if my mother transfers everything . . ."

FIGURE 6.1. "You will not be an owner." The privatization of municipal housing that Labkovsky describes led to a variety of interesting new practices, some of which were visible from the street. This image shows the effects of one resident's decision to renew the exterior paint of his or her balcony. Photo by the author.

"Yes," said Labkovsky, "she can will it to your sister, and nothing will be left for you, for example."

Appreciating the stakes, Vladimir knows that in relinquishing his right to privatize, he would be in a sense owned by his mother, affecting not only his property but his identity. "And what does it mean then if my sister demands that I leave? I leave, and then I end up homeless [*bomzh*]?"

"The decision is yours to make," Labkovsky said a third time, emphasizing that Vladimir, too, is his own boss.

Fifty-four-year-old Tatiana, in contrast, described her successful ownership in terms that suggest not only her sense of self-possession but also her ability to structure others into relations of dependence. "I settled my own housing question, so that I have, excuse me, a well-deserved [*dostoinaia*] apartment just under eighty [square] meters. I can be in charge of it from now on [*dal'she rasporiazhat'sia*] so that I will have some inheritance for [my children] and hold them like flies on a string" (May 7, 2005, caller 9).

There were many examples where privatization and psychotherapeutic techniques were enfolded to constitute a sense of self: the man wondering when he is truly free of his ex-wife given that the property he attained after the divorce was obtained with some portion of their money; the husband who feels himself a victim for having been bilked out of ownership by his own wife; the divorced father who asked, "How shall we divide the child?" The constitution of the esteemed, possessed self appeared throughout the program, including in programs about addiction, dependence, divorce, domestic disputes, and communication. Samootsenka thus grounded an ethics by which one should decide for oneself. In and through this practical ethics, and its constitution of the self as a territorial domain and a locus of control, it also constituted what we might think of as a privatized self. As will become clear in the next section, this privatized self became, through Labkovsky's liberalism, the site of political action.

Political Intimacy and Publics

The critique is often made that techniques like self-esteem have no politics. Yet it is clear from Labkovsky's program that self-esteem was a profoundly political matter. Recall the program on "changing yourself." Referencing the bad habit of complaining about politics but not doing anything to change things, Labkovsky proposed that his listeners consider redirecting their political dissatisfaction to self-transformation. He suggested that since the only thing that complaining about our surroundings will accomplish is our "gradual irritation," we should look to those places where we *do* have power.[21] Labkovsky's techniques of the self facilitated a fluid exchange between the personal and the political, which is reminiscent of what Cruikshank calls "liberation therapy," by which "personal fulfillment becomes a social obligation," and "revolutions within" become closely tied to political transformation (1996, 232).[22] The question, then, is, what politics did Labkovsky's form of liberation therapy enable and constrain? How did the politics of self extend into political registers?

In social contexts, samootsenka could also problematize relations of intimacy with family, among friends, and with strangers, in organizing politically. Here

I draw on Lauren Berlant's (2000) sense of intimacy as an experience of closeness, attachment, or desire between people that is also always-already mediated by legal institutions, public discourse, and medical technologies and therapies, and expressed through concepts like responsibility, (im)propriety, and (ab)normality. Read in this way, reinscriptions of the relations of intimacy are also tied to particular governing projects and cruel attachments (see also Berlant 2011). On *For Adults about Adults*, the way that samootsenka could be used to transform the norms governing intimate relations also touched on notions of citizenship. The problematization of different forms of intimacy opened onto alternative conceptions of sociality, politeness, community, political action, rights, and membership.

For example, when on New Year's Day Labkovsky devoted a program to "problems with *obshchenie* [communication; socializing]," he was not invoking any old word for sociality but a culturally thick, almost sacred concept of communion among close friends. As Dale Pesmen (2000) notes, obshchenie is part of the Russian discourse of dusha (soul) that inscribes the who (svoi, or one's intimate circle), where (the kitchen table), and how (obshchenie) of intimacy. Pesmen quotes an informant: "Life, success, money, even success with women, as shocking as it sounds, none of these are the main thing. The main thing in this system of values is 'the feeling of *elbows*.' The feeling that people will . . . come to your aid. . . . In a close circle of friends that feeling appears, that impression of oneness, unity of dusha" (2000, 165; see also Yurchak 2006, 102–8). Despite this soulful meaning, on Labkovsky's show host and caller referred to its more mundane sense of "socializing," in effect renegotiating the nature of intimate social interactions.

Consider Ivan (January 1, 2005, caller 12), a caller who was eager to give others advice. After telling listeners that obshchenie can happen not only in one's inner circle but also "in line at a store," he suggested that to be "successful" in obshchenie, (male) listeners need, first, to attend to self-presentation and hygiene because "women pay attention to shoes." He then got into the psychological nitty-gritty: referencing the "doubts that interfere with saying something, and missing a chance," Ivan recommended using "the three-second rule": "Count to three, wait and speak. When you start to speak, it gets easier; the main thing is to take the first step. If a person is interested in conversation, the person smiles, says something, makes a so-called return connection." He added that psychological techniques could also assist in controlling the social context: on the premise of owning the interaction, one should define the terms of obshchenie by creating a "structure of communication" and a "system of relationships" within which to converse. "To immediately become a master of obshchenie," Ivan concluded, "is impossible. You need to study how to converse [obshchat'sia], learn to move past yourself [perekhodit' cherez soboi], to quell your fears [podavliat' svoi strakhi], your limiting beliefs, inner dialogue."

Through this interplay of social anxiety and an almost businesslike approach to the self, intimate obshchenie was transformed into a competitive, self-centered, and gendered form of social interaction. This not only eroticized a platonic mode of sociality but also expanded the sites appropriate for intimate interactions while simultaneously isolating the self from its social constitution.

Other reinscriptions of intimacy with more explicitly political implications were seen on the program on May 14, which Labkovsky had devoted entirely to the new housing laws: after years of inept state control of housing, Russians were now allowed to form their own Apartment Owner's Association (TSZh) to manage their housing fees for, say, the hiring of private services for building maintenance. "Citizens often complain about the excessive influence of the state on their private life," Labkovsky began. "The new [housing law] is a rare opportunity for citizens to show their independence, their civic position, and that they are a kind of civil society. The state has, literally, given our citizens a chance to show their civic activism." Labkovsky continued, "But the prognosis is rather pessimistic, and I don't know that our citizens will demonstrate that activity in order to live better. Most of all, I feel that everything will end with robbery by state companies, and nothing new will come into our lives." Referencing this "litmus test for our activity," Labkovsky issued a challenge to his listeners: "Will you build your homes, or will, as always, the state do it?"

Over the course of two hours, Labkovsky laid out the foundations of civic activism, beginning with techniques of the self: civic activism was initially a question of mentality. He claimed that "our psychology" and "historical makeup" interfered because Russians had a certain "relation to affairs" (otnoshenie k delu). Civic activism rested on an alternative, psychologically mediated, practical ethics that should then cascade over social relations, shifting attitudes about intimacy. Speaking directly to the matter of the home, Labkovsky complained, "We only consider our own homes as being behind the closed door. We don't consider, for example, our building entrance . . . , the elevator, much less our courtyard. No one organizes to do the so-called evro-remont (Euro-standard remodel) in their own building entrance; meanwhile, people continue, well, to piss and shit [there]. In general, the impression one gets from the entrance is always worse than from the apartment. This probably reflects our relationship to the home." (See figure 6.2.)

FIGURE 6.2. "This probably reflects our relationship to the home." This is a particularly run-down example of a Saint Petersburg apartment entry. While most that I visited are in better shape, it was generally the case, as Labkovsky says, that the entryway was an abandoned space. Photo by the author.

Labkovsky's appeal to civic activism, joint decision making, shared responsibility, and a regard for the commons was an attempt to expand people's ideas about the home to include unfamiliar neighbors. His appeal was also posed against the logic of *blat*, or the personal connections on which one relies to get things done in Russia. Blat is about social networks held together by an informal moral economy of favors and personal trust; Labkovsky was advancing forms of civic action that, while personal, were more formal and rationalized (Rivkin-Fish 2005, 155).

If intimate relations were in this case expanded into what might be called the political intimacy of liberal civil society, they were contracted when it came to physical proximity. For example, in a program on mental health, fifty-four-year-old Galina said that when in public, respectful distance was most appropriate (April 9, 2005, caller 2). "We have a neurotic society," she began, citing the "elbow culture" (*loktevaia kul'tura*) of crowded Russian cities (recall Pesmen's informant's love of the elbow). "Liberate [*osvobodite*] and create around yourself a living space [*sozdaite vokrug sebia zhiznennoe prostranstvo*]," she said.

In the dance between caller and host, this intimate prescription eventually moved from public space, to the person, to the home. Labkovsky began by framing her complaint in cultural terms: he cited a psychological study about the norms governing "the average space between people." While with close friends the average space is the same cross-culturally, there is variation when it comes to strangers. Whereas in Scandinavia it ranges from 150 centimeters to 20 meters, in Russia it's just around 20 centimeters. Invoking the sociality of dusha, Labkovsky said, "We have a soulful people [*narod dushevnyii*], and so tactile contact is demanded everywhere, even if there are no crowds."

This cultural explanation gives Galina no solace. For her, the lack of respect for personal space was a sign of poor upbringing, "psychic illness," and even an "inadequate reflection of reality [*neadekvatnoe kakoe-to otrazhenie deistvitel'nosti*]." Adopting a psychologized biblicism, she noted that you ought to "relate to another as to yourself [*vy k drugomu otnosites' tak zhe, kak k samomu sebe*]."

Going along, Labkovsky put in, "Perhaps a lack of respect for the other is a sign that we don't respect ourselves," a sentiment he also expressed on the program on housing associations.

"Yes, exactly. We don't respect ourselves, and so we don't respect our surroundings. And so we have such an elbow culture. Who brushed whom. Speech is [also] like that, you know, a reaction, whose words brushed whom."

Moving into the home, Labkovsky then asked, "Do you relate to your family as 'healthy people'?"

"Of course I do," she said, "although . . . this neurosis . . . hasn't passed by our family. Fatigue from work, from life. . . . It seems to me that even in the family sometimes we need to keep back from each other a bit more."

"Well, in any case, each member of the family ought to have personal space [*lichnoe prostranstvo*]. I absolutely agree," concluded Labkovsky.

Erving Goffman (1971) suggests that in liberal societies personhood is at issue in contestations around personal space. That is, personal space marks "the role the individual is allowed in determining what happens to his claim [for personal space]" (60). This and other preserves composing the "territories of the self" (28) are actually sites for the performance of rituals for demonstrating self-determination, which he says is crucial to what it means to be a "full-fledged person" (61). To think with Goffman, Galina's desire for elbow room would then express the importance of self-determination to her own sense of personhood. But we can also go further: personal space for Galina does not designate only a site for liberal autonomy. It also links together into a vision of Scandinavian civility certain kinds of public behavior, notions of self-respect and selfhood, family relations, and ultimately relations with strangers, all of which is measured against a pathologized social (dis)order.

On discussions about public transit, this desire for civility (and the realignment of intimate relations it entailed) collided with competing senses of manners—a collision, I suggest, that highlights a crucial political subtext, the question of citizenship.[23] On May 7, two days before Victory Day, a holiday of national unity honoring the defeat of the Fascists in World War II and the sacrifices of the older generations, Labkovsky invited listeners to ponder the "tradition of relations between generations." Surprisingly, despite this disarming introduction, discussions quickly deteriorated into a shouting match over manners on public transit. Elderly callers accused young riders of rudeness, or *khamstvo*, for ignoring the custom of giving up their seat for the infirm.[24] "This rudeness [of the young], we need to struggle with it," said an elderly Tatiana (May 7, 2005, caller 9). "It's written right there [in all the buses] 'for invalids, the aged.' But no, he sits [there], and really sits, hanging his scarf on half of the next spot." Young riders countered that each paying rider was equally entitled to a seat; moreover, the elderly were rude and pushy. A listener who signed himself or herself "a twenty-two-year-old" (May 7, 2005, caller 18) retorted, "Permit me to disagree with Tatiana. If we look at the metro, there are these elderly people who can tear you to pieces. Or at the bus stop a crowd of grannies can just trample you. I've seen it many times myself."

Whereas the older callers were more preoccupied with the rude ignoring of social obligation than with personal space per se, the young tended to view rudeness in terms of a breach of the personal space that Galina described above. These views of rudeness and public intimacy expressed different conceptions of citizenship. That is, the pensioners' adherence to social custom was met with the young's advocacy of a consumer model of equal rights to public space and a stripping away of social obligations: one rider, one seat; first come, first served. The discussions were no doubt stoked by the recent monetization of pensioner benefits. These neoliberal reforms sought to give pensioners small cash payments in lieu of benefits such as free metro rides; to the surprise of the Putin administration, these changes triggered a "grey revolution," and pensioners marched to protest the comparatively miniscule value of the cash payment. The debate on *For Adults about Adults* highlighted how the former benefits had also anchored a sense of social debt, manifested in the ritual of respect of giving up a seat on a crowded bus. The rolling back of these benefits, an elderly Aleksandr (May 7, 2005, caller 3) complained, seemed to have also rolled back the manners that had taken shape around the benefits system. Citing the "completely boorish behavior of the young on public transportation," he asserted, "Attitudes to the elderly are administered from the top, and that's why we have this atmosphere in society."

Alaina Lemon (2000, 18) has suggested that the Moscow metro is a "place trope" where "ontologies of a society in transition" are contested. In times of instability, public transit can become an index of evolving social relations, attitudes about those relations, and the dynamics of unraveling and reform. Not only the exchanges about public transit on *For Adults about Adults* but also the radio show more broadly is a place trope. The calculating, sovereign self entailed in Ivan's version of obshchenie; Labkovsky's appeal to the expanded political intimacy of the housing association; Galina's call for civility and personal space; and young transit riders' rejection of social customs—these all indicated how Labkovsky's conception of selfhood anchored a much larger set of social and political relations and assembled them into a social formation consistent with a neoliberal political rationality. In particular, he advanced a view of the autonomous, partitioned, choosing, and socially unobligated subject. Meanwhile, Labkovsky's advocacy of civil activism through increased political intimacy invoked forms of governance that aimed to replace social programs with assemblages of "uncoordinated" actions by autonomous actors that scale up to functional, efficient, self-administrative wholes.

As Andrea Barry, Thomas Osborne, and Nikolas Rose (1996) assert, neoliberal techniques aim to "produce a degree of 'autonomization' of entities of government from the State" (11–12), resulting in an "autonomization of society" (27). Replacing state bureaucratic structures, this autonomization of society turns entities, organizations, and individuals into self-governing machines by creating "chains of enrolment, 'responsibilization' and 'empowerment' to sectors and agencies distant from the centre, yet tied to it through a complex of alignments and translations" (12). In this sense, the Apartment Owners' Association was one such chain of enrollment, whereas personal space, along with the host of other techniques of the self that were discussed, was a site for constituting the autonomous subject in relation to other autonomous subjects.

For Adults about Adults therefore evinced a complex assemblage of neoliberal techniques. This was not intentional but resulted from the happenstance convergence of Labkovsky's efforts to deconstruct socialist discourses, his liberal politics, and the neoliberal rationality that continued to circulate in Russia during the early Putin period. Even the talk show itself reproduced neoliberal technologies by turning Labkovsky's discursively constituted public of political action into a performative one: in calling the radio show and just talking, listeners took a first step toward the practical ethics of self-esteem and at the same time re-created this public in virtual form.[25] That is, they performed the Kantian ideal of the subject who speaks freely in public. They enabled the individualizing and totalizing force of pastoral power to work around and through them.[26] In the act of hearing, with its sensual, immersive quality, people became part of a neoliberal public.[27] And, finally, in completing the link between the care of self and the political, they became autonomized circuits.

Social Problems

What, then, is one to make of a simmering reluctance to accept the linking of politics, publics, and the esteem, possession, presentation, and spatial requirements of the self? Motivating psychotherapeutic discourse against itself, one caller said, "Changing yourself is the straightest path to neurosis. Is your program a provocation?" (March 5, 2005, caller 26). Another asked, "Doesn't depression result from the successful change of your character, exterior, and relations?" (March 5, 2005, caller 52). Masha suggested that political improvement is not at all a matter of self-change: "Mikhail, people are divided into creators, contemplators, and philistines. The lousy philistines are nothing. They need to change" (March 5, 2005, caller 17). These calls highlight the limited appeal of the self-esteem model.

One of the most profound communication gaps between host and caller came when the self-esteem model encountered social life itself. In the face of discomfort, the esteem of self was driven further down the road of self-possession, to self-control. This imperative to control oneself resisted Labkovsky's other rearticulations of intimate relations. A caller named Lara said, "I have tormented myself all of my conscious life; I change, and [still] I dislike everything about myself. I am convinced that given what's left of my life, changing myself isn't possible [*nel'zia*], fundamentally" (March 5, 2005, caller 49). "Sometimes," she added haltingly, "it seems that, well, I am already completely different. . . . But a moment arises, and everything returns to its place [*na krugi svoia*]. No, you can't change yourself. No way. You had some advice, 'If there is some kind of problem, you need to change your relationship [to it].' Well, that's like telling a nervous person not to be nervous."

"No, you didn't understand," Labkovsky replied. "It's not my advice, it's a Freudian saying, very famous and wise. On the contrary, it's not a suggestion to the nervous person not to be nervous, but a suggestion that he himself accept the nervousness. It's not the same. You didn't understand the sense of this phrase."

"Yes, maybe I didn't quite put it right, I just . . . ," Lara trailed off. "Inasmuch as I am an emotional person, I get overwhelmed by my own words [*ia sebia zakhlestivaiu svoimi slovami*]. I only want to say, um, I told myself a hundred times, I will be calm, and if in my militaristic frontline life, now a respite comes, I think, 'Oh, I became calm.' Baloney. A moment hits that disturbs me, and again everything flies off. . . . Then I am sorry . . . why am I screaming . . . well . . ."

Drawing on the dual meaning of the word *nel'zia*, which can be used by a parent wagging a finger at a child (as in, "you mustn't") or to signify that which is ontologically impossible, Lara suggested that self-transformation was hopeless. Moreover, her efforts at self-control were constantly undermined by the hard life she said she had at home, even by language itself, which "overwhelmed" her.

Another response to the self-esteem model was the sense that others lacked self-control. On the program promoting the Apartment Owner's Association, despite Labkovsky's suggestion that self-transformation and civic activism might be paired through the rearticulation of attitudes about intimacy and the home, Kira complained that others can't be trusted to control themselves: "Eventually all these members of the [association] will try to gnaw each others' throats at the general meeting in order to put their own person by the cashier and snatch a piece of the general funds. Everything that you speak of is complete nonsense" (May 14, 2005, caller 16).

"Kira just reflects, I think, the opinion of the masses [*mnenie mass*], not our listeners, but those apartment owners," Labkovsky said resignedly. "Here, with such a psychology, with such relations to affairs, our endless history awaits us regarding the . . . eternal dissatisfaction with life."

Others expressed a similar difficulty mapping the self-esteem model onto the realities of their daily experiences in that their attempts to be oriented primarily inward were constantly undermined by the khamstvo of others.

"What do I want to change in myself?" asked sixty-nine-year-old Alla Pavlovna (March 5, 2005, caller 37). "I'm not reserved. I often yell at people. True, it's for [legitimate] things, but nevertheless that's not allowed. And so it really bothers me. I would even like to apologize publicly." Adding that "life has not been easy," she said, "I can't calmly regulate myself in response to khamstvo. My voice rises." She gave the example of how fellow residents continually drop their litter absentmindedly in the building courtyard. "I am really bothered [by this]," she said. "Are there really those who live by handling themselves like that?" (See figure 6.3.) Then Alla Pavlovna checked herself: "I don't know . . . I . . . I'm saying, now that I've gotten through to you, whoever hears me, who knows me, I am sorry for my unreservedness [*nesderzhannost'*]."

Khamstvo and its response, a defensive self-control, even turned self-esteem into a contradictory proposition. In Elena's call, it was as if only half of the formula was actualized: "I would change in myself my vulnerability to negligible external actions. And I would increase my reaction in response to khamstvo" (March 5, 2005, caller 8). That is, while striving to be less oriented to outside disturbance and more reserved, she nevertheless wanted to be more aggressive in response to khamstvo.

Others cited the daily scenes of cruelty, neglect, and sorrow that troubled their efforts to esteem and possess themselves. "I would like to learn to say 'no,' " one listener wrote in. "It turns out to be very hard because people are often sad when they are denied" (March 5, 2005, caller 34). As if in response, Masha asked rhetorically, "How can I handle the negative when I see beggars on the metro? You can give or not give money, but these people emotionally violate all the passengers [*no eti liudi nasiluiut emotsional'no vsekh passazhirov*]" (March 5, 2005, caller 81).

Such calls pointed to the way that social relations—whether in the form of distrust (e.g., with regard to the corruption or irresponsibility of others), battles at home, or pity—constantly challenged Labkovsky's model of the autonomous subject and the imperative to locate inner reserves and attain order *within* oneself. Tugging at the threads holding self-esteem together, the grinding everyday threatened to unravel it and its particular structure of relations between the self and the social world. But more than that, these calls also highlighted how the practical ethics of self-esteem existed alongside others (e.g., selfless giving, socialist residues of self-control), just as Labkovsky's normative view of the public, civil society, and citizenship existed alongside others (the publics of svoi, or one's inner circle, for instance; or the nonpublic of what's outside one's front door).[28]

FIGURE 6.3. "Are there really those who live by handling themselves like that?" In her call to the radio program, Alla Pavlovna cited those whose trash doesn't make it into the dumpster as exhibing the kind of rudeness that drives her crazy. Photo reproduced with the kind permission of Emily Newman.

Perhaps the greatest challenge to Labkovsky's recipe for political change through a revolution within was posed by Dasha, who asked how self-work would help her to relieve the distress she experienced from feeling pity for homeless animals and witnessing cruelty. "How can I not notice [abuse]?" (March 5, 2005, caller 62).

"Dasha, a hard question, very hard." In following the "logic of conscience," Labkovsky reasoned, one would have to take in every homeless animal, despite having limited means. Clearly this is unsustainable. "But if we dig deeper," he said philosophically, "then life in general according to its definitions isn't just. It's set up in this way, and you simply need to accept this as a fact. You need to try to resolve this question of justice inside yourself, while bearing in mind that each person has limited possibilities. [*I vopros spravedlivosti nuzhno re-shat' pytat'sia vnutri sebia, pri etom imet' vidu, shto u kazhdogo cheloveka est' svoi, kakie-to ogranichennye vozmozhnosti.*] And you need not try to take on more than you can handle because you just won't be able to bear it."

In the absence of justice, Labkovsky could only resort to the default position of the inward turn—ethical and political questions and practices need to be decided "inside yourself," where there are also limitations. This shows not only how the messiness of social relations limited the politico-ethical viability of self-esteem but also how many in Labkovsky's audience had trouble imagining themselves as the kinds of autonomous subjects he was advocating. Met with competing understandings of subjectivity, family, compassion, emotion, obligation, responsibility and a whole range of other objects and practices, the political reach of the psychotherapeutic subject turned out to be less extensive than Labkovsky hoped.

Conclusion

> To recognize that subjectivity is itself a matter of the technologizing of humans is not to regard this process as amounting to some kind of crushing of the human spirit under the pressure of a corset of habits, restrictions and injunctions. Human capacities are . . . inevitably and inescapably technologized. An analytics of technology has, therefore, to devote itself to the sober and painstaking task of describing the consequences, the possibilities invented as much as the limits imposed, of particular ways of subjectifying humans.
>
> —Andrew Barry, Thomas Osborne, and Nikolas Rose, introduction to *Foucault and Political Reason*

Talk shows, and their psychologies, do not dehumanize; they *re*humanize. This chapter has shown how *For Adults about Adults* was involved in the production of techniques of the self that linked up with neoliberal governing practices and publics. But as the critical engagements show, these techniques were hardly all-consuming. Rather, they appeared as one of several options for the management of life. This reflects the fact that neoliberal reforms do not involve a wholesale substitution of values but specific mechanisms that are articulated, as Stephen Collier notes, with "old biopolitical forms, and the actual substantive fabric of human communities" (2005, 388).

This view also helps to place Labkovsky's subjectivizing and public-making endeavors in the broader context of federal politics. On the one hand, Labkovsky's models of self-esteem were consonant with the kinds of subjects inculcated by the legislation on Apartment Owner's Associations and the monetization of benefits, both of which could be described as neoliberal reforms. On the other hand, his appeals to political transformation through self-government, and his liberal-democratic vision of a future Russian civil society, sat uneasily with policies under Putin that have been hostile to grassroots movements, opposition parties, outspoken journalists, and so forth. The neoliberal articulations of Labkovsky's particular psychological techniques of the self, therefore, are not examples of top-down implementation. Rather, they reflect instances where the liberal assemblage he advanced—largely a liberal-democratic vision of the sovereign, self-esteeming, self-possessing, empowered, civically minded, polite subject—coincided symbiotically with a slightly different assemblage of liberal technologies. At this point of productive *coincidence* (in both senses of this homonym), a range of normative visions—civility, civil society, neoliberal subjectivity—were articulated with one another, bringing diverse governing projects into alignment. Such forms of coincidence are also, to use a central concept in this book, instances of commensurability. These governing projects ranged from self-governance to Apartment Owners' Association, and from the regulation of public behavior through politeness to the transformation of citizenship.

But what kinds of political options did these psychological techniques of the self open up? Given that efforts to learn how to manage one's life, to be more self-sufficient, to get along with others, to be happier, helped to constitute a particular liberal assemblage, what kinds of politics were actually enabled? Did pedagogies of self-work in fact open up political possibility in Russia, or did they rather lead to depoliticization? This book has mentioned various instances in which practitioners have described self-work as a political endeavor, at least potentially so. These have included particular "civilizing" missions among commercial psychologists working with children of the elite; the work of precarious care delivered in state institutions; and the psychosocialities pursued by psychologists interested in rearticulating the social. These, I have suggested, were instances of the incommensurability of psychotherapeutic projects with biopolitical norms.

On the basis of Labkovsky's program, however, it is clear that political technologies like self-esteem can also become paradoxically *antipolitical* when discontent is obscured by the endeavor of psychological engagement, and the zone for political work remains at the level of the self. As was seen in Labkovsky response to a call from Andrei, if you are unhappy because you have to work two jobs to pay for the family apartment, you come home grumpy, and then find yourself irritated by "small things," the problem is nonetheless not the way your life is structured by certain demands; "it's [your] own choice" (March 5, 2005, caller 36). Or, as Michele Rivkin-Fish (2005) argues, when liberal solutions like self-empowerment fail to address complex dilemmas tied to structural inequalities, blame is often placed on the victims, who, in not exercising their power, are seen as enacting a moral failure.

In the rather apolitical atmosphere of Putinism, it is perhaps not surprising that the most common concern of callers was the search for an ethics of *control* of self, of person, of others, of things. This interest in self-control is linked to the autonomization of subjects referenced above—where the self is turned into a domain of government and where self-governing individuals are encouraged to constitute networks of self-governing machines such as housing associations. But it also dovetails with another key term in Russia, stabil'nost' (discussed in the previous chapter), which was also being used as a justification for Putin's "managed democracy" (Anderson 2007). According to this logic, a sustained political and social calm and the related guarantee of personal economic possibility and success far outweigh the benefits of "democracy without quotation marks" (Ryzhkov 2008), the formation of which would presumably require the sacrifices of instability. The search for self-control seems to constitute the self as another governed realm subsumed by the logic of stability, where citizenship, understood as a relationship of obligation and responsibility between state and population, is the privileged object of sacrifice—a sacrifice made at the altar of the economy.

As was evident in the final exchange between Dasha and Labkovsky above, this politics of the self was therefore not always so easily translated into political terms for a host of reasons extending from personal ethics, to historically constituted citizen-state relations, to a general lack of the "chains of enrollment" through which those subjects should operate politically. In the absence of organizations meant to give political voice to the techniques of self, what is left is a neoliberalism without liberals. This arrangement points to an effect of contemporary capitalism: the reliance on market technologies, privatization, and the farming out of state activities to nongovernmental sectors, if those even exist, may act as an antipolitics machine (Ferguson 1994), distancing citizens from the political machinery that might otherwise be mobilized for their benefit.

Is psychological self-work antipolitical, then? Does the intimate elaboration of a feeling subject in Russia replace political practices with the management of affects? The preceding chapters of this book have argued against this conclusion. Rather, there is a surplus of politics in self-work. For example, tied to new state biopolitics, psychotherapeutic care has become incorporated into the state's management of its young populations. In the area of commercial work, a range of practitioners pursue projects that combine self-realization with broader social-reform goals, including a loosely articulated engagement with social inequality. Finally, as a more purely personal project, psychological self-work also evidences a tentative exploration of new socialities. The question is not "Is self-work political?" but "What are its politics, and what are the effects of those politics?"

In the conclusion of this book, I take up this final question as a way to meditate on the psychotherapeutic turn as I have observed it more recently, putting it in the context of events in between 2012 and 2015. As this chapter has shown, psychotherapeutic work remains a vibrant site for thinking through the personal and social effects of a politics of the self, pointing to both a nascent public promise and deep political risks.

FIGURE POSTLUDE.1. "Roaming for Travelers": billboard for the Megafon cell phone company. Photo by the author.

Subjects of Freedom

While researching the scope of contemporary psychotherapeutic services in Saint Petersburg, I came across the following quotation by a therapist:

> *For decades the primary concern of Soviet theorists in psychotherapy had been "ideological purity," i.e. conforming to materialistic ideas and limiting the influence of "hostile" theories and practices. Psychotherapy was used essentially as a tool for "re-forming" patients and correcting "wrong" behavior. The requirements for professional work, therefore, were formal techniques. The concepts of internal human experience and humane therapeutic relationships were notably missing. It was out of the need for learning in this field—promoting and teaching humanistic psychology—that [our] Institute was founded by a group of friends and colleagues.*
>
> *With years of experience we began to understand that, in Russia, our work served not only a psychological but also a social task. Paraphrasing Chogyam Trungpa, who noted years ago that "Buddhism will come to the West as psychology," it is possible to say that humanistic/existential psychology is coming to Russia as a power for social change.*

The psychotherapist went on to quote one of his students on the role and importance of their institute:

> You Americans think we are free now, you think we are building a new market society, that independence is now here. It is impossible to say that it starts like that. It is a process. In the beginning, what is important in order to become free? People have to experience this freedom inside themselves. Everyone has to become free at first. But history has examples where people have had to learn to be free. One of the very famous examples is when Moses was leading his people for forty years in the desert. In order to gain new values you need time. Of course I don't want us to spend forty years traveling in the desert and just look to the new generations in the future. I want to be learning now.

/ / /

These statements, ranging over history, subjective transformation, different conceptions of freedom, and conversion, offer an argument for psychotherapy's social and political relevance in Russia—this time by linking "learning to be free" with social transformation. This argument reiterates an idea I found among many practitioners: psychotherapy has a social and political purpose in Russia. In the conclusion I turn to a final question: so what? What analytic and political difference do these sorts of claims make, particularly in the face of the psychotherapeutic turn's complicity with social inequality? What kind of freedom is this, anyway?

CONCLUSION
And Yet . . . So What?

Something revealing happened at the border with Aleksandr. We had sailed through the snowy Russian-Karelian countryside, over hill and dale, discussing democracy with a small *d*. Then, as we approached the border zone, traffic slowed significantly. Eventually we came to a grinding halt. The line of cars into neighboring Finland seemed endless. An hour passed. We sat. Occasionally a shiny black Land Rover with tinted windows—the kind that oligarchs and mafiosi drove—flew past, driving against traffic in the other lane. Another thirty minutes, another hundred meters. Aleksandr kept the car idling to run the heat, and the cloying smell of petrol crept inside. Aarno woke up from his nap and became cranky. After another thirty minutes he completely lost it. The checkpoint was still two miles up the road. Aarno stood up on the back seat and started screaming, looking tearfully at the cars behind us. Suddenly there was a knock on the window. The driver behind us, a woman, had noticed Aarno and told us that since we had an infant we could drive to the front of the line. Aleksandr shrugged his shoulders and shifted into drive, and we did what the fancy Land Rovers had done, only much more cautiously. We approached the border patrol nervously, not knowing whether we would be scolded and sent back, but we were quickly waved through. It was well below freezing outside, and the guards made a point of rushing Aarno back into the car. Within ten minutes we were sailing smoothly again. Unfortunately, the Finnish checkpoints were also snarled with traffic. Unlike the Russian side, which had one lane, they had multiple lanes—several for European Union citizens (all empty) and a few for Russians (packed). We wondered whether, as people with an infant, we might also have special privileges there. I exited the car in search of a guard but could find no one. On a whim, we decided to pass through the European Union gate since Aarno and I are also European Union citizens. The guard eyed us and then made a vague gesture. We interpreted it as a green light, and Aleksandr started driving. After a minute of uncertain passage, a gate swung closed, blocking our path. A large car with sirens came flying toward us. We were routed back and asked to pass through the appropriate channel. Neither Aleksandr's Russian passport nor Nicole's US one could pass through that particular gate.

We did, then, make it through fairly easily. But the point is not about access, or even the differential treatment of nationality, but rather the possibility (or lack thereof) for negotiation in biopolitical contexts. (What is a border guard if not a biopolitical figure?) In liberal political theory, negotiations like these are often discussed in terms of administrative failure or corruption. But over the years in Russia I came to appreciate the flexibility of "administrative failure." When rules can be negotiated and interpreted, accommodations can be made. True enough, too often accommodations are made just because you drive a fancy Land Rover. But the fact that many in Russia allow room for negotiation when it comes to social need is a sign, I would argue, of a healthy society. It is also a sign of a moral economy. As many scholars have noted, a wide range of informal social practices took shape under socialism: noncommoditized forms of gift exchange, barter, extralegal arrangements. These practices even had a special vocabulary—*blat* (pull), *vziatka* (bribe), and getting something *cherez znakomykh* (through acquaintances) (Wanner 2005; Patico 2008; Caldwell 2004; Humphrey 2002; Rivkin-Fish 2005; Volkov 2002). As elements of a moral economy, these practices were often strategies of adaptation to economies of shortage under socialism (Verdery 1996), but they were also means of maintaining social relations. Under postsocialism they have persisted, now as countercurrents to the hyperrationalization and commodification of daily life. As the whizzing Land Rovers of the elite make clear, this countercurrent is hardly unproblematic. Yet I want to draw attention to the fact that this moral economy of human relations is of a piece with the incommensurable practices of precarious care described in this book. Whether the person was working to promote empathy among the elite through their children, or circumventing legal norms to provide more holistic care, or seeking alternative kinds of sociality and public life through psychotherapy, these were ultimately moments where a person, not an official or an entrepreneur, stepped out from behind the uniform. In such moments, people enter into relations of exchange that are irreducible to simple profit motive, normative orders, or rational-choice models. Such moments entail, instead, culturally specific modes of social being.

Summary of the Argument

In many ways, *Shock Therapy* has aimed to identify the traces of the moral economy in domains normally analyzed as hopelessly colonized by neoliberal rationalities, while at the same time attending closely to those very processes of colonization. Colonization first: this book's title is of course a play on the neoliberal reforms in Russia in the 1990s (privatization, marketization, price liberalization, shrinking social expenditures). As analysts noted after Russia's 1998 recession, shock therapy turned out to be "too much shock, and too little therapy" (Ledeneva 2006, 10). The reforms disrupted everyday life massively. Production slowed. Currency devaluation meant that the few fancy things for sale in stores were beyond reach. Wages for public workers were often in arrears. Meanwhile, a demoralizing mass theft took place in which a few well-positioned people seized public property for their personal use. In a few years, Russia was transformed from a society with relative income equality to one with extremely high wealth inequality. For those left out, there were reminders everywhere of their social position—black Land Rovers (again), glitzy unaffordable restaurants, expensive food products. These transformations also shuffled the meanings attached to work: for example, teachers, once held in very high esteem, found themselves in a position of subservience to the class of New Russians (Patico 2008). If there was no political-economic "therapy," there was, at least, psychotherapy. To a degree, the psychotherapeutic turn of the 1990s and 2000s worked as a transfer point for neoliberal rationalities, conveying the familiar normative cluster—self-esteem, responsibility, life as a career requiring investment, competition, new coordinates of blame, and so forth—into the very heart of the psyche.

My main argument, however, has been that the psychotherapeutic turn is not simply a symptom, or function, of neoliberal governmentality. Instead, it has inaugurated a form of *precarious care* that intersects with some, but not all, of the forms of rule specific to neoliberal states. That is, while reiterating self-governing modalities like self-esteem, psychotherapists' work has also been animated by other rationales, meanings, and aims specific to the post-socialist context. These include the humanization of doctor-patient relations, the demedicalization of therapeutic care and the shift from "patient" to "client," a democratization of psychological knowledge, the creation of new work opportunities for women, the belief that the care one offers should not be ideologically constrained, efforts to transform the managerial class and care for those left out of the postsocialist economy, and, finally, a set of loosely articulated social agendas tied to psychosociality and public intimacy. I am not saying that these specific meanings obviate a critique of psychotherapy-as-neoliberal-governmentality but rather that care is a far more complex enterprise than that kind of account allows for.

The psychotherapeutic turn in Russia is better described as postsocialist. Its rationales, meanings, and aims are determined not by an imported liberalism but by a set of experiences specific to Russia at the end of the last century and the start of this one. As my informants explained, those experiences included a feeling of inertia and frustration during late socialism but also, in the post-Soviet years, a nostalgic yearning for the "freedom from money," as one acquaintance put it, that the socialist period had also entailed. There were also reflections on the political collapse's promise of a more democratic society, as well as the disappointment that the ensuing years under Boris Yeltsin and Vladimir Putin ended up bringing. And those experiences included the still barely burning embers of desire for a yet-to-be-named postsocialist (and perhaps postliberal?) democratic society. To call this complex assemblage "neoliberal governmentality" misses important details. And yet (and now the phrase operates in the reverse fashion) the effects of neoliberal capitalism on this democratic desire cannot be ignored either. And what of care? In similar fashion, care was sometimes aligned (commensurable) with, and sometimes at odds (incommensurable) with, the biopolitical. I suggested that this on-again, off-again dynamic is precisely what makes the psychotherapeutic turn of ethnographic and analytic interest.

In making this claim, it was important for me to begin by showing that the (in)commensurability of care was also a feature of socialist psy-ence. In the first chapter, I traced a genealogy of applied psychology, the precursor to the contemporary psychotherapy boom, in order to show three things. First, from the point of view of political ideology and practice in the 1930s, a Freudian elaboration of human experience was deemed inconsistent with a properly dialectical Marxism and the materialist orientation in social science. This strongly shaped the development of psychology as a practice in Soviet Russia, limiting its non-biomedical forms to the research laboratory. By extension, mental disturbance was typically framed in pathological terms, and applied behavioral work was left in the hands of pedagogues. Second, the psychotherapeutic turn in the 1990s was part of a much longer elaboration of interiority, emotions, relations, and personality in Russia over the course of the twentieth century. There were several periods when an interest in the "subjective factors of human behavior" (Bauer 1959, 67) emerged in Soviet psy-ence—the 1920s, 1960s, and 1980s. Third, whereas an ideological history of Soviet psy-ence says one thing, interviews with psychotherapists say another: practitioners nearly always employed a diversity of incommensurable practices, attitudes, and approaches in their work, including at times of heightened ideological scrutiny.

Part II followed the initial, late-socialist interest in humanization into work with children in the first decade of the 2000s—a time of postsocialist capitalism under Putin. In the 1980s there were already concerns that the more differentiated—and psychologized—approach to education would lead to heightened inequality. The arrival of market capitalism amplified those tendencies. As practitioners incorporated psychological knowledge into post-Soviet government and the harnessing of human capital, they also accentuated, in psychological terms, the social differences emerging from the marketization of society. As participants in an expanding "domestic services" market, psychotherapists essentially became enrolled in providing treningi (trainings) for Russia's new elite in personal growth (*lichnyi rost*) and samo-otsenka (self-esteem). In contrast, psychologists working in state institutions faced resource constraints and precarity and ended up reproducing the category of the problem child and graduated forms of psychological citizenship (see Ong 2006). How did this happen? Psychological difference, I suggested, resulted from psychotherapists' efforts to make their work commensurable with biopolitical and economic norms, including the state's interest in young citizens as engines of economic resurgence, the politics of the demographic crisis and pronatalism, and the neoliberal austerity measures under modernization. The signs of commensuration were different in each case: commercial psychotherapists tried to leverage an anxiety-inducing language of success in their work; state psychologists, by contrast, deployed the defensive diagnostics of social risk. One historical irony here is that late-socialist humanization has survived, but only in a commercial form that has intensified the risks of psychological difference. Meanwhile, state services appear to have resuscitated the pathologization of mental distress that had for so long dominated Soviet mental health. This amounts to the *commodification of emotionality* and the *pathologization of precarity*. Finally, I also explored the desires, aims, and aspirations of the psychotherapists themselves. These I found to be at least partly incommensurable with the effects just mentioned. Tamara Grigorievna and her staff at ReGeneration wove a democratic desire into psychological education, seeing it as a way to constitute greater empathy and tolerance among Russia's elite. And practitioners at the PPMS Center became quite adept at navigating bureaucratic constraints in order to deliver more holistic forms of care. While the PPMS Center and ReGeneration worked with different segments of the population, in both cases the psychotherapists elaborated a form of care that was, at least loosely, political.

In part III I elaborated on the "loosely political." Turning to personal-growth seminars for adults and the mass media, I explored some of the social and political values that psychotherapists expressed. Nikolai's and Olessia's work (harmonious relations and systemic constellation) unfolded socially expansive aspects of self-work—what I termed *psychosociality*. To borrow Miriam Ticktin's description of biosociality, psychosociality is "the socially framed choice to draw on one's [psychology]" (2006, 35) as a means toward some ends. Drawing on idioms like *energiia, garmoniia*, and *dusha*, Nikolai and Olessia offered participants technologies for resisting the market economy's domination of value, as well as the increasingly isolating and fear-laden atmospheres of Russia's managed democracy. Mikhail Labkovsky, the host of the radio program *For Adults about Adults*, also drew on psychological technologies as a basis for social change, promoting an orientation to self-esteem that could scale up to a democratic polity in which even the notion of home might be expanded into a new public, a public intimacy. Each example of incommensurable care was, however, precarious—at risk of either commodification or biopoliticization. In the case of psychosociality, the use of psychology as a social resource could also have differentiating effects, particularly as psychological knowledge became incorporated into the market in divergent ways: as a useful skill set for personal advancement, on the one hand, or as a way to identify signs of trouble in others, on the other. *For Adults about Adults* also revealed some of the tensions within and among a psychologically attuned democratic politics. While Labkovsky's messages were not in the service of a singular political rationality—neoliberal, socialist, or otherwise—the antipolitical undercurrent of his ideas was apparent: in the face of injustice and structural problems, the host could only say, "Start with yourself and those things that you can control."

One observation that cuts across all of these materials is that the psychotherapeutic turn as seen in Saint Petersburg in 2005–13 has created spaces, practices, and discourses by which people have broached political, ethical, social, and personal questions at a time of social change. These include questions about the relationship between the individual, the social, the public, and the political. In that sense, this ethnography of psychotherapeutic practice has offered a glimpse of how people, living in one part of Russia in the new millennium, were thinking about their country's future, all the while becoming embroiled in the business of its state-capitalist present. The question I deferred in the introduction, though, remains: to what ends? What is the use of pointing to incommensurability in the face of social inequality? One way to begin answering that is through an update on what has happened since my first focused bout of fieldwork in 2005–6.

Psychology Boom . . . and Bust?

The events between 2012 and 2015 suggest that psychotherapeutic care has been both increasingly absorbed into biopolitics and also, in some cases, erased. In addition, as modernization has become "conservative modernization" during Putin's third term, the liberal-democratic rhetoric of cultivating citizens has diminished and been replaced with more traditionalist emphases on patriotism and labor as constitutive of full citizenship.[1] There are many possible explanations for this, and answering the question of why is beyond the scope of this book. However, I conjecture that the humanizing kernel, and the conjuncture of emotional well-being and democratic personhood at the heart of the psychotherapeutic turn, is at odds with Putin's, and United Russia's, vision of the country.

One can see this, for example, in the events surrounding Labkovsky's removal from the air: Labkovsky's last show of *For Adults about Adults* aired on September 1, 2012, the same day that a law designed to protect children from explicit content took effect. The station director, Aleksandr Venediktov, explained that the station feared that the show would fall under the sway of the conservative law. Called "On the Protection of Children from Information Harmful to Their Health and Development" (O zashchite detei ot informatsii, prichiniaiushchei vred ikh zdoroviiu i razvitiiu), the law was part of a slate of conservative legislative acts issued to purify the public sphere. (Also passed at the time was the well-known law against gay propaganda, as well as laws restricting the right of assembly.) The fear, as Venediktov noted on Twitter, was that some of the content of Labkovsky's program would be seen as corrupting minors. Whereas Labkovsky's program *About That* (*Pro Eto*) was specifically about sexual relations (and was appropriately scheduled late at night; it was also removed from the air), *For Adults about Adults* was actually G-rated. Labkovsky discussed the daily struggles of people in their marriages, at work, with their children and others, and when alone. Why would such a show be a threat to children? If there were any threat, it was more likely to be Labkovsky's views on Russian politics and society. Never particularly pointed in his critique of federal politics, his commentaries nevertheless almost always touched on an everyday rot at the heart of Russian life: corruption and graft among the elite, unfairness, and injustice, as well as a host of other structural factors that impacted well-being.

As I was finishing a revised draft of this manuscript, I found Labkovsky's final show archived on the Internet. On it, I could hear the host introducing the show's theme in the usual way. The topic was, as expected, G-rated: "Should parents be involved in their children's schoolwork—assuring they do their homework, checking their copybooks—or is it better to give them more independence?" After the theme was announced, a song played as usual while the first calls and text messages started rolling in—this time Morcheeba's "Even Though," which faded out with an ominous chorus, sung in English:

> Even though we know it's forever changing
> Even though we know we lie and wait
> Even though we know the hidden danger
> I hope it's not too late

Then Labkovsky returned to the air. "My friends," he said, "I have a request. Don't write and don't call about why the program is ending." He reminded listeners of the theme of the day and then briefly described the reason for the end of his show: "The program is closing because of a well-known . . . a sad and well-known law." With that, Labkovsky invited his listeners to "return to our children."

Press coverage about the show's end offered some clues as to what had happened. In an interview in the online magazine *Lenta.ru*, Venediktov (2012) remarked, "We think that a law that is written sloppily and with many possible loopholes has made it possible for any program about the family to be affected. . . . As long as this law is not changed, no director will risk [other] programs. Because when the Duma [the Russian Parliament] works in the mode of a mad printer, there is no telling what it will do next." The law, in other words, could put the entire station—one that has a reputation of being a fairly regular critic of Putin—in jeopardy because one program's legal troubles could lead to a suspension of the station's broadcast license. Another article linked the law to a broader trend of censorship of the Russian media (BBC 2012), and an irate Russian blogger attributed the law to "our Orthodox Taliban," referring to the rising influence of the Orthodox Church (znatokin 2012).

On the basis of these and other accounts, it is possible to read the end of Labkovsky's program as symptomatic of a larger shift in Russia over the last decade in which there has been a swing away from democratic discourses of any kind—including those enfolded into psychological models of personhood—and toward a toxic combination of patriarchy, social conservatism, and unapologetic inequality. Under those conditions, any forms of speech that appear anathema to Russia's resurgent national identity have become punishable by law. It is part of the same movement that swept the members of Pussy Riot into two years of hard labor for singing a protest song in a church. And it is part of the same movement that put the upstart politician Alexei Navalny under house arrest. Making matters more complex, Putin and United Russia now parrot liberal-democratic discourses of tolerance in their aggressive policies. Pussy Riot was put away for "religious hatred," and laws like the one that ended Labkovsky's program are phrased in terms of protection. Finally, it is part of the same movement that has fostered increasingly jingoistic performances of Russian national identity constructed around the heteronormative family, patriotic feeling, and ethnochauvinism. Under conservative modernization, the space for alternative points of view has become quite narrow. The transformation to a "neoliberalism without liberals" appears complete, leaving a form of clientelistic capitalism that is also present, albeit less explicitly, in the United States, for instance—a capitalist oligarchy in which the governed are isolated from power (Parfitt 2014). In thinking about psychotherapeutic discourses of empathy, self-knowledge, inner freedom, and psychosociality, and also about the general liberal attitude of those in psychotherapeutic circles, this book has continually asked whether there are aspects of the political in psychotherapeutic care, especially in light of Putin's aggressive state capitalism. This is only speculative, but the turn against Labkovsky suggests that there might well be something to this point.

How have the psychotherapists I came to know—at ReGeneration, at the PPMS Center, at Verity, and elsewhere—fared in the time of conservative modernization? In 2012 I went back to all of my key sites. More research would have to be done to trace the connections between the particulars of Putin's policies and the course of psychological services in Saint Petersburg; however, my impression was that the tendencies visible in the 2000s—in particular, those tied to psychological difference—had continued. In the PPMS Center, whereas in 2007 I was surprised to see my psychologist friend Igor Filippovich appear from behind a bit of broken drywall wearing a dust mask (to save money, the organization was handling its own renovations), by 2012 the center had secured a better location, nestled inside a school in a remoter area of the region. This shift was consistent with the use of public funds around the city to repair playgrounds, as well as to build new soccer fields at every school. Tatiana Fedorovna, the director of the PPMS Center, told me that they now had five times the space they once did. From an infrastructural point of view, they had managed to improve the center. Having completed renovations, they had also been able to bring staffing levels within the legal norms—one specialist for every 750 children in the region—and also to bring the total number of cases back to fourteen hundred per year, closer to the maximum allowed. A conversation with a Russian social scientist in 2014, however, indicated that some context was needed to make sense of these kinds of improvements. As she explained, the Putin government had indeed expanded social spending, but it had focused almost entirely on infrastructure as opposed to qualitative changes within institutions. In her view, they were just "throwing money at a problem without really fixing what underlies it." Her points were consistent with conservative modernization's focus on institutions. They also confirmed what Tatiana Fedorovna had told me about the challenges they were now facing: infrastructural improvements notwithstanding, the mental health of the children in the region was worse than it was six years earlier. As to whether the earlier shift from emotion to cognition as the focus of intervention had remained, that was not something I was able to determine.

When I visited ReGeneration, they had just concluded two camps held simultaneously in southern Europe. Tamara Grigorievna, the director, told me that they were now attracting children from places as far-flung as Vladivostok, Irkutsk, Israel, Turkey, and the Czech Republic—mostly from émigré Russian families interested in having their children spend time speaking their native tongue. Their services were in high demand. Their psychological camps were booked six months ahead, and many parents paid fully in advance. ReGeneration had also hired an office manager and an accountant to make the business side of the work less intermixed with the psychotherapeutic. While their competition has grown, Tamara said there were plenty of clients to go around. Staffing changes notwithstanding, it seemed that it had become even harder to keep therapeutic and economic aims distinct. Even though they remained committed to helping children in "communicating with others, being comfortable in the world," Tamara Grigorievna explained that parents ask that their trainings focus exclusively on promoting leadership, improving schoolwork, and resolving behavioral issues. Vadim, a staff psychologist at ReGeneration, complained that poor behavior was not a problem but a symptom of something else—usually an issue in the home. They could work with the child in the camp, but when the child returned to the "old system" at home, the same patterns resulted. Parents somehow expected them to "rebuild the child from zero." ReGeneration's earlier ambitions to intervene in elite social reproduction appeared to be challenged by the consumer desires of those very elites.

ReGeneration's work also seemed to have become less explicitly political. At least on that visit, I heard little about democracy or the rebuilding of society. Meanwhile, ReGeneration had won a big contract with the federal government to participate in the state's program in "tolerance." They led seventeen trainings with heads of schools to teach them how to promote communication among staff and students in order to help mitigate interethnic conflicts. ReGeneration was recently awarded a contract to do an additional seventy trainings. Yet the notion of a program in tolerance sponsored by a state that continues to allow, and even at times foment, ethnically based discrimination, raises questions about the sincerity of such a state program.

Others I met in 2005 had found more lucrative work in psychological training. Aleksandr and Zhenya, the two psychologists I came to know best at ReGeneration, had moved on to other work and were organizing trainings for multinational corporations with offices in Russia, and traveling a great deal internationally in the process. As they described it, the multinational corporate clients want them to translate a team-building ethos for their Russian compatriots. Perhaps the only people for whom there seemed to have been little change were Nikolai and Olessia, who were continuing their work with Verity, and Vitya Markov and his colleague Vladimir Mikhailovich. That work seemed unabated, and Nikolai continued to try to translate his vector system to US markets.

What should one make of this update? While the public-policy relevance of the promotion of humanistic psychotherapy appears to have faded in the last decade, its relevance to building human capital in commercial work has grown. Psychological training, personal growth, psychosociality—these are important in the biopolitical economy only to the degree that they generate capital. It is not that the interest in things psychotherapeutic has waned, but it has become more normalized. Self-work has become part of the normal practices of doing business and managing populations; its unruliness vis-à-vis the hegemony of stabil'nost' appears remoter than at the start of my fieldwork. From that perspective, the questions explored in this book about care's complicity with structures of inequality, and its potential as a form of social and political work, must be shifted to a new ground—one of narrowed biopolitical horizons and commensuration. My impression is that commercial psychotherapy is now, more than before, a form of middle-class culture building that includes an interest in self-promotion. Meanwhile, its linkages to democratic politics appear diminished. Putin's broader attack on public speech and the channeling of potentiation into narrowly market-cum-national forms have solidified the sense that psychotherapeutic talk was, perhaps only for a time, also a place to explore alternate kinds of political subjectivity—kinds that, it turns out, have not accorded with the dominant view of the new Russia. Whether there are discursive spaces within psychotherapeutic care that continue to critique the various political abuses of the Putin era is, it would seem, a topic for another project. My suspicion is that, beneath the surface of things, care remains precarious, and psychotherapists continue to probe the outsides of biopolitical and economic legibility.

Implications and Future Directions

What do I hope that readers will take away from this study? My point, once again, is that thinking about care as precarious creates an important analytic space. Specifically, it enables one to see the incommensurable, politico-ethical face of care, alongside its regressive effects. Perhaps more important, thinking about care as precarious also hones in on the breakage points within biopolitical schemes—the points where subjection does not take form. A critical anthropology need not simply reinforce analytically the vision of domination that powerful states seek to promote (see Tsing 2000; Gibson-Graham 2006). It is not that the critique of neoliberalism as a political rationality that promotes selfishness, heightened inequality, and crushed social supports is invalid, only that assessments of the macro- and micropolitical effects of those policies do not smoothly scale down to those working in the interstitial zones between government and everyday life. People are not effects of power. Rather, they (and we) are compromised agents, and the things that they (and we) do with and for others—whether as Soviet or post-Soviet psychotherapists or anthropologists—are messy, precariously interfaced with power, and therefore politico-ethical.

Now, about that little story at the border: how might attention to the moral economy help clarify the double valence of psychotherapeutic care? Apart from the fact that, for better and for worse, there often seems to be a way to get what one needs in Russia, regardless of the law, the informal practices of the moral economy appear relatively resistant to both the capitalization of daily life and depersonalization:[2] Caroline Humphrey (2002), Catherine Wanner (2005), and Michele Rivkin-Fish (2005) describe how in the early years of wild capitalism, people continued to hold on to certain moral orientations that separated the bribe (vziatka) from pull (blat) because of the foreignness of the money form to social relations. At the time of my main fieldwork, this social aversion to money still held sway. The exchange of cash among friends was terribly awkward, and I found that traditions of charity and social care were strong over and above the accumulation of things (see Caldwell 2016). While some informal practices—for instance, firms that sell semilegal ways to circumvent Russia's bureaucracy—have been capitalized, the legacy of the moral economy lives on. Douglas Rogers (2009, 245) suggests that the "incontrovertible economic logic with no consideration of any human values, practices, or consequences" that arrived in Russia will continue to be "remoralized." And Serguei Oushakine (2009, 15–78) suggests that in trying to make sense of the changes of the last two decades, people have "repatriated" capitalism in ways that incorporate other kinds of sociality and values. Might Russia's persisting moral economy be not only a source of corrupt officials and Land Rovers cutting in line but also a way of imagining Russia's political and social life? At stake is an analytic imperative to seek breakage points between the everyday and its instrumentalization via abandonment in the form of cost-effectiveness, profit seeking, ethnonationalism, and other socially corrosive practices.

In this book, I have found Michel Foucault's (1988, 1990b, 1997a, 2005) writings on the "ethical practices of freedom" a particularly helpful resource—especially because that late work grew out of earlier writings on discipline, power/knowledge, governmentality, and biopolitics. James Laidlaw (2002) has drawn on Foucault's late writings to subvert social (or economic) control theses of human conduct, in order to shift from anthropological discussions of agency to an attention to ethics and freedom. He suggests that the focus on agency has narrowed the view of human action to one of effectiveness—a mode of being that, even if oppositionally, is always-already prefigured by power. Agents are always seen to be succeeding (or failing) at something, inscribing their wishes in the structures of power. He writes, "As an index of freedom, the concept of agency is preemptively selective. Only actions contributing towards what the analyst sees as structurally significant count as instances of agency. Put most crudely, we only mark them down as agency when people's choices seem to us to be the right ones" (315). In contrast to this approach, Laidlaw argues that a Foucauldian inquiry into the ethical pursuit of freedom may offer a more comprehensive view of human conduct based not on some outcome but on the active practices of self, based on "models," or available repertoires (as Douglas Rogers puts it). Laidlaw writes, "The freedom of the ethical subject, for Foucault, consists in the possibility of choosing the kind of self one wishes to be" (324)—a choosing that, of course, takes place within constraints.[3]

The politico-ethical face of care in Russia, however, is far less self-centered than this particular strand of late Foucauldianism. The views expressed by various psychologists and psychotherapists about the social dimensions of self-realization were versions of freedom of a different sort. As anthropological studies of Russia have shown, freedom (*svoboda*) has a more social dimension than in liberal societies. Humphrey (2007) points out that the word *svoboda*, which is derived from *svoi*, or "ours," has historically connoted a form of "freedom with." Thus, it is less "I am free" than "we are free together." She notes that this is often vis-à-vis an "alien other," but not in every case. Another important part of the discourse of freedom in Russia is the notion of the community, or *mir*, which can ideally have a limitless reach. One need not be free only with one's people (and in opposition to some other); one can also become free in a sense of cosmic oneness, in keeping with an "image of the universalized community" (4).[4] Humphrey is not alone in her reading of Russian ideas about freedom. In his research on late-socialist forms of sociality, Alexei Yurchak (2006) has described forms of close togetherness (obshchenie) in which identities were mutually dependent on those of others. These groupings were known as *svoi*, which has the same root word as *svoboda*. Through svoi, people established "deterritorialized milieus" in which they could practice a form of daily life—freely, as it were—among intimates. Crucially, these milieus were not "free from" Soviet society but were very much free within it. They were *vnye*, or simultaneously inside and outside Soviet culture. Similarly, the many anthropological studies of the Russian moral economy have noted how people rely on others to make ends meet. As described by Alena Ledeneva (2006), Vadim Volkov (2002), and others, blat, or pull, was an essential survival strategy and therefore anchored social identities within economies of favors. Even more recently, the members of the punk protest group Pussy

Riot invoked the need for "inner freedom" in their outspoken objection to Putinism (Alyokhina, Samutsevich, and Tolokonnikova 2012; see also Nikitin 2012). Therefore, in Russia there is a certain social-moral orientation toward freedom that diverges from both the atomized self-interested individual and the money form—two ideal-type touchstones of liberal societies.

According to Humphrey, however, in the post-Soviet period svoboda has been resignified under capitalism. "Svoboda-freedom has a new content, widely seen to come from the West: namely contested elections, privatization, consumer choice, religious revivals, NGOs, environmental movements, gender consciousness." Moreover, this "new *svoboda* is available to anyone with the wealth or resources to exercise it." This has led to a situation in which poorer Russians are unable to afford those freedoms. "People are worried that this new 'freedom' is not really freedom at all, but the downside of endless openness, namely 'limitlessness' (*bespredel*)" (2007, 8). The ambiguity I find in the psychologists' work—namely, the participation in the entrenchment of elite power through psychological difference, and the pursuit of social change—contains these two svobodas. I raise the issue of the moral economy and the ethical practice of freedom in Russia because they frame the work of Russia's psychotherapists as an ongoing struggle between different assumptions about freedom, value, social life, and personhood that plays out through precarious care. That is, one of the virtues that Russian psychotherapists seek to cultivate for themselves, as well as their clients, is this plural kind of freedom, one based, first of all, in a "we" that is held together by particular kinds of moral exchange. If their efforts are, without question, tied to the reproduction of problematic class and gender formations, then this may be a way to better understand how they also strain to work otherwise, in the face of the confounding promise of democracy. By resisting the commensurability of value and virtue, of the political and the economic, of care and biopolitics, it is possible to consider, and perhaps also carefully support, the complex intertwinement of projects, hopes, dreams, and technologies of rule that characterizes contemporary life, not only in Russia, but in many other places as well.

NOTES

PRELUDE

1. Soon after this study began in 2005–6, anthropologists argued that the post-Soviet was a "vanishing referent" (Boyer and Yurchak 2008) and did not resonate with those who had come of age after the collapse (Thelen 2011). My research, however, suggests that the Soviet Union remains an important referent in public discourse in Russia.

2. For fascinating parallel cases of psychologization, see Kleinman and Kleinman (1985) and Zhang (2017) on China, and Kitanaka (2011) on Japan.

INTRODUCTION

1. Throughout this book I use pseudonyms to ensure confidentiality and protect people's identities. I also observe the Russian custom of using the first name and patronymic in formal relationships marked by social distance (e.g., Tamara Grigorievna), and the first name only, sometimes in diminutive form, in more intimate relations (e.g., Aleksandr, or Sasha). These pseudonyms reflect my actual relations in the field, as well as the types of formality and informality I had to observe in different institutional spaces and encounters. Finally, I have used the real names of those few figures described in the media; they are identified by their first and last names (without the patronymic).

2. As I discuss in chapter 1, there are important political and ideological reasons for the near absence in the USSR of a psychotherapy habit similar to that found in the United States. In the 1930s, psychology's "bourgeois" heritage, its vulnerability to the

charge of subjectivist idealism, and its unpalatable research results put it under increasing ideological pressure. Applied work was especially severely curtailed and began to reappear only in the 1970s.

3. At the time of my fieldwork, various psychotherapeutic practices for groups were called *"trening"* (plural: *treningi*), which translates as "training." The term summons similar phenomena in Russian as in English, merging physical exercises with ethical or ideological types of self-work. This latter meaning was particularly in evidence during the Soviet period (see Hellbeck 2006). Throughout the text I use the direct English translation "training(s)," and sometimes the transliterated "trening(i)," to preserve these meanings.

4. For key examples and perspectives in this literature, see Foucault (1991), Ferguson and Gupta (2002), Kipnis (2008), Ong (2006), and Rose (1990, 1996a).

5. I am grateful to one of Duke Press's anonymous reviewers for this elegant phrasing.

6. My fieldwork focused most closely on commercial and state-municipal work with children. In commercial services, I worked in one children's organization and participated in its long-term trainings (treningi), which lasted from several days to two weeks. I also worked in one of the city's regional Psycho-pedagogical Medico-social (PPMS) Centers, where I interviewed the staff, attended meetings, and attended therapy sessions for both staff and local teachers. Unlike in the commercial sector, their work with children was off-limits to me. I supplemented this fieldwork with interviews with sixty different practitioners in commercial, public, and nongovernmental services in which I explored the history and status of applied psychology, and collected life histories. I also conducted fieldwork in adult-oriented group therapy settings as well as in a Psychoneurological Clinic (PND). To come to grips with psychology's popular forms, I collected printed materials (popular self-help books, glossy psychology magazines, brochures promoting self-work, website materials), analyzed TV and radio programs, and visited a product expo on childhood as a strategy to assess the broader market ecology in which children's psychological services were situated. I also attended local conferences on psychology and conflict resolution. Finally, I collected materials at the Library of the Academic Sciences in Saint Petersburg. These were primarily Soviet-era documents, conference proceedings on pedagogy and psychology, and dissertations on the history of psychology. I have used these materials to supplement my interviews on Soviet psychotherapeutic practice. I combined this work with extensive secondary-source reading on the historiography of Soviet psychology, psychiatry and psychotherapy, as well as follow-up trips in 2007, 2010, 2012, and 2013. The result is a broad and yet also ethnographically grounded transect through the psychotherapeutic turn in Saint Petersburg beginning with Putin's second term and extending through to 2013. The conclusion to this book provides some updates in the period from 2013 to 2015.

7. I draw inspiration from Mariana Valverde's work. Writing on the bourgeois tinge of confessional practices in women's consciousness-raising groups, Valverde argues that such practices are not necessarily purely psychological and therefore antipolitical: "A woman can also proceed to unburdening herself in ways that construct a sociolog-

ical or economic cause of the violent situation rather than one rooted in some deep psychological truth" (2004, 83). In other words, people may engage in them for a variety of reasons, including political ones.

8. I find Mikhail Bakhtin's notion of unfinalizability (*nezavershennost'*) helpful here. Literally translated as "not completed, finished, ended or finalized," the concept describes the complexity and open-endedness of events, acts, and the most basic of encounters—the dialogue. Bakhtin writes evocatively, "Nothing conclusive has yet taken place in the world, the ultimate word of the world and about the world has not yet been spoken, the world is open and free, everything is still in the future and will always be in the future" (1984, 166). As an analytic, this is paradoxical. As Morson and Emerson note (1990, 6), Bakhtin's concept is "a highly rational attempt to imagine the world as incommensurate with systems." But the paradox is also what makes it fruitful for a critical anthropology. *Unfinalizability* names a productive tension between systematization and the everyday, and between theory and ethnography. Theorization totalizes; ethnography unravels.

9. Liisa Malkki writes in this spirit, noting that for people involved in humanitarian work, "it was not as 'global citizens,' 'worldly nomads,' or 'cosmopolitans' but as specific social persons with homegrown needs, vulnerabilities, desires, and multiple professional responsibilities that people sought to be a part of something greater than themselves, to help, to be actors in the lively world" (2015, 4). My account differs from Malkki's in the sense that she asks, *who* is the humanitarian? My question is, *how* do care providers negotiate conflicting commitments in their work?

10. "Blasphemy," writes Donna Haraway, "has always seemed to require taking things very seriously. I know no better stance to adopt from within the secular-religious, evangelical traditions of US politics, including the politics of socialist-feminism. Blasphemy protects one from the moral majority within, while still insisting on the need for community. Blasphemy is not apostasy. Irony is about contradictions that do not resolve into larger wholes, even dialectically, about the tension of holding incompatible things together because both or all are necessary and true. Irony is about humor and serious play. It is also a rhetorical strategy and a political method, one I would like to see more honoured within socialist-feminism" (1991, 149).

11. See Rabinow (1996) for a discussion of biosociality. To borrow the words of Anne Allison, psychosociality effected a "revaluing of life as wealth of a different kind, based on the humanness of a shared precariousness and shared efforts to do something about it" (2013, 179).

12. In contrast with Kantian ethics as a system of norms, "practical ethics" follows an Aristotelian vein. In relation to the care of the self, Foucault distinguishes between practices that seek to discover an authentic content or self-identity, which he compares to "mortification" (2000a, 311), and practices that aim to *create* a self-content (2005, 56–57). It is these latter practices that Foucault affiliates with the practice of freedom—a freedom that does not simply resist, but takes shape in and through power relations where the care of the self "is a way of limiting and controlling power" (1997a, 288). Scholars have wondered whether Foucault's turn to ethics and the care of the self betrays his

earlier work on discipline and power/knowledge. But Foucault consistently saw these inquiries as related. The study of discipline was a study of the structures of coercion and domination—an approach that bracketed the question of practices—and his later work was an attempt to think the question of practices and subjectivity alongside his earlier insights about capillary power. See Foucault (2000b, 1994), as well as Povinelli (2012), Koopman and Matza (2013).

13. See Mahmood (2005), Laidlaw (2002), Faubion (2011), and Lambek (2010). In the anthropology of Russia, see D. Rogers (2009) and Zigon (2011).

14. Joel Robbins (2013) and Sherry B. Ortner (2016) identify a tension in anthropology between the "suffering slot" and the anthropology of the good (Robbins), and between "dark anthropology" and the anthropology of ethics (Ortner). This study walks the line between these analytic practices.

15. Several historical factors contributed to this shift, including exchanges with Eastern European psychologists following World War II (Vasilyeva 2005; Elena Kazakova, personal communication, October 12, 2007); "citizen diplomats," including psychotherapists and psychologists, who visited the Soviet Union in the 1970s and 1980s (see Hassard 1990); and perestroika-era liberalization. As scholars have pointed out, popular psychology in Russia has been a site of hybridization, merging American and European strands of psychotherapy with the emotional styles (Lerner 2011) and socialities (Leykin 2015) of postsocialism.

16. Even at the height of Russia's oil boom in the early 2000s, 20 million people, or 15 percent of the population, were considered poor, living on less than 5,083 rubles ($169) a month, and another 25 percent were considered vulnerable to poverty, hovering just above the poverty line (World Bank 2009b, 17–18).

17. One of the interesting features of success is its uneasy fit with other, historically sedimented categories of social distinction in Russia, particularly those tied to the liberal intelligentsia, such as *kul'turnost'* (culturedness) and *intelligentnost'* (intelligence or good upbringing). On intelligentsia class discourses, see Rivkin-Fish (2009) and Patico (2005). For studies that merge a Marxian attention to structural position with a Weberian focus on status and symbolic production, see, for example, Bourdieu (1984), Willis (1977), Frykman and Löfgren (1987), and Ortner (2006).

18. This pattern recapitulates a broad, perhaps even global trend, whereby unremunerated or poorly remunerated affective labor is also feminized. On the normative gendering of the workplace, marriage, and family life in Russia, see, for example, Zdravomyslova (2010); Rotkirch, Temkina, and Zdravomyslova (2007); Zdravomyslova and Temkina 2003; and Rivkin-Fish (2010).

19. In this and other translations in this book, the use of the pronoun "himself" reflects common usage in Russian, whereby the masculine pronoun, he (*ego*), is used as a universal, standing for both men and women. In other instances, such as the common phrase "New Soviet Man" (*Novyi Sovetskii Chelovek*), I translate the word *chelovek* (also *person*) as "man" in order to reflect the gendering of personhood that typified Soviet discourses and that is still quite common in Russia today. Finally, in instances where I am, myself, referring to the broad category of persons, I use the phrase *he or she* to counter androcentric discourses.

20. The tests mentioned refer, respectively, to the Stanford-Binet Intelligence Scales, which test intellectual and developmental delays in children, and the Hand Test, which is used to forecast aggressive behavior.

21. On the productive power of discourse, see Foucault (1990a, 1995). On the relevance of these arguments to the psychological expertise, see Rose (1996b) and Hacking (1995).

22. This bifurcation of care is part of a global phenomenon whereby the management (and production) of affect has become a crucial site for the circulation of capital. The service industry, branding, and the mantra "have a nice day" are emblematic of contemporary efforts to harness affect for the ends of accumulation. Often termed *immaterial* or *affective labor* (Lazzarato 1996; Hardt 1999; Negri 1999), the forms of work that have arisen around affect channel interiority toward ever more sensuous capitalist experiences (Gill and Pratt 2008). In Russia this is seen in the importance placed on soft skills in customer service, and the role of psychologists in helping develop these and other skills. Psychological education in the commercial sector thus draws clients into new forms of immaterial labor by teaching them to convert affect into capital. But its contrasting forms—in municipal services—also indicate the social limits of the affect economy.

23. *Modernization* refers to a set of reforms undertaken by Putin that began in his first term and have been directed at social and political institutions. For an overview of Putin's "conservative modernization" (and a comparison with the competing "liberal modernization") in Russia, see Urnov (2012).

24. These tactics are the small maneuvers of making do with what has been given (see Caldwell 2004), a kind of "escape without leaving" (Farquhar and Zhang 2005) not unlike the politics of *vnye*, of living simultaneously inside and outside, that Alexei Yurchak (2006) describes in late socialism. This analytic language supports inquiries that avoid reducing *being* a subject to undergoing processes of subjectification—in Michel de Certeau's (1988) language, confusing *production* with *use*.

25. During the Lüscher color test, subjects are presented with cards consisting of a range of colors and asked to choose the favorite, until none are left. The test is used to assess personality types on the basis of particular assumptions about how color preference, presumed to be unconscious, correlates with personality.

26. Discussions of democracy in postsocialist contexts are vexed and crowded, both in the more prescriptive social science fields and in anthropology. Chris Hann, Caroline Humphrey, and Katherine Verdery (2002; see also Hann and Dunn 1996) and Michael Burawoy and Katherine Verdery (1999) have noted a tendency among political scientists to let normative assumptions drive analyses of Russia, leading in some cases to echoes of Francis Fukuyama's (1992) "end of history" and the triumph of liberal capitalism. In contrast, anthropologists working in postsocialist and postcolonial contexts have been critical of the liberal triumphalism that has been promoted in Russia and elsewhere. Critiques have been leveled at the reform policies' lack of fit with cultural or institutional conditions, the cynical use of democratic rhetoric to secure an entrenched elite's hegemony (Paley 2001), and the paradoxical silencing effects of certain liberal politics and their invocations of freedom, equality, and human

rights (see Spivak 1988; Said 1994; Mahmood 2005; Englund 2006). When it comes to Russia, this polarized field obscures as much as it reveals about the complexities of post-Soviet transformation.

27. In making these arguments, I join other recent anthropologies about therapeutics, which take us helpfully through, and also beyond, the biopolitical's "remedial institutions" (Favret-Saada 1989). E. Summerson Carr (2011) discusses how many self-help practices involve clients learning certain metalinguistic practices to remake themselves. Yet Carr argues that while such practices take place within specific discursive and institutional contexts, clients often "flip the script" in their favor. Rebecca J. Lester's (2007) work poses the therapeutic as a rite of passage by which clients are moved (or move themselves) to an institutionally more desirable state of being grounded in "values deemed important to recovery (such as personal responsibility)" and "specific practices (such as requiring clients to make the bed each morning)" (370). Again, though, as a ritual practice the therapeutic also entails a *reconfiguration* of cultural proscriptions—a "critical therapeutics" that decomposes the therapeutic in ways not unlike critical analytics. Finally, Angela Garcia (2010) underscores the sociality of care: it rests on both intimate interrelations and a felt dependence between people rooted in broader understandings of responsibility. Viewed as a dependency, care can lead one person, along with another, into harm's way (as with intergenerational drug use). But dependency can also be an engine of mutual responsibility that sustains sociality.

1. THE HAUNTING SUBJECT IN SOVIET BIOPOLITICS

1. The research context for Bauer's work is important, especially since his book (based on his doctoral thesis) has influenced subsequent histories. Bauer, a social psychologist and historian, was a researcher in the Harvard Project for the Study of Soviet Society (HPSSS), helmed by Clyde Kluckholn and undertaken in cooperation with the US Air Force in the 1950s. Bauer gathered most of his materials via interviews with Soviet refugees in the 1950s. At the time, the functionalist theories of Talcott Parsons, who trained Kluckholn and whose Harvard center may have also influenced the scope and methodology of the HPSSS, were an influential social science paradigm. This may explain part of the rationale for focusing so much on the functional relationships among philosophical debates, ideology, and party decisions—an approach appropriate to certain kinds of research interests and topics but not others. (I am indebted to Sylvia Yanagisako for making this point.) Another reason was certainly the paucity of available sources. In the course of the project, Bauer interviewed many psychologists, psychiatrists, and doctors, who supplied him with materials for his history of Soviet psychology. These transcripts, now available online through Harvard's Davis Center, show that Bauer was keenly interested in finding support for his theory that the debates in philosophical Marxism in the late 1920s and 1930s were the central driver of psychological theory and practice. Generally, his respondents confirmed this view, strengthening his claim that these fields were politicized because they touched on politically sensitive issues such as the relationship of human capacity to socialist environments, the tension between social position and nationality, and also the relationship of theory and practice.

But there are also a number of responses in Bauer's archive that don't accord with this. One of his informants suggested that the "determinism" orientation of some psychologists in the 1920s (i.e., the mechanistic idea that social environment determined personality and consciousness) was completely spontaneous and not decreed from above (HPSSS n.d., 4). This informant added that the research directions people adopted were less a matter of decree than funding: people would read the party discussions for clues as to how to orient their work (HPSSS n.d., 7). Meanwhile, Bauer's own notes following his interviews underscore his interest in high-level philosophical debates and the ideological character of psychological work. These points suggest that Bauer's focus on ideology and policies is but one historical approach. See, for instance, Anna Krylova's (2000) essay on the "tenacious liberal subject" in Soviet history, which argues that the work of many US historians has been guided by a tacit search for signs of a "liberal subjectivity" (120) that would resist the communist Russian state.

2. Elizabeth Lunbeck, Emily Martin, and Louis Sass coined the term the "psy-ences" in a seminar series entitled "The Psy-ences Project" in order to explore the social history of disciplines such as psychiatry, psychology, psychoanalysis, and psychopharmacology. Eugene Raikhel and Dörte Bemme (2016) elaborated on the term *psy-ences* in relation to postsocialism.

3. With regard to the historiography on the Soviet Union, Alexander Etkind (1997, 225) argues, "Western literature . . . tends to attribute a disproportionate significance to the ideological debates that took place at the end of the 1920s. In an oblique way, Western scholars are in agreement with the Soviet [philosophical] debaters they study, many of whom really believed that the force and ideological purity of their arguments could shape something tangible in the future." In response, this chapter also draws on studies that show how the Stalinization and ideologization of the field did not continue unabated beyond the 1950s. Rather, psychologists and psychotherapists both tested the edges of their field, promoting alternative humanisms, exploring supposedly forbidden literatures, and inserting a variety of proto–talking cures into psychiatric work.

4. I have referred to the formation of Soviet psychology as being *biopolitical*. By this I mean to highlight the way that the psy-ences fit into the USSR's broader objectives in managing its population as an object of social policy. In the words of Thomas Lemke (2008), biopolitics is linked to that instance "when life is taken into account by political strategies, when population emerges as an object for politics, as something that can be transformed, that can be optimised, on which one can intervene, which can be used to achieve certain ends." While Michel Foucault's concept was primarily developed via a genealogy of liberalism, Stephen J. Collier (2011) has recently described what he calls "socialist biopolitics" in Russia. He shows that in the Soviet Union biopolitics was premised on a teleological political ontology of "total planning." This involved the precise calculation of social norms and needs, and the meeting of those norms and needs in and through decisions on social policy. This planning paradigm can be contrasted with Foucault's explorations of liberal biopolitics in Europe. Foucault argues that the French physiocrats, for example, established the boundaries of government and the calculation of social norms and needs by way of the recognition of various regularities (demand, mortality rates, etc.). Social policy under these conditions was what Collier

might call "genetic," as opposed to "teleological." The point is that the Soviet Union, which had not undergone a bourgeois revolution, established different kinds of biopolitical arrangements among population, production, and welfare.

Nikolas Rose (2007) uses the neologism *ethopolitics* to denote the management of the population's psychology. This distinction is interesting, if problematic inasmuch as it assumes a split between mind and body. As a reading of the history of Soviet psychology shows, the seat of human psychology was in constant debate—oscillating between materialist conceptions of the brain and subjectivist conceptions of the mind or psyche. For these reasons, the production of a difference between biology and psychology is itself internal to biopolitics. (Some of these ideas were developed in conversation with Kevin Lewis O'Neill.)

5. Discussions of the practices and even the concrete institutions of Soviet psychology are commonly excluded from the historical literature. Getting a sense of the applied fields is difficult. Instead, the historical literature has tended to focus on philosophical and theoretical debates within Marxism and psychology, and on the party politics of the 1920s and 1930s. Nonetheless, since the main contours of Soviet psychology—both its theoretical and applied forms—were drawn at that time, a kind of partial view of practice does come into view. My discussion of the first decades of Soviet psychology relies on Raymond Bauer's *The New Man in Soviet Psychology* (1959), David Joravsky's *Russian Psychology: A Critical History* (1989), Alex Kozulin's *Psychology in Utopia: Toward a Social History of Soviet Psychology* (1984), Martin Miller's *Freud and the Bolsheviks: Psychoanalysis in Imperial Russia and the Soviet Union* (1998), Loren Graham's *Science, Philosophy, and Human Behavior in the Soviet Union* (1987), Joseph Wortis's *Soviet Psychiatry* (1950), and Artur V. Petrovsky's *Psychology in the Soviet Union: A Historical Outline* (1990). These texts provide a good sense of how the evolving ideological positions on the discourses of self, person, consciousness, and the psyche impacted applied work.

6. With the exception of hygiene campaigns, the "civilizing missions" linked to taste, consumption, and self-fashioning would come later (see Dunham 1990; Hellbeck 2006).

7. See also Fitzpatrick 1999.

8. The sciences were initially dominated by the Soviet intelligentsia (Suny 2011, 226–31; see also Beer 2008). Facing the post–Civil War economic collapse, Lenin had advised not to fear using "bourgeois specialists" (Suny 2011, 75). Stalin's purges changed this.

9. Even before the October Revolution, Russian psychology had been trending toward objectivism and away from an introspectionist approach concerned with subjective reactions to experiences. Such was also the case abroad. According to Joravsky (1989), psychology around the world had been in crisis since the late nineteenth century, when a division between objectivism and subjectivism had been heightened. As an object of hard science, the psyche had been deemed empirically unreachable. This already-existing unease in the sciences of mind was thus compatible with the Bolshevik's fetishism of science as well as the orthodox Marxist determinism that held sway in the late 1920s.

10. Bauer (1959) suggests that this disagreement was linked to the much broader Marxist doctrinal conflict between spontaneity and consciousness, which he glosses

as spontaneity versus intervention, or genetics versus teleology. At the level of politics, the former was allied with a deterministic attitude according to which the laws of history would bring about the development of Soviet society and thus no intervention was required. The latter was a call for social planning. For a consideration of the relationship between genetic versus teleological understandings in Soviet biopolitics, see Stephen Collier (2011).

11. These shifts foreshadow the development of structural Marxism—for example, Louis Althusser's theory of the relative autonomy of the superstructure.

12. The relationship that Stalin prescribed between party-mindedness (*partiinost'*) and the scientific rigor (*nauchnost'*) changed over time. In the 1930s, partiinost' had been determinative of nauchnost' under the premise that even objective science could be corrupted by bourgeois idealism, and also that theory should follow praxis. This had played out in agriculture with the installation of Lysenko, whose disavowal of genetics is well known (see Pollock 2009), and also Stalin's own interventions in linguistics (see Yurchak 2006). Before the end of this life, however, Stalin reversed course, insisting that certain things are subject to "objective laws" that cannot be determined by policy. This undoubtedly shielded psychologists from what could have been another brutal swing against their field in the name of objectivity and materialism. And when de-Stalinization began in 1953, the last assault on psychology by physiology was brought to an end.

13. Joravsky notes of the early use of intelligence tests by pedologists: "[In Russia the pioneers of IQ testing] shared the populist ideology that prevailed in the educational profession of their country, the conviction that poor people at the bottom did not put themselves there, that great talents were imprisoned within the uncivilized (*nekul'turnye*) masses, to be set free by revolutionary abolition of social constraints and by educators bearing modern culture to the liberated masses" (1989, 346). Speaking of post-Soviet psychology, Albert Gilgen and Carol Gilgen argue that "taking the test away from psychologists deprived them of a tool that no doubt greatly inhibited the growth of the discipline in the USSR" (1996, 14).

14. The term *psychodynamic* is a broader term than *psychoanalytic* and encompasses the latter. Freud is generally considered to have coined one of the first psychodynamic theories of mind. Psychodynamic theory emphasizes the interplay of different psychic elements, whether cognition and emotion, or, in Freud's case, the ego-id-superego constellation. According to one historian, dynamic psychology "conceives of psychological problems as resulting from intrapsychic conflicts, unconscious motivations, and the interplay of external demands with components of the personality structure" (Hunt 1993, 564).

15. Miller cites a article from 1923 by Bernard Bykhovskii, a Bolshevik philosopher, which articulated a theory of Freudomarxism. As Miller summarizes,

> [Bykhovskii] argued . . . that Freud's thesis can be interpreted from a materialist point of view. The conflict between our psychological needs and the social demands placed upon us, which is censored, mediated, and transformed ('displaced' or 'transferred' to other acceptable realms of everyday existence) in our unconscious, moves irrevocably toward some resolution. . . . The structure of conflict resolution Bykhovskii found to be, if not analogous to the social class struggle in historical

periods, at least consistent with it methodologically. . . . Closer examination of the links between Freud's emphasis on 'psychic sources' of conflict and Marx's stress on the oppressive nature of social class conflict could only expand our efforts to improve the world of the postrevolutionary order, Bykhovskii concluded. (1985, 629)

16. These arguments anticipate those made in the antipsychiatry movement of the 1960s and 1970s in the United States, as well as some critiques of the psy-ences in critical anthropology.

17. For an overview of Pavlov and Russian narcology, see Raikhel (2016). Raikhel shows how a similar focus on mechanism over etiology was common in alcohol treatment at this time. Quite fascinatingly, Soviet psychiatry's materialist orientation prefigures the current "age of the brain" in the United States and Europe (Rose and Abi-Rached 2013).

18. Soviet rational psychotherapy bears a similarity to the now-popular cognitive-behavioral therapies in the United States. For a discussion of cognitive-behavioral therapies' origins and relationship to psychoanalysis in the United States, see Smith (2009).

19. For a more substantive discussion of rational psychotherapy, see Lauterbach's *Soviet Psychotherapy* (1984).

20. I thank Michele Rivkin-Fish for bringing my attention to this crucial dimension of Eisenberg's story.

21. In this book, published by the Marxist press International Publishers, Wells distinguishes the Soviet Union from the West by the orientation of each's psychologies. Wells notes that in the USSR, China, and Eastern Europe, "the Pavlovian conditioned reflex approach is having a profound influence on diverse sciences and institutions," whereas in the West, especially the USA, "the Freudian psychoanalytic approach today . . . spreads throughout the world wherever it can penetrate" (1956, 12).

22. *Samizdat*, literally "self-published" or "self-made," is the Soviet term for censored texts that were copied by hand and distributed through social networks; they were often first obtained by people who had visited other countries.

23. As of 1961, the psychology faculty had been closed for nearly three decades, and the psychological disciplines had been folded into the philosophy department. That Eisenberg was wandering between psychiatry and psychology already suggests a loosening of the boundaries between the two.

24. Others put the engagement with Freud differently. Another female practitioner educated in the 1970s told me that a common way to read Freud was through "bourgeois criticism" (*burzhuaznaia kritika*)—that is, discussions of Freud were permissible when framed by perfunctory remarks about the superiority of Marxist-Leninist psychology (see Miller 1998, 140–46). See also Yurchak (2006) on the "performative shift" under late socialism.

25. To illustrate his theory of activity, Leontiev gave the example of a child playing in the same way as an adult. In the example of a child playing with a doll, Leontiev argued that what is important is neither the doll's appearance, nor the way the child sees the doll, but the social relationship the child establishes with it. The child is imitating an activity or practice that she or he has seen among adults. Here, previous activity became important. Leontiev denied the existence of an "innate human personality" and instead

asserted the formative influence of social activity on personality. A baby at birth is only an individual, not a personality. He was also critical of psychologists who developed theories of personality based on human needs like sex or hunger (i.e., Freud). "Personality cannot develop within the framework of need; its development necessarily presupposes a displacement of needs by creation, which alone does not know limits" (quoted in Graham 1987, 212–13).

26. There was also a large international congress organized around the unconscious and in relation to Uznadze's work in 1979 in Tblisi, Georgia. According to Miller, "the conference on the unconscious was a triumph for those professionals in the Soviet Union, particularly among psychologists, who had fought for the demythologizing of Pavlovian doctrine and for the rehabilitation of the study of psychoanalytic theory" (1998, 147–48).

27. Interestingly, such insights anticipate recent discussions among affect theorists and psychologists about prediscursive (but not presocial) sensations in human experience (Massumi 2002), as well as discussions in the neurosciences about the role of nonconscious neural activity in shaping perception and behavior (Rose and Abi-Rached 2013).

28. The piatyi punkt is a designation in one's passport ostensibly denoting religious belief. In actuality, it was based not on belief but on blood.

29. Eugene Raikhel's (2010) study of narcology is consistent with what I heard from practitioners: narcology had a low status among medical fields, primarily because of the target population (alcoholics were viewed unsympathetically in the Soviet Union) and secondarily because of the routine set of treatment tools (hypnosis, drug treatments, and placebo therapies).

30. For more on podshivka, see Chepurnaia and Etkind 2006; Raikhel 2016.

31. Miller (1998, 120) makes the interesting point that Miasishchev received many honors for his work, but never from the Academy of Medical Sciences (only from the Academy of Pedagogical Sciences). This is intriguing given that this tension between medical and educational expressions of psychological work has been recapitulated in the post-Soviet period.

32. Oleg Kharkhordin (1999, 184–201) notes that in the nineteenth century, influenced by the translation of Jean-Jacques Rousseau's works and the Russian Enlightenment, the term lichnost' developed a dual meaning—one "high," one "low." The high meaning referred to the notion of a unique individual; the low to a basic notion of the person. He argues that in the Soviet Union this duality was extended and rechanneled. The tension between the high sense of lichnost' and bourgeois individualism was addressed in the early Soviet period by asserting that it is socialist society that gives rise to developed, harmonious, and unique individuals, thus preserving the fundament of individualism. This was extended under Stalin, when stories of the heroes of socialism became common. Still, argues Kharkhordin, becoming an exceptional individual was not necessarily a mass phenomenon, and the average person remained a lichnost' in the low sense. This basic lichnost', however, became important in the "mass individuation" of the postwar period, when the collective was deployed by educators like Anton Makarenko to create, not spectacular individuals, but, as Kharkhordin puts it, a person "that socialist society needs" (200).

33. The literal translation of *telefon doveriia* is "trust line"; Vladimir here emphasizes the word *trust* (*doveriia*).

34. Makarenko (1888–1939) became the director of a labor colony of war orphans and juvenile delinquents in 1920. Makarenko's success at "civilizing" waifs, delinquents, and addicts attracted the attention of the party, and he eventually became a kind of Soviet Dr. Spock (Bronfenbrenner 1970), providing parents advice on *vospitanie*, a word that implies "upbringing" with a moral cast (Bozhovich and Slavina 1967). His books became "the bible of Soviet education" and psychology (Joravsky 1989, 350). Consider, for example, this passage from his hugely popular book *Road to Life*:

> I ventured to question the correctness of the generally accepted theory of those days [the 1920s and early 1930s], that punishment of any sort is degrading, that it is essential to give the fullest possible scope to the sacred creative impulses of the child, and that the great thing is to rely upon self-organization and self-discipline. I also ventured to advance the theory, to me incontrovertible, that, so long as the collective, and the organs of the collective, had not been created, so long as no traditions existed, and no elementary habits of labor and mores had been formed, the teacher was entitled—nay, was bound!—to use compulsion. I also maintained that it was impossible to base the whole of education on the child's interests, that the cultivation of the sense of duty frequently runs counter to them, especially as these present themselves to the child itself. I called for the education of a strong, toughened individual, capable of performing work that may be both unpleasant and tedious, should the interests of the collective require it.
>
> Summing up, I insisted upon the necessity of a strong, enthusiastic, if necessary a stern collective, and of placing all hopes on the collective alone. My opponents could only fling their pedological axioms in my face, starting over and over again from the words "the child." (Quoted in Joravsky 1989, 351)

35. The exchange of psychological knowledge was complemented by the exchange of mass-mediated confession in the form of the *Phil Donahue Show*, which aired on Soviet television in 1987 after a series of so-called US-Soviet telebridges connecting live studio audiences.

36. The American Association for Humanistic Psychology hosted numerous diplomatic trips to the USSR in the 1980s and included numerous accounts in its journal, the *Journal of Humanistic Psychology*. See Bondarenko (1999), Greening (1984, 1989), Hassard (1990), Macy (1987), and C. Rogers (1987).

37. Cole (1986) explored this question through observation of Soviet "family clubs" based on the popular teachings of Boris Nikitin. These involved practices like physical fitness, vegetarianism, spending time in the countryside, home birth, herbal medicine, tai chi, Erhard Seminars Training (EST), and meditation, and a general interest in freeing "hidden human potential" (70).

38. I am grateful to Nima Bassiri for the phrase *conditions of acceptability* in place of the usual Foucauldian *conditions of possibility*. As this chapter demonstrates, it was not so much epistemological limits as political-ideological constraint that shaped the Soviet psy-ences.

39. Similar to what Saiba Varma (2012) describes in Kashmir, in Russia the late-socialist psychosocial approaches to care remained institutionally subordinate to medical psychiatry. The interplay among biological, psychological, and social approaches to mental distress, nicely framed by Junko Kitanaka (2011), is connected to the ways in which health and personhood are conceived and reconceived under shifting social and political conditions.

2. THE SUCCESS COMPLEX AND PSYCHOLOGICAL DIFFERENCE

1. The fact that ReGeneration's lagery focused on Russian youth and merged leisure and learning had a cultural resonance with the Soviet period. Communist youth groups like the Pioneers had also organized lagery, in some cases in the same locations outside the city, to cultivate future citizens. Tamara Grigorievna explained that ReGeneration hoped to become known as a place where children from influential families rub shoulders. She compared their camps to Artek, a very famous Soviet pioneer camp for the party elite's children.

2. *Modernization* refers to a set of reforms undertaken by Putin beginning in his first term, directed at social and political institutions. For an overview of Putin's "conservative modernization" (and a comparison with the competing "liberal modernization") in Russia, see Urnov (2012).

3. A focus on ethnicity is also relevant here but is beyond the scope of this chapter.

4. As a well-known educator and writer, Simon Soloveychik, wrote in 1985 in the newspaper *Novyi Mir* (New World), parents needed to leave behind the Soviet pedagogical formulas for upbringing, which he called the "street-traffic model" of teaching rules, the "vegetable-garden" approach of treating the child's soul like a plot in need of weeding, and the "carrot and the stick" (1987, 10–13). Instead, drawing on Lev Vygotsky's ideas, Soloveychik (1987) advocated lovingly cultivating the child's soul. For a compendium of Soviet-era worries over children and families, see Kelly (2007).

5. As Suvi Salmenniemi (2013) notes, while the Soviet Union was classless with regard to economic capital, other types of capital (political, social, and cultural) were mobilized to create class distinctions. Thus, when Eklof and Dneprov (1993, 5) argue that the debate within the APN essentially played out a long-standing class-based conflict within Soviet society between the middle classes, who were disinclined toward leveling, and the margins of the educational community, what is meant is a conflict among those with varying degrees of access to political, social, and cultural capital.

6. Following Soviet-era terminologies, Attwood (1990, 2) uses the phrase "psychological sex" instead of gender. For purposes of clarity, I opt for the latter.

7. *Soprovozhenie* can be translated as guidance, accompaniment, or support. As Anna Pavlovna Ovcharova (2012, 71) notes, it generally denotes "an action, which accompanies some phenomenon [*deistvie, soputstvuiushchee komu-libo iavleniiu*]." She continues, "Etymologically it comes from the verb 'to accompany' [*soprovozhdat'*], which has several meaningful interpretations. The meaning of the interpretation depends on the context, but it generally refers to simultaneously occurring phenomena, or actions. It is interesting that the use of this verb with the reflexive suffix '*sia*' [as in *soprovozhdat'sia*] . . . shifts the focus to a form of oversight [*kuriruemyi*] . . . as in 'to

entail as a direct continuation or consequence,' 'to be implemented or equipped with something.'" For the purposes of this book, I translate soprovozhdenie as "guidance" in order to retain a general link between this practice and guidance counseling approaches in Europe and the US. Nonetheless, I think that the notion of being side-by-side contained in the translation *accompaniment* retains an important dimension of this practice. This should be kept in mind when reading the history of soprovozhdenie in Russia.

8. In the striking words of one Russian acquaintance, from 1991 on Russia had been "kicked like a street dog" by the United States and its allies. As anthropologists have noted, a sense of national shame appears in an everyday discourse of permanent crisis (Shevchenko 2009), despair, and conspiracy theory (Oushakine 2009).

9. Russia's annual GDP growth rate in 2008 was -7.8 percent, compared to -1.5 percent for South Africa, -0.3 percent for Brazil, 8.5 percent for India, and 9.2 percent for China. The world GDP fell by 2.1 percent for 2008 (World Bank 2016).

10. In 2007, at the time of my main fieldwork, life expectancy at birth had still not returned to 1990 levels (see Anderson 1997). The average male life expectancy at birth was sixty, putting Russia among the lowest in the former Soviet bloc and at the level of many much poorer nations around the world (WHO 2009a, 44). Women's life expectancy was also low. In 2006, suicide rates for men were 53.9 per 100,00 (tied for second highest in the world with Lithuania) (WHO 2009b). Combined with low fertility rates (1.3 children per woman), the Russian population as a whole had been contracting by 0.4 percent per year since 1997 (WHO 2009a, 136–37).

11. Valerie Sperling (2015, 150) notes that in the actual address, when Putin asked his question "what is most important for our country," a male voice—Putin's then Defense Minister, Sergei Ivanov—called out, "Love!" "Correct!" said Putin, before continuing his address. The official version of the address does not include this exchange.

12. Legislation approved by the Duma in 2008 increased the surveillance of young men in the country by forcing them to report to a local military commissariat if they will be absent from home for more than fifteen days. This was presumably intended to cut down on draft dodging. Journalist Paul Goble (2008) posited that these steps were in response to Russia's demographic problems: "The number of draft-age males has been falling for the last decade and will reach a level next year that will not permit Moscow to fill the ranks unless it changes existing draft rules."

13. In the months following the speech, Putin encouraged the Duma to implement the "basic mother's capital" incentive, which would pay out 250,000 rubles for a mother of two children, to be paid out gradually. The program went into effect on January 1, 2007, though some have written that the cash payments have often been delayed (see Rotkirch, Temkina, and Zdravomyslova 2007). As columnist and former Putin adviser Vladimir Frolov (2008) wrote in 2008, these efforts did have a positive, if moderate, effect on birth rates. The first half of 2007 showed a 5 percent increase in the number of children born compared to the same period the previous year, and also more than all preceding years since 1999. But Frolov asserts that this is "far from sufficient to stop the population decline": birth rates would need to grow by 50 percent over current levels to achieve that. Short of what he calls a "massive shift in social behavior," or an unsustainable boost in the government's "hiring out [of] women to

produce children," this "is simply not in the cards." He asserted that Russia's population decline can be reversed only through the much more difficult task of reducing death rates, which are "mind-blowing by a developed economy's standards." He added, "Russia is the only developed country in the world that has seen a decline in life expectancy during the last 40 years, while death rates in certain working age groups have increased twofold." This raises the interesting point that the child may prove a more effective biopolitical target than the adult, who poses for the state a far more vexing set of issues, including risky sexual behavior, addiction, and other patterns of unhealthy living, as well as costs associated with professional retraining in cases of unemployment. From the point of view of not just boosting numbers but also altering norms and behavior, children thus give the state a chance at a fresh start, while those for whom it is too late are at risk of being written off by the state as a lost generation.

14. The federal focus on biological reproduction has continued in the years since I began my fieldwork. Various social programs promote family life, with particular emphasis on women. The year 2008 was named the "Year of the Family," and a variety of pro-family events, media campaigns, and a website were launched. The mother's-capital initiative is ongoing; as of 2012, it paid families 387,640 rubles (approximately $12,000) for child-related expenses for each additional child after the firstborn. More recently, federal officials created a new national holiday called the Day of Family, Love, and Fidelity (Den' Sem'i, Liubvi i Vernostei). Attended, in my experience, mostly by elderly women, the new holiday uses the Orthodox saints Peter and Fevronia as a model married couple to promote the heteronormative, biologically reproductive marriage. In conjunction with the Orthodox Church, Putin's administration has promoted the campaign against abortion, and legislation during his third term banned the foreign adoption of Russian children in countries where gay marriage is legal. Most famously, in the lead-up to the Sochi Olympics in 2014, Russia also banned any form of "gay propaganda."

15. Putin/Medvedev/Putin refers to the widely shared view that, on many important issues of policy, Medvedev's presidency was essentially a "seat-warming" term for Putin (Ioffe 2011).

16. Modernization has also taken shape through "national projects," or *natsproekty*. First announced on September 5, 2005, and focused on four areas of reform—agriculture, education, housing, and health care—the natsproekty have become touchstones in the administration's casting of itself as socially concerned. The public figure first appointed to lead the natsproekty, Dmitry Medvedev, would later become Putin's appointed heir. Lilia Shevtsova describes the natsproekty that Medvedev has overseen as "a populist formula of stability" that has been used to "divert . . . attention to consumer aspirations" (2007, 87).

17. Povinelli's (2011) main concern with commensuration is how the vital challenges that radical worlds pose to the liberal diaspora are domesticated by means that are neither bloodless nor innocent but are nonetheless taken as normal and even just.

18. As Douglas Rogers's (2015) work on energy politics in the Perm region of Russia shows, partnerships between the state and the market continue to be a viable area of cultural development and programming in other places as well.

19. Elizabeth Dunn (2008), citing Paul Manning (2007), writes of the perceived need for consumer guidance in postsocialist countries following the semiotic and material collapse of the state and its standards. The problem of trust became real in many areas. One psychologist working on the issue of professional standards told me that their organization has co-opted the old name "Gosstandard," or "State Standard," dating from the Soviet period, in their documents. As she put it, "the state" is still "a brand" (*brend*) that people trust.

20. This particular form of celebrating the child was distinctly post-Soviet. According to Catriona Kelly (2007, 374), while beauty contests for children were becoming popular in prerevolutionary Russia, the Soviet ideal of gender egalitarianism had ended this trend. Children were often displayed in Soviet publications but usually as social representatives rather than individualized icons. According to Elizabeth Waters (1993), the first Soviet beauty contests did not appear until the late 1980s.

21. Domestic services also existed in the USSR. Well-off families could hire nannies, known as *domrabotnitsy*, or "home workers," who were supposedly unionized and had work contracts (Kelly 2007, 408–15). But compared to the current range of services, the Soviet precursor operated at a smaller, and of course less commercial, scale. In a paradoxical way, then, the supposed liberation from domestic drudgery that formal labor contracts and unions had promised women resulted for many in an embrace of motherhood as the proper way to raise one's children.

22. An article by the news service ITAR-TASS reported that bribes at Russian universities were on the rise (ITAR-TASS 2008). According to UNESCO, bribes in Russian universities totaled $520 million in 2007. The article reported that law, finance, and international relations departments (i.e., the best-remunerated professions) were the most corrupt. An official at the All-Russia Education Fund, Sergei Komkov, explained that "the universities specializing in technologies and arts are the least affected by corrupt practices. This is because those professions have middling prestige. Artists and engineers are usually low-paid specialists in this country." The chairman of the education committee of the Moscow City legislature, Yevgeny Bunimovich, contrasted Russian students with those in the West, who "realize their future career hinges on the quality of knowledge they get, and that's why bribery doesn't flourish there." Russian students, in contrast, "need graduation certificates just for the sake of a mere formality."

23. There are many ethnographies demonstrating this. Some good examples of works concerned specifically with mental health include Biehl (2005), Garcia (2010), and Davis (2012).

24. Anagnost (2006, 510–11) draws on this suzhi discourse to argue that the desire to be recognized as a body of high value draws rural migrants to turn themselves into "willing bodies for exploitation," as in the case of increased blood donation in exchange for money.

25. Donzelot (1979) argues that psychotherapists offered workable solutions to the state's liberal problematic—how shall freedom be governed?—by replacing the atmosphere of penality and judicial action that had characterized sovereign power with the soft power of the social worker, the psychohygienist, the therapist. These professions respected the boundaries of the private family, while at the same time opening up its internal rela-

tions to a series of psychotherapeutic interventions. The mantle of blame for dysfunction was placed on the relational rather than the personal, channeling the therapeutic into the "regulation of images" rather than the discipline of particular subjects.

26. The biopolitical economy under Putin is not part of a liberal problematic but rather of a distinctly postsocialist one bringing together neoliberal reforms and statism, capitalist self-styling and the remains of socialist welfare.

27. To put this in the terms Aihwa Ong (2006) uses, just as neoliberal techniques loosen the spatial link between citizen and nation-state through emphases on flexible citizenship, so, too, are some "excepted," that is to say left out. She writes, "Variations in individual capacities or in performance of market skills intensify existing social and moral inequalities while blurring political distinctions between national and foreign populations" (16).

3. CIVILIZING MISSIONS AND DEMOCRATIC DESIRE

1. I am thinking with Elizabeth Povinelli here of liberalism not in terms of policies or political institutions but rather as "subjective, institutional, and discursive identifications, dispersions and elaborations of the enlightenment idea that society should be organized on the basis of rational mutual understanding" (2002, 6).

2. Parents learn about this organization largely through *sarafannoe radio* (word of mouth) but also via expos and print advertising. To some extent, parents' aims can be inferred from how practitioners frame the programs. What seems most pressing is the problem of idle time, which poses a threat to the child's mood and safety but also his or her future. To address this problem, the camps merge "pleasant rest" with "development"—providing a "useful vacation." Fieldwork suggests that many parents find psychological education (*psikhologicheskoe obrazovanie*) unfamiliar and even suspect. Calling the programs *lagery*, or camps, the advertisements work to overcome this by tying them to the familiar—"the great tradition of children's pioneer camps"—and also tout the chance to make "true friends." The international locales (e.g., Finland) and extra-curricular activities (e.g., skiing) add value but are not central. In sum, these advertisements reflect familiar parental concerns, but also new emphases on child development.

3. I explore the formation of the PPMS Center network in Russia in terms of a shift in governmentality from the late-socialist to the postsocialist period. By *governmentality* I refer to Michel Foucault's (1991, 2007) concept, which brings into one analytic frame state institutions, techniques, and those who are governed. In other contexts, this approach has been used to argue that in *modern* governmentality the constitution of particular kinds of subjectivities has become one of the primary aims and methods of governance. The contemporary example to which scholars often point is the spread of neoliberal reforms like privatization, which are premised principally on the replacement of relations of so-called welfare dependency with personal responsibility and autonomy. This is taken to be a sign of governing "from a distance" (Rose 1996a) through freedom (Burchell 1996).

4. Scholars have written about competitive forms of upbringing around the world, with China being a particularly striking parallel (see, especially, the contributions by Anne Anagnost and others in Jennifer Cole and Deborah Lynn Durham's *Figuring*

the *Future: Globalization and the Temporalities of Children and Youth* [2008]; see also Stephens 1995). This literature highlights how, under economic globalization, children have been revalued as both future adult producers and present-day consumers (Allison 2008), shifting the line between childhood/youth and adulthood ever earlier.

5. This was not inconsistent with Soviet pedagogies of self-training, which were premised on a model of the conscious actor. Moreover, thanks to the ideological rejection of the Freudian unconscious under Stalin, Soviet pedagogies of the self were even less tied to emotions. See chapter 1.

6. This phenomenon can be seen throughout the world, whether through the development of prudentialism in western Europe (Rose 1996a, 1996b), cosmopolitan desire in China (Rofel 2007), entrepreneurialism in Indonesia (Rudnyckyj 2009), audits in Poland (Dunn 2004), or emotional control in drug rehabilitation in Russia (Zigon 2011). Interestingly, Jarrett Zigon (2011) finds similar technologies at work at the opposite end of the social scale—not elite clientele but among HIV-infected drug users in rehabilitation. This is consistent with my findings in relation to psychological services among the poor and working class.

7. The semantic anchoring of discourses of freedom and possibility in the West has a long history in Russia, starting at least from Peter the Great, and extending from Lenin's push for electrification to the late-Soviet period. As Alexei Yurchak (2006) points out, the "imaginary West" was a key site of "internal emigration" in times when physical travel was impossible. Western jazz and rock 'n' roll, Wrangler jeans, and other cultural products became imbued with desire and cachet. After the collapse of communism, this "elsewhere" became more attainable, at least for some, yet the West retained its symbolic value. Visiting Saint Petersburg as a student in 1994, I still remember the ubiquitous baseball caps on Nevsky Prospect that read "USA California," and the card tables set up on various corners selling tickets to the US green-card lottery. Throughout the first post-Soviet decade, monetary value was uncertain; therefore, many spent their money as soon as they had it on imported goods, or converted it immediately to dollars (Lemon 1998; Oushakine 2009, 7).

8. Michele Rivkin-Fish makes a similar point in her discussion of post-Soviet sex educators, whose offering of an alternative to repressive Soviet pedagogies of sexuality and pleasure, while problematically yoked to gender-essentialist categories, nonetheless provided "strategic, if limited, emancipatory effects" (2005, 94).

9. Foucault's inquiry into self-care as an ethical practice of freedom is specific to the Greco-Roman world; however, in an interview he extended this research to present political concerns: "The [politico-ethical] problem is not to try to dissolve [power relations, discipline] in the utopia of completely transparent communication but to acquire the rules of law, the management techniques, and also the morality, the *ethos*, the practice of the self, that will allow us to play games of power with as little domination as possible" (1997a, 298). This "new ethics" is "the hinge point of ethical concerns and the political struggle for respect of rights, of critical thought against abusive techniques of government and research in ethics that seeks to ground individual freedom" (299).

10. This argument is indebted to the work of other anthropologists who, moving from Foucault's late work, carved out ways to view "problematic" pursuits ("freedom,"

women's Muslim piety) anew—as a pursuit of virtue within constraints (see Laidlaw 2002; Lambek 2010; Mahmood 2005). Recently, in the anthropology of Russia, both Douglas Rogers's (2009) "ethical repertoire" and Zigon's (2011) framework of moral breakdown and ethical practice have further refined this approach. In this chapter, I hew closer to a Foucauldian language because of my interest in thinking governmentality alongside ethics and subjectivation.

11. The psychologists' pathologization of the Soviet period recapitulates both the views of the Western reformers who descended on Russia in the 1990s and what Alexei Yurchak (2006, 4–10) has termed "binary socialism." However, while there is a formal similarity here, once one locates the genesis of their critique in the perestroika moment, it becomes inadequate to describe their characterizations as neoliberal. Such statements have their own genealogies—and this is a key point of this book. By way of this history, the projects of self-work can be read, following Foucault, as a contextually specific "refusal of what we are" (Foucault 2000b, 336; see also Koopman and Matza 2013).

12. After the wild capitalism of the 1990s, which resulted in the dissolution of the state, a moral vacuum, elite reentrenchment, and a decade of unbridled capitalism (Volkov 2002; Wedel 1998), many of the terms of liberal theory are tainted in Russia. This sheds light on Aleksandr's reference to Russia's "own course" as well as a general avoidance of liberal terminology. Indeed, according to a survey conducted jointly by the EU-Russia Centre and the Levada Center in 2007, Russians had "confused and often contradictory" understandings of democracy, liberalism, freedom, and human rights, and they "see little application of these values to their own lives" (EU-Russia Centre/Levada Center 2007, 6).

13. Humphrey (2007) points out that "freedom" in Russia is often more social than in liberal democracies. ReGeneration's pedagogy accents individualizing freedoms, but their rationales for this work also contain the sociality of svoboda.

14. This was not the only statement that reinforced the we-they division. I was warned at one point to be careful not to enable the children to taunt another psychologist in English, a language they spoke but he did not. Aleksandr also often referred to the children as "clients," and the psychologists as the "people who work for the parents."

15. As Rivkin-Fish puts it, the intelligentsia had "a 'sacred' quality, merging and condensing the symbolism of kul'turnost' (culturedness), high education, and the attendant respect and authority that derive from honesty and moral righteousness" (2009, 81). According to Patico (2005, 480, 490), kul'turnost' continues to be a very salient "trope of value" by which a person's moral worth is judged.

16. The question of whether this elite constitutes a "new middle class" is disputed. Neoliberals argued that the middle class would be the keystone of the formation of civil society in Russia. As Edmund Mokrzycki (1996) pointed out in the 1990s, this designation is less a social reality than a vision of those who would lead Russia's economic march to the future and reform society. So far, the middle class is less a broad-based group whose wealth has prompted grassroots politics and institution building than a repackaging of the old elite, bound to the Putin-Medvedev tandem through a

hegemonic stasis. (The "tandem" refers to Medvedev's seat-warming term, in which he continued many of Putin's main priorities, while allowing Putin to return to power.) Its most visible members have been the New Russians, a category of description rather than self-identification that, as Humphrey (2002) notes, designates the envied (and reviled) nouveaux riches. This is the social group ReGeneration targets.

Middle-classness has a different significance in the Soviet period, and it is helpful to put current class politics in historical context. Starting in the post–World War II period, the intelligentsia (and also well-positioned part officials) had become accustomed to a middle-class quality of life that largely disappeared in the 1990s at the same time that a new petite bourgeoisie—the New Russians—were ascendant. If the former group have maintained their place as the moral standard-bearers of Russian culturedness (kul'turnost'), the latter have been defined by philistinism (see Boym 1994; Dunham 1990; Volkov 2002). In the Soviet period, critiques of the bureaucratic elite known as the *nomenklatura* were common among dissident intellectuals. In the post-Soviet period, then, those that remain a part of this loose category of the intelligentsia continue the critique the low culture of the nouveau riche. Without presuming any neat boundaries or homology, it is reasonable to assert that many of the psychologists working with children in Saint Petersburg, both in the public and the private or nongovernmental sectors, could be counted among this group of mass intelligentsia.

17. This economy of comparison and desire also draws on several centuries of etiquette campaigns in the prerevolutionary Russian Empire. The entire era following Peter the Great's so-called Westernization of seventeenth-century Russia was marked by an effort to overcome Russian "backwardness" (*otstalost'*) through the imitation of European lifestyles, including speaking French, cultivating an aristocratic country life, and attending balls—things vividly described in Leo Tolstoy's nineteenth-century novels. The Soviet period, too, had its civilizing campaigns. According to the historian Francine Hirsch, "the Bolsheviks took state-sponsored evolutionism very seriously, putting far more effort into realizing its ends than the European colonial empires had put into their own civilizing missions. Characterizing 'backwardness' as the result of sociohistorical circumstances and not of innate racial or biological traits, Soviet leaders maintained that all peoples could 'evolve' and thrive in new Soviet conditions" (2005, 9). Stalin also attempted to redefine the notion of kul'turnost' by separating it from the nineteenth-century intelligentsia's polished sensibilities and turning it into a virtue for the Soviet elite (see Volkov 2000). On the history of etiquette in Russia, see Kelly (2001). On Soviet kul'turnost', see Dunham (1990) and Boym (1994). On the intelligentsia in Soviet film, see Faraday (2000). As Patico (2005) notes, the party sought the twin imperatives of kult'urnost' and *tsivilizovannost'* (civilizedness) through consumer goods.

18. As Elena Zdravomyslova and Anna Temkina (2003) and Michele Rivkin-Fish (2010) have noted, demographic concerns have played a particularly important role in Russia since the 1960s, prompting a neotraditional conception of femininity and motherhood, as well as an anxiety about the crisis of masculinity.

19. Slavoj Žižek (1997) has suggested that there is no inconsistency between the norms of tolerance and capitalism (see also Salecl 1994). Here, by contrast, my as-

sumption is that there is no natural relationship between capitalist self-formation and tolerance. I prefer to take Wendy Brown's (2003) genealogical, as well as strategic, view that the political and the economic need not be collapsed into one another.

20. Recent studies of humanitarianism demonstrate how care and compassion, too, can be channeled in undesirable directions, and they caution against a blanket valorization of "regimes of care" outside a particular sociopolitical context (see Ticktin 2011; Malkki 2010).

4. TACTICAL GUIDANCE AT A SOCIAL MARGIN

1. Balint groups were held regularly at the PPMS Center. Based on the work of Hungarian psychoanalysts Michael and Enid Balint, Balint groups are meetings of practitioners that are designed to bring the emotional and relational contexts of doctor-patient relations to the surface. At the PPMS Center, Balint groups focused on one practitioner's difficult case.

2. See Giordano (2014) on the conundrums of therapeutic translation and cultural difference in ethnopsychiatry.

3. For a variety of critiques of the biomedicalization of psychiatry, see Luhrmann (2000), Biehl (2005), Martin (2007), and Kleinman (1995).

4. Perhaps more important, poverty is "shallow," with many clustered just around the subsistence line: if the subsistence line were raised 10 percent (just 508 rubles, or $17, per month), an additional 4 million (2.5 percent of the population) would fall under it (World Bank 2009a, 17).

5. For a good overview of the post-Soviet housing boom, and the (failed) attempt to create a mortgage market, see Zavisca (2012).

6. By *affect* I mean a feeling in the raw or, to put it in more theorized terms, what Brian Massumi (2002) posits as an embodied and prediscursive sensation that flows through us. *Emotion* is something else. It is discursive; it is named; it is culturally rooted. Literary traditions rest on normative conceptions of love or happiness. *Affect* instead refers to the spirit of the crowd that overtakes the sports fan, or the way one feels the atmosphere of a room (Brennan 2004). It is also intersubjective and experienced in the body (Spinoza 1993).

7. Soprovozhdenie as a concept can be traced to the work of Oleg Semenovich Gazman, a member of the VNIK-Shkola group who had a hand in the development of the Pedagogy of Cooperation, which helped initiate the psychological turn in Soviet education and upbringing (see Eklof and Dneprov 1993).

8. Such imperatives also place these services in relation to transformations in managed care that prioritize short-term efficacy and research over longer-term therapy, as well as the movement for Global Mental Health (GMH) that confronts limited mental health care resources (Saxena et al. 2007). In Kashmir, for instance, Saiba Varma (2012, 528) found that even if they were not sure what it meant, psychosocial counselors liked to describe their work as a form of cognitive-behavioral therapy (CBT). She wrote, "CBT had cache [*sic*] power, and the listeners expressed their desire to possess it." The Russian case, though, is a bit different: in the PPMS Center the use of cognitive-behavioral approaches was less about empowerment than bureaucratic

defense—that is, the cognitive shift seemed to me to be a way of rendering psychosocial care in forms that would seem more accountable and legible in bureaucratic contexts.

9. The interest here was not only on behalf of the child, but also in adding legitimacy to the PPMS system. This was because attestation would effectively ensure that PPMS Centers were in compliance with norms and held accountable.

10. Iasiukova's system, which is sold as a psychodiagnostic system in Russia, was used extensively at the PPMS Center. The system uses a variety of tests, including the Amthauer Intelligence Test, Raven's Progressive Matrices, and others to assess intelligence, memory, and other cognitive functions.

11. Collier's book makes an important contribution to the anthropology of postsocialism and also neoliberalism. Collier is at pains to specify what neoliberalism is, beyond being something "we are against." He claims that neoliberalism is not a political rationality that lacks social aims but is one with particular social aims expressed through different sorts of rationality. Inasmuch as I make no claim that Russia is "neoliberal" without qualification, this study is consistent with Collier's points about Russia. However, I diverge from Collier's account of neoliberalism, which can appear to substitute political rationality for political effects. In other words, his is a book about how neoliberal theorists conceived of neoliberalism, but not about the ways in which aspects of that rationality have negatively impacted people's lives in Russia.

12. Raikhel notes that, in combination with the registry (uchet) (a tracking mechanism whereby a person's residence permit was a prerequisite for treatment), the use of dispensaries (outpatient clinics) "provided a grid through which state actors attempted to manage the health of populations" (70).

13. This amounts to a different kind of "bureaucratic writing" than the sort that Akhil Gupta (2012) documents in his study of state institutions.

14. It is not that some form of oversight was a bad idea. As many cases showed, practitioners had tremendous power that could be exercised through normalizing judgment. Diagnosis was a delicate and uncertain process, and the specialists had only small amounts of time to spend with each client, yet their assessments could carry significant weight. In many instances, because practitioners lacked the medical authority to address particularly severe cases, they were expected to forward these on to the city's PNDs. These were the province of doctors in white coats, where I also did some fieldwork. Apart from these being unnerving places, such referrals could potentially taint a child's record: being seen at a PND can also mean being put *na uchet* (on the registry), which most Russians assumed meant you were crazy and which could impact one's future employability. Thus, there was a significant disincentive for making referrals that also placed a heavy burden on case decision making. Warranted or not, however, the effect of the impending attestation, as I gathered from the numerous outbursts and grumblings during the konsilium, was primarily one of unproductive anxiety resulting from internal procedures that were ill matched to the audit procedures.

15. This discussion is also indebted to Heath Cabot, Peter Locke, and Saiba Varma, who in 2013 organized a panel at the American Anthropological Association meetings on a related term, *indeterminacy*. They asked, "How might a focus on 'indeterminacy' in aid

encounters—and in particular the role of individual imagination in reshaping them—enhance our understanding of such work? But also, do we risk under-emphasizing the power relationships that shape (and may *over*determine) such encounters?" (Aid and Indeterminacy, American Anthropological Association Annual Meeting, Washington, DC, November 22, 2013).

16. The relationship between state formation and various kinds of private, informal, and sometimes-semilegal actions is discussed by Vadim Volkov (2002) in relation to the security industry.

17. It occurred to me while writing this chapter that, following modernization, the PPMS Center would also have difficulty offering this service.

5. PSYCHOSOCIALITY UNDER PUTIN

1. Energy is a foundational concept in psychoanalysis. In Freud's theories, psychic energy is the source of our drives and takes two forms—libidinal energy and the death instinct. The primary goal of therapy is the redirection of misdirected energies away from neurotic responses. In fieldwork it was not clear that it was specifically this kind of energy that was being discussed. As to whether there is a Russian vernacular form of energiia, Serguei Oushakine's (2009, 115–29) study suggests that the term has a nationalist dimension in the form of a post-Soviet "ethnovitalist" movement, in which patriotic sentiment has warned against the dissipation of "energies" in the face of the "Russian tragedy" of diminishing birth rates, abortion, and swelling immigration. Yet neither of these specific kinds of energy was ever cited. Thus, it seems more empirically appropriate to view energiia as a floating signifier. As the accounts here suggest, the invocation of energiia could be various and sometimes contradictory; however, in most cases energiia was part of a rhetorical strategy used to anchor the claim that was being made in a kind of psychobiologized nature.

2. *Psychosociality* repurposes Paul Rabinow's (1996) concept of biosociality. Rabinow's essay is a meditation on a broader epistemic shift, with the dissolution of modernist society, from the sociobiological to the biosocial. He writes, "If sociobiology is culture constructed on the basis of a metaphor of nature, then in biosociality, nature will be modeled on culture understood as practice. Nature will be known and remade through technique and will finally become artificial, just as culture becomes natural. Were such a project to be brought to fruition, it would stand as the basis for overcoming the nature/culture split" (99). The part of this essay that is relevant here relates to the cultural and social implications of new technologies. Rabinow points out how, in the face of genetic testing and diagnosis, new kinds of sociality are formed: "In the future, the new genetics will cease to be a biological metaphor for modern society and will become instead a circulation network of identity terms and redistribution loci, around which and through which a truly new type of autoproduction will emerge, which I call 'biosociality'" (99). He writes that biosocialities entail "groups whose members meet to share their experiences, lobby for their disease, educate their children, redo their home environment, and so on. . . . Such groups will have medical specialists, laboratories, narratives, traditions and a heavy panoply of pastoral keepers to help them experience, share, intervene in, and 'understand' their fate" (102). In

contrast, psychosocialities are united not by pathology but by a sense of shared generalizable distress, a particular enthusiasm for expert-mediated "ethics of the concern for self" (Foucault 1997a), or some combination of these.

3. According to Whitney Duncan (2017), "family constellation" has also gained popularity in Oaxaca, Mexico, as a means for thinking through family relationships.

4. The discourses of self-purging bear a resemblance to Soviet-era self-cultivation practices, as outlined by Jochen Hellbeck (2006), who finds evidence in Stalin-era diaries of great anxiety about bourgeois residues in one's family. The nature of self-work, under those conditions, was closely tied to anxieties about the past.

With regard to historical memory, Alexander Etkind (2009) has noted a lack of historical reckoning in Russian popular culture; he points to the curious proliferation of zombies and the undead in post-Soviet films and novels. Turning temporality in a different direction, Oushakine (2000) reads the past as an erstwhile available linguistic repertoire that has been inadequate to describing a transformed, post-Soviet reality. He relates his informants' experiences of speechlessness in the 1990s to aphasia.

5. However, it is worth noting that Hellinger's focus on the reproduction of trauma transgenerationally has also been particularly influential in post-Holocaust Germany. Scholars interested in post-Soviet memory practices have drawn on the German reconciliation process as a contrast to the lack of post-Stalinist processing in Russia (Etkind 2009).

6. While this is not necessarily related, at the time I attended my first Systemic Constellation session, the news was full of unsettling stories. The kangaroo-court proceedings for Putin's political rival and oil magnate, Mikhail Khodorkovsky, were under way, even as the mass media were continuing to fall under state control. Strategic industries (especially oil and gas) increasingly padded the pockets of political allies, and everyone knew it. The shift from gubernatorial elections to appointments across Russia under Putin's bid for vertical power (*vertikal'naia vlast'*) indicated a general narrowing of political competition that went hand in hand with the use of legal obstacles to block political challengers to Putin's political party, United Russia. Finally, tensions with Ukraine in response to its Orange Revolution—early indicators of the conflicts that began in 2014—were also surfacing and were fought out on the ground of petropolitics.

7. Many scholars have noted the particular temporality of Soviet modernity, which fused a sense of a future that was already present with a past, 1917, that was constantly celebrated in the origin stories of the Soviet Union (see Buck-Morss 2000). This was said to produce a "modal schizophrenia," where the "is" and the "ought to be" were constantly being forced, ideologically speaking, into an uneasy equivalence (Clark 1981). This temporality also anchored a sense of certainty and social order that was disrupted with the Soviet collapse. Alexei Yurchak's (2006) book title summons this sentiment nicely: *Everything Was Forever, Until It Was No More.*

8. It is interesting to consider this energiia as an alternative formulation of agency. What is interesting about systemic constellations are the ways in which the capacity to act was articulated in and through social relations—a kind of distributed will in which the capacity to act emerges from elsewhere. This stands in opposition to willpower, an internal engine.

9. To take up genetics expertise as a parallel example, Rabinow (1996, 100) points out that the shift to direct-to-consumer medical knowledge that personalized genotyping enabled not only reshaped medical practices through the "minimization of direct therapeutic intervention and arrival of preventative administrative management of risk" but also triggered the "promotion of working on oneself to produce an efficient and adaptable subject," as well as "the certain formation of new group and individual identities and practices arising out of these new truths" (100).

10. Yurchak (2006, 126–27) explains the difference as being between deep, cosmic truths (istina) and political or "clear" ones (pravda).

11. For discussions of the sociality of dusha in Russia, see Pesmen (2000) and Wierzbicka (1992).

12. Citing the many Russian Slavophile writings of the nineteenth century that rail against the soullessness (*bezdushie*) of the West, Wierzbicka (1992, 61–62) suggests that in the West, where rationality has gradually replaced emotional worlds, the concept of the soul has become less and less privileged as compared to mind, whereas in Russia dusha has retained a central cultural significance, particularly in a psychological sense. Wierzbicka for some reason does not emphasize the cosmic (or, in her language, "transcendental") dimension of dusha; perhaps this is because she was writing closer to the Soviet period. She suggests that Soviet materialism denied this meaning of the soul, citing a Soviet kindergarten rhyme: "but science teaches us that the soul doesn't exist" (*no nauka dokazal shto dushi ne sushchestvuet*). Nonetheless, dusha in its psychological meaning would be used by party officials to refer to the *moral* aspects of a personality—as in the case of a "spirit" that cannot be broken and should not be softened (1992, 37).

13. Someone who tested as having a strong "visual character" would be very interested in aesthetics and the natural world; persons with a "nasal character" would be interested in food.

14. This led to not only political instability but also many experiences of personal instability resulting from wage freezes, dispossession, the transformation of cultural value, and the loss of markers of status, identities, social institutions, and the rules of the game (see Collier 2005; Patico 2005; Shevchenko 2009; Wanner 2005).

15. The Soviet collapse unmoored many of the anchors of social and personal value. For instance, Jennifer Patico (2008) found that schoolteachers in Saint Petersburg experienced a profound sense of social dislocation as the politico-ethical commitments of socialism (see Yurchak 2006) were trumped by the material. Melissa Caldwell (2004) describes how, in the face of depersonalized kinds of exchange, many turned even more deliberately to informal social networks, anchored as they were by forms of established trust. Since the turn of the century, economic value has become even more entrenched as a measure of quality in Russian life.

16. Biosociality is also double edged. As Miriam Ticktin points out, while biosociality, as a "socially framed choice to draw on one's biology" (2006, 35), may open up access to certain medical services, it can come with steep costs. In her research she finds the *sans papiers* (undocumented) in France seeking out HIV infection as a way to stay in the country.

6. TALK-SHOW SELVES AND PUBLIC INTIMACY

1. The genealogy of the Russian talk show can be traced to Mikhail Gorbachev's policy of glasnost, initiated in 1985, which entailed a "reevaluation of values" (*pereot-senka tsennostei*) that was to take place primarily through the mass media (Mickiewicz 1999, 11). At this time, "lively, hard-hitting programs" appeared that broke from more conservative broadcasting to discuss edgy topics like "rock culture, drug abuse, prostitution, youth disaffection, violence, and corruption with unprecedented candor and energy" (Stites 1992, 189–90). In addition to offering audiences fresh faces and formats, these programs also opened novel arenas in public discourse, new ways of relating to media and publics, and new political imaginaries.

What differentiated Soviet talk shows from the American ones was a much-diminished focus on personal detail. While in the United States talk shows had opened into new, tabloid-style confessionals on *Donahue* and *Oprah*, in the Soviet Union producers were drawn to the format because its participatory and spontaneous qualities could be used to push political issues, not explore personal affairs. This difference was made particularly clear when Phil Donahue's programs with Soviet audiences on Soviet soil aired in the USSR in 1987 (Broadcasts 1987a, 1987b). Providing the lead-in was Donahue's Soviet counterpart, Vladimir Pozner, who said, "The questions which Donahue asks. The questions, let's put it this way, are unusual for us; they touch on intimate aspects of family life, and, as a rule, we don't take this sort of question onto TV screens. In America it's the opposite; they don't just take them, but at times they relish them" (Broadcasts 1987a). The Soviet collapse in 1991 brought about an "American effect" (Mickiewicz 1999, 21), and American-style programming continues to hold a central place in Russian TV. For more on the history of the talk show and its links to psychological confession, see Matza (2009, 491–92). For more on the Citizens' Summits (also called space bridge [*telemost*] by Soviets), see Mickiewicz (1988, 43–56).

2. Warner (2002) argues that mass publics attract subjects because of a "utopian desire" for self-abstraction that is always, also, potentially self-fulfilling. This utopianism is genealogically rooted in the bourgeois public sphere, where a "privileged public disembodiment" (i.e., white and male) was the condition of public participation. In the era of virtual reality, mass publics no longer negate bodies through self-abstraction but rather allow one to "trade [one's body] in for a better model" (176). Talk radio is thus a related, albeit elementary, form of virtual reality in which the dialectic between self-abstraction and self-fulfillment is experienced through a mass (psychologized) self.

3. Michel Foucault's phrase "techniques of the self" refers to a set of practices, or arts of existence, through which self-cultivation is practiced and which both constrain and enable subjects (see Foucault 1988, 1990b, 2005). When deployed through a talk show, these are given greater potential force. Michael Warner's (2002) nonnormative concept of a public is useful here. He defines it as a contingent, self-perpetuating relation among strangers that relies on circulating texts—or, in this case, radio programs— that are "reflexive." Like techniques of the self, such publics also mediate subjectivity by shaping ways of relating to oneself and others through participation, in this case

psychotherapeutically mediated forms of public intimacy. Moreover, they are of social import because they "make stranger relationality normative." This is what gives publics their "expansive force [as] cultural forms" (76). Andrew Barry, Thomas Osborne, and Nikolas Rose (1996) extend Foucault's notion of techniques of the self to his concept of governmentality (Foucault 1991). Combining an examination of techniques of the self with a focus on the practices, regulatory mechanisms, and disciplinary mechanisms of government, these scholars have opened a space of inquiry into how the voluntary processes of becoming a subject are mediated by relations of power, expert knowledge, and the management of populations.

4. In light of the history of Soviet psychotherapy (discussed in chapter 1) and the limited exposure most Russians have had to therapy, the popularity of psychological advice on talk shows is striking.

5. All quotations are taken from the shows' promotional materials on the web (Pervyi Kanal 2008a, 2008b). Both aired on Russia's state-run Channel One. *Lolita: Without Complexes* went off the air in 2007, but returned again to another channel in 2014. *Understand. Forgive.* remained in the air until 2014. All translations are my own unless otherwise noted.

6. Figures calculated as of April 13, 2007. The category of advice talk shows included psychological and lifestyle programs, plus several health-advice shows that include "the soul" as a target.

7. Nikolas Rose (1996b) has drawn connections between the marketization (or degovernmentalization) of state functions and the outsourcing of the government of citizens to the citizen himself or herself by the constitution of the self as a domain of government. Here, power is exercised not on subjects but through them, aligning their energies and desires for liberation with the pursuit of a more efficient polity. "Neoliberal techniques of the self," then, typically entail an increased attention to feelings, employing the skills of psychological and social experts in the development of more fulfilled (and therefore effective) persons.

8. Wendy Brown (2003) makes a useful distinction between political liberalism (liberal democracy, freedom, rights) and classical economic liberalism (free trade, state nonintervention in the economy). These are part of neoliberalism's genealogy; however, neoliberalism's liberalism hews much more closely to the economic rationality of laissez-faire. Moreover, neoliberalism extends market rationalities (cost-benefit analysis, efficiency, "morally neutral" evaluations based on dollars) to politics, society, and the very fabric of the citizen's being.

9. For more on the assemblage as an analytic of global process, see Ong and Collier (2005).

10. Brown notes, "Liberal democracy cannot be submitted to neo-liberal governmentality and survive. There is nothing in liberal democracy's basic institutions or values—from free elections, representative democracy, and individual liberties equally distributed, to modest power-sharing or even more substantive political participation—that inherently meets the test of serving economic competitiveness or inherently withstands a cost-benefit analysis" (2003, 46).

11. The Echo of Moscow's corporate structure embodies a political tension important to this chapter. At the time of my research it was owned by *Kommersant*, one of the more liberal newspapers in Russia, but its largest stakeholder is the state-majority-owned oil and gas giant Gazprom. Nevertheless, Echo of Moscow was one of the first liberal radio stations in Soviet Russia and remains a critical voice in a political landscape otherwise dominated by state-controlled media. It first went on the air in August 1990 and featured straightforward political commentary and even call-in shows (Remnick 2008). In 2008 roughly a third of its programs were call-in programs. Twelve were advice programs; Labkovsky's was the only one concerned with psychological issues. (The major state-run national stations, Radio of Russia and Radio Maiak, have similar figures.) Psychotherapists have a stronger presence on television; nevertheless, this chapter focuses on radio because of the analytic possibilities offered by a higher volume of caller-host interactions that medium contains, as well as the immediacy and spontaneity of the therapeutic interactions.

12. The law, "On the Protection of Children from Information Harmful to Their Health and Development" (O zashchite detei ot informatsii, prichiniaiushchei vred ix zdoroviu i razvitiiu), went into effect on September 1, 2012. It was part of a broader slate of conservative legislative acts intended to "purify" the public sphere. Among the other laws passed at the time is the well-known law against so-called gay propaganda.

13. The program would eventually move an hour later, starting at eleven o'clock. Labkovsky also started another show, called *The Night Program*, about sex, broadcast early Monday morning from midnight to two in the morning.

14. The shows aired between January and July 2005, and analysis was based on transcripts posted on the Echo of Moscow website (http://www.echo.msk.ru/programs /psychology/archive/3.html). In addition to performing content analysis, I created a database indexing call content and, when possible, caller sex and age. I recorded socioeconomic status using a basic scheme that was crudely subjective and based on uneven information—for example, ownership of property or a business, capital, family or personal situation, and/or profession. Finally, I grouped and counted call types to assess patterns in how listeners responded to each week's theme. Unaccounted for in any substantive way in this analysis, but worthy of mention, is that calls were screened, yielding a particular sample of people with particular issues.

15. Gilles Deleuze (1988) uses the metaphor of the fold to describe the process of subjectivation. The dynamic is one where "the relations of an outside folded back upon themselves to create a doubling, to allow a relation to oneself to emerge, and to constitute an inside which is hollowed out and develops its own unique dimension" (100). Instead of having an essence, our interiors reflect relations of force, or rule; particular understandings of the body or flesh; and regimes of truth.

16. *Samootsenka* can also be translated as "self-appraisal," suggesting a neutral evaluative relation to the self. I translate *samootsenka* as "self-esteem" because of its explicit use as a psychological concept.

17. Attempts to draw too clear a distinction between Soviet selves and post-Soviet selves risks caricature and the conflation of pedagogy and practice, not to mention the ethical quandary of attributing total penetration to party power. Recent historical

scholarship that uses Foucault to study Soviet subjectivity under Stalin has been criticized for this. See chapter 1, as well as Etkind (2005), and the discussions in the journal *Ab Imperio*, especially Boym (2002).

18. Property is hardly postsocialist. As Katherine Verdery (2003, 46–48) notes, property was fundamental to socialist institutions and functioned as a form of social capital that grounded systems of informal exchange and reciprocity, and that organized power and social relations. Soviets had personal use rights to their apartments (known as private property, or *chastnaia sobstvennost'*) and also to possessions such as clothing, cars, and books (personal property, or *lichnaia sobstvennost'*). In an economy of scarcity, those possessions took on hugely personal meanings. Soviets thus had possessions, yet, in the last instance, only the state owned things. The difference this makes as a matter of folded interiority and self-self relations correlates with Labkovsky's inversion of socialist samootsenka.

19. Labkovsky fielded an immense number of questions about the new property regime. For instance, on a May 28 program concerned with family relations (where law was one of six possible areas of inquiry), twenty-nine of the forty-two calls concerned property. This was common across all the programs. "With . . . sadness," Labkovsky commented on April 30, "I can establish that 90 percent of the questions . . . concern kicking someone out, taking away something from someone, giving away something, and, in general, all of this turns around apartments."

20. In Russia apartment registry is the guarantor of one's ability to live and work somewhere. In desirable places like Moscow, apartments can be hard (or expensive) to come by. Registration is distinct from ownership; only the latter provides the right to sell or to determine who lives in a flat. If he loses his right of ownership, Vladimir is also risking having his registration (and right to live there) revoked.

21. Rose notes that contemporary technologies of subjectivity do not promise "liberation from social constraints but render psychological constraints on autonomy conscious, and hence amenable to rational transformation. Achieving freedom becomes a matter not of slogans or political revolution, but of slow, painstaking, and detailed work on our own subjective and personal realities, guided by an expert knowledge of the psyche" (1990, 213).

22. Cruikshank reports the logic of revamped state programs, citing the language of the California Task Force to Promote Self-Esteem and Social and Personal Responsibility: " 'Government and experts cannot fix these problems [of crime, poverty, and inequality] for us. It is only when each of us recognizes our individual personal and social responsibility to be part of the solution that we also realize higher self-esteem' " (1996, 232).

23. Scholars of postsocialism have adopted different understandings of citizenship. Adriana Petryna (2002, 202) thinks of citizenship as consisting of two kinds of rights—claims (including on a biological basis) rights and liberty rights. The former include the rights to a job, material well-being, and education, which the state is obligated to provide to its citizens. The latter are more abstract rights, including, in Western democracies, the rights to liberty, fair trials, and privacy. In contrast, Humphrey (2002, 75–76) views citizenship as a matter of state-imposed *obligations and categorizations*, where being a citizen means carrying the necessary documentation (internal

passport, work record, etc.) and observing the rules of border crossings. The discussion of citizenship on *For Adults about Adults* concerned all three of these—rights, obligations, and categorizations—and debates about public conduct revolved around the displacement of one citizenship regime by another.

24. *Khamstvo* is a flexible term, having both a pejorative meaning of lacking culture and manners that is linked to Stalin's answer to the intelligentsia—*kul'turnost'*—and also a positive meaning of soulful authenticity that resists Western forms of false politeness. In either meaning, the term is often associated with the sovok (the quintessential boorish Soviet person).

25. See Silverstein (2008) on the links among media, performance, and disposition.

26. Foucault (2000b, 2007) uses the phrase *pastoral power*, in analogy to the intense attention a shepherd gives to each and every member of his or her flock, to describe modern forms of state power. This power is both individualizing (in that it focuses analytic attention on the human) and totalizing (in that its calculative practices govern populations).

27. As Charles Hirschkind (2006, 13–16) notes in his study of cassette-tape sermons in Egypt, Enlightenment philosophers perceived the intimate quality of hearing to be dangerous because it involved immersion, passive reception, and engulfment, as opposed to the ocular values of distance, judgment, and reason.

28. Alexei Yurchak (2006, 117) defines the public of svoi as "a kind of deterritorialized public" that was "self-organized not through an oppositional counterdiscourse of one's 'interests and needs' but through the performative shift of authoritative discourse. Explicit opposition, just like explicit support, was avoided" (117). As an example of *performative shift*, Yurchak points to young Komsomol (Young Communist League) members who participated in state sanctioned activities, and, without necessarily negating the authoritative state discourse, were nonetheless able to redirect that discourse in directions that served their own needs.

CONCLUSION

1. Mark Urnov writes that conservative modernization "reduces 'the problem of changing values and motivations' to 'an increase in work motivation' and the need for 'civic education, patriotic upbringing of youth, [and] the promotion of legal, cultural and moral values among young people'" (2012, 43). By comparison, liberal modernization (as expressed during Putin's first terms, and by former president Dmitry Medvedev) had "propose[d] a much more radical version of human capital modernization, based on the assumption that changing institutions is a function of changing the culture (values)" (43). Thus, Putin's conservative modernization "treats changes in the value system as a function of changes in formal institutions" (43).

2. Moral economies have also been described in other contexts. In Africa, for instance, James Ferguson argues that a scientific capitalism bent on efficiency and driven by cost-benefit analyses can be demoralizing (in the sense of removing moral considerations from the calculation; Ferguson 2007, 69–88) as well as antipolitical (in the sense that common citizens are distanced from the levers of power by a gray bureaucratic language; Ferguson 1994).

3. Laidlaw (2002, 327) writes, "Wherever and in so far as people's conduct is shaped by attempts to make of themselves a certain kind of person, because it is as such a person that, on reflection, they think they ought to live, to that extent their conduct is ethical and free. And to the extent that they do so with reference to ideals, values, models, practices, relationships, and institutions that are amenable to ethnographic study, to that extent their conduct becomes the subject matter for an anthropology of ethics."

4. As Humphrey notes (2007, 3–4), this link between the free "we" and cosmic unity became an integral part of the communist project, which sought to promote its own forms of internationalism and freedom.

REFERENCES

Adams, Vincanne. 2013. "Evidence-Based Global Public Health: Subjects, Profits, Erasures." In *When People Come First: Evidence, Actuality, and Theory in Global Health*, edited by João Biehl and Adriana Petryna, 54–90. Princeton, NJ: Princeton University Press.

Adams, Vincanne, Michelle Murphy, and Adele E. Clarke. 2009. "Anticipation: Technoscience, Life, Affect, Temporality." *Subjectivity* 28 (1): 246–65.

Ahmed, Sara. 2004. "Affective Economies." *Social Text*, no. 79 (Summer): 117–39.

Alexievich, Svetlana. 2016. *Secondhand Time: The Last of the Soviets.* New York: Random House.

Allison, Anne. 2008. "Pocket Capitalism and Virtual Intimacy: Pokemon as Symptom of Postindustrial Youth Culture." In *Figuring the Future: Globalization and the Temporalities of Children and Youth*, edited by Jennifer Cole and Deborah Lynn Durham, 179–96. Santa Fe: School for Advanced Research Press.

———. 2013. *Precarious Japan.* Durham, NC: Duke University Press.

Althusser, Louis. 1971. "Ideology and Ideological State Apparatuses." In *Lenin and Philosophy and Other Essays*, 121–73. New York: Monthly Review Press.

Alyokhina, Maria, Yekaterina Samutsevich, and Nadezhda Tolokonnikova. 2012. "Pussy Riot Closing Statements." Translated by Marijeta Bozovic, Maria Corrigan, Chto Delat, Elena Glazov-Corrigan, Maksim Hanukai, Katharine Holt, Ainsley Morse, and Sasha Senderovich. *n+1*, August 13. http://nplusonemag.com/pussy-riot-closing-statements.

Anagnost, Anne. 2006. "Strange Circulations: The Blood Economy in Rural China." *Economy and Society* 35 (4): 509–29.

———. 2008. "Imagining Global Futures in China: The Child as a Sign of Value." In *Figuring the Future: Globalization and the Temporalities of Children and Youth,* edited by Jennifer Cole and Deborah Lynn Durham, 49–72. Santa Fe: School for Advanced Research Press.

Anderson, David. 1997. "The Russian Mortality Crisis: Causes, Policy Responses, Lessons." Policy and Research Papers, No. 11, International Union for the Scientific Study of Population. https://iussp.org/sites/default/files/PRP11.pdf.

Anderson, Perry. 2007. "Russia's Managed Democracy: Why Putin?" *London Review of Books* 29 (2), January 25. https://www.lrb.co.uk/v29/n02/perry-anderson/russias -managed-democracy.

Asmolov, Aleksander. 2005. "Lichnost' Na Trone Kul'tury: A. G. Asmolov" [The Personality on the Throne of Culture: A. G. Asmolov]. Interview by M. G. Zaitseva. *Psikhologicheskaia Gazeta,* no. 5 (May): 10–13.

Attwood, Lynne. 1990. *The New Soviet Man and Woman: Sex-Role Socialization in the USSR.* Bloomington: Indiana University Press.

Bakhtin, Mikhail. 1984. *Problems of Dostoevsky's Poetics.* Minneapolis: University of Minnesota Press.

Barry, Andrew, Thomas Osborne, and Nikolas Rose. 1996. Introduction to *Foucault and Political Reason,* edited by Andrew Barry, Thomas Osborne, and Nikolas Rose, 1–17. Chicago: University of Chicago Press.

Bauer, Raymond A. 1959. *The New Man in Soviet Psychology.* Cambridge, MA: Harvard University Press.

BBC. 2012. "Russia Internet Blacklist Takes Effect." BBC, November 1. http://www.bbc .com/news/technology-20096274.

Beer, Daniel. 2008. *Renovating Russia: The Human Sciences and the Fate of Liberal Modernity, 1880–1930.* Ithaca, NY: Cornell University Press.

Berlant, Lauren. 2000. "Intimacy: A Special Issue." In *Intimacy,* edited by Lauren Berlant, 1–8. Chicago: University of Chicago Press.

———. 2011. *Cruel Optimism.* Durham, NC: Duke University Press.

Biehl, João. 2005. *Vita: Life in a Zone of Social Abandonment.* Berkeley: University of California Press.

Bloch, Sydney and Peter Reddaway. 1984. *Soviet Psychiatric Abuse: The Shadow over World Psychiatry.* London: V. Gollancz.

Bondarenko, Alexander F. 1999. "My Encounter with Carl Rogers: A Retrospective View from the Ukraine." *Journal of Humanistic Psychology* 39 (1): 8–14.

Bornstein, Erica, and Peter Redfield. 2011. *Forces of Compassion: Humanitarianism between Ethics and Politics.* Santa Fe: School for Advanced Research Press.

Bourdieu, Pierre. 1984. *Distinction: A Social Critique of the Judgment of Taste.* Cambridge, MA: Harvard University Press.

Boyer, Dominic. 2008. "Thinking through the Anthropology of Experts." *Anthropology in Action* 15 (2): 38–46.

Boyer, Dominic, and Alexei Yurchak. 2008. "Postsocialist Studies, Cultures of Parody and American Stiob." *Anthropology News* 49 (8): 9–10.

Boym, Svetlana. 1994. *Common Places: Mythologies of Everyday Life in Russia.* Cambridge, MA: Harvard University Press.

———. 2002. "Kak Sdelana 'Sovetskaia Sub'ektivnost'?" [How Is 'Soviet Subjectivity' Made?] *Ab Imperio,* no. 3: 285–96.

Bozhovich, L. I., and L. S. Slavina. 1967. "Fifty Years of Soviet Psychology of Upbringing." *Voprosy Psikhologii* 13 (5): 51–70.

Brennan, Teresa. 2004. *The Transmission of Affect.* Ithaca, NY: Cornell University Press.

Briggs, Jean L. 2000. "Emotions Have Many Faces: Inuit Lessons." *Anthropologica* 42 (2): 157–64.

Broadcasts, BSoW. 1987a. TV *Discussion of Family Problems.*

———. 1987b. TV *Discussion of Refuseniks, Antirefusniks, the Military and Chernobyl.*

Bronfenbrenner, Urie. 1970. *Two Worlds of Childhood: U.S. and U.S.S.R.* New York: Russell Sage Foundation.

Brown, Wendy. 2003. "Neo-liberalism and the End of Liberal Democracy." *Theory and Event* 7 (1): 1–21.

Buchowski, Michal. 2004. "Hierarchies of Knowledge in Central-Eastern European Anthropology." *Anthropology of East Europe Review* 22 (2): 5–14.

Buck-Morss, Susan. 2000. *Dreamworld and Catastrophe: The Passing of Mass Utopia in East and West.* Cambridge, MA: MIT Press.

Bulakhtin, Vladislav. 2017. Aktsiia 'Belyi Vagon'_kak eto bylo ran'she/ orientirovochno 2012/ [White Metro Car Rally_how it was before/ roughly 2012]. YouTube, May 27. https://youtu.be/XHfQ7v2hI3A.

Burawoy, Michael, and Katherine Verdery. 1999. *Uncertain Transition: Ethnographies of Change in the Postsocialist World.* Lanham, MD: Rowman and Littlefield.

Burchell, Graham. 1996. "Liberal Government and Techniques of the Self." In *Foucault and Political Reason,* edited by Andrew Barry, Thomas Osborne, and Nikolas Rose, 19–36. Chicago: University of Chicago Press.

Butler, Judith. 1997. *The Psychic Life of Power: Theories in Subjection.* Stanford, CA: Stanford University Press.

———. 2010. *Frames of War: When Is Life Grievable?* London: Verso.

Cabot, Heath. 2014. *On the Doorstep of Europe: Asylum and Citizenship in Greece.* Philadelphia: University of Pennsylvania Press.

Caldeira, Teresa. 2000. *City of Walls: Crime, Segregation and Citizenship in São Paulo.* Berkeley: University of California Press.

Caldwell, Melissa. 2004. *Not by Bread Alone: Social Support in the New Russia.* Berkeley: University of California Press.

———. 2016. *Living Faithfully in an Unjust World: Compassionate Care in Russia.* Berkeley: University of California Press.

Carr, E. Summerson. 2011. *Scripting Addiction: The Politics of Therapeutic Talk and American Sobriety.* Princeton, NJ: Princeton University Press.

Castel, Robert. 1991. "From Dangerousness to Risk." In *The Foucault Effect: Studies in Governmentality with Two Lectures by and an Interview with Michel Foucault*, edited by Graham Burchell, Colin Gordon, and Peter Miller, 281–98. Chicago: University of Chicago Press.

Certeau, Michel de. 1988. *The Practice of Everyday Life*. Berkeley: University of California Press.

Chambers, Samuel A. 2011. "Jacques Rancière and the Problem of Pure Politics." *European Journal of Political Theory* 10 (3): 303–26.

Chan, Sewell. 2017. "Russia's 'Gay Propaganda' Laws Are Illegal, European Court Rules." *New York Times*, June 20. https://www.nytimes.com/2017/06/20/world /europe/russia-gay-propaganda.html?_r=0.

Chepurnaia, Ol'ga and Alexander Etkind. 2006. "Intrumentalizatsiia Smerti. Uroki Antialkogol'noi Terapii" [The Instrumentalization of Death: Lessons from Anti-Alcoholic Therapy]. *Otechestvennye Zapiski* 2 (29). http://www.strana-oz.ru/2006/2 /instrumentalizaciya-smerti-uroki-antialkogolnoy-terapii#_ftn1.

Clark, Katerina. 1981. *The Soviet Novel: History as Ritual*. Chicago: University of Chicago Press.

———. 1995. *Petersburg: Crucible of Cultural Revolution*. Cambridge, MA: Harvard University Press.

Cohen, Dan Booth. 2006. " 'Family Constellations': An Innovative Systemic Phenomenological Group Process from Germany." *Family Journal* 14 (3): 226–33.

Cole, Jennifer, and Deborah Lynn Durham, eds. 2008. *Figuring the Future: Globalization and the Temporalities of Children and Youth*. Santa Fe: School for Advanced Research Press.

Cole, Michael. 2006. "Introduction: The Historical Context." In *The Making of Mind: A Personal Account of Soviet Psychology*, edited by Michael Cole and Sheila Cole, 1–16. Mahwah, NJ: Lawrence Erlbaum.

Cole, Sheila. 1986. "Soviet Family Clubs and the Russian Human Potential Movement." *Journal of Humanistic Psychology* 26 (4): 48–83.

Collier, Jane F., and Sylvia J. Yanagisako. 1987. *Gender and Kinship: Essays toward a Unified Analysis*. Stanford, CA: Stanford University Press.

Collier, Stephen J. 2005. "Budgets and Biopolitics." In *Global Assemblages: Technology, Politics, and Ethics as Anthropological Problems,* edited by Aiwha Ong and Stephen J. Collier, 373–90. Oxford: Blackwell.

———. 2011. *Post-Soviet Social: Neoliberalism, Social Modernity, Biopolitics*. Princeton, NJ: Princeton University Press.

Cruikshank, Barbara. 1996. "Revolutions Within: Self-Government and Self-Esteem." In *Foucault and Political Reason*, edited by Andrew Barry, Thomas Osborne, and Nikolas Rose, 231–51. Chicago: University of Chicago Press.

———. 1999. *The Will to Empower: Democratic Citizens and Other Subjects*. Ithaca, NY: Cornell University Press.

Dave, Naisargi. 2011. "Indian and Lesbian and What Came Next: Affect, Commensuration, and Queer Emergences." *American Ethnologist* 38 (4): 650–65.

Davis, Elizabeth Anne. 2012. *Bad Souls: Madness and Responsibility in Modern Greece.* Durham, NC: Duke University Press.

Dean, Mitchell. 1996. "Foucault, Government and the Enfolding of Authority." In *Foucault and Political Reason*, edited by A. Barry, T. Osborne, and Nikolas Rose, 209–30. Chicago: University of Chicago Press.

Deleuze, Gilles. 1988. *Foucault.* London: Athlone.

———. 2007. "On Spinoza." *Lectures by Gilles Deleuze*, February. htp://deleuzelectures .blogspot.com/2007/02/on-spinoza.html.

DeLillo, Don. 1997. *Underworld.* New York: Scribner.

Donzelot, Jacques. 1979. *The Policing of Families.* New York: Pantheon Books.

Douglas, Mary. 1990. "Foreword." In *The Gift: The Form and Reason for Exchange in Archaic Societies*, by Marcel Mauss, vii–xviii. New York: W. W. Norton.

———. 2002. *Purity and Danger: An Analysis of Concepts of Pollution and Taboo.* London: Routledge.

Dubois, Paul. 1905. *The Psychic Treatment of Nervous Disorders: (The Psychoneuroses and Their Moral Treatment).* New York: Funk and Wagnalls.

Duncan, Whitney. 2017. "An Alternative Therapy Hits Home in Mexico." SAPIENS, March 15. http://www.sapiens.org/culture/family-constellations-oaxaca -mexico/.

Dunham, Vera S. 1990. *In Stalin's Time: Middle-Class Values in Soviet Fiction.* Durham, NC: Duke University Press.

Dunn, Elizabeth. 2004. *Privatizing Poland: Baby Food, Big Business, and the Remaking of Labor.* Ithaca, NY: Cornell University Press.

———. 2008. "Postsocialist Spores: Disease, Bodies and the State in Postsocialist Georgia." *American Ethnologist* 35 (2): 243–58.

Dunstan, John, and Avril Suddaby. 1992. "The Progressive Tradition in Soviet Schooling to 1988." In *Soviet Education under Perestroika*, edited by John Dunstan, 1–13. London: Routledge.

Eklof, Ben, and Edward Dneprov. 1993. *Democracy in the Russian School: The Reform Movement in Education since 1984.* Boulder, CO: Westview.

Englund, Harri. 2006. *Prisoners of Freedom: Human Rights and the African Poor.* Berkeley: University of California Press.

Espeland, Wendy Nelson, and Mitchell L. Stevens. 1998. "Commensuration as a Social Process." *Annual Review of Sociology* 24 (1): 313–43.

Etkind, Alexander. 1997. *Eros of the Impossible: The History of Psychoanalysis in Russia.* Boulder, CO: Westview.

———. 2005. "Soviet Subjectivity: Torture for the Sake of Salvation?" *Kritika: Explorations in Russian and Eurasian History* 6 (1): 171–86.

———. 2009. "Post-Soviet Hauntology: Cultural Memory of the Soviet Terror." *Constellations* 16 (1): 182–200.

EU-Russia Centre/Levada Center. 2007. "Voices from Russia: Society, Democracy, Europe." eu-russiacentre.org, February. http://www.eu-russiacentre.org/assets/files /EU-RC%20Levada%20Research%20Commentary.pdf.

Fabian, Johannes. 1996. *Remembering the Present: Painting and Popular History in Zaire.* Berkeley: University of California Press.

Faraday, George. 2000. *Revolt of the Filmmakers: The Struggle for Artistic Autonomy and the Fall of the Soviet Film Industry.* University Park: Pennsylvania State University Press.

Farquhar, Judith, and Qicheng Zhang. 2005. "Biopolitical Beijing: Pleasure, Sovereignty, and Self-Cultivation in China's Capital." *Cultural Anthropology* 20 (3): 303–27.

Faubion, James. 2011. *An Anthropology of Ethics.* Cambridge: Cambridge University Press.

Favret-Saada, Jeanne. 1989. "Unbewitching as Therapy." *American Ethnologist* 16 (1): 40–56.

Fedotova, Tamara Iur'evna. 2006. "Sluzhbe—Byt'!" ["Help Is on the Way!—Interview with Tamara Iur'evna Fedotova." By Ol'ga Reshetnikova. *Shkol'nyi Psikholog*, no. 9. http://psy.1september.ru/article.php?ID=200600915.

Ferguson, James. 1994. *The Anti-politics Machine: "Development," Depoliticization, and Bureaucratic Power in Lesotho.* Minneapolis: University of Minnesota Press.

———. 2007. *Global Shadows: Africa in the Neoliberal World Order.* Durham, NC: Duke University Press.

Ferguson, James, and Akhil Gupta. 2002. "Spatializing States: Toward an Ethnography of Neoliberal Governmentality." *American Ethnologist* 29 (4): 981–1002.

Fitzpatrick, Sheila. 1999. *Everyday Stalinism: Ordinary Life in Extraordinary Times; Soviet Russia in the 1930s.* Oxford: Oxford University Press.

Fomichev, A. P. 1946. "Concerning the Pedological Distortions in the System of the Peoples Commissariat of Education." *Sovietskii Pedagog*, no. 7: 11–20.

Foucault, Michel. 1988. *The Care of the Self.* Vol. 3 of *The History of Sexuality.* New York: Vintage Books.

———. 1990a. *The History of Sexuality: An Introduction.* New York: Vintage Books.

———. 1990b. *The Use of Pleasure.* Vol. 2 of *The History of Sexuality.* New York: Vintage Books.

———. 1991. "Governmentality." In *The Foucault Effect,* edited by Graham Burchell, Colin Gordon, and Peter Miller, 87–104. Chicago: University of Chicago Press.

———. 1994. "(Auto)biography Michel Foucault, 1926–1984." In *Michel Foucault: Critical Assessments,* edited by B. Smart. Vol. 7, 257–60. London: Routledge.

———. 1995. *Discipline and Punish: The Birth of the Prison.* New York: Vintage Books.

———. 1997a. "The Ethics of the Concern for Self as a Practice of Freedom." In *Ethics: Subjectivity and Truth,* edited by Paul Rabinow, 281–302. New York: New Press.

———. 1997b. "Technologies of the Self." In *Ethics: Subjectivity and Truth,* edited by Paul Rabinow, 223–51. New York: New Press.

———. 2000a. "'Omnes et Singulatim': Toward a Critique of Political Reason." In *Power,* edited by James D. Faubion, 298–325. New York: New Press.

———. 2000b. "The Subject and Power." In *Power,* edited by James D. Faubion, 326–48. New York: New Press.

———. 2005. *The Hermeneutics of the Subject: Lectures at the Collège de France, 1981–82.* New York: Palgrave Macmillan.

———. 2007. *Security, Territory, Population: Lectures at the Collège de France, 1977–78.* New York: Palgrave Macmillan.

FRED. 2018. "Federal Reserve Bank of St. Louis Economic Research: Gini Index for the Russian Federation." https://fred.stlouisfed.org/series/SIPOVGINIRUS.

Frolov, Vladimir. 2008. "Analysis and Opinion: Endangered Hopes." *Expat.ru*, October 28. https://www.expat.ru/analitics.php?item=500.

Frykman, Jonas, and Orvar Löfgren. 1987. *Culture Builders: A Historical Anthropology of Middle-Class Life.* New Brunswick, NJ: Rutgers University Press.

Fukuyama, Francis. 1992. *The End of History and the Last Man.* New York: Free Press.

Gal, Susan, and Gail Kligman. 2000. *The Politics of Gender after Socialism: A Comparative-Historical Essay.* Princeton, NJ: Princeton University Press.

Garcia, Angela. 2010. *The Pastoral Clinic: Addiction and Dispossession along the Rio Grande.* Berkeley: University of California Press.

Gaudiano, Brandon A. 2008. "Cognitive-Behavioural Therapies: Achievements and Challenges." *Evidence-Based Mental Health* 1 (1): 5–7.

Gessen, Masha. 2013. "When Putin Declared War on Gay Families, It Was Time for Mine to Leave Russia." *Slate*, August 26. http://www.slate.com/blogs/outward/2013/08/26/when_putin_declared_war_on_gay_families_it_was_time_for_mine_to_leave_russia.html.

Gibson-Graham, J. K. 2006. *The End of Capitalism (As We Knew It): A Feminist Critique of Political Economy.* Minneapolis: University of Minnesota Press.

Gilgen, Albert R., and Carol K. Gilgen. 1996. "Historical Background, Analytical Overview and Glossary." In *Post-Soviet Perspectives on Russian Psychology*, edited by Vera A. Koltsova, Yuri N. Oleinik, Albert R. Gilgen, and Carol K. Gilgen, 3–52. Westport, CT: Greenwood.

Gill, Rosalind, and Andy Pratt. 2008. "In the Social Factory? Immaterial Labour, Precariousness and Cultural Work." *Theory, Culture and Society* 25 (7–8): 1–30.

Giordano, Cristiana. 2014. *Migrants in Translation: Caring and the Logics of Difference in Contemporary Italy.* Berkeley: University of California Press.

Goble, Paul. 2008. "Shortage of Draft-Age Men Prompts Duma to Tighten Registration Requirements." *Window on Eurasia*, March 26. http://windowoneurasia.blogspot.com/2008/03/window-on-eurasia-shortage-of-draft-age.html.

Goffman, Erving. 1971. *Relations in Public: Microstudies of the Political Order.* New York: Basic Books.

Gorbachev, Mikhail. 2010. "Perestroika Lost." *New York Times*, March 13. http://www.nytimes.com/2010/03/14/opinion/14gorbachev.html.

Gordon, Colin. 1991. "Governmental Rationality: Introduction." In *Foucault Effect*, edited by Graham Burchell, Colin Gordon, and Peter Miller, 1–52. Chicago: University of Chicago Press.

Graham, Loren. 1987. *Science, Philosophy, and Human Behavior in the Soviet Union.* New York: Columbia University Press.

Greening, Tom. 1984. "AHP Delegation to the Soviet Union." *Journal of Humanistic Psychology* 24 (1): 7–8.

———. 1989. "The Journal of Humanistic Psychology and the AHP Soviet-American Exchange Program." *Journal of Humanistic Psychology* 29 (3): 367–69.

Gupta, Akhil. 2012. *Red Tape: Bureaucracy, Structural Violence, and Poverty in India.* Durham, NC: Duke University Press.

Gutiérrez, María. 2011. "Making Markets out of Thin Air: A Case of Capital Involution." *Antipode* 43 (3): 639–61.

Hacking, Ian. 1995. *Rewriting the Soul: Multiple Personality and the Sciences of Memory.* Princeton, NJ: Princeton University Press.

Halley, Janet. 2006. *Split Decisions: How and Why to Take a Break from Feminism.* Princeton, NJ: Princeton University Press.

Hann, Chris, and Elizabeth Dunn. 1996. *Civil Society: Challenging Western Models.* London: Routledge.

Hann, Chris, Caroline Humphrey, and Katherine Verdery. 2002. "Introduction: Postsocialism as a Topic of Anthropological Investigation." In *Postsocialism: Ideals, Ideologies and Practices in Eurasia,* edited by Chris Hann, 1–28. London: Routledge.

Haraway, Donna. 1991. "A Cyborg Manifesto: Science, Technology, and Socialist-Feminism in the Late Twentieth Century." In *Simians, Cyborgs and Women: The Reinvention of Nature,* 149–81. New York: Routledge.

Hardt, Michael. 1999. "Affective Labor." *boundary 2* 26 (2): 89–100.

Hardt, Michael, and Antonio Negri. 2005. *Multitude: War and Democracy in the Age of Empire.* Reprint, New York: Penguin Books.

HPSSS (Harvard Project on the Soviet Social System). n.d. Schedule B, Vol. 02, Case 382 (interviewer R.B.). Widener Library, Harvard University, Cambridge, MA.

Hassard, Jack. 1990. "The AHP Soviet Exchange Project." *Journal of Humanistic Psychology* 30 (3): 6–51.

Hellbeck, Jochen. 2006. *Revolution on My Mind: Writing a Diary under Stalin.* Cambridge, MA: Harvard University Press.

Hemment, Julie. 2004. "The Riddle of the Third Sector: Civil Society, International Aid, and NGOs in Russia." *Anthropological Quarterly* 77 (2): 215–41.

Herzfeld, Michael. 1992. *The Social Production of Indifference.* New York: Berg.

Hirsch, Francine. 2005. *Empire of Nations: Ethnographic Knowledge and the Making of the Soviet Union.* Ithaca, NY: Cornell University Press.

Hirschkind, Charles. 2006. *The Ethical Soundscape: Cassette Sermons and Islamic Counterpublics.* New York: Columbia University Press.

Höjdestrand, Tova. 2009. *Needed by Nobody: Homelessness and Humanness in Postsocialist Russia.* Ithaca, NY: Cornell University Press.

Hosking, Gregory. 1993. *The First Socialist Society: A History of the Soviet Union from Within.* Cambridge, MA: Harvard University Press.

Humphrey, Caroline. 2002. *The Unmaking of Soviet Life: Everyday Economies after Socialism.* Ithaca, NY: Cornell University Press.

———. 2007. "Alternative Freedoms." *Proceedings of the American Philosophical Society* 151 (1): 1–10.

Hunt, Morton. 1993. *The Story of Psychology.* New York: Doubleday.

Iarskaia-Smirnova, Elena, and Pavel Romanov. 2013. "Doing Class in Social Welfare Discourses: 'Unfortunate Families' in Russia." In *Rethinking Class in Russia*, edited by Suvi Salmenniemi, 85–106. London: Ashgate.

Iasiukova, L. A. 2005. *Zakonomernosti Razvitiia Poniatiinogo Myshleniia I Ego Rol' v Obychenii* [The Laws of Development of Conceptual Thinking and Its Role in Learning]. Saint Petersburg: Imaton.

Illouz, Eva. 2008. *Saving the Modern Soul: Therapy, Emotions, and the Culture of Self-Help*. Berkeley: University of California Press.

Ioffe, Julia. 2011. Twilight of a Seat-Warmer: Medvedev's Worst Week Ever Just Keeps Going." *Foreign Policy*, October 4. http://foreignpolicy.com/2011/10/04/twilight-of-a-seat-warmer/.

ITAR-TASS. 2008. "Palm-Greasing at Russian Universities Continues Swelling." www.sras.org, February 4. http://www.sras.org/bribery_at_russian_universities.

Jackson, Michael. 2011. *Life within Limits: Well-Being in a World of Want*. Durham, NC: Duke University Press.

Joravsky, David. 1989. *Russian Psychology: A Critical History*. Oxford: Blackwell.

Kaganovsky, Lilya. 2008. *How the Soviet Man Was Unmade: Cultural Fantasy and Male Subjectivity under Stalin*. Pittsburgh: University of Pittsburgh Press.

Karpenko, Oksana. 2014. "Preserving Independence and Freedom in Russian Sociology: An Interview with Oksana Karpenko, CISR." By Michele Rivkin-Fish. *NewsNet* 54 (4): 6–9.

Kelly, Catriona. 2001. *Refining Russia: Advice Literature, Polite Culture, and Gender from Catherine to Yeltsin*. Oxford: Oxford University Press.

———. 2007. *Children's World: Growing Up in Russia, 1890–1991*. New Haven, CT: Yale University Press.

Kharkhordin, Oleg. 1999. *The Collective and the Individual in Russia: A Study of Practices*. Berkeley: University of California Press.

Kipnis, Andrew. 2008. "Audit Cultures: Neoliberal Governmentality, Socialist Legacy, or Technologies of Governing?" *American Ethnologist* 35 (2): 275–89.

Kitanaka, Junko. 2011. *Depression in Japan: Psychiatric Cures for a Society in Distress*. Princeton, NJ: Princeton University Press.

Kleinman, Arthur. 1995. *Writing at the Margin: Discourse between Anthropology and Medicine*. Berkeley: University of California Press.

Kleinman, Arthur, and Joan Kleinman. 1985. "Somatization: The Interconnections in Chinese Society among Culture, Depressive Experiences, and the Meanings of Pain." In *Culture and Depression: Studies in the Anthropology and Cross-Cultural Psychiatry of Affect and Disorder,* edited by Arthur Kleinman and Byron Good, 429–90. Berkeley: University of California Press.

Kollontai, Alessandra. 1990. "Make Way for Winged Eros." In *Bolshevik Visions: First Phase of the Cultural Revolution in Soviet Russia*, edited by William G. Rosenberg, 67–76. Ann Arbor: University of Michigan Press.

Koopman, Colin, and Tomas Matza. 2013. "Putting Foucault to Work: Analytic and Concept in Foucaultian Inquiry." *Critical Inquiry* 39 (4): 817–40.

Kozulin, Alex. 1984. *Psychology in Utopia: Toward a Social History of Soviet Psychology*. Cambridge, MA: MIT Press.

Kripal, Jeffrey. 2007. *Esalen: America and the Religion of No Religion*. Chicago: University of Chicago Press.

Krylova, Anna. 2000. "The Tenacious Liberal Subject in Soviet Studies." *Kritika: Explorations in Russian and Eurasian History* 1 (1): 119–46.

Kuhn, Thomas S. 1996. *The Structure of Scientific Revolutions*. 3rd ed. Chicago: University of Chicago Press.

Laidlaw, James. 2002. "For an Anthropology of Ethics and Freedom." *Journal of the Royal Anthropological Institute* 8 (2): 311–32.

Lambek, Michael. 2008. "Value and Virtue." *Anthropological Theory* 8 (2): 133–57.

———, ed. 2010. *Ordinary Ethics: Anthropology, Language, and Action*. New York: Fordham University Press.

Lauterbach, Wolf. 1974. "Clinical Psychology in the Soviet Union." *Comprehensive Psychiatry* 15 (6): 483–93.

———. 1984. *Soviet Psychotherapy*. Oxford: Pergamon.

Laszlo, Ervin. 2004. *Science and the Akashic Field: An Integral Theory of Everything*. Rochester, VT: Inner Traditions.

Lazzarato, Maurizio. 1996. "Immaterial Labour." In *Radical Thought in Italy*, edited by Paulo Virno and Michael Hardt, 132–46. Minneapolis: University of Minnesota Press.

Ledeneva, Alena. 2006. *How Russia Really Works: The Informal Practices That Shaped Post-Soviet Politics and Business*. Ithaca, NY: Cornell University Press.

Lemke, Thomas. 2008. "An Interview with Thomas Lemke: Michel Foucault Today; On the Theoretical Relevance of Foucauldian Concepts of 'Governmentality' and 'Biopolitics.'" By Stéphane Baele. *Émulations* 2 (4). http://www.revue-emulations .net/interviews/interviews2/thomaslemke-foucaulttoday.

Lemon, Alaina. 1998. "'Your Eyes Are Green like Dollars': Counterfeit Cash, National Substance, and Currency Apartheid in 1990s Russia." *Cultural Anthropology* 13 (1): 22–55.

———. 2000. "Talking Transit and Speaking Transition: The Moscow Metro." In *Altering States: Ethnographies of Transition in Eastern Europe and the Former Soviet Union*, edited by Daphne Berdahl, Matti Bunzl, and Martha Lampland, 14–39. Ann Arbor: University of Michigan Press.

Lerner, Julia. 2011. "TV Therapy without Psychology: Adapting the Self in Post-Soviet Media." *Laboratorium: Russian Review of Social Research* 3 (1): 116–37.

———. 2015. "The Changing Meanings of Russian Love: Emotional Socialism and Therapeutic Culture on the Post-Soviet Screen." *Sexuality and Culture* 19 (2): 349–68.

Lester, Rebecca J. 2007. "Critical Therapeutics: Cultural Politics and Clinical Reality in Two Eating Disorder Treatment Centers." *Medical Anthropology Quarterly* 21 (4): 369–87.

Leykin, Inna. 2015. "*Rodologia*: Genealogy as Therapy in Post-Soviet Russia." *Ethos* 43 (2): 135–64.

Liechty, Mark. 2003. *Suitably Modern: Making Middle-Class Culture in a New Consumer Society*. Princeton, NJ: Princeton University Press.

Luhrmann, Tanya. 2000. *Of Two Minds: The Growing Disorder in American Psychiatry*. New York: Knopf.

Lukacs, Gabriella. 2010. *Scripted Affects, Branded Selves: Television, Subjectivity, and Capitalism in 1990s Japan.* Durham, NC: Duke University Press.

Lutz, Catherine. 1988. *Unnatural Emotions: Everyday Sentiments on a Micronesian Atoll and Their Challenge to Western Theory.* Chicago: University of Chicago Press.

Macpherson, C. B. 1962. *The Political Theory of Possessive Individualism: Hobbes to Locke.* Oxford: Clarendon.

Macy, Francine. 1987. "The Legacy of Carl Rogers in the U.S.S.R." *Journal of Humanistic Psychology* 27 (3): 305–8.

Mahmood, Saba. 2005. *Politics of Piety: The Islamic Revival and the Feminist Subject.* Princeton, NJ: Princeton University Press.

Makarenko, Anton. 1967. *The Collective Family: A Handbook for Russian Parents.* Garden City, NJ: Anchor Books.

Malia, Martin. 1999. *Russia under Western Eyes: From the Bronze Horseman to the Lenin Mausoleum.* Cambridge, MA: Belknap Press of Harvard University Press.

Malkki, Liisa. 2010. "Children, Humanity, and the Infantilization of Peace." In *In the Name of Humanity: The Government of Threat and Care*, edited by Ilana Feldman and Miriam Ticktin, 58–85. Durham, NC: Duke University Press.

———. 2015. *The Need to Help: The Domestic Arts of International Humanitarianism.* Durham, NC: Duke University Press.

Manning, Nick, and Nataliya Tikhonova. 2009. *Health and Health Care in the New Russia.* Farnham, England: Ashgate.

Manning, Paul. 2007. "Rose-Colored Glasses? Color Revolutions and Cartoon Chaos in Postsocialist Georgia." *Cultural Anthropology* 22 (2): 171–213.

Martin, Emily. 2007. *Bipolar Expeditions: Mania and Depression in American Culture.* Princeton, NJ: Princeton University Press.

Marx, Karl. 1990, *Capital: A Critique of Political Economy.* Vol. 1. Translated by Ben Fowkes. New York: Penguin Books.

Maslow, Abraham. 1987. *Motivation and Personality.* New York: Harper & Row.

Massumi, Brian. 2002. *Parables for the Virtual: Movement, Affect, Sensation.* Durham, NC: Duke University Press.

Matza, Tomas. 2009. "Moscow's Echo: Technologies of the Self, Publics and Politics on the Russian Talk Show." *Cultural Anthropology* 24 (3): 489–522.

———. 2012. "Allan Chumak." *Frequencies*, January 16. http://frequencies.ssrc.org /2012/01/16/allan-chumak/.

———. 2014. "The Will to What? Class, Time, and Re-willing in Post-Soviet Russia." *Social Text*, no. 120 (Fall): 49–67.

McFaul, Michael, and Karen Stoner-Weiss. 2008. "The Myth of the Authoritarian Model." *Foreign Affairs* 87 (1): 68–84.

Mendelson, Sarah. 2008. "Dreaming of a Democratic Russia: Memories of a Year in Moscow Promoting a Post-Soviet Political Process, an Undertaking That Now Seems Futile." *American Scholar* 77 (1): 35–43.

Mickiewicz, Ellen. 1988. *Split Signals: Television and Politics in the Soviet Union.* New York: Oxford University Press.

———. 1999. *Changing Channels: Television and the Struggle for Power in Russia.* Durham, NC: Duke University Press.

Miller, Martin. 1985. "Freudian Theory under Bolshevik Rule: The Theoretical Controversy during the 1920s." *Slavic Review* 44 (4): 625–46.

———. 1990. "Psychoanalysis and the Problem of the Unconscious in Russia." *Social Research* 57 (4): 875–88.

———. 1998. *Freud and the Bolsheviks: Psychoanalysis in Imperial Russia and the Soviet Union.* New Haven, CT: Yale University Press.

Mokrzycki, Edmund. 1996. "A New Middle Class?" In *Culture, Modernity and Revolution: Essays in Honor of Zygmunt Bauman,* edited by R. Kilminster, 184–99. London: Routledge.

Molostov, Aleksandr N. 2015. "Psikhologo-pedagogicheskoe Soprovozhdenie: Istoriografiia Voprosa i Osobennosti v Protsesse Formirovaniia u Kursantov Vuzov MVD Tolerantnogo Povedeniia" [Psycho-pedagogical Accompaniment: Historiography of the Topic and Features of the Training Process in Tolerant Behavior among Cadets in the Ministry of Internal Affairs]. *Sovremennye Problemy Nauki i Obrazovaniia* 1 (1). https://www.science-education.ru/ru/article/view?id=17222.

Morson, Gary, and Caryl Emerson. 1990. *Mikhail Bakhtin: Creation of a Prosaics.* Stanford, CA: Stanford University Press.

Muckle, James. 1990. *Portrait of a Soviet School under Glasnost.* New York: St. Martin's.

Muehlebach, Andrea. 2012. *The Moral Neoliberal: Welfare and Citizenship in Italy.* Chicago: University of Chicago Press.

Negri, Antonio. 1999. "Value and Affect." *Boundary 2* 26 (2): 77–88.

Nikitin, Vadim. 2012. "The Wrong Reasons to Back Pussy Riot." *New York Times,* August 20. http://www.nytimes.com/2012/08/21/opinion/the-wrong-reasons-to-back-pussy-riot.html.

Obeyesekere, Gannath. 1985. "Depression, Buddhism and the Work of Culture in Sri Lanka." In *Culture and Depression: Studies in the Anthropology and Cross-Cultural Psychiatry of Affect and Disorder,* edited by Arthur Kleinman and Byron Good, 134–52. Berkeley: University of California Press.

OECD. 2017a. "Life Expectancy at Birth (Indicator)." doi: 10.1787/27e0fc9d-en (accessed March 29, 2017).

———. 2017b. "Suicide Rates (Indicator)." doi: 10.1787/a82f3459-en (accessed March 29, 2017).

———. 2018. "OECD Data: Income Inequality, 2005–2015." https://data.oecd.org/inequality/income-inequality.htm.

Ong, Aihwa. 1999. *Flexible Citizenship: The Cultural Logics of Transnationality.* Durham, NC: Duke University Press.

———. 2006. *Neoliberalism as Exception: Mutations in Citizenship and Sovereignty.* Durham, NC: Duke University Press.

Ong, Aihwa, and Stephen Collier. 2005. *Global Assemblages: Technology, Politics, and Ethics as Anthropological Problems.* Oxford: Blackwell.

Ortner, Sherry. 1974. "Is Female to Male as Nature Is to Culture?" In *Woman, Culture, and Society,* edited by Michelle Rosaldo and Louise Lamphere, 68–87. Stanford, CA: Stanford University Press.

———. 2006. *Anthropology and Social Theory: Culture, Power, and the Acting Subject.* Durham, NC: Duke University Press.

———. 2016. "Dark Anthropology and Its Others: Theory since the Eighties." *HAU: Journal of Ethnographic Theory* 6 (1): 47–73.

Oushakine, Serguei. 2000. "In the State of Post-Soviet Aphasia: Symbolic Development in Contemporary Russia." *Europe-Asia Studies* 52 (6): 991–1016.

———. 2004. "The Flexible and the Pliant: Disturbed Organisms of Soviet Modernity." *Cultural Anthropology* 19 (3): 392–428.

———. 2009. *The Patriotism of Despair: Nation, War, and Loss in Russia.* Ithaca, NY: Cornell University Press.

Ovcharova, Anna P. 2012. "Poniatie 'Psikhologo-pedagogicheskoe Soprovozhdenie Detei Mladshego Shkol'nogo Vozrasta' kak Pedagogicheskaia Kategoriia" [The Concept of 'Psycho-pedagogical Accompaniment of Primary School Children' as a Pedagogical Category]. *Vestnik Leningradskogo Gosudarstvennogo Universiteta Im. A. C. Pushkina* 4 (3): 70–78. Saint Petersburg: GAOU VO LO "LGU im. A. C. Pushkina." https://cyberleninka.ru/article/n/ponyatie-psihologo-pedagogicheskoe-soprovozhdenie-detey-mladshego-shkolnogo-vozrasta-kak-pedagogicheskaya-kategoriya.

Pakhomova, Evgeniia V. 2007. "Psikhologo-pedagogicheskoe Soprovozhdenie Rebenka s Oslablennym Zdorov'em Obrazovatel'noi Srede Doshkol'nogo Uchrezhdeniia" [Psycho-pedagogical Accompaniment of the Child with Poor Health in Preschools]. Stavropol' State University. Scientific library of dissertations and abstracts, http://www.dissercat.com/content/psikhologo-pedagogicheskoe-soprovozhdenie-rebenka-s-oslablennym-zdorovem-v-obrazovatelnoi-sr#ixzz4v1qhxhPA.

Paley, Julia. 2001. *Marketing Democracy: Power and Social Movements in Post-Dictatorship Chile.* Berkeley: University of California Press.

Parfitt, Tom. 2014. "New Left Review—Gleb Pavlovsky: Putin's World Outlook." *New Left Review*, no. 88 (August). http://newleftreview.org/II/88/gleb-pavlovsky-putin-s-world-outlook.

Patico, Jennifer. 2005. "To Be Happy in a Mercedes: Tropes of Value and Ambivalent Visions of Marketization." *American Ethnologist* 32 (3): 479–96.

———. 2008. *Consumption and Social Change in a Post-Soviet Middle Class.* Washington, DC: Woodrow Wilson Center Press.

Pervyi Kanal. 2008a. "Arkhivnye Programmy: *Lolita. Bez Kompleksov.*" http://www.1tv.ru/owa/win/ort5_peredach.peredach?p_shed_name_id=5686&p_alphabet_id=.

———. 2008b. "Arkhivnye Programmy: *Poniat'. Prostit'.*" http://www.1tv.ru/owa/win/ort5_peredach.peredach?p_shed_name_id=5713&p_alphabet_id=.

Pesmen, Dale. 2000. *Russia and Soul: An Exploration.* Ithaca, NY: Cornell University Press.

Petrovskaia, I. 2006. "Smotrite Televizor: 29 Mai–4 Iun" [Watch TV: May 29–June 4]. *Izvestia*, May 26.

Petrovsky, Artur V. 1990. *Psychology in the Soviet Union: A Historical Outline.* Moscow: Progress.

Petryna, Adriana. 2002. *Life Exposed: Biological Citizens after Chernobyl.* Princeton, NJ: Princeton University Press.

Pollock, Ethan 2009. "From *Partiinost'* to *Nauchnost'* and Not Quite Back Again: Revisiting the Lessons of the Lysenko Affair." *Slavic Review* 68 (1): 95–115.

Povinelli, Elizabeth. 2001. "Radical Worlds: The Anthropology of Incommensurability and Inconceivability." *Annual Review of Anthropology* 30 (1): 319–34.

———. 2002. *The Cunning of Recognition: Indigenous Alterities and the Making of Australian Multiculturalism.* Durham, NC: Duke University Press.

———. 2011. *Economies of Abandonment: Social Belonging and Endurance in Late Liberalism.* Durham, NC: Duke University Press.

———. 2012. "The Will to Be Otherwise/ The Effort of Endurance." *South Atlantic Quarterly* 111 (3): 453–75.

Prangishvili, A. S., A. E. Sherozia, and F. V. Bassin. 1978. *Bessoznatel'noe* [The Unconscious]. Tbilisi: Metzniereba.

Procacci, Giovanna. 1991. "Social Economy and the Government of Poverty." In *Foucault Effect,* edited by Graham Burchell, Colin Gordon, and Peter Miller, 151–68. Chicago: University of Chicago Press.

Putin, Vladimir. 2006. "Address to the Federal Assembly of the Russian Federation" [Poslanie Federal'nomu Sobraniiu Rossiiskoi Federatsii]. kremlin.ru, May 10. http://kremlin.ru/events/president/transcripts/23577.

Rabinow, Paul. 1996. "Artificiality and Enlightenment: From Sociobiology to Biosociality." In *Essays on the Anthropology of Reason,* 91–111. Princeton, NJ: Princeton University Press.

Raikhel, Eugene. 2010. "Post-Soviet Placebos: Epistemology and Authority in Russian Treatments for Alcoholism." *Culture, Medicine and Psychiatry* 34 (1): 132–68.

———. 2016. *Governing Habits: Treating Alcoholism in the Post-Soviet Clinic.* Ithaca, NY: Cornell University Press.

Raikhel, Eugene, and Dörte Bemme. 2016. "Postsocialism, the Psy-ences, and Mental Health." *Transcultural Psychiatry* 53 (2): 151–75.

Rajan, Kaushik Sunder. 2006. *Biocapital: The Constitution of Postgenomic Life.* Durham, NC: Duke University Press.

Rancière, Jacques. 1992. "Politics, Identification, and Subjectivization." *October* 61: 58–64.

Rawles, Richard E. 1996. "Soviet Psychology, Perestroika, and the Human Factor." In *Post-Soviet Perspectives on Russian Psychology,* edited by V. A. Koltsova, 101–15. Westport, CT: Greenwood.

Remnick, David. 2008. "Echo in the Dark: A Radio Station Strives to Keep the Airwaves Free." *New Yorker,* September 22. https://www.newyorker.com/magazine/2008/09/22/echo-in-the-dark.

Ries, Nancy. 1997. *Russian Talk: Culture and Conversation during Perestroika.* Ithaca, NY: Cornell University Press.

Rivkin-Fish, Michele. 2005. *Women's Health in Post-Soviet Russia.* Bloomington: Indiana University Press.

———. 2009. "Tracing Landscapes of the Past in Class Subjectivity: Practices of Memory and Distinction in Marketizing Russia." *American Ethnologist* 36 (1): 79–95.

———. 2010. "Pronatalism, Gender Politics, and the Renewal of Family Support in Russia: Toward a Feminist Anthropology of 'Maternity Capital.'" *Slavic Review* 69 (3): 701–24.

Robbins, Joel. 2013. "Beyond the Suffering Subject: Toward an Anthropology of the Good." *Journal of the Royal Anthropological Institute* 19 (3): 447–62.

Rofel, Lisa. 1999. *Other Modernities: Gendered Yearnings in China after Socialism.* Berkeley: University of California Press.

———. 2007. *Desiring China: Experiments in Neoliberalism, Sexuality, and Public Culture.* Durham, NC: Duke University Press.

Rogers, Carl. 1987. "Inside the World of the Soviet Professional." *Journal of Humanistic Psychology* 27 (3): 277–304.

Rogers, Douglas. 2009. *The Old Faith and the Russian Land: A Historical Ethnography of Ethics in the Urals.* Ithaca, NY: Cornell University Press.

———. 2014. "Energopolitical Russia: Corporation, State, and the Rise of Social and Cultural Projects." *Anthropological Quarterly* 87 (2): 431–51.

———. 2015. *The Depths of Russia: Oil, Power, and Culture after Socialism.* Ithaca, NY: Cornell University Press.

Rosaldo, Michelle Z. 1984. "Toward an Anthropology of Thought and Feeling." In *Culture Theory: Essays on Mind, Self and Emotion,* edited by Richard Shweder and Robert LeVine, 137–57. New York: Cambridge University Press.

Rose, Nikolas. 1990. *Governing the Soul: The Shaping of the Private Self.* London: Routledge.

———. 1996a. "Governing 'Advanced' Liberal Democracies." In *Foucault and Political Reason,* edited by Andrew Barry, Thomas Osborne, and Nikolas Rose, 37–64. Chicago: University of Chicago Press.

———. 1996b. *Inventing Our Selves: Psychology, Power, and Personhood.* Cambridge, MA: Cambridge University Press.

———. 2007. *The Politics of Life Itself: Biomedicine, Power and Subjectivity in the Twenty-First Century.* Princeton, NJ: Princeton University Press.

Rose, Nikolas, and Joelle M. Abi-Rached. 2013. *Neuro: The New Brain Sciences and the Management of the Mind.* Princeton, NJ: Princeton University Press.

Rosen, Seymour. 1971. *Education and Modernization in the USSR.* Reading, MA: Addison-Wesley.

Rotkirch, Anna, Anna Temkina, and Elena Zdravomyslova. 2007. "Who Helps the Degraded Housewife? Comments on Vladimir Putin's Demographic Speech." *European Journal of Women's Studies* 14 (4): 349–57.

Rudnyckyj, Daromir. 2009. "Spiritual Economies: Islam and Neoliberalism in Contemporary Indonesia." *Cultural Anthropology* 24 (1): 104–41.

Russian Federation. 1998. *Tipovoe Polozheniie Ob Obrazovatel'nom Uchrezhdenii Dlia Detei, Nuzhdaiushchikhsia v Psikhologi-Pedagogicheskoi I Medico-Sotsial'noi Pomoshchi* [Standard Statute on Educational Institutions for Children in Need of Psycho-pedagogical and Medico-social Help]. http://pravo.gov.ru/proxy/ips/?docbody=&nd=102054699&rdk=&backlink=1.

———. 2002. "Prikaz: O Kontseptsii Modernizatsii Rossiiskogo Obrazovaniia na Period do 2010 Goda" [Order: On the Concept of Modernization in Russian Education through the Year 2010]. No. 393, February 11. http://www.edu.ru/db/mo/Data /d_02/393.html.

———. 2004. "Educational System in Russia: The National Report of the Russian Federation." Report presented at the 47th Session of the International Conference on Education, United Nations, September 8–11, 1–31. Geneva. http://www.ibe .unesco.org/International/ICE47/English/Natreps/reports/russia_ocr.pdf.

———. 2010. *Semeinyi Kodeks Rossiiskoi Federatsii* [Family Code of the Russian Federation]. Novosibirsk: Sibirskoe universitetskoe izdatelstvo.

Ryzhkov, Vladimir. 2008. "Oppozitsiia bez Sprosa" [Opposition without Demand]. *Novaia Gazeta*, May 8. https://www.novayagazeta.ru/articles/2008/05/08/38159 -oppozitsiya-bez-sprosa.

Said, Edward. 1994. *Orientalism*. New York: Vintage Books.

Saint Petersburg State University. n.d. "Istoria Fakulteta" [History of the Department]. Accessed October 3, 2017. http://www.psy.spbu.ru/department/history.

Salecl, Renata. 1994. *The Spoils of Freedom: Psychoanalysis and Feminism after the Fall of Socialism*. London: Routledge.

Salmenniemi, Suvi. 2013. "Introduction: Rethinking Class In Russia." In *Rethinking Class in Russia*, edited by Suvi Salmenniemi, 1–22. London: Ashgate.

Sartan, Mark. 2002. "O Razvitii Sistemy Psikhologo-Pedagogicheskoi Mediko-Sotsial'noi Pomoshchi Uchashchimsia v Kontekste Zadach Modernizatsii Rossi-iskogo Obrazovaniia" [On the Development of the System of Psycho-pedagogical Medico-social Assistance for Students in the Context of the Problem of the Modernization of Russian Education]. *Shkol'nyi Psikholog*, no. 17. http://psy.1september .ru/article.php?ID=200201707.

Saxena, Shekhar, Graham Thornicroft, Martin Knapp, and Harvey Whiteford. 2007. "Resources for Mental Health: Scarcity, Inequity, and Inefficiency." *Lancet* 370: 878–89.

Scott, David, and Charles Hirschkind. 2006. *Powers of the Secular Modern: Talal Asad and His Interlocutors*. Stanford, CA: Stanford University Press.

Severov, Mikhail. 2001. "S Obryva v Mogilu i Obratno" [From the Precipice into the Grave and Back]. *Argumenty i Fakty* 23 (408). http://www.spb.aif.ru/gazeta /number/29240.

Sheldon, Brian. 1995. *Cognitive-Behavioural Therapy: Research, Practice, and Philosophy*. London: Routledge.

Sheldrake, Rupert. 1995. *The Presence of the Past: Morphic Resonance and the Habits of Nature*. Rochester, VT: Park Street Press.

Shevchenko, Olga. 2009. *Crisis and the Everyday in Postsocialist Moscow*. Bloomington: Indiana University Press.

Shevtsova, Lilia. 2007. *Russia—Lost in Transition: The Yeltsin and Putin Legacies*. Washington, DC: Carnegie Endowment for International Peace.

Shlapentokh, Vladimir. 1989. *Public and Private Life of the Soviet People: Changing Values in Post-Stalin Russia*. New York: Oxford University Press.

Silverstein, Brian. 2008. "Disciplines of Presence in Modern Turkey: Discourse, Companionship, and the Mass Mediation of Islamic Practices." *Cultural Anthropology* 23 (1): 118–53.

Smith, Daniel. 2009. "The Doctor Is In." *American Scholar*. https://theamericanscholar .org/the-doctor-is-in/#.WcxUzUyZORs.

Soloveychik, Simon. 1987. " 'Goo Goo' and the Bogeyman: Pedagogical Reflections." *Soviet Psychology* 26 (2): 3–50.

Spacebridges. 2013. "Spacebridge—'Citizens Summit'—Leningrad-Seattle—1985." YouTube, April 12. https://www.youtube.com/watch?v=-GcP-asqXP4.

Sperling, Valerie. 2015. *Sex, Politics, and Putin: Political Legitimacy in Russia*. New York: Oxford University Press.

Spinoza, Benedictus de. 1993. *Ethics*. Edited by G. H. R. Parkinson. Translated by Andrew Boyle. London: New Edition.

Spivak, Gayatri. 1988. "Can the Subaltern Speak?" In *Marxism and the Interpretation of Culture*, edited by C. Nelson and L. Grossberg, 271–313. Basingstoke, UK: Macmillan Education.

Standing, Guy. 2011. *The Precariat: The New Dangerous Class*. London: Bloomsbury Academic.

Stepanova, N. 2006. "Televedushchii Andrei Malakhov: My Ne Pretenduem Na To, Shtoby Lechit' Vsiu Stranu" [TV Host Andrei Malakhov: We Aren't Pretending to Cure the Whole Country]. *Izvestia*, April 18. https://iz.ru/news/313019.

Stephens, Sharon. 1995. *Children and the Politics of Culture*. Princeton, NJ: Princeton University Press.

Stevenson, Lisa. 2014. *Life beside Itself: Imagining Care in the Canadian Arctic*. Berkeley: University of California Press.

Stewart, Kathleen. 2012. "Precarity's Forms." *Cultural Anthropology* 27 (3): 518–25.

Stites, Richard. 1992. *Soviet Popular Culture*. Cambridge: Cambridge University Press.

Strathern, Marilyn. 2000. *Audit Cultures: Anthropological Studies in Accountability, Ethics and the Academy*. London: Routledge.

Suny, Ronald Grigor. 2011. *The Soviet Experiment: Russia, the USSR, and the Successor States*. 2nd ed. New York: Oxford University Press.

Taussig, Michael. 1987. *Shamanism, Colonialism, and the Wild Man: A Study in Terror and Healing*. Chicago: University of Chicago Press.

Thatcher, Margaret. 1987. "Interview for *Woman's Own* ('No Such Thing as Society')." By Douglas Keay. Margaret Thatcher Foundation, September 23. http://www .margaretthatcher.org/document/106689.

Thelen, Tatjana. 2011. "Shortage, Fuzzy Property and Other Dead Ends in the Anthropological Analysis of (Post)socialism." *Critique of Anthropology* 31 (1): 43–61.

Ticktin, Miriam. 2006. "Where Ethics and Politics Meet." *American Ethnologist* 33 (1): 33–49.

———. 2011. *Casualties of Care: Immigration and the Politics of Humanitarianism in France*. Berkeley: University of California Press.

Tolkachev, Viktor. 2008. *Roskosh' Sistemnogo Samopoznaniia: Osnovy Sistemno- Vektornogo Psiokhoanaliza* [The Splendor of Systematic Self-Knowledge: The

Fundamentals of Systematic Vector Psychoanalysis]. Saint Petersburg: Academy of Systems Thinking V. K. Tolkachev.

Tsing, Anna. 2000. "The Global Situation." *Cultural Anthropology* 15 (3): 327–60.

United Nations. 2016. "National Accounts Main Aggregates Database." United Nations Statistics Division. http://unstats.un.org/unsd/snaama/selbasicFast.asp.

Urnov, Mark. 2012. "Russian Modernization Doctrines under Debate." In *Waiting for Reform under Putin and Medvedev*, edited by Lena Jonson and Stephen White, 38–58. Hampshire, England: Palgrave Macmillan.

Valverde, Mariana. 2004. "Experience and Truth-Telling in a Post-humanist World: A Foucauldian Contribution to Feminist Ethical Reflections." In *Feminism and the Final Foucault*, edited by Dianna Taylor and Karen Vintges, 67–90. Champaign: University of Illinois Press.

Varma, Saiba. 2012. "Where There Are Only Doctors: Counselors as Psychiatrists in Indian-Administered Kashmir." *Ethos* 40 (4): 517–35.

Vasilyeva, Anna V. 2005. "The Development of Russian Psychotherapy as an Independent Medical Discipline in the Second Half of the Twentieth Century." *International Journal of Mental Health* 34 (4): 31–38.

Venediktov, Aleksandr. 2012. " 'Ekho Moskvy' zakrylo peredachu 'Vzroslym I Vzroslykh' Iz-Za Zakona O Detiakh." ['Echo of Moscow' Closes the Program 'For Adults about Adults' Due to the Law on Children]. *lenta.ru*, August 28. http://lenta.ru/news/2012/08/28/fired/.

Verdery, Katherine. 1996. *What Was Socialism, and What Comes Next?* Princeton, NJ: Princeton University Press.

———. 2003. *The Vanishing Hectare: Property and Value in Postsocialist Transylvania.* Ithaca, NY: Cornell University Press.

Volkov, Vadim. 2000. "The Concept of *Kul'turnost'*: Notes on the Stalinist Civilizing Process." In *Stalinism: New Directions*, edited by S. Fitzpatrick, 210–30. London: Routledge.

———. 2002. *Violent Entrepreneurs: The Use of Force in the Making of Russian Capitalism.* Ithaca, NY: Cornell University Press.

Wanner, Catherine. 2005. "Money, Morality and New Forms of Exchange in Postsocialist Ukraine." *Ethnos* 70 (4): 515–37.

Warner, Michael. 2002. *Publics and Counterpublics.* New York: Zone Books.

Waters, Elizabeth. 1993. "Soviet Beauty Contests." In *Sex and Russian Society*, edited by Igor Kon and James Riordan, 116–34. Bloomington: University of Indiana Press.

Wedel, Janine. 1998. *Collision and Collusion: The Strange Case of Western Aid to Eastern Europe, 1989–1998.* New York: St. Martin's.

Wells, Harry K. 1956. *Pavlov and Freud.* New York: International Publishers.

Wierzbicka, Anna. 1992. *Semantics, Culture, and Cognition: Universal Human Concepts in Culture-Specific Configurations.* New York: Oxford University Press.

Willis, Paul. 1977. *Learning to Labor: How Working Class Kids Get Working Class Jobs.* New York: Columbia University Press.

WHO. 2009a. *World Health Statistics.* Geneva: WHO Press. http://www.who.int/whosis/whostat/EN_WHS09_Full.pdf?ua=1.

———. 2009b. "Suicide Rates (per 100,000), by Gender, Russian Federation, 1980–2006." who.int. http://www.who.int/mental_health/media/russ.pdf.

World Bank. 2009a. *Russian Economic Report*. No. 18. Washington, DC: World Bank. http://documents.worldbank.org/curated/en/214911468294637283/Russian -economic-report.

———. 2009b. *Russian Economic Report*. No. 20. Washington, DC: World Bank. https://siteresources.worldbank.org/INTRUSSIANFEDERATION/Resources /305499-1245838520910/rer20fulltext_eng.pdf.

———. 2012. "World Development Indicators: Distribution of Income or Consumption." http://wdi.worldbank.org/table/1.3.

———. 2016. "GDP Growth (Annual %)." http://data.worldbank.org/indicator/NY .GDP.MKTP.KD.ZG.

Wortis, James. 1950. *Soviet Psychiatry*. Baltimore: Williams and Wilkins.

Yaroshevsky, Mikhail. 1996. "Marxism in Soviet Psychology: The Social Role of Russian Science." In *Post-Soviet Perspectives on Russian Psychology*, edited by Vera Koltsova, Yuri Oleinik, Albert Gilgen, and Carol Gilgen, 161–86. Westport, CT: Greenwood.

Young, Allan. 1997. *The Harmony of Illusions—Inventing Post-traumatic Stress Disorder.* Princeton, NJ: Princeton University Press.

Yurchak, Alexei. 2003. "Russian Neoliberal: The Entrepreneurial Ethic and the Spirit of 'True Careerism.'" *Russian Review* 62 (1): 72–90.

———. 2006. *Everything Was Forever, Until It Was No More: The Last Soviet Generation.* Princeton, NJ: Princeton University Press.

Zabrodin, Yuri, and A. G. Watts. 2003. "Public Policies and Career Development: A Framework for the Design of Career Information, Guidance and Counseling Services in Developing and Transition Countries." Country Report on Russia, 1–53. World Bank, May. http://siteresources.worldbank.org/INTLL/Resources/Public -Policies-and-Career-Development-Policy/Russia_Report.pdf.

Zavisca, Jane R. 2012. *Housing the New Russia*. Ithaca, NY: Cornell University Press.

Zdravomyslova, Elena. 2010. "Working Mothers and Nannies: Commercialization of Childcare and Modifications in the Gender Contract (A Sociological Essay)." *Anthropology of East Europe Review* 28 (2): 200–225.

Zdravomyslova, Elena, and Anna Temkina. 2003. "Gosudarstvennoe Konstruirovanie Gendera v Sovetskom Obshchestve" [The State Construction of Gender in Soviet Society]. *Zhurnal Issledovanii Sotsial'noi Politiki* 1 (3–4): 299–322.

Zhang, Li. 2017. "The Rise of Therapeutic Governing in Postsocialist China." *Medical Anthropology* 36 (1): 6–18.

Ziferstein, Isidore. 1966. "The Soviet Psychiatrist: His Relationships to His Patients and to His Society." *American Journal of Psychiatry* 123 (4): 440–46.

———. 1968. "'Pathogenic' (Dynamic) Psychotherapy in the Soviet Union." *American Journal of Psychiatry* 125 (5): 129–30.

———. 1969. "Soviet Psychiatry: Past, Present and Future." In *Social Thought in the Soviet Union*, edited by Alex Simirenko, 328–59. Chicago: Quadrangle Books.

Zigon, Jarrett. 2011. *HIV Is God's Blessing: Rehabilitating Morality in Neoliberal Russia.* Berkeley: University of California Press.

Zimina, Olga. 2003. "Attestatsiia PPMS-Tsentrov Kak Mekhanizm Upravleniia Sistemnoi Kompleksnoi Spetsializirovannoi Pomoshchi Detiam" [Attestation of PPMS Centers as a Mechanism to Manage an Integrated System of Specialized Care for Children]. Report. Saint Petersburg: Saint Petersburg Committee for Education of Saint Petersburg (SPbAPPO).

Žižek, Slavoj. 1997. "Multiculturalism, or, The Cultural Logic of Multinational Capitalism?" *New Left Review*, no. 225: 28–51.

znatokin. 2012. "Vsroslym o Vsroslykh—Peredacha dlia Iunykh Zakonodatelei" [For Adults about Adults—A Show for Young Legislators]. livejournal.com, September 8. http://znatokin.livejournal.com/338847.html.

INDEX

abortion, 48, 82, 174, 175, 189, 196, 257n14, 265n1. *See also* demographic crisis

abuse: domestic, 138–140, 158, 200; in narrative of Soviet past, 13, 54, 63–64, 88, 123, 191

Academy of Pedagogical Sciences. *See* APN

addiction, 22–23, 76, 140, 152–154, 160–161, 204, 209, 254n34, 257n13, 268n1. *See also* alcoholism

Adler, Alfred, 45, 85

advertisement, 3, 6, 18, 25, 74–76, 87–93, 102, 128, 133, 259n2. *See also* consumer culture

affect: in care, 8, 29, 38, 99, 102, 110, 118–123, 131, 136, 140–141, 144–148, 162, 179, 222, 247n22; and incommensurability, 26–29, 253n27, 263n6; affective labor, 108, 155, 162, 179–180, 184, 193–194, 246n18, 247n22. *See also* dusha; energiia

agency: circumscribed, 121, 156, 161–163, 180, 238–240, 266n8; liberating, 42, 65, 97, 121, 238–240, 266n8. *See also* svoboda; volia

Agenstvo domashnego personala (domestic personnel agencies), 90–91, 127, 258n21

alcoholism, 13–14, 17, 53–56, 62, 80, 82, 138–139, 149, 158, 176, 200–201, 252n17, 253n29. *See also* addiction

Alexievich, Svetlana, 4–5, 17

Allison, Anne, 189, 194, 245n11, 260n4

All-Russia Education Fund, 258n22

Althusser, Louis, 23, 251n11

ambivalence, 4, 34, 64, 127–129, 192

Amthauer Intelligence Test, 264

Anagnost, Anne, 99, 119, 258n24, 259n4

antipolitics, 8–11, 221–222, 232, 244n7, 272n2. *See also* neoliberalism

APN (Academy of Pedagogical Sciences), 58–59, 72, 78, 80, 124, 253n31, 255n5

applied psychology, 64, 230, 244n6; historiography of, 39–62

Asmolov, Aleksander, 60, 78, 124

assemblage, 3–5, 121, 200, 202, 215–216, 221, 230, 269n9

civility, 28, 129, 132, 199, 214–215, 221

civilizing project, 25, 125–126, 221, 250n6, 251n13, 254n34, 262n17

civil society, xx, 84, 128, 202, 206, 211, 212, 218, 221, 261n16

class. *See* consumer culture; elite; middle class; poverty; psychological difference; social inequality; social mobility; vospitanie; working class

cognition, 25, 137, 144, 145, 148, 236, 251

cognitive-behavioral therapy (CBT), 118, 149, 252n18, 263n8. *See also* behavior

Cold War, 6, 31, 33, 60, 64, 104

Cole, Sheila, 61, 254n37

collectivism, 35, 42–44, 175

Collier, Stephen J., 4, 121, 149, 220, 249n4, 251n10, 264n11, 269n9

commensurability. *See* (in)commensurability

communication. *See* obshchenie

communism, xx, 4, 59–60, 104, 124, 206, 249n1, 255n1, 260n7, 272n28, 273n4

Communist Party, 59, 62, 82

competition: and care, 23, 29, 76, 85, 89, 94, 103, 110, 118–120, 129–130, 192, 211, 229, 259n4; economic, 81, 85, 269n10; and ethics, 10; under socialism, 43, 79. *See also* success complex; uspekh

confession, 110, 244n7, 254n35, 268n1

confidence. *See* samouverennost'

consciousness. *See* soznanie

consumer culture, 8, 17–18, 29, 51, 67, 74, 76, 79, 80, 89, 95, 121, 124, 133, 144, 149, 190–194, 214, 228, 231–232, 237, 241, 257n16, 258n19, 260n4, 262n17, 267n9. *See also* elite

control. *See* samoupravlenie

corruption, 28, 124, 125, 188, 194, 218, 228, 234, 239–240, 258n22, 268n1

counseling. *See* konsul'tirovaniie

critical anthropology, 11, 109, 238, 245n8, 252n16

critical-complicit, 108–109, 121, 127–130, 132

critique, 9–11, 30, 247n26; of psy-ence, 46–47, 51, 55–56, 64–65, 78, 252n16, 263n3; through psy-ence, 27, 38–39, 65, 105, 108–110, 119–121, 124–125, 163, 192, 194–196, 199, 209, 220, 230, 234, 238, 248n27, 261n11,

262n16, 270n11. *See also* abuse; critical anthropology; critical-complicit

Cruikshank, Barbara, 3, 8, 29, 110, 199, 205, 209, 271n22

culturedness. *See* kul'turnost'

danger. *See* risk

Davis, Elizabeth Anne, 26

Defense Ministry, 82, 83, 256n11

Deleuze, Gilles, 180, 202, 270n15

democracy, xx–xxi, 5, 8, 104–106, 188, 199–202, 222, 227, 232–233, 241, 247n26, 261n12–13, 269n8, 269n10, 271n23; and care, 16, 25, 29, 46, 59, 67, 70, 78, 104–110, 120–131, 146, 230–232, 235, 237–238, 261n13. *See also* tactics

demographic crisis, 61, 79–83, 88, 102, 127, 141–143, 231, 256n12, 256n13, 262n18, 265n1. *See also* pronatalism

demoralization, 9, 229, 272n2. *See also* antipolitics; moralizing

depression, 26, 29, 38, 80, 115, 140, 182, 191, 202, 216

de-Stalinization, 49–52, 251n12. *See also* Soviet historiography

determinism, 40–42, 63, 249n1, 250n9, 251n10

diagnosis, 8, 25, 45, 55, 60, 80–81, 97, 110, 126, 139–140, 148, 155, 159, 162, 171, 231, 264n14, 265n2

dialectics, 42–44, 47, 56, 64, 230, 245n10, 268n2. *See also* Soviet historiography

discipline, 102; as organized knowledge, 42, 48, 65, 67, 85, 146, 249n2, 251n13, 252n23, 259n25, 260n9, 269n3; as subject formation, 23, 43, 45, 47, 49, 59, 110, 117–119, 122, 124, 129, 179–180, 239, 246n12, 254n34, 259n25, 260n9, 269n3

displacement. *See* psychotherapy

disposition, 10, 102, 119, 131, 184, 191, 272n25

divorce, 12, 17, 80, 125, 138, 180, 200–202, 209

Donahue, Phil, 254n35, 268n1

Donzelot, Jacques, 98, 100, 133, 258n25

Douglas, Mary, 30, 127, 188

dreams, 48, 89, 115, 194–195, 241

Duma, 234, 256n12, 256n13

Dunn, Elizabeth, 119, 258n19

dusha (soul), 29, 62, 128, 181–185, 193–196, 210, 213, 232, 255n4, 267n11, 267n12, 269n6

Echo of Moscow, 28, 168, 197, 200, 270n11, 270n14. *See also* For Adults about Adults; tok-shou

elite: post-Soviet, 81, 119–120, 125, 201, 221, 228, 231, 234, 241, 247n26, 261n12, 261n16; Soviet, 45, 51, 129, 262n16, 262n17. *See also* Childhood Planet; ReGeneration

emotion, xxi, 8, 124, 126, 180, 251n14, 260n5–6, 263n1, 263n6, 267n12; and management, 4, 19, 21, 25–26, 70, 76–81, 92–102, 104, 111–119, 127, 131, 136, 139–140, 145–148, 155, 157, 162, 176, 181–182, 187, 217–220, 231–233, 236, 246n15; and need, 39, 59–60, 64–65, 72. *See also* affect

empathy, 29, 37, 101, 120, 130–132, 228, 232, 235

energiia (energy), 28, 171–175, 179–186, 191–196, 232, 265n1, 266n8

Enlightenment, 116, 253n32, 259n1, 272n27

epistemology, 86, 174, 254n38

Esalen Institute, 60–61. *See also* human potential movement

Espeland, Wendy Nelson, 86

ethics. *See* care, precarious; (in)commensurability; politico-ethical

ethnonationalism, 41, 82, 178, 186, 235, 239

Etkind, Alexander, 249n3, 266n4, 266n5

European Union, 119, 227–228, 261n12

everyday, 9–13, 29, 34, 73, 89, 102, 121, 163, 169, 178, 197, 199, 204, 218, 229, 234, 238–239, 245n8, 251n15, 256n8

experts and expertise: in anthropology, 10–11, 120–121, 145; pedagogical, 45, 94; psychological, 15–16, 59, 80, 95, 122–123, 131, 136–137, 146, 191, 198, 201, 247n21, 271n21; structuring care, 18–19, 23, 40, 74, 97–103, 110, 121–122, 195, 198, 266n2, 267n9, 269n3, 269n7, 271n21–22. *See also* critical anthropology; critical-complicit; psychological difference

Fabian, Johannes, 35

family. *See* childhood; children; demographic crisis; parent; pronatalism

family constellation. *See* psychotherapy

fear. *See* strakh

femininity. *See* gender

feminism, 78, 102, 120, 127, 245n10

Ferguson, James, 9, 121, 163, 222, 272n2

Finland, 6, 19, 22, 72, 77, 89, 104, 105, 107, 122, 155, 188, 227, 259n2

For Adults about Adults, 8, 28, 196, 199–202, 207, 210, 215–216, 220, 232–234, 272n23. *See also* Echo of Moscow; tok-shou

Foucault, Michel: discipline, 85, 179, 188, 205, 220, 246n12, 247n21, 254n38, 270n17; ethics, 10, 13, 121, 195, 239–240, 245n12, 260n9, 260n10, 261n11, 266n2, 268n3; governance, 110, 137, 244n4, 249n4, 259n3, 269n3, 272n26

freedom. *See* agency; svoboda; volia

Freud, Sigmund, 251n14; in post-Soviet psychology, 2, 71, 85, 184, 217, 265n1; in Soviet psychology, 14, 41, 45–46, 49–50, 52, 56, 62, 230, 251n15, 252n24, 253n25, 260n5; in Western psychology, 55, 252n21. *See also* unconscious

Fukuyama, Francis, 247n26

functionalism, 97, 102, 145, 248n1

future. *See* children; democracy; past; present; temporality; trevoga; uspekh

gambling, 140

Garcia, Angela, 119, 248n27, 258n23

garmoniia (harmony), 14, 173, 182, 184–186, 188, 190–196, 232, 253n32

Gazman, Oleg Semenovich, 263n7

gender, 11, 17–18, 23, 27, 73–74, 76, 78–83, 88–90, 98–103, 107, 109, 120, 129–132, 165, 175, 179, 186–192, 195–196, 200–201, 207, 211, 241, 246n18–19, 255n6, 258n20, 260n8; femininity, 126–127, 162, 262n18; masculinity, 83, 102, 119, 127, 162, 190, 262n18; neotraditional roles, 80, 91–92, 131, 262n18. *See also* critical-complicit; feminism; heteronormativity; homosexuality; sex and sexuality

genealogy, 39–40, 58, 172–175, 230, 249n4, 261n11, 263n19, 268n1, 268n2, 269n8

Gestalt, 62

gift, 30, 109, 228. *See also* charity

Girard, René, 188

glasnost, 268n1

Goffman, Erving, 213–214

Gorbachev, Mikhail, 37–39, 59, 61, 78, 124, 146, 190, 268n1

Graham, Loren, 61, 253n25

gumanizatsiia (humanization), 38–40, 59, 65, 67, 76–81, 99–100, 124, 136, 146–148, 220, 229–233

habitus, 12, 22, 101, 126

Hand Test, 22, 247n20

Haraway, Donna, 245n10

harmony. See garmoniia

Harvard Project for the Study of Soviet Society, 248n1

haunting, 38, 63, 174–176, 193

Hellinger, Bert, 172, 174–175, 266n5

heteronormativity, 83, 129, 179, 235, 257n14

Hirschkind, Charles, 272n27

homosexuality, 178, 233, 257n14, 270n12. See also On the Protection of Children

housing law, 202, 211

humanistic psychology, 60–62, 64, 71, 146, 200, 225, 237, 254n36. See also human potential movement

humanization. See gumanizatsiia

human potential movement, 2, 55, 60–61, 124, 181, 254n37. See also humanistic psychology

Humphrey, Caroline, xxi, 119, 125, 144, 205–207, 239–241, 261n13, 262n16, 271n23, 273n4

hypnosis, 48, 55–57, 253n29

Iasiukova, Liudmila A., 148–149, 264n10

idealism, 38, 46–47, 244n2, 251n12

ideology, 16, 23, 34–35, 38, 44, 49–50, 61, 63, 78, 92, 100, 104, 109, 123, 206, 225, 230–231, 243n2, 244n3, 248n1, 249n3, 250n5, 251n13, 254n38, 260n5, 266n7

improvisation, 24, 125, 155–163. See also attestatsiia; bureaucracy; (in)commensurability; indeterminacy; norms

(in)commensurability, 9–10, 16, 23–29, 35, 58, 63, 65, 76, 86–87, 94, 98–103, 108, 119, 130–132, 137, 155–156, 161–165, 195, 221, 228–233, 238, 241, 245n8, 257n17. See also affect; care, precarious

indeterminacy, 264n15; legal, 156–158, 160–161; therapeutic, 156, 158–161. See also

attestatsiia; bureaucracy; improvisation; (in)commensurability; norms

individualism, 4, 10, 30, 35, 37, 58, 64, 84, 98, 100, 105, 110, 118, 123, 131–132, 140, 183–184, 186, 190, 202, 206–207, 216, 253n32, 258n20, 261n13, 272n26. See also dusha; garmoniia; psychosociality

intelligentsia, 124–125, 246n17, 250n8, 261n15, 262n16, 262n17, 272n24

interiority, 270n15; after socialism, 22–23, 40, 92, 94, 101, 110–111, 123, 187, 199–200, 202–204, 231, 247n22; under socialism, 38, 64, 271n18. See also individualism; lichnost'; unconscious

Jackson, Michael, 163, 194

Joravsky, David, xxi, 43–45, 250n9, 251n13, 254n34

Jung, Carl, 71, 85

justice and injustice, 219–220, 232, 234

Kazakova, Elena, 80, 147, 246n15

Kelly, Catriona, 255n4, 258n20, 258n21, 262n17

KGB, 14, 56, 64

khamstvo (rudeness), 214, 217–218, 272n24

Kharkhordin, Oleg, 206, 253n32

khoziaistvo (property/household), 205, 207. See also property

Khrushchev, Nikita, 49

Kitanaka, Junko, 146, 255n39

Kleinman, Arthur and Joan, 243n2

konsilium (weekly meeting), 22, 24, 137, 141, 154, 160–161, 177, 264n14

konsul'tirovaniie (counseling), 3, 12, 43, 57, 71–72, 133, 138, 181, 256n7, 263n8

Kripal, Jeffrey, 58, 60

kul'turnost' (culturedness), 246n17, 251n13, 261n15, 262n16, 262n17, 272n24

Kurpatov, Andrei, 198

Labkovsky, Mikhail, 28, 168–169, 199–222, 232–235, 270n11, 270n13, 271n18, 271n19

labor: capitalist, 4, 18, 23, 81, 102, 127, 183, 189, 233, 235; socialist, 13, 39, 44, 52, 61, 78, 127, 254n34, 258n21. See also affect; capitalism

lagery (camps), 3, 19, 22, 72, 77, 89, 93, 101, 104–126, 129–130, 155, 165, 236–237, 255n1, 259n2. See also ReGeneration

sovereignty, 215, 221, 258n25
Soviet Academy of Pedagogical Sciences (APN), 58–59, 72, 78, 80, 124, 255n5
Soviet collapse, xxi, 4, 15, 51, 81, 266n7, 267n15, 268n1. *See also* post-Soviet
Soviet historiography, 6, 31, 34–35, 38–63, 244n6, 249n3
Soviet medicine, 13–14, 16, 38, 48, 53–54, 57, 62
sovok (Soviet boor), 131, 272n24
soznanie (consciousness), 41–47, 50, 64, 175, 249n1, 250n10. *See also* unconscious
Spinoza, Baruch, 180, 263n6
stabil'nost' (stability), 27, 35, 147–148, 173, 186–190, 202, 215, 222, 238, 257n16, 267n14
Stalin, Joseph: psychology after, 38, 49–53, 61–64, 249n3, 251n12, 266n5; psychology under, 39–40, 44–49, 56–57, 250n8, 251n12, 253n32, 260n5, 262n17, 266n4, 270n17, 272n24
Stanford-Binet Intelligence Scales, 22, 247n20
state. *See* APN; attestatsiia; austerity; biopolitics; Defense Ministry; Ministry of Education; modernizatsiia; Pedagogy of Cooperation; public; Putin, Vladimir; Stalin, Joseph; welfare
Stevenson, Lisa, 8, 11
Stewart, Kathleen, 9
strakh (fear), 173, 176–178, 211
subjectivation (Foucault), 121, 129, 131, 205, 261n10, 270n15. *See also* civilizing project
subjectivity: liberal, 3–5, 8, 27–28, 35, 84, 106, 109–110, 121, 126, 147, 155, 196–199, 202, 207, 220–221, 226, 238, 249n1, 259n1, 259n3, 268n3, 270n14, 271n21; Soviet, 37–43, 56, 61–65, 146, 231, 244n2, 249n1, 250n4, 250n9, 270n17. *See also* bourgeois; civilizing project; lichnost'; modernizatsiia; neoliberalism; subjectivation
success complex, 86–94, 102. *See also* uspekh
suicide, 1, 17, 138–143, 256n10. *See also* demographic crisis
svoboda (freedom), 106, 109–118, 122–123, 213, 240–241, 261n13. *See also* agency; volia
svoi (us/ours), 74, 183, 203, 210–211, 217–220, 240, 272n28
symptom, 3, 23, 26, 38, 50, 53, 61, 131, 140, 171–174, 193, 229, 235, 237

Systemic Constellation. *See under* psychotherapy

tactics, 23–27, 65, 103, 105, 110, 119, 188, 247n24. *See also* democracy; improvisation
teaching, 4, 30, 48, 59, 63, 86, 130, 146, 184, 186, 225, 247n22, 254n37, 255n4
techniques of the self, 116–117, 198–199, 209, 211, 215, 220–222, 268n3, 269n7
temporality, 93–94, 98, 102, 126, 266n4, 266n7. *See also* nostalgia; past; present; Soviet collapse
terapiia (therapy), 3–4, 11–16, 23–28, 39, 43, 48–53, 57, 62–64, 71, 85, 98, 110, 136, 140, 157–159, 173, 180–181, 193–194, 198, 229, 244n6, 263n8, 265n1, 269n4. *See also* improvisation; indeterminacy
third sector, 128–129
Ticktin, Miriam, 11, 108, 232, 263n20, 267n16
tok-shou (talk show), 197–199, 202–209, 216, 220, 268n1, 268n3, 269n4, 269n6. *See also* Echo of Moscow; For Adults about Adults
tolerance, 105, 109, 120, 129, 131–132, 189, 232, 235, 237, 262n19. *See also* civility
trauma, 8, 28, 139, 175–178, 266n5
trening (training), xix, 2–4, 14–16, 24–28, 69–72, 74–75, 87, 95, 101, 116, 138, 144, 148, 158, 169, 179, 184–187, 191–193, 206, 231, 237, 244n3, 244n6
trevoga (anxiety), 26, 38, 72–74, 76, 81–82, 94, 99, 103, 110, 121, 126, 132, 140, 151, 173, 176–177, 180, 189, 201, 207, 211, 231, 264n14, 266n4
Trotsky, Leon, 45
trust, 54, 118, 125–126, 160, 212, 217–218, 254n33, 258n19, 267n15

Ukraine, 266n6
unconscious, 2, 45–48, 51–52, 65, 175, 179, 247n25, 251n14, 251n15, 253n26, 260n5. *See also* Freud; interiority; subjectivity
unemployment, 40, 144, 257n13. *See also* demographic crisis
unfinalizability, 10–11, 245n8
United Russia, 233, 235, 266n6
United States, 2, 52, 77, 86, 104–105, 119, 122, 142, 228, 235, 237, 245n10, 252n21, 256n8,

260n7, 268n1; psychology in, 14, 38, 44–45, 60–61, 64, 74, 85, 191, 205, 243n2, 246n15, 248n1, 252n16–18, 254n35–36, 256n7. *See also* human potential movement; West

upbringing. *See* vospitanie

urban, 7, 40, 51–52, 86, 99, 142, 172–173, 188, 195

Urnov, Mark, 247n23, 255n2, 272n1

uspekh (success), 72, 79, 92–97, 118, 186. *See also* success complex

Uznadze, Dmitri, 52, 253n26

value, 9–10, 99–101, 105, 124–128, 173, 175, 182–183, 190–196, 204–205, 220, 226, 232, 248n27, 260n7, 261n15, 267n14–15, 268n1, 272n1, 272n27. *See also* consumer culture; garmoniia; human potential movement; (in)commensurability; middle class; politico-ethical; samootsenka; uspekh

Valverde, Mariana, 244n7

Varma, Saiba, 255n39, 263n8, 264n15

Verity, 12, 14, 28, 173, 186, 192, 235, 237. *See also* PPMS Center; ReGeneration

violence, 8, 14–15, 40, 173, 177–178, 188, 245n7, 268n1

Vnik-Shkola (Temporary Research Committee on the Schools), 59–60, 263n7

volia (will), 41, 113, 124, 180, 182, 195, 206–207, 266n8. *See also* agency; svoboda

Volkov, Vadim, 51, 240, 261n12, 262n16, 262n17, 265n16

vospitanie (upbringing), 78, 83, 122–123, 205, 254n34. *See also* middle class

vulnerability, 10, 38, 42, 243n2; and care, 12, 17, 102, 132, 136, 218, 245n9; economic, xx, 81, 88, 141–145, 152, 246n16

Vygotsky, Lev, 41, 44, 52, 60, 79, 255n4

vziatka (bribe). *See* corruption

Warner, Michael, 180, 197, 268n2

Weber, Max, 9, 246n17

welfare, xxi, 9, 11, 108, 158, 200, 250n4, 259n3, 259n26

well-being, 13, 143; and care, 5, 17, 65; of children, 70, 160; mental/emotional, 16, 67, 94, 147–148, 173, 184–185, 189, 193–194, 233–234; physical/material, 74, 271n23

West, 5–6, 33–34, 271n23; interventions of, xx, 128; as object of desire, 119, 123, 126, 241, 258n22, 260n7, 261n11, 262n17; psychology in/of, 3, 35, 38–40, 44–45, 47, 49–50, 55, 62, 64, 110, 124, 225, 249n3, 252n21; stance against, xxi, 105, 267n12, 272n24. *See also* consumer culture; United States

whole child, 99, 103, 144

Wierzbicka, Anna, 182–184, 267n11, 267n12

willpower. *See* volia

working class, 40–41, 51, 76, 100–101, 151, 162, 260n6. *See also* middle class; poverty; social mobility

World War I, 40

World War II, 45, 51, 140, 175, 214, 246n15

Yalom, Irvin, 2

Yeltsin, Boris, xx, 125, 230

Yurchak, Alexei, 29, 52, 64, 120, 127, 131, 183, 210, 240, 243n1, 247n24, 251n12, 252n24, 260n7, 261n11, 266n7, 267n10, 267n15, 272n28

Zdravomyslova, Elena, 82–83, 149, 246n18, 256n13, 262n18

Zelind, Vadim, 181

Zhang, Li, 243n2, 247n24

Ziferstein, Isidore, 48, 55

Zigon, Jarrett, 121, 260n6, 261n10

Žižek, Slavoj, 262n19